In the Gospels & Acts we se

The King of the Jews (Matthew). Photo: *"Where is the one who has been born king of the Jews? We saw his star in the east..."* (Matt. 2:1-2).

The Servant who came to redeem us (Mark). Photo: *"If anyone would come after me, he must deny himself and take up his cross and follow me"* (Mark 8:34).

The Son of Man and Savior for all (Luke). Photo: *"For the Son of Man came to seek and to save what was lost"* (Luke 19:10).

The Son of God who gives eternal life to all who believe in Him (John). Photo: *"I am the resurrection and the life. He who believes in me will live, even though he dies"* (John 11:25).

The One who empowers believers to witness for Him (Acts). Photo: *"But you will receive power when the Holy Spirit comes on you; and you will be my witnesses..."* (Acts 1:8).

The One standing at the Father's right hand (Acts). Photo: In Antioch, Syria, there was a temple to Apollo. Antioch became the base for Paul's three missionary trips.

In the Salvation (Soteriological) Epistles we see Christ as:

Our Righteousness, and the One who delivers us from being slaves of sin (Romans). Photo: The Colosseum in Rome, where thousands of believers died for their faith (Rom. 8:33-34)

The firstfruits from among the dead and the One made sin for us (1 & 2 Corinthians). Photo: As death came through a man, the resurrection of the dead comes through a man (1 Cor. 15:20-21).

The End of the Law (Galatians). Photo: *"So the law was put in charge to lead us to Christ...Now that faith has come, we are no longer under...the law"* (Gal. 3:24-25).

In the Prison Epistles we see Christ as:

The Head over all powers and authorities for the Church (Ephesians). Photo: Old theater near Ephesus (modern Turkey). Authorities forced some believers to fight wild beasts in theaters (1 Cor. 15:32).

The One through whom God supplies all our needs (Philippians). Photo: In Philippi they beat Paul and Silas and put them in stocks in the prison (Acts 16:24; Phil. 4:19).

The Head of the Body, the Church (Colossians). Our Lord and Master (Philemon). Photo: Old stone aqueduct near Laodicea, north of Colosse

In the Eschatological & Pastoral Epistles we see Christ as:

Our returning Lord who will judge the world (1 & 2 Thess.). Photo: The Egnatian Way linked the Macedonian cities of Thessalonica and Philippi to Rome. Roman roads helped spread the gospel.

The only Mediator between God and man who gives crowns to faithful believers (Timothy). Photo: The main street at Ephesus led to the harbor. Paul left Timothy there to teach the truth (1 Tim. 1:3).

Our great God and Savior who gives us grace to be holy (Titus). Photo: Knossos Palace on the island of Crete. Paul left Titus at Crete to direct the church (Titus 1:5).

In Hebrews & the General Epistles we see Christ as:

Our Great High Priest who offered His own blood (Hebrews). Photo: The ministry Jesus has received is as superior to other high priests as the new covenant is superior to the old (Heb. 8:6).

The One who demands faith that works; the Healer of the sick (James). Photo: Jesus still heals the sick today as believers pray with faith in Him (James 5:14-15).

The Shepherd of our souls who suffered for us (1 Peter). Photo: Ruins of the temple of Apollos in Asia Minor. James and Peter wrote to believers scattered in Pontus, Galatia, Cappadocia, Asia, and Bithynia.

The patient Lord who will return to judge the earth (2 Peter). Photo: Ruins of an old temple in Pergamum, Asia Minor (modern Bergama in Turkey). See 1 Peter caption.

Our Standard for truth and practice, in contrast to the Gnostics (Epistles of John). Photo: *"That which was from the beginning, which we have heard, ... seen ... proclaim concerning the Word of life"* (1 John 1:1).

The Judge who is returning to judge all false teachers and sinners (Jude). *"See the Lord is coming with thousands upon thousands of his holy ones to judge everyone..."* (Jude 14-15).

In the Apocalyptic book we see Christ as:

The One walking among the seven lampstands (Rev. 1:12-21).

Lion of the tribe of Judah and the Lamb (Rev). *"Do not weep! See, the Lion of the tribe of Judah...is able to open the scroll...Then I saw a Lamb..."* (Rev. 5:5-6).

KING OF KINGS AND LORD OF LORDS (Revelation). *"I saw heaven standing open and there before me was a white horse, whose rider is called Faithful and True"* (See Rev. 19:11-16).

Survey of the New Testament

Cover Photo

The cross is one of the main symbols of Christianity. It was there that the Lamb of God died to take away the sins of the world. But the empty tomb is also an important symbol. A large, circular, heavy rock sealed the grave. It stood like a proud, silent soldier guarding the body of a dead Savior. But angels rolled away the stone to reveal that Christ conquered death. Hallelujah! The cross reminds us that the blood of Jesus brought a new covenant. And the empty tomb assures us that one day we will live with Him forever.

Components That Complement This Book

Visit www.FaithAndActionSeries.org to see components with this book:

Teacher's Guides—To purchase a TG a person must submit our online form and be approved as a teacher, pastor, or administrator.
www.faithandactionseries.org/teachers.html

eVisuals—all figures in color with captions for projection in classroom. Download from our website.

2 **Kindle** versions available from Amazon:

Version on left is a color version of the printed book. Suitable for your computer or large tablet

Version on right is a typical Kindle format. Suitable for your tablet or phone or computer

To find us on Amazon search Faith & Action Team.
www.amazon.com (search Faith & Action Team)

Contact Information

Order your copy from:

Faith & Action Team
429 U.S. Hwy 65
Walnut Shade, Missouri 65771 U.S.A

Telephone: 417-881-4698

E-mail: Orders@FaithAndActionSeries.org

Web: www.FaithAndActionSeries.org

SURVEY OF THE NEW TESTAMENT

Student Manual

by Dr. John Wesley Adams,
Dr. Quentin McGhee,
and Dr. Willard Teague

Instructional Design by
Dr. Quentin McGhee,
Senior Editor

PUT YOUR FAITH TO WORK!

Faith & Action Series

Faith Action
429 U.S. Hwy 65
Walnut Shade, Missouri 65771 U.S.A.

Photo Credits

	Figure #	Color Page
Ken Berg	2.1, 2.12, 3.1, 5.7, 5.20, 10.1, 10.3, 12.1	Matthew, Mark, Luke, Galatians, Hebrews, 1 John
Robert E. Cooley	1.11, 2.8, 3.2, 3.11, 4.2, 5.12, 6.1, 7.3, 7.4, 7.6, 7.18, 7.22, 8.3, 11.1, 11.4, 11.10, 13.4, 13.6	1 & 2 Thessalonians, 2 Peter, Timothy
Corel Photo Stock	1.7, 5.8, 9.1, 9.5, 9.6, 10.23, 10.25, 11.5	Acts-b, Romans, Ephesians, Colossians, Titus, 1 Peter
Gustave Doré	0.1, 1.1, 2.14, 4.1, 5.1, 7.1, 8.1, 10.26, 12.10, 12.13	
Ralph W. Harris	6.4	
ICI	7.11, 7.23	John, Philippians, James
Jerry Rausin	3.9	
Rockafellow Studios		Acts-a
Pat M. Smith	8.7, 11.11, 11.18, 13.1, 13.8, 13.14-15, 13.17-18	Acts-a, Jude, Revelation a-c
Lucinda Zilverberg		Corinthians

Copyright Information

First Edition 2002
Fifth Edition 2018

Course # BIB1013
ISBN 978-1-60382-236-7
Item # 4415-11E0

Table of Contents

List of Maps and Charts

Faith & Action Series Overview

Bible	Theology	Church Ministries
Survey of the Old Testament	Theology 1: The Bible, God & Angels	Evangelism & Discipleship
Survey of the New Testament	Theology 2: Man, Sin, Christ & Salvation	Marriage & Family
Pentateuch	Theology 3: The Holy Spirit & the Church	Pastoral Ministry
Historical Books	Hermeneutics 1: General Principles for Interpreting Scripture	Ministerial Ethics
Poetic Books	Hermeneutics 2: Interpreting Genres of Scripture	Homiletics 1: Preparing Biblical Messages
Major Prophets	Unlocking the Treasures of Your Fire Bible	Homiletics 2
Minor Prophets		Principles of Teaching
Synoptic Gospels: Life & Teachings of Christ		Biblical Counseling
Gospel of John		Children's Ministry
Acts of the Holy Spirit		Youth Ministry
Romans & Galatians		Missions 1
First & Second Corinthians		Missions 2: Cross-Cultural Communications
Prison Epistles		Teaching Literacy: Read the Light
Paul's Eschatological & Pastoral Epistles		Leadership 1: Loving God & People
Hebrews		Leadership 2: Skills to Empower, Govern & Administrate
General Epistles		Church History 1: Christ to Reformation
Revelation & Daniel		Church History 2: Reformation to Present

Faith & Action Series
Three-Year Bible School Plan (95 credits)

First Year

First Semester

Course #	Title	Credits
BIB1013	Survey of the New Testament	3
BIB1023	Pentateuch	3
BIB1033	Synoptic Gospels: Life & Teachings of Christ	3
THE1012	Theology 1: The Bible, God & Angels	2
THE1023	Hermeneutics 1: General Principles for Interpreting Scripture	3
MIN3023	Children's Ministry	2
		16

Second Semester

Course #	Title	Credits
BIB1043	Survey of the Old Testament	3
BIB1052	Gospel of John	2
BIB1063	Acts of the Holy Spirit	3
THE1032	Theology 2: Man, Sin, Christ & Salvation	2
MIN1013	Homiletics 1: Preparing Biblical Messages	3
MIN1033	Evangelism & Discipleship	3
		16

Second Year

First Semester

Course #	Title	Credits
BIB2013	Romans & Galatians	3
BIB2023	Historical Books	3
BIB2072	Hebrews	2
MIN2012	Church History 1: Christ to Reformation	2
MIN2023	Missions 1	3
MIN3073	Marriage & Family	3
		16

Second Semester

Course #	Title	Credits
BIB2043	First & Second Corinthians	3
BIB2052	Prison Epistles	2
BIB2062	Poetic Books	2
MIN2032	Church History 2: Reformation to Present	2
THE2042	Theology 3: The Holy Spirit & the Church	2
MIN2042	Leadership 1: Loving God & People	2
THE2033	Hermeneutics 2: Interpreting Genres of Scripture	2
		15

Third Year

First Semester

Course #	Title	Credits
BIB3012	Paul's Eschatological & Pastoral Epistles	2
BIB3022	General Epistles	2
BIB3033	Major Prophets	3
MIN3012	Pastoral Ministry	2
MIN1032/ MIN1042	Teaching Literacy/ Unlocking the Treasure of Fire Bible	2
MIN3033	Missions 2: Cross-Cultural Communications	3
MIN3043	Homiletics 2	2
		16

Second Semester

Course #	Title	Credits
BIB3043	Revelation & Daniel	3
MIN3053	Biblical Counseling	3
BIB3053	Minor Prophets	2
MIN3063	Principles of Teaching	2
MIN3072	Ministerial Ethics	2
MIN3082	Youth Ministry	2
MIN3092	Leadership 2: Skills to Empower, Govern & Administrate	2
		16

About This Book

1. **The Lesson Headings** divide each chapter into several parts. Each of these lessons focuses on principles related to one theme. We number the lessons consecutively throughout the book.
2. **The Lesson Goals** are listed at the beginning of each chapter. Also, when a lesson begins, the goal for that lesson is printed there. You will find that there is at least one goal for each lesson.
3. **Key Words** are defined in a section called "Definitions" at the end of the book. The symbol * comes before all words that are defined. To help some students, we have also defined a few words that are not key words.
4. **Teaching Method:** These courses are designed for the *guided discovery* method of learning. This method focuses on the student, rather than the teacher. When this course is used in a classroom, lectures are not intended. Rather, most of the class time should be used for students to discuss the questions in the margins and related questions from the teacher and other students. At least 25% of the student's grade should be on how faithfully the student has tried to answer questions *before* class.

   It is VERY important for each student to own his or her book. We encourage Bible schools to require students to buy their texts at the time they pay tuition. It is a shame for students to leave school without their books, because they need them for a lifetime of ministry. Owning the book enables a student to write notes in it and underline important ideas. Also, when students own their books, they do not waste class time by copying things that are already written in the text. Rather, they spend their time discussing questions related to the Bible and ministry.

   In a classroom the teacher and students should discuss key questions together. The best teachers never answer their own questions. Some students will complain at first when the teacher requires them to think, read, and search for answers. But a good teacher knows that children who are always carried never learn to walk. And students who are always told the answer learn to memorize, but not think and solve problems. In many ways, a good teacher is like a coach—guiding others to succeed.

   The questions in this course are like a path that leads straight to the goal. If the questions are too hard for a student, the teacher can ask easier questions that are like stairs toward harder questions. Also, the teacher should ask questions that guide students to apply the text to local issues. Often, a good teacher will add a story or illustration that emphasizes a truth for students.
5. **Schedule:** Most *Faith & Action Series* courses have up to 40 lessons. For a Bible school course, it is good to plan for 40 contact hours between the teacher and students. This allows 1 lesson for a class hour.
6. **The Questions.** Most questions in the margins are identified by the hammer and nail symbols. Questions are steps toward a goal. As a student answers the questions, he or she is sure to reach the goals. The hammer introduces *content questions* and the nail precedes *application questions.* Our logo for this book includes the hammer hitting the nail. A student must grasp content before being able to apply it. The answers to all content questions are in the text, near the question. We encourage students to answer nail or application questions from their local settings.

   In some books there is the symbol of a shovel before certain questions. Questions beside the shovel symbol are inductive questions. The word *induce* means "to lead." These questions lead students to discover truth for themselves. The shovel symbol alerts students that it is time to dig in and discover truth for themselves. *All students studying this course alone should complete the shovel questions.* Such students miss the 40 or more hours in a classroom that resident or extension students receive. The shovel questions will help these correspondence students get more out of the course. *When this book is used in a classroom setting, students will still benefit from answering the shovel questions. Teachers may require students to answer all shovel questions outside of class, or they may guide students to complete these questions in class; or they may replace some shovel questions with other work.*
7. **The Illustrations**, such as stories and examples, are preceded by the candle symbol.
8. **Figures** include pictures, photos, charts, and maps. We number the figures in order throughout the chapter. For example, the first three figures in chapter one are numbered 1.1, 1.2, and 1.3. There is a list of figures near the front of the book.

9. **The Test Yourself** questions come at the end of each chapter and are indicated by the balance symbol. There are always ten of these questions. As a rule, there are two test questions for each goal in the chapter. If students miss any of these questions, they need to understand why they missed them. Knowing why an answer is right is as important as knowing the right answer.

10. **Essay Test Topics** are at the end of each chapter, indicated by the pencil symbol. Note that these essay topics are the lesson goals of the chapter. A student should be able to summarize these goals, writing 50-100 words on each one. These essay topics test students at a much higher level than the multiple choice, Test Yourself questions.

11. **Sample Answers** to the hammer questions, some comments on the nail questions, and answers for the Test Yourself questions and Essay Topics are in the Teacher's Guide. Students should answer questions so they will grow and become strong in their mental skills.

12. **Bible quotations** are usually from the New International Version (NIV). We also use the New Century Version (NCV), New American Standard Bible (NASB), and the King James Version (KJV). We encourage students to compare biblical passages in several versions of the Bible.

13. **The Scripture List** includes key Scripture references in this course. It is located near the back of the book.

14. **The Bibliography** is near the endnotes page. It is a complete list of books the author refers to in this course. Some students will want to do further research in these books.

15. **Endnotes** identify the sources of thoughts and quotes. They are listed by chapter at the end of the book.

16. **The Unit Exams and Final Exam** are in the Teacher's Guide. In the Teacher's Guide there are also other useful items for the teacher and potential projects for the students.

17. **Who Said It?** These quotes are at the end of the book, after chapter 13. This is a good game for two or more students to play. A student or teacher can read a quote to a student or a class, without mentioning a Scripture reference. Then, the listener can try to answer three questions: 1) Who said it? 2) To Whom? 3) Why? If the listener cannot identify the quote, the reader can give the Scripture reference that goes with it. These quotes are a great way to review the New Testament. Even students who cannot identify the quotes the first time will soon come to know them well. Games like this increase attention and learning! Give a prize to the best student.

18. **Course Description:** (BIB1013) This course is an introduction and overview of the 27 books in the New Testament. It begins by exploring the historical background and geography of the New Testament. The study proceeds to examine book by book: the author, readers, date, literary style, context, outline, theme, purpose, and key passages. An effort is made to integrate the books, using Jesus Christ and His Church as unifying themes, and to show how the various books became part of the canon. There is an emphasis on principles and how to apply them throughout the course.

19. **Global Goals** for the entire course are listed below. The goals in each chapter will enable a student to reach these broader goals. By the end of this book, a student should be able to:

- Explain how God used the Jews, Greeks, and Romans to prepare the world for His Son.
- Analyze the political, social, and religious characteristics of New Testament times.
- Explain the formation of the New Testament canon.
- Identify 5 nations, 5 districts, 10 cities, and 5 bodies of water related to New Testament times.
- Divide the New Testament into 4 groups, listing the books and characteristics of each group.
- Summarize how Jesus Christ is a unifying theme of the New Testament.
- Analyze the authorship and historical context of each New Testament book.
- Explain and apply the theme and purpose of each New Testament book.

20. **Authors**

Dr. John Wesley Adams is Professor of Biblical Studies at All Nations Training Center in Kansas City. He has four earned degrees in biblical and theological studies: B.A., Southern Nazarene University (Bethany, Oklahoma); M.A., Southern Nazarene University (Bethany, Oklahoma); M.Div., Nazarene Theological Seminary (Kansas City, Missouri); Ph.D., Baylor University (Waco, Texas).

Dr. Adams served as a professor in New Testament at Mid-America Nazarene University in Olathe, Kansas for 6 years. He has 10 years pastoral ministry, including planting a new church that is thriving.

He spent 2 years (1997-99) in ministry in England.

Dr. Adams has authored numerous journal articles, is a contributing author to the *Beacon Dictionary of Theology*, is co-author and associate editor of the internationally translated *Full Life Study Bible,* and is chairman of the revision committee for the *Full Life Study Bible* 10th anniversary edition published under the new title *Life in the Spirit Study Bible* (March 2003). He has also written commentaries on Ephesians and Hebrews for the *Full Life Bible Commentary.*

Dr. Quentin McGhee is the founder and senior editor of the *Faith & Action Series*. He earned a B.A. from Southwestern College in Oklahoma City, and a B.S. from Oral Roberts University (ORU). Later he completed an M.Div. at the Assemblies of God Theological Seminary. There he taught beginning Greek and was selected by the faculty for "Who's Who Among Students in American Colleges and Universities." He earned a D.Min. from ORU in 1987.

Dr. McGhee and his wife, Elizabeth, pioneered a church in Oklahoma. They went on to serve as missionaries in Kenya for 15 years, where they helped start many churches, developed an extension Bible school for full-time ministers, and assisted in curriculum development. Currently, Dr. McGhee serves with the Assemblies of God World Missions as Director for the *Faith & Action Series* under the Latin America/Caribbean field.

Dr. Willard Teague currently serves as Academic Dean of the School of Bible and Theology at Global University. He earned a B.A. from Southwestern Assemblies of God University, an M.A. and M.Div. from the Assemblies of God Theological Seminary, and a D.Min. from Denver Seminary. He has a diploma in French Studies from Lemania College in Lausanne, Switzerland. He began his ministry as a youth evangelist in Texas and later became a pastor in Oklahoma. During this time, he did graduate work at Texas Christian University in Fort Worth and at Phillips University in Enid, Oklahoma.

As an appointed Assemblies of God missionary and field chairman of the missionary body in the Ivory Coast, he conducted evangelistic meetings with his student-pastors and planted several churches in different cities. In 1973 he became director of the new Bible school in San Pedro and set up the first ICI office. From 1986 to 1998 he served as president of West Africa Advanced School of Theology in Lomé, Togo, founded the WAAST International Chapel, and began a program of distance education.

21. Contributors and Consultants

Dr. Stanley M. Horton approved this course for biblical and theological accuracy. His degrees include a B.S. from the University of California, an M.Div. from Gordon-Conwell Theological Seminary, an S.T.M. from Harvard University, and a Th.D. from Central Baptist Theological Seminary. He is Distinguished Professor of Bible and Theology Emeritus at the Assemblies of God Theological Seminary in Springfield, Missouri. Dr. Horton has written 400 articles and book reviews, and authored 46 books on topics such as Genesis, Amos, Matthew, John, Acts, 1 & 2 Corinthians, Revelation, and the Holy Spirit.

Dr. Robert E. Cooley provided many photos for this series and confirmed this course's historical and cultural accuracy. His degrees include a B.A. in Biblical Studies and Archaeology from Wheaton College, an M.A. in Religious Education from Wheaton College Graduate School, and a Ph.D. in Hebrew Studies and Near Eastern Archaeology from New York University. Dr. Cooley served as President and Professor of Biblical Studies and Archaeology at Gordon-Conwell from 1981-97. He currently serves in many outstanding positions, including Distinguished Professor of Biblical Archaeology, Jerusalem University; Counsel to the President for Strategic Leadership, Eastern Nazarene College; Distinguished Visiting Scholar, and Counsel to the President, Bethel College and Seminary; Chancellor and Professor of Biblical Studies and Archaeology at Gordon-Conwell Theological Seminary. He has written articles in publications such as *The Bulletin of the Near East Archaeological Society, The New Encyclopedia of Archaeological Excavations in the Holy Land, Theological Education,* and *The Oxford Encyclopedia of Archaeology in the Near East.*

Figure 00.1 The Nativity, or birth of Christ, as shown by the famous French artist Gustave Doré
*"The Word became flesh and made His dwelling among us.
We have seen His glory, the glory of the One and Only,
who came from the Father, full of grace and truth"* (John 1:14).

Unit 1:
The Gospels and Acts

Chapter 1 is an overview. One of our goals is to help you learn the books of the New Testament. To reach this goal, we will introduce you to a song of the New Testament books. Also, you will learn to draw the House of New Testament books. The song and the house will make it easy for you to remember the 27 books of the New Testament.

- *Other goals of this chapter include:*
- *Explain how God used the Jews, Greeks, and Romans to prepare the world for His Son.*
- *Define or describe key words such as Pharisees, Sadducees, Sanhedrin, Septuagint, Herod's family, high priest, temple, and synagogues.*
- *Summarize three pictures of Christ from each group of New Testament books.*

Chapter 2 focuses on the Synoptic Gospels. Synoptic means "seeing together." We call Matthew, Mark, and Luke Synoptic Gospels because they look at the life and teachings of Christ from the same point of view.

- *In Matthew, you will learn to explain his purpose, and how he fulfilled it. We will teach you to identify the five teaching pillars of his Gospel. Also, you will study about Matthew's emphasis on the kingdom of heaven, and learn ways in which he stressed it.*
- *In Mark, you will learn that his purpose and method were different from Matthew's. We will emphasize several ways that Mark helped Gentile readers.*
- *In Luke, you will discover 45 new teachings that neither Matthew nor Mark presents. You will learn to appreciate Luke's theme: Jesus, the Savior of all.*
- *Before we leave the Synoptics, we will summarize and apply four reasons why Jesus taught in parables. We will define the kingdom of God and explain its two phases. And we will explain why Jesus healed and did miracles, as He still does today.*

Chapter 3 deals with the Gospel of John. This apostle wrote after the Synoptics had been written. So he omitted many things about which Matthew, Mark, and Luke had written. There are several things about John's Gospel that are different from the Synoptics.

- *He organized his Gospel into five parts.*
- *His purpose was to help people believe in Jesus Christ. So he emphasized words like signs, believe, and life.*
- *He included no parables, but built his Gospel around seven signs and their meanings.*
- *He gave us seven "I am" statements of Jesus.*
- *He emphasized the way Jesus took time to talk with people.*

Chapter 4 covers the book of Acts. In this chapter you will learn to:

- *Analyze the title, author, date, and outline of this book.*
- *Summarize five purposes of Acts.*
- *Analyze three steps in which believers witnessed for Jesus from Jerusalem to Rome.*

Chapter 1:
An Overview of the New Testament

Figure 1.1 In a dream, an angel warned Joseph and Mary to take Jesus and flee to Egypt. They left at once during the night (Matt. 2:13-15). (by Doré)

Introduction

God plans ahead.

- He told Abraham that his descendants would be slaves for 400 years (Gen. 15:13). But He promised to deliver them (Gen. 15:14-16). God plans ahead.
- He gave Joseph dreams about ruling when the youth was only 17 years old (Gen. 37:2). These dreams were not fulfilled until Joseph was 30 (Gen. 41:46). God plans ahead.
- He made every nation of people from one man. The Almighty planned the times for each nation and the places where each nation would live (Acts 17:26). God plans ahead.
- He showed Daniel that the Medes and Persians would conquer the Babylonians. Then the Greek kingdom would arise, but in time be conquered by the Romans. Finally, God said that an eternal kingdom would rise above the ruins of all human kingdoms (Dan. 2:24-47). God plans ahead.

Therefore, we are not surprised that He planned for our salvation. He allows each person to accept or reject the gospel. But God made a plan to save us before He created us (Matt. 25:34; 2 Tim. 1:9; 1 Pet. 1:18-20).

For he chose us in him before the creation of the world to be holy and blameless in his sight (Eph. 1:4).

[4]*But when the time had fully come, God sent his Son, born of a woman, born under law,* [5]*to redeem those under law, that we might receive the full rights of sons* (Gal. 4:4-5).

In this chapter we will look at some of the ways God prepared the world for Jesus through the Jews, the Greeks, and the Romans.

Lessons:

1 Preparation for the New Testament

Goal A: *Define Pharisees, Sadducees, Sanhedrin, and Septuagint.*

Goal B: *Explain how God used the Jews, Greeks, and Romans to prepare the world for His Son.*

2 Books of the New Testament

Goal A: *Describe 6 rulers of Herod's family, the high priest, the temple, and synagogues.*

Goal B: *Sing the books of the New Testament.*

Goal C: *Draw a house that shows the 4 groups of New Testament books.*

3 Christ in Every Book of the New Testament

Goal: *Summarize 3 pictures of Christ from each group of New Testament books.*

Key Words

Caesars	Pharisees	Jews	monotheism	Sanhedrin	General Epistles
Maccabean	Romans	Greeks	Septuagint	Sanhedrin	apocalyptic
		Babylon	Sadducees		

Lesson 1 Preparation for the New Testament

Goal A: *Define Pharisees, Sadducees, Sanhedrin, and Septuagint.*

Goal B: *Explain how God used the Jews, Greeks, and Romans to prepare the world for His Son.*

Setting

Welcome to our study of the New Testament. Rome ruled the world at the time of the New Testament. The top Roman rulers were called *Caesars or emperors. Like kings, they had great authority. But a child was born in a small town of *Palestine. That child changed the world.

Period (B.C.)	Date	Explanations
Persian (450-330)	430-420	Malachi was a prophet who wrote during the time of Nehemiah. He wrote the last book of the Old Testament. The Persians controlled Judah for about 100 years after Nehemiah. But they allowed the Jews to worship God.
Greek or *Hellenistic (330-166)	334-323	Alexander the Great conquered the Persian armies in Macedonia. Then he gained control of Europe and the Middle East. He allowed the Jews to follow their religion.
	323	At Alexander's death in 323 B.C., his kingdom split. Two of his generals, Ptolemy and Seleucus, started *dynasties. That is, they started kingdoms where one family ruled for several generations.
	320-198	Ptolemy and the kings who ruled after him reigned in Egypt. They controlled Israel during these years. Still, they allowed Jews to worship the God of Israel.
	198-166	Seleucus set up his kingdom in Antioch, Syria. The Seleucids gained control of Palestine in 198. For a time, they gave the Jews religious freedom. Then a terrible Syrian ruler named Antiochus IV Epiphanes began to rule (175-164 B.C.). His name meant "God revealed." He tried to Hellenize the Jews. That is, he tried to force them to forsake Jewish ways and follow Greek (Hellenistic) ways. He tried to destroy all copies of the *Torah or Pentateuch. This caused most Jews to rebel in 167.
*Maccabean or Hasmonean (166-63)	167	A messenger from Antiochus IV ordered a Jewish priest named Mattathias to offer a Greek sacrifice. He refused. When another Jew stepped forward to offer it, Mattathias killed him and the king's messenger. The priest and his five sons destroyed the Greek altar and fled to the mountains. Thus began the Maccabean revolt. The term *Maccabeus* means "hammer." It was the name some gave to Judas, one of the five sons of Mattathias. Others refer to this period as the Hasmonean period, based on the name Hasmon. He was the great-grandfather of Mattathias. Another Jewish group of this period was the *Hasidim,* which means "holy ones." Members of this group were loyal to the law of Moses. They joined with the Maccabeans and opposed being forced to follow the Greek way of life.[1] In time, the Hasidim seem to have split into two groups. The small group was the Essenes. They withdrew from society and lived alone. The larger group from the Hasidim was the *Pharisees.[2]
Roman (63 through the time of Christ)	63	The Roman General Pompey conquered Jerusalem. Then the provinces of Palestine came under Rome. Herod the Great was the ruler of all of Palestine when Christ was born.

Figure 1.2 Four periods of time from Malachi to Christ[3]

Jesus lived, died, rose from the dead, and ascended to heaven. But He sent His Spirit back to take His place. On the Day of Pentecost 120 believers were filled with the Spirit. The Spirit gave them power to witness for Jesus. They witnessed through words, deeds of kindness, and supernatural signs and wonders. The Church began as a group so small it met in one upper room. But it grew and spread all over the Roman Empire. The Church began as one Jewish group of one language and culture. But it grew to be an international Church of many languages and cultures.

The books of the New Testament were written for groups of believers. The Gospels teach believers about the life and teachings of Christ. Acts records the growth of the

Church. The Epistles, *Romans through Jude, teach how to live the Christian life. The last book, Revelation, predicts the final victory of God over His enemies.

God prepared the world for hundreds of years before He sent Jesus. *"When the time had fully come, God sent his Son"* (Gal. 4:4). Before Christ's birth, God was at work in the nations. God prepared the world for Christ by using three groups: the *Jews, the *Greeks, and the Romans. Let us look at how God used each group.

A. The Jews

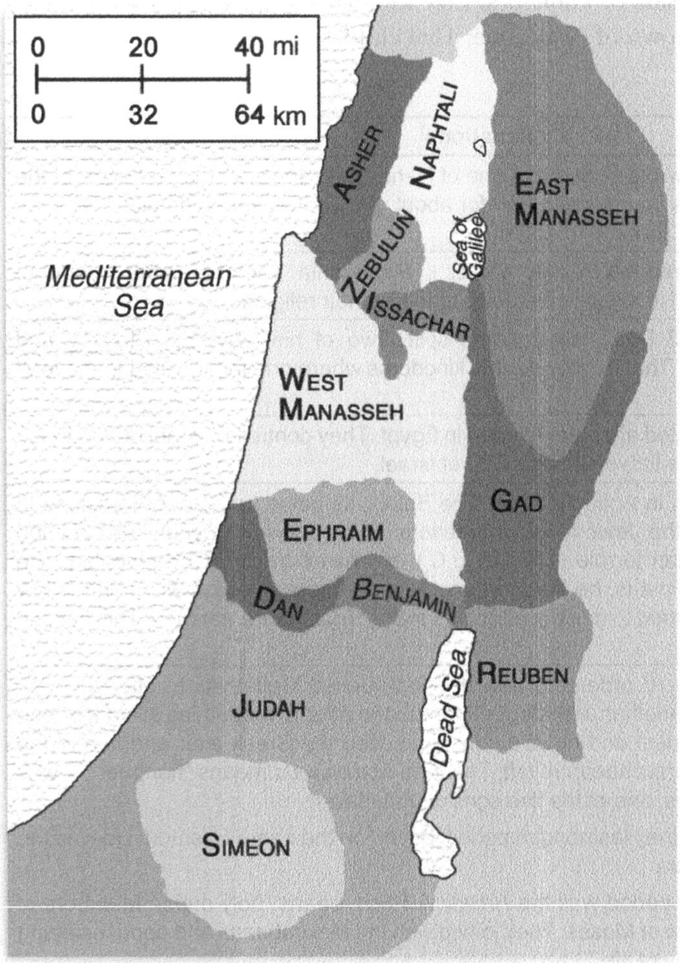

Figure 1.3 Location of the 12 tribes of Israel in Canaan or Palestine

The people of Israel were special to God. He chose them to be a kingdom of priests and a holy nation (Exod. 19:6). God wanted them to be His messengers to the nations around them. But they failed! They continually disobeyed God and worshiped idols. So God punished them.

There were 12 tribes in Israel. Ten of these tribes lived in the northern part of Palestine. These 10 tribes are often called Israel or the Northern Kingdom. The Southern Kingdom was called Judah. It included the tribes of Judah, Simeon,+ and part of Benjamin. *Assyria conquered the northern tribes of Israel in 722 B.C. We hear little of these tribes after that. Later, *Babylon conquered Judah in 586 B.C. Nebuchadnezzar, king of Babylon, carried the nation of Judah away as captives.

Captivity in Babylon changed the Jewish people in many ways. After this captivity, many Jews returned to Palestine. Some remained in Babylon. Others moved to various nations. All of these Jews told others they were worshipers of Yahweh (Jehovah), the one true God.

Two things made the Jews different from other people. *First*, the Jews believed in only one God. We refer to this as *monotheism. In the Greek language, *mono* means "one" and *theism* refers to God. The *second* way the Jews were different was that they believed in the law of Moses. These two beliefs of Judaism helped prepare the way for Christ and the gospel. When Jesus was born, the world knew about the God of Israel and the Messiah. Thus the words, ideas, and message of the gospel were not completely new. Many people outside of Palestine had heard about God and Moses. The Jews had told them.

Q 1 *Explain 2 ways the Jewish religion prepared the world for Christ.*

Q 2 *What is the Septuagint?*

Q 3 *What was the Sanhedrin?*

Old Testament Scriptures were written in Hebrew. But these Hebrew Scriptures were translated into Greek between the years 250-150 B.C. This translation was called the *Septuagint. *Septuagint* is from a Latin word that means "the Seventy." Seventy scholars translated the Hebrew Old Testament into Greek. Why was the translation helpful? Greek was the common language of the world at that time. This Greek translation made the Old Testament teachings available to every educated person. Many Gentiles read about the God of Israel. Also, many Jews studied their Scriptures in Greek. This shows us that they were thinking in new ways. The book of Hebrews quotes often from the Septuagint.

The Jews developed two groups of strong religious leaders about 200 years before Christ. They were called the Pharisees and *Sadducees. We read about them often in

---

\+ Simeon's land and inheritance were within the territory of Judah (Josh. 19:1).

Matthew through Acts. The Pharisees were the larger of the two groups. They were mainly the students and teachers of the Old Testament.

Q 4 How did the beliefs of the Pharisees and the Sadducees differ?

The Sadducees were powerful political leaders. The high priest and the leading officials of the *Sanhedrin were Sadducees. The Sanhedrin was the highest Jewish court. It was made up of 70 elders and the high priest. There were both Pharisees and Sadducees who were members of the Sanhedrin.

The Pharisees had very strong religious beliefs. They accepted all of the Old Testament as God's Word. Pharisees believed in angels, spirits, and life after death. In contrast, the Sadducees did not believe in the resurrection, angels, and spirits (Acts 23:6-8). Yet it was the Pharisees who most often challenged Christ's teaching. They believed the Old Testament, but were legalists. The Pharisees were more concerned with small details than the more important parts of the Law (Matt. 23:23-24). They became angry with Jesus for healing on the Sabbath, eating with unwashed hands, and having mercy on sinners.[4]

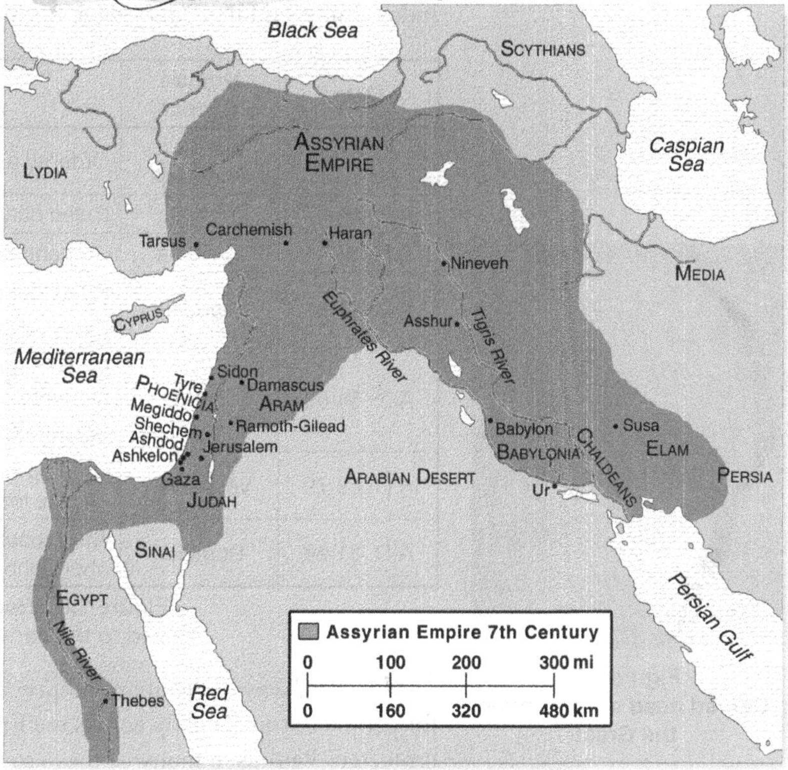

Figure 1.4 The kingdom of Assyria

B. The Greeks

One language for the whole world. That was the dream of young Alexander. He was the son of King Philip of Greece. This was more than 300 years before the birth of Christ. Alexander began to make his dream come true in 334–323 B.C. His army quickly conquered the known world. He then made Greek the official language of the people he conquered. He set up Greek cities and Greek culture. Greek customs became the way of life for everyone. Alexander's great kingdom fell apart soon after he died at the age of 33. However, the Greek language and way of life remained.

All of these events happened long before Christ's birth. How did they relate to the gospel and the New Testament? Greek became the common language of the world. This made it easier to tell the good news. The apostles preached mostly in Greek. Also, the authors of the New Testament books wrote in Greek.

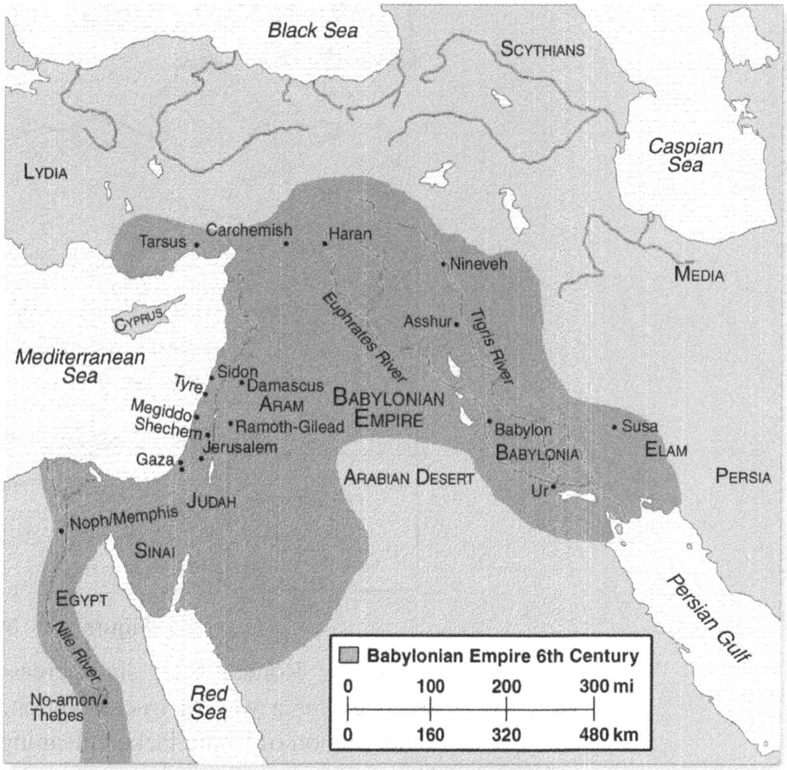

Figure 1.5 The kingdom of Babylon

C. The Romans

The Romans conquered the known world after Alexander's kingdom fell apart. They organized the world into a great empire. The Romans ruled from the western end of the Mediterranean Sea to the Euphrates River in the East. (See Figure 1.8.) Local governors ruled over provinces and districts. In God's plan, the Romans also prepared the world in important ways for the coming of Christianity.

Q 5 How did God use the Greeks to prepare the world for His Son?

Q 6 *Name 2 ways that God used the Romans to prepare the world for Christ.*

First, the Romans brought law and order. They had a large army that brought peace to the world during the rule of Caesar Augustus. Jesus was born in the little village of Bethlehem during this time. This village was near Jerusalem in the Roman province of Judea. Luke said that Mary gave birth to her firstborn son (Luke 2:1-7) in Bethlehem.

Date	Roman Caesar	Explanation	Bible Reference
30 B.C.-A.D. 14	Caesar Augustus	Ordered a census at the time Jesus was born	Luke 2:1
A.D. 14-37	Tiberius	Ruled during the ministry and death of Jesus	Luke 3:1
A.D. 37-41	Caligula	Demanded that people worship him	
A.D. 41-54	Claudius	Ruled during a great famine Expelled the Jews from Rome	Acts 11:28 Acts 18:2
A.D. 54-68	Nero	Persecuted Christians; Peter and Paul were martyred during his rule Was the Caesar at Paul's trial	2 Tim. 4:16-17 Acts 25:10-12 Acts 27:24
A.D. 69-79	Vespasian	Ordered his son, Titus, to destroy Jerusalem and the temple in A.D. 70	Luke 21:20
A.D. 81-96	Domitian	Was probably the Caesar persecuting believers when John wrote Revelation	Rev. 17:8-11

Figure 1.6 Roman Ceasars or emperors related to the early years of the New Testament

Figure 1.7 Carved head of Alexander the Great

A *second* way the Romans helped was with their roads. These roads made it possible for people to travel easily across the Empire. The roads were built well and were usually protected. Paul used many of these roads as he traveled across Achaia and Macedonia.

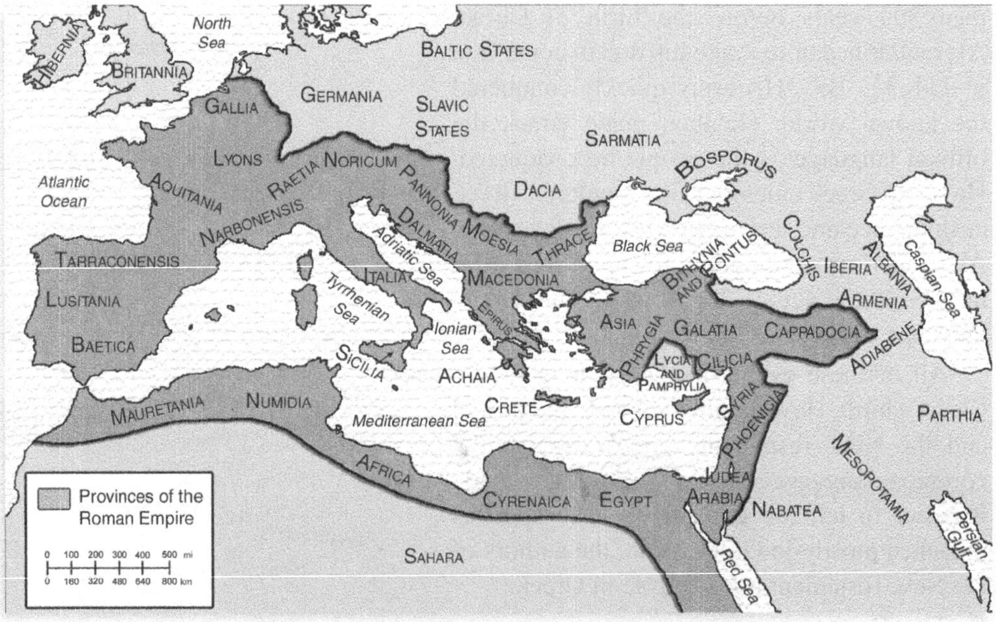

Figure 1.8 Map of the Roman Empire

During Roman rule, sin increased greatly. Helpful religion decreased. People searched for a way of true salvation. Many were losing faith in their old gods. The state religion of Rome lacked meaning. It could not satisfy the heart. People felt empty. Various "mystery" religions promised salvation and fellowship with the gods. However, these did not satisfy the hearts of people either. People were ready for a Savior.

Jesus came into a world prepared for Him. He was born *"when the time had fully come"* (Gal. 4:4).

Lesson 2

Books of the New Testament

Goal A: *Describe 6 rulers of Herod's family, the high priest, the temple, and synagogues.*
Goal B: *Sing the books of the New Testament.*
Goal C: *Draw a house that shows the 4 groups of New Testament books.*

Setting: Palestine in the first century

At the beginning of Christianity, **Herod the Great** and his family ruled in Palestine. The Romans appointed this Herod to be the king of the Jews. He ruled from 37 B.C. to 4 B.C. Herod the Great ordered the killing of all babies in Bethlehem (Matt. 2). This Herod had several family members who ruled after him. We'll look at five of them (See Figure 1.10).

Q 7 *Fill in the empty boxes in Figure 1.9.*

Ruler	Place	Dates	Scriptures
Herod the Great	Palestine		
Archelaus			
Herod Philip II			
Herod Antipas			
Herod Agrippa I			
Herod Agrippa II			
Pontius Pilate			

Figure 1.9 Seven rulers in Palestine

Archelaus was the son of Herod the Great. He ruled in Judea, Idumea, and Samaria (4 B.C. to A.D. 6). Joseph and Mary avoided Judea because he was ruling there (Matt. 2:19-23).

Herod Philip II was another of Herod the Great's sons. He ruled the northeast territories of Iturea and Trachonitis (4 B.C. to A.D. 34). Caesarea Philippi was within his realm.

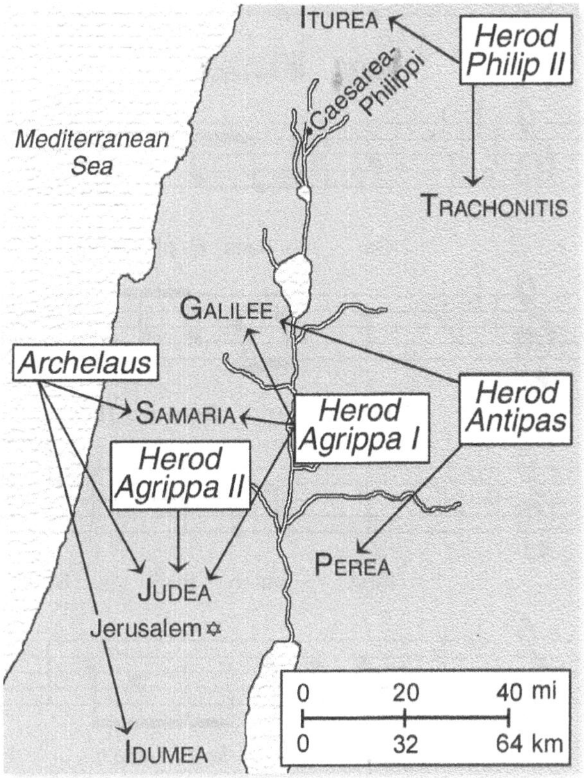

Figure 1.10 Map showing the districts of Palestine where the family of Herod ruled

Herod Antipas ruled as governor of Galilee and Perea from 4 B.C. to A.D. 39. We often read about him in the Gospels. John the Baptist accused this Herod of adultery. Herod married his own sister-in-law, Herodias. This cost John his life (Matt. 14:1-2). Jesus called Herod Antipas *"that fox"* (Luke 13:32). Antipas was also involved in Christ's trial in Jerusalem (Luke 23:7-12).

After Antipas, **Herod Agrippa I** ruled over Galilee, Samaria, and Judea. He was the grandson of Herod the Great. Agrippa ruled from A.D. 37-44 before he suddenly died. Acts 12 tells that he murdered James, the son of Zebedee, and also put Peter in prison. Then Acts briefly tells about this Herod's death (Acts 12:21-23).

Figure 1.11 A writing of Pilate found at Caesarea

Herod Agrippa II was the last member of Herod's family to rule (A.D. 50-100). He was the great-grandson of Herod the Great. His name is found in Acts 25–26 at the time of Paul's trial before Festus in Caesarea. Agrippa II was king of Judea. He agreed with Festus that Paul should be released (Acts 26:31-32).

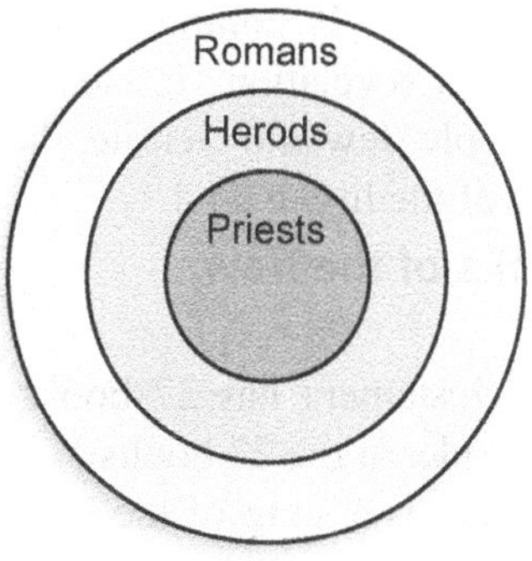

Figure 1.12 Three levels of rulers in Palestine

Pontius Pilate was the Roman governor of Judea at the time of Christ (A.D. 26-36). Pilate is important in history because of his part in the trial of Christ. Pilate condemned the Lord after first saying that Jesus was "not guilty" (John 18:38–19:6). Shortly after Christ's death, the Romans removed Pilate from office. He was ordered to appear before the Emperor (A.D. 36). We do not know what happened to Pilate after this.

Q 8 *How did Pilate's position differ from that of Herod Antipas?*

Q 9 *In Christ's time, how did Jews use the temple and synagogues?*

Q 10 *What did the Jews believe about the Old Testament Scriptures?*

The Jewish high priest and the Sanhedrin ruled over Jewish religious matters in these difficult times. The New Testament tells about three of these high priests. We read in John of Annas and Caiaphas, who was the high priest at the time of the trial of Christ (John 18:13). Caiaphas was married to the daughter of Annas, the former high priest. The third high priest, Ananias, is named in Acts 23:2.

The *temple in Jerusalem was the center of religious life for the Jews. The Jews came from near and far to worship and offer sacrifices there. They kept the religious feasts of Judaism, especially the Feasts of *Passover, *Pentecost, and *Tabernacles.

Q 11 *Learn to sing the books of the New Testament from memory.*

Figure 1.13 Song of the books of the New Testament

*Synagogues were also important in the religious life of the Jews. There were no priests or sacrifices in the synagogues. But the synagogues were schools, community centers, and places to teach the Scriptures on the Sabbath. Many Jews lived far from Jerusalem. These seldom went to the temple. But they could attend the local synagogues often. All synagogues were places of prayer and religious instruction. The people offered prayers at certain times during the synagogue worship service. Both Jesus and the early Christians worshiped often in synagogues (Luke 4:16-30; Acts 13:14; 26:11). Those far from Jerusalem often focused on the synagogues rather than the temple.

The Old Testament was the Book of God for the Jews. They believed it contained God's Law and God's will. It taught that there is only one God. It also taught that all of life is under His control. The Jewish people believed that God would help and save them in time of need (Luke 2:25). This is what the Jews believed when Christ was born.

The New Testament is based upon the Old Testament. It completes the record of God's revelation. It clearly teaches all people, Jew and Gentile, the eternal truths of the living God.

The 27 books of the New Testament

The New Testament has 27 books. An easy way to learn the 27 books is to sing them. There is a song of the New Testament books in Figure 1.13. This is an English song. The tune is based on the old song, "Bring Them In." If you do not sing in English, create a song that will work in your language. Choose the melody of a song you already know. Then work on singing the books of the New Testament to that melody. If this is too hard for you, find a musical person to help you. Once you learn a song of the New Testament books, you will probably remember it all of your life. Music turns memorizing from work to play. Practice singing the song each day that you study this course.

We can divide the New Testament into four groups of books. An easy way to remember these four groups is to relate them to a house (Figure 1.14).

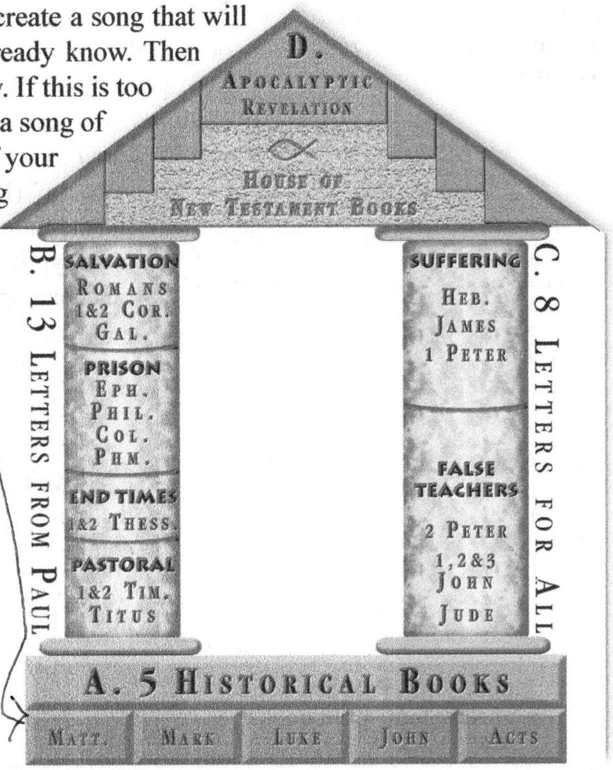

Figure 1.14 House of New Testament books

A. The four Gospels and Acts (Matthew–Acts)

Matthew shows Jesus Christ as the "*King of the Jews*." This book gives the fulfillment of many Old Testament prophecies about the coming of the Messiah. The teachings of Christ are the most important part of the book.

Mark pictures Jesus as "the Servant of the Lord," busy doing His Father's work and will. Mark emphasizes Christ's work, especially the work of redemption.

Luke emphasizes Jesus as "*the Son of Man*," the perfect example of man. Jesus gave His life *to "seek and to save what was lost"* (Luke 19:10). The love and compassion of Christ are important thoughts in this Gospel.

John presents Jesus as "*the Son of God*." Jesus is the eternal Word who came to reveal God to all. This Gospel shows the relationship of Christ to those around Him. It tells about the people He met and the way that He changed their lives. People received eternal life when they realized that He was really the Son of God.

The book of Acts continues Luke's Gospel. It shows the risen Christ working through His apostles, who have new power by the Holy Spirit. Acts describes the beginning of the Church and its growth "*to the ends of the earth*." It is the first Church history textbook.

Q 12 *How does each of the 5 historical books describe Jesus?*

Q 13 *Sing the 5 history books.*

B. 13 letters from Paul (Romans–Philemon)

The New Testament letters (Epistles) explain who Jesus is and what He did. They show believers how to apply His teachings to their lives. The apostle Paul wrote 13 of the New Testament Epistles. Figure 1.15 shows that we may divide Paul's letters into four groups. Do not try to memorize this now. We will spend more time on Paul's letters later in this course.

New Testament Group	Letters
Letters about salvation	Romans, Galatians, 1 and 2 Corinthians
Letters from prison	Ephesians, Philippians, Colossians, Philemon
Letters about the future	1 and 2 Thessalonians
Letters for pastors	1 and 2 Timothy, Titus

Figure 1.15
We may divide Paul's letters into four groups.

C. 8 letters to all (Hebrews–Jude)

Various people wrote the remaining New Testament letters. We can divide these letters into two groups:

- Letters to those who are suffering: Hebrews, James, 1 Peter
- Letters about false teachers: 2 Peter; 1, 2, and 3 John; Jude

Q 14 *Sing the 5 historical books and Paul's 13 letters.*

The two problems of suffering and false teachers became worse as time passed. Persecution of Christians came first from the non-Christian Jews. After A.D. 64, the Roman government also began persecuting believers. Jesus had warned His followers that false christs and false prophets would come (Matt. 24:24). Paul also warned the elders of the Ephesian church about this threat (Acts 20:29-30). Later, the Gnostics created great problems in the Church. Gnostics were false teachers who claimed to have special spiritual knowledge. John's letters were written to correct their false teaching.

Q 15 *Sing the song of all the New Testament books.*

D. Apocalyptic: Revelation

Revelation is a blend of three types or forms of writing.

Q 16 *Explain 3 forms of writing in Revelation.*

Q 17 *Use Figure 1.16 to learn to create Figure 1.14 from memory.*

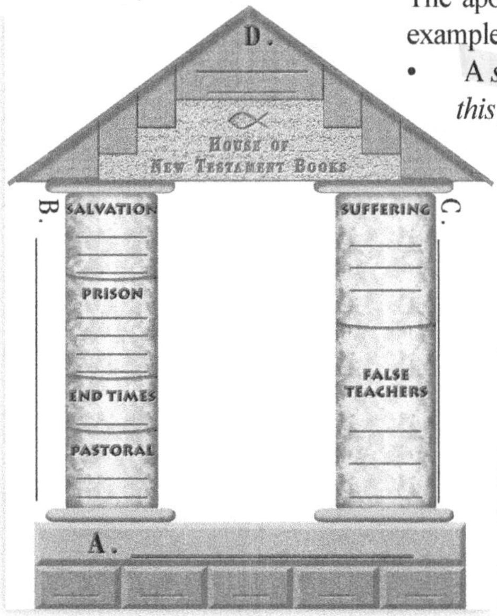

Figure 1.16 Practice house of New Testament books

- The *first* form is **apocalyptic*. This final book of the Bible begins with *"The Revelation,"* or *apokalupsis* (Rev. 1:1). *Apokalupto* is a Greek word that means "to unveil or reveal." The apocalyptic form of writing uses visions and symbols to unveil the future. Other examples of apocalyptic writings are Ezekiel, Daniel, and Zechariah.
- A *second* form of writing in Revelation is *prophetic*. John refers to *"the words of this prophecy"* (Rev. 1:3). Prophetic writings give the Word of God about the present and the future. Prophetic writings usually have fewer visions and symbols than apocalyptic writings. The Major and Minor Prophets of the Old Testament are other examples of prophetic writings.
- A *third* form of writing in Revelation is *letter*. John wrote Revelation as a letter *"to the seven churches"* (Rev. 1:4). From the greeting through chapter 22, Revelation is a letter. Other examples of letters in the Bible are the letters of Paul and Peter.

Revelation is mainly about the judgments of God in the last days. It shows the final victory of God over Satan and good over evil. Revelation shows the completion of redemption. Paul wrote that God's purpose was *"to bring all things...together under one head, even Christ"* (Eph. 1:10). John understood this as he recorded the words he heard during his vision of heaven:

The kingdom of the world has become the kingdom of our Lord and of his Christ, and he will reign for ever and ever (Rev. 11:15).

Lesson 3

Christ in Every Book of the New Testament

Goal: *Summarize 3 pictures of Christ from each group of New Testament books.*

The Bible contains 66 books. Yet it is one book with one main theme: Jesus Christ. Figure 1.17 summarizes how each section of the Bible relates to Jesus Christ.[5]

Group of Books	Relationship to Christ, the Theme of the Bible
	Old Testament
Law (Gen.–Deut.)	The Law was the foundation for Christ. It was the schoolteacher that taught us our need for the Savior (Rom. 3:20-22; Gal. 3:23–4:7).
History (Josh.–Esther)	The Historical Books tell of the preparation for Christ. They tell us how God was preparing a way for the Messiah to come. He came through David, Israel's greatest king. Nehemiah was written near the close of the Old Testament. At that time, we see the Jews rebuilding their temple and nation. As the Old Testament closes they are waiting in Jerusalem for their Messiah.
Poetry (Job–Song of Songs)	The Poetic Books express our desire for Christ. He is the One who will put an end to suffering like Job had. He is the Creator, Deliverer, and Judge that the psalmists worship. He is the true Shepherd. He is our Wisdom. He alone is the Lover of our souls.
Prophecy (Isa.–Mal.)	The Prophets foretold the coming of Christ. They wrote about Israel's coming Messiah. He is the One who will restore Israel and judge the nations.
	New Testament
History (Matt.–Acts)	The Gospels record the appearance of Christ. They tell the story of Christ working in flesh. Acts of the Holy Spirit show the continuing ministry of Christ. Acts tells the story of Christ working through His body, the Church.
The Epistles (Rom.–Jude)	The Epistles interpret and apply Christ. They tell us the meaning of His death and resurrection. They explain and apply redemption and sanctification. They defend our freedom in Christ. They explain our sufferings for Christ. They tell about our blessings in Christ.
Prophecy (Rev.)	Revelation announces the return of Christ as King of kings. Christ is the mountaintop of all history. He is the highest part. Genesis records what God started through Christ. Revelation records what God will finish through Him. Christ will complete what God started in Eden. Christ will judge evil. All of creation will worship Him.

Figure 1.17 Christ is the theme of each group of books in the Bible.

Our *Survey of the Old Testament* course suggests pictures of Christ in each Old Testament book. Now let us look at pictures and descriptions[6] of Jesus in each book of the New Testament.[7]

A. The Gospels and Acts

Q 18 *Describe Christ from each of the 5 historical books.*

Book	Picture or Description of Christ	Reference
Matthew	the King of the Jews	2:1-2; 27:37
Mark	The Servant who came to redeem us	entire book
Luke	The Son of Man and Savior for all	6:5; 19:10
John	The Son of God who gives eternal life to all who believe in Him	3:16-17
Acts	The One who baptizes believers in the Holy Spirit The One who empowers believers to witness for Him The ascending Lord The One standing at the Father's right hand	1:5; 2:4 1:8 1:9 7:56

Figure 1.18 Pictures of Christ in the Gospels and Acts

B. The letters of Paul: Romans through Philemon

Q 19 *Explain at least 5 pictures of Christ in Paul's Epistles.*

Book	Picture or Description of Christ	Reference
Romans	Our righteousness The One who delivers us from being slaves of sin	3:22 6:15-18
1 Corinthians	The Firstfruits from among the dead	15:20
2 Corinthians	The One who was made to be sin for us	5:21
Galatians	The End of the Law	3:10, 13
Ephesians	The Head over all powers and authorities for the Church	1:20-23
Philippians	The One through whom God supplies all our needs	4:19
Colossians	The Image of the invisible God The Creator The Head of the Body, the Church	1:15-18 2:9 3:3
1 Thessalonians	Our returning Lord	4:15-18
2 Thessalonians	The world's returning Judge	1:6-10
1 Timothy	The only Mediator between God and man	2:5
2 Timothy	The Giver of crowns to faithful shepherds & believers	4:8
Titus	Our great God and Savior who gives us grace to be holy	2:13
Philemon	Our Lord and Master	entire book

Figure 1.19 Pictures of Christ in the 13 letters from Paul

C. 8 letters for all: Hebrews and the 7 *General Epistles

Q 20 *Identify 5 pictures of Christ from Hebrews and the General Epistles.*

Book	Picture or Description of Christ	Reference
Hebrews	The One who represents God perfectly & is better than all Our Great High Priest who offered His own blood	1:3 9:11-15
James	The One who demands faith that works The Healer of the sick	1–5 5:15
1 Peter	The Shepherd of our souls who suffered for us	2:22-25
2 Peter	The patient Lord who will return to judge the earth	2:8-10
1 John	The Word of life who came by water and blood Our Standard for truth and practice	1:1; 5:6 1:5-7; 3:3,16; 4:17
2 John	The union of truth and love	3
3 John	The One who changed the "Son of Thunder" into the apostle of love and truth	entire book
Jude	The Lord coming with thousands upon thousands of His saints	14

Figure 1.20 Pictures of Christ in the 8 letters for all

Q 21 *Summarize 3 pictures of Christ in Revelation.*

D. Apocalyptic: Revelation

Book	Picture or Description of Christ	Reference
Revelation	The One coming with clouds whom all nations will see	1:7
	The One walking among the lampstands, who was dead but is alive for ever and ever	1:13, 18
	The One who holds the keys of death and Hades	1:18
	The One who hates the deeds of the Nicolaitans	2:6
	The One with a sharp two-edged sword	2:12
	The Son of God with eyes like blazing fire and feet like polished bronze	2:18
	The Lamb who takes the scroll from the Father's right hand	5:6-7
	Israel's Son who will rule the nations with an iron rod	12:5
	The Bridegroom who will come for His bride	19:7
	The "King of kings and Lord of lords"	19:16
	The Alpha and the Omega, the First and the Last, the Beginning and the End	22:13

Figure 1.21 Pictures of Christ in Revelation

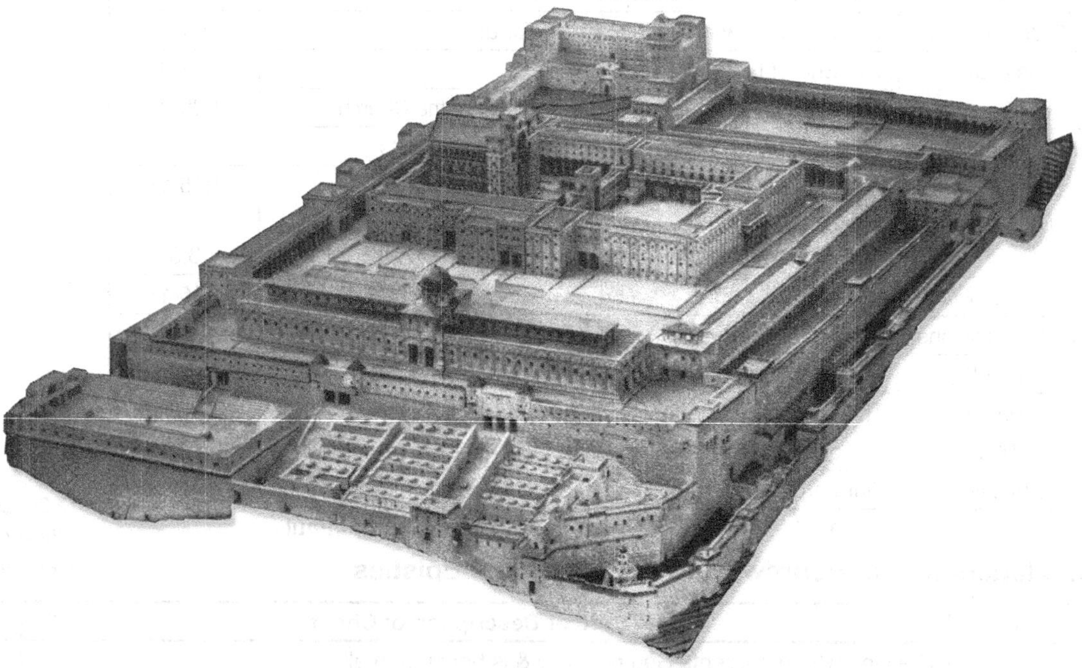

Figure 1.22 The temple in Jerusalem was the center of Jewish worship.

Test Yourself: Circle the letter by the ***best*** completion to each question or statement.

1. What was the name of the highest Jewish court?
a) Supreme Court
b) Septuagint
c) Sanhedrin
d) Areopagus

2. Who built roads to prepare the world for Christ?
a) The Greeks
b) The Romans
c) The Samaritans
d) The Jews

3. The Greeks prepared the world for Christ by
a) emphasizing one religion.
b) emphasizing one government.
c) emphasizing one army.
d) emphasizing one language.

4. Which of these is in the correct biblical order?
a) Mark, John, Luke
b) Ephesians, Galatians, Philippians
c) John, Acts, Romans
d) Hebrews, James, Revelation

5. The leading officials of the Sanhedrin were
a) Pharisees.
b) Sadducees.
c) Levites.
d) Zealots.

6. How many letters did Paul write?
a) 5
b) 8
c) 13
d) 15

7. Which group of books contains Acts?
a) Synoptics
b) Historical books
c) General Epistles
d) Letters to all

8. Herod Agrippa II listened to the trial of whom?
a) Jesus
b) Stephen
c) Peter
d) Paul

9. Who was the high priest when Jesus was on trial?
a) Annas
b) Ananias
c) Gamaliel
d) Caiaphas

10. Which book pictures Christ as our Righteousness?
a) 2 Peter
b) Hebrews
c) Romans
d) Galatians

Essay Test Topics: Write 50-100 words on each of these goals that you studied in this chapter.

Preparation for the New Testament

Goal: *Define Pharisees, Sadducees, Sanhedrin, and Septuagint.*

Goal: *Explain how God used the Jews, Greeks, and Romans to prepare the world for His Son.*

Books of the New Testament

Goal: *Describe 6 rulers of Herod's family, the high priest, the temple, and synagogues.*

Goal: *Draw a house that shows the 4 groups of New Testament books.*

Christ in Every Book of the New Testament

Goal: *Summarize 3 pictures of Christ from each group of New Testament books.*

Chapter 2:

The Synoptic Gospels: Matthew, Mark, and Luke

Figure 2.1 The Son of Man was delivered into the hands of sinful men and crucified for our salvation (Luke 24:7).

Introduction

A Bible school student in Finland named Kai was once a policeman. He tells about studying a crime or a car accident. He explains, "If everyone describes what happened in exactly the same words, the policeman knows that there is a problem. On the other hand, if each witness tells what happened from a slightly different point of view, it has the sound of truth."

In London, in the National Gallery of Art, there are three paintings of King Charles I. All three of these paintings are together, in one picture, within one frame. In the first painting, his head is turned to the left. But his head is turned to the right in the second painting. In the third painting King Charles is looking straight ahead. An artist named Van Dyck painted these three views of the king for someone who wanted to make a stone statue of the king. Having three different views of the king was a great help.[1]

Likewise, the Synoptic Gospels allow us to learn about Jesus Christ from three different points of view. The Synoptics, together with John, give us a complete picture of Jesus. Matthew emphasizes that Jesus was a king, but Mark shows that He was a perfect servant. Luke shows that Jesus was the Son of Man, but John emphasizes that He was the Son of God.

Lessons:

The Gospel of Matthew

4

Goal A: *Explain Matthew's purpose, and the main way he fulfilled it.*

Goal B: *Identify and explain the 5 teaching pillars of Matthew.*

Goal C: *Explain why Matthew emphasized the Kingdom. State 3 ways he stressed it.*

The Gospel of Mark

5

Goal A: *Explain Mark's purpose and how he fulfilled it.*

Goal B: *Give 2 examples of how Mark helped Gentile readers.*

The Gospel of Luke

6

Goal A: *Contrast the purposes of Matthew and Luke.*

Goal B: *Identify 5 things found only in Luke that emphasize his theme of Jesus, the Savior of all.*

Characteristics of the Synoptics

7

Goal A: *Summarize and apply 4 reasons Jesus taught in parables.*

Goal B: *Define the kingdom of God and explain its 2 phases.*

Goal C: *Explain why Jesus healed and did miracles. Apply this to today.*

Key Words

synoptic

Messiah

Son of Man

genealogy

parables

kingdom of heaven

Aramaic

Lesson 4 The Gospel of Matthew

Goal A: *Explain Matthew's purpose, and the main way he fulfilled it.*
Goal B: *Identify and explain the 5 teaching pillars of Matthew.*
Goal C: *Explain why Matthew emphasized the Kingdom. State 3 ways he stressed it.*

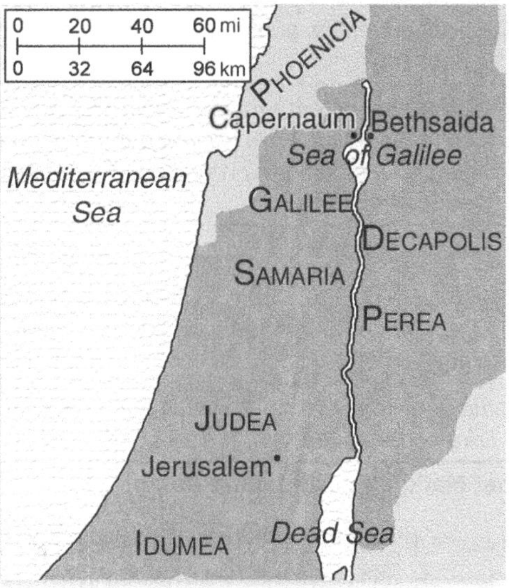

Figure 2.2 Map of Palestine in the time of Christ

Setting

The first three Gospels are called the *Synoptic Gospels. *Synoptic* means "seeing together." Matthew, Mark, and Luke tell similar stories about the life of Christ. They present Christ from a different point of view than John does.

Figure 2.3 summarizes some of the things we will learn about the Synoptic Gospels.

Gospel	Readers	Purpose and Theme
Matthew	Jews	Jesus is the *Messiah, King of the Jews
Mark	Romans	Jesus is the Servant of the Lord, busy working
Luke	Greeks	Jesus is the *Son of Man, the perfect human

Figure 2.3 The Synoptic Gospels: their readers and purposes

We will look briefly at each of the Synoptics, beginning with Matthew.

A. Author, date, and theme

Matthew was one of the twelve disciples of Christ. He wrote the book that is placed first in the New Testament. He probably wrote it about A.D. 60-69. At one time, Matthew was a man whom no one liked. He was a Jew who collected taxes for the Roman government. Then Jesus called him (Matt. 9:9; Mark 2:14). He left his job as a tax collector and followed Jesus (Matt. 9:9-13). Later, he wrote his Gospel to Jewish readers. The *theme* of Matthew is Jesus, the Messiah and King of the Jews. What a change Jesus made in his life. Today, people who never met Matthew love him. Thousands have given their children his name.

Q 1 *What does synoptic mean?*

Q 2 *Identify the author and theme of Matthew.*

B. Readers and purpose

Matthew wrote his Gospel mainly to Jewish readers. His main purpose was to prove to Jewish readers that Jesus was the Messiah. This helped believers and unbelievers. The family tree was very important to Jews. So Matthew began his Gospel with the *genealogy of Jesus. He showed that Jesus was a son of David and a son of Abraham (Matt. 1:1).

All of the Gospel writers quoted from the Old Testament. But Matthew included nine quotes from the Old Testament that Mark, Luke, and John did not. His main purpose was to show that Jesus was the Jewish Messiah. And his main method was to show how Jesus fulfilled the Old Testament Scriptures (See Figure 2.4).

Q 3 *Put these books in the biblical order: Luke, Matthew, Acts, John, Mark.*

Q 4 *What was Matthew's main purpose?*

Q 5 *Give 3 examples of how Matthew showed that Jesus was the Messiah.*

Matthew	Quote from the Old Testament
1:22-23	*All this took place to fulfill what the Lord had said through the prophet: "The virgin will be with child and will give birth to a son, and they will call him Immanuel"—which means, "God with us."* [Isa. 7:14]
2:15	*where he stayed until the death of Herod. And so was fulfilled what the Lord had said through the prophet: "Out of Egypt I called my son."* [Hos. 11:1]
2:17-18	*Then what was said through the prophet Jeremiah was fulfilled: "A voice is heard in Ramah, weeping and great mourning, Rachel weeping for her children and refusing to be comforted, because they are no more."* [Jer. 31:15]

Continued on next page

Continued from previous page

2:23	*and he went and lived in a town called Nazareth. So was fulfilled what was said through the prophets: "He will be called a Nazarene."*
4:14-16	*to fulfill what was said through the prophet Isaiah: "Land of Zebulun and land of Naphtali, the way to the sea, along the Jordan, Galilee of the Gentiles—the people living in darkness have seen a great light; on those living in the land of the shadow of death a light has dawned."* [Isa. 9:1-2]
8:17	*This was to fulfill what was spoken through the prophet Isaiah: "He took up our infirmities and carried our diseases."* [Isa. 53:4]
12:17-21	*This was to fulfill what was spoken through the prophet Isaiah: "Here is my servant whom I have chosen, the one I love, in whom I delight; I will put my Spirit on him, and he will proclaim justice to the nations. He will not quarrel or cry out; no one will hear his voice in the streets. A bruised reed he will not break, and a smoldering wick he will not snuff out, till he leads justice to victory. In his name the nations will put their hope."* [Isa. 42:1-4]
13:35	*So was fulfilled what was spoken through the prophet: "I will open my mouth in parables, I will utter things hidden since the creation of the world."* [Ps. 78:2]
21:4-5	*This took place to fulfill what was spoken through the prophet: "Say to the Daughter of Zion, 'See, your king comes to you, gentle and riding on a donkey, on a colt, the foal of a donkey.' "* [Zech. 9:9]
27:9-10	*Then what was spoken by Jeremiah the prophet was fulfilled: "They took the thirty silver coins, the price set on him by the people of Israel, and they used them to buy the potter's field, as the Lord commanded me."* [Jer. 32:6-9]

Figure 2.4 Matthew includes nine quotes from the Old Testament that Mark, Luke, and John do not.

The Gospel of Matthew is like a bridge between the Old and the New Testaments. It joins together the prophecies of the coming Messiah with Christ's fulfillment of those prophecies. Matthew often quoted from the prophets to show Jesus was the Messiah. He connected their words with the life and ministry of Jesus. Matthew first gave us the Old Testament message, "He is coming." Then he added his own message, "He is here!"

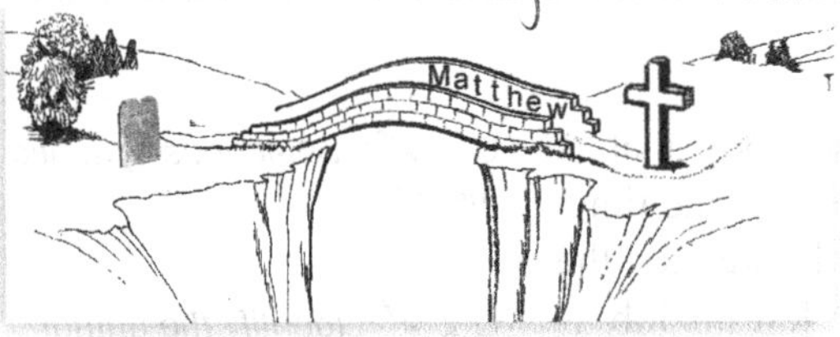

Figure 2.5 Matthew is like a bridge between the Old and New Testaments.

Matthew writes 33 times about the **kingdom of heaven* (See point E. that follows).[2] He was the only Gospel writer to use these words. Why? The Jews believed that the word *God* was very holy. It was so holy to them that they rarely said it. Therefore, Matthew usually avoided using the word *God*. Mark and Luke write about the kingdom of God. But Matthew substitutes the word *heaven* for God. This was important because he was writing to Jewish readers.

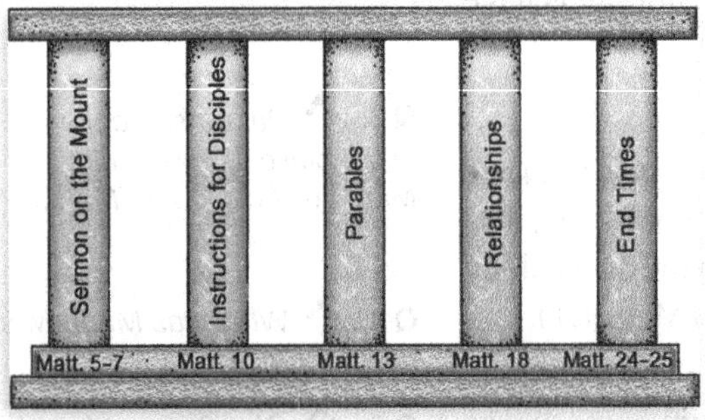

Figure 2.6 Five sermons or teaching pillars in Matthew

C. The five sermons or teaching pillars in Matthew

There are five places in Matthew that contain long portions of the teachings of Jesus (See Figure 2.6). These five places are chapters: 5–7, 10, 13, 18, and 24–25. Matthew closes each of these sections with words like, "*When Jesus had finished saying all these things.*" The best students of the Bible should know that Matthew contains these five major sections of teachings. Also, they should be able to summarize some of the teachings in each of these five places. These five places are like five pillars that help hold up the book of Matthew.

Q 6 *Draw the 5 teaching pillars of Matthew. Identify the chapters and theme of each.*

Q 7 *Explain what is happening just before each of the 5 pillars.*

Note how the Holy Spirit guided Matthew to plan his writing. Matthew used the five pillars of teaching to help organize his Gospel. The *first* pillar of teaching is Matthew 5–7. Matthew uses this as a smooth way to move from the private life of Jesus (Matt. 1–4) to His public ministry. The *second* pillar of teaching is Matthew 10. Just before it are the ten miracles of chapters 8 and 9. After it comes the rising conflict between Jesus and the religious leaders (Matt. 11–12). Then Matthew gives us the *third* pillar in chapter 13. It includes eight *parables. Just past this third pillar, we find Jesus ministering in Galilee. The conflict between Jesus and Jewish leaders continues to rise (Matt. 14–17). The *fourth* pillar of teaching is Matthew 18. It marks the time that He turned from Galilee and started toward Judea. Finally, the *fifth* pillar of teaching is Matthew 24–25. It comes just before the Last Supper, the Crucifixion, and the Resurrection.

D. Outline

Theme	Matthew
A. The Messiah's Birth and Early Years	**1–2**
His family tree	1:1-17
His birth	1:18–2:12
His escape to Egypt	2:13-23
B. The Messiah's Background for Ministry	**3:1–4:11**
His announcement by John	3:1-12
His baptism	3:13-17
His temptation	4:1-11
C. The Messiah's Ministry in and Around Galilee	**4:12–18:35**
The beginning of ministry in Galilee	4:12-25
The Sermon on the Mount	5–7
Miracles of the Messiah	8–9
The commission of the twelve apostles	10
Ministry throughout Galilee	11–12
Parables of the Kingdom	13
Opposition rises against the Messiah	14–17
Teachings on life in the Kingdom	18
D. The Messiah's Ministry in Judea and Perea	**19–20**
Teachings about divorce, little children, and entering the Kingdom	19
Teachings about the vineyard, the Lord's death, and being a servant	20:1-28
The healing of blind Bartimaeus at Jericho	20:29-34
E. The Messiah's Final Week of Ministry in Jerusalem	**21–27**
The King enters Jerusalem, cleanses the temple, and rebukes the leaders	21–23
The end-time sermon on the Mount of Olives	24–25
The arrest, trial, crucifixion, and burial of the Messiah	26–27
F. The Messiah's Resurrection and Great Commission	**28**
The Resurrection	28:1-15
The Great Commission	28:16-20

Figure 2.7 Outline of Matthew

E. The kingdom of heaven

Q 8 *Explain why Matthew emphasized the Kingdom. State 3 ways he stressed it.*

The kingdom of heaven is a big theme in Matthew. Matthew's purpose was to prove to the Jews that Jesus was the Messiah. The Jews expected the kingdom of God to come to earth when their Messiah came. They thought the Messiah would conquer the Romans. Why did they believe this? Because under the kings of the Old Testament, Israel conquered her enemies. That is how they possessed the land of Palestine. Also, the prophets had predicted that the Messiah and God's kingdom would come to the earth. The Jews did not recognize that there were two phases of the Kingdom. They did not discern that the Messiah would come first to suffer (Isa. 53). Then He would return to set up God's kingdom on the earth.

Figure 2.8 Workers harvesting grain

The Jews linked the Messiah to the Kingdom. Therefore, Matthew mentioned the kingdom of heaven twice as often as any other Gospel writer.[3] He showed that the Kingdom was near or at hand. Likewise, he included many teachings about the Kingdom. He emphasized the righteous standards of the Kingdom (Matt. 5–7). He showed the present power of the Kingdom over sin, sickness, demons, and even death. He wrote about the future triumph of the Kingdom at the end of the age (Matt. 24–25).

Q 9 *Complete Figure 2.9.*

In addition to the teachings mentioned above, Matthew included 12 of the Messiah's parables about the Kingdom. Most of these parables begin with the words *the kingdom of heaven is like* (Figure 2.9).

Parable	Matthew	Your main thought on the kingdom of heaven
The weeds	13:24-30	
The mustard seed	13:31-32	
The yeast	13:33	
The hidden treasure	13:44	
The pearl	13:45-46	
The net	13:47-50	
The workers in the vineyard	20:1-16	
The two sons	21:28-32	
The wicked renters	21:33-46	
The wedding banquet	22:1-14	
The ten virgins	25:1-13	
The talents	25:14-30	

Figure 2.9 Twelve parables in Matthew about the kingdom of heaven

For a thorough study of Matthew, study the *Faith & Action* course *The Life & Teachings of Christ.*

Lesson 5

The Gospel of Mark

Goal A: *Explain Mark's purpose and how he fulfilled it.*

Goal B: *Give 2 examples of how Mark helped Gentile readers.*

Q 10 *What are 4 reasons Mark knew much about Jesus?*

Q 11 *Illustrate 2 different ways Mark especially helped Gentile readers.*

A. Author, date, and theme

Mark, the author, was not one of the twelve apostles. However, he lived in Jerusalem (Acts 12:12). He was a friend of Simon Peter (1 Pet. 5:13). And he was a cousin of Barnabas (Col. 4:10). Also, Mark, sometimes called John Mark, worked with Paul and the other apostles (Acts 12:25). So he was close to all of the apostles. He knew much about the life of Christ and the life of the early church.

Jewish custom or Aramaic word	Explanation for Romans and other Gentile readers	Mark
Boanerges	This Aramaic word means *"Sons of Thunder."* It is the name Jesus gave to James and John.	3:17
"Talitha koum!"	These Aramaic words mean *"Little girl, I say to you, get up!"*	5:41
Washing of hands	The Pharisees and all Jews do not eat without washing their hands. Their tradition also guides them to wash cups, pitchers, and kettles.	7:2-4
Corban	A Hebrew word meaning *"a gift devoted to God."*	7:11
"Ephphatha"	An Aramaic word that means *"be opened."*	7:34
Golgotha	An Aramaic word which means *"The Place of the Skull."*	15:22
"Eloi, Eloi, lama sabachthani?"	An Aramaic sentence meaning *"My God, my God, why have you forsaken me?"*	15:34
Preparation Day	This means it was the day before the Jewish Sabbath.	15:42

Figure 2.10 Mark explained Jewish customs and Aramaic words to help Roman and other Gentile readers.

Mark may have been written first, before the other three Gospels. Most scholars date it in the late 50's or early 60's.

The *theme* of Mark is Jesus the servant. Mark gives us no genealogy of Jesus. Why? Because no one is concerned about the ancestors of a servant! What people want from a servant is work. So Mark shows Jesus in action.

B. Readers and purpose

Mark wrote his Gospel mainly to Roman readers. He knew that

Romans and other Gentiles did not understand Jewish culture or the *Aramaic language Jews spoke. So he explained Jewish customs and many Aramaic words (Figure 2.10).

Q 12 *What word does Mark use often to show that Jesus was a busy servant?*

His purpose was to show Jesus at work as "*the Servant of the Lord.*" Forty-two times in this Gospel we see Christ doing things "*immediately.*" This shows us that the Servant was busy doing His Father's work. Mark used almost half of his Gospel to tell of the death and resurrection of Christ (Mark 11:1–16:18). He showed that Jesus served us most as the Savior who died and rose for us.

C. Outline

Q 13 *Summarize how Jesus served in Galilee (Mark 1–9).*

Matthew emphasized what Jesus said. But Mark focused on what Jesus did. Therefore, we have created an outline that emphasizes Jesus in ministry.

Theme	Mark
A. The Background of Jesus' Ministry	**1:1-13**
His messenger	1:1-8
His baptism	1:9-11
His temptation	1:12-13
B. Jesus' Early Ministry in Galilee	**1:14–3:12**
He called the first disciples	1:14-20
He drove out demons and healed diseases in Capernaum.	1:21-34
He ministered throughout Galilee—first trip.	1:35-45
He returned to Capernaum: healed a paralytic, called Levi, and taught on fasting and the Sabbath.	2:1–3:22
C. Jesus' Later Ministry in Galilee	**3:13–7:23**
He chose the Twelve, taught about Beelzebub, told parables, and calmed a storm.	3:13–4:41
He freed a man from a Legion, raised a dead girl, and healed a sick woman.	5
He visited Nazareth, sent out the twelve, fed 5,000, and walked on the water.	6
He taught what makes a person clean or unclean.	7:1-23
D. Jesus' Ministry Beyond and in Galilee	**7:24–9:50**
In Phoenicia: He shared some bread crumbs with a Gentile woman.	7:24-30
In Decapolis: He healed a man who was deaf and mute, then fed 4,000.	7:31–8:10
Around Caesarea Philippi: He taught about yeast, touched a blind man twice, heard Peter's confession, predicted His death, was transformed on a mountain, and freed a demon-possessed boy.	8:11–9:32
Back in Galilee: He taught about being a servant, accepting others, and loving children.	9:33-50
E. Jesus' Ministry in Judea and Perea	**10**
He taught on divorce, children, and the danger of riches.	10:1-31
He predicted His death and responded to the request of James and John.	10:32-45
He healed the eyes of blind Bartimaeus.	10:46-52
F. The *Passion Week	**11–15**
Sunday: He rode into Jerusalem—The *Triumphal Entry.	11:1-11
Monday: He cleansed the temple and cursed a fig tree.	11:12-19
Tuesday: He taught on faith, authority, tenants, four questions, the end times, and Mary's gift.	11:20–14:11
Thursday: He ate the Last Supper with the Twelve.	14:12-25
Friday: He traveled from Gethsemane to *Calvary.	14:26–15:47
G. The Resurrection	**16**

Figure 2.11 Outline of Mark

Lesson 6 The Gospel of Luke

Goal A: *Contrast the purposes of Matthew and Luke.*

Goal B: *Identify 5 things found only in Luke that emphasize his theme of Jesus, the Savior of all.*

Q 14 *Which 2 Gospels were not written by apostles?*

Q 15 *Contrast the purposes of Matthew and Luke.*

Q 16 *Which verse in Luke do you think states his purpose best?*

A. Author, date, and theme

Luke, the author, was a doctor (Col. 4:14). He was also a friend of Paul (Phm. 24). He wrote two books of history. He wrote his Gospel on the life of Christ. Most scholars think he wrote Luke about A.D. 60-63. His second book, Acts, is the history of the early church. Luke, like Mark, was not one of the twelve apostles. But he gives us a sure account of the life and teachings of Jesus (Luke 1:1-4).

His *theme* is Jesus, the Savior of all.

B. Readers and purposes

Figure 2.12 Jesus came to seek and save what was lost (Luke 19:10; John 3:17).

Matthew was a Jew who wrote to the Jews. But Luke was a Greek who wrote to the Greeks. He had at least two related purposes for writing us a history of the Lord's life and ministry.

First, Luke's main purpose was to present Jesus as the Savior of all. Matthew's purpose was to prove Jesus was the Jewish Messiah who fulfilled the Old Testament prophecies. But Luke emphasizes that Jesus came *"to seek and save what was lost"* (Luke 19:10). We see Luke's emphasis on Jesus the universal Savior in many places.

- Gabriel told Mary to name her child *Jesus,* which means "Savior" (Luke 1:31).
- The angels told the shepherds [10] *"...good news...for all the people...* [11] *...a Savior has been born"* (Luke 2:10-11).
- Simeon held the baby Jesus and praised God, saying [30] *"my eyes have seen your salvation,* [31] *which you have prepared in the sight of all people,* [32] *a light...to the Gentiles and...to your people Israel"* (Luke 2:30-32).
- *"The Son of Man came to seek and to save what was lost"* (Luke 19:10).

People Jesus came to save	Luke
Samaritans, even though Jews and Samaritans hated each other	9:51-55; 10:30-37; 17:11-19
Gentiles	2:11, 31-32; 3:6, 38; 4:25-27; 7:9; 10:1; 24:47
Jews	1:33; 2:10, 31-32; 19:9-10
Publicans (tax collectors), sinners, and those society casts out	3:12; 5:27-32; 7:37-50; 19:2-10; 23:43
Respected people	7:36; 11:37; 14:1
The poor	1:53; 2:7; 6:20; 7:22; 14:21
The rich	14:2; 23:50
Women and men	7:36-50; 19:1-10

Figure 2.13 Luke shows that Jesus came to be the Savior of all people.[4]

Matthew emphasized that Jesus was the Messiah. But Luke wrote good news for the whole world. Luke is truly the *Global Gospel!* Figure 2.13 shows that Jesus came to save all people.

Matthew traces the Lord's genealogy through David and back to Abraham. But Luke's family tree of Jesus goes all the way back to Adam, the son of God (Luke 3:38). Thus Luke shows that Jesus is related to all people. Figure 2.17 lists 45 things found only in Luke. These will help you see Luke's emphasis on salvation. Note especially Luke 15. This trio of parables tells about the lost sheep, the lost coin, and the lost son. Heaven rejoices when the lost are saved. Luke wrote that Jesus came so "*all mankind will see God's salvation*" (Luke 3:6).

Q 17 *How do the genealogies recorded by Matthew and Luke relate to their purposes?*

Q 18 *Summarize how Luke shows that Jesus was perfect in relationship to man.*

Second, Luke emphasized that Jesus was the perfect man. The highest goal of the Greeks was to find the ideal or perfect man. All educated Greeks sought the perfect person.[5] So Luke showed that Jesus was the complete, perfect man.

In relation to humans, Jesus was above the highest Greek standards. He was born fully human. From a child to an adult He "*grew in wisdom and stature, and in favor with*

God and men" (Luke 2:52). Jesus showed love for the sinful, like the immoral woman He forgave. But He showed righteousness when He cleansed the temple. He was tender, but also powerful. He was humble, but fearless. He was wiser than the wisest teachers of the day.

Jesus was also perfect in His relationship to God. Luke emphasized this in two ways: through prayer and being filled with the Spirit. More than any other Gospel, Luke emphasized Christ's attitude toward prayer. And Luke also stresses that Jesus depended on the Spirit. Why was the Savior able to preach good news, free the prisoners, heal the blind, and release the oppressed? Because the Spirit of the Lord was upon Him (Luke 4:18-19). Luke shows us that Jesus was a model for us in character, prayer, and being filled with the Spirit. As the Son of Man, Jesus was the best man in every way. Thus Luke presents the perfect "*Son of Man* [who] *came to seek and to save what was lost*" (Luke 19:10).

Figure 2.14
The Good Samaritan (Luke 10:25-37)

C. Outline

Theme	Luke
Introduction to Luke's Gospel	**1:1-4**
A. The Savior's Background	**1:5–2:52**
Announcement about John	1:5-25
Announcement about the Savior	1:26-56
Birth of John	1:57-80
Birth and childhood of the Savior	2
B. The Savior's Preparation	**3:1–4:13**
His messenger	3:1-20
His baptism	3:21-22
His genealogy	3:23-38
His temptation	4:1-13
C. The Savior's Ministry in Galilee	**4:14–9:50**
He is rejected at Nazareth, but heals many in Capernaum.	4:14-41
A tour of Galilee: He calls Simon, James, John, and Levi; heals a leper and a paralytic.	4:42–5:39
He heals a man's hand on the Sabbath and chooses the Twelve.	6:1-16
The sermon on the plain	6:17-49
He heals a centurion's servant and raises a widow's son.	7:1-17.
Jesus and John the Baptist	7:18-35
Faith in Jesus saves a sinful woman.	7:36-50
The Savior's teachings: the sower, a lamp, and His family	8:1-21
The Savior's power: calms a storm, frees a man from demons, raises a dead girl, heals a woman	8:22-56
He sends the Twelve, feeds 5,000, is glorified, frees a boy from a demon, and teaches on greatnes	9:1-50
D. The Savior's Ministry on the Final Journey to Jerusalem	**9:51–19:27**
The Savior reaches out to Samaritans, and sends out the 72.	9:51–10:24
The Good Samaritan	10:25-37
Mary and Martha	10:38-42
Prayer, Beelzebub, Jonah, the eye, and 6 woes	11
Fear, riches, worry, watching, division, and the end times	12

Continued on next page

Q 19 *In what 2 ways was Jesus perfect in relation to God?*

Q 20 *What lesson near the calling of Levi (Matthew) illustrates Luke's theme (Luke 5:27-31)?*

Continued from previous page

Repentance, compassion, the Kingdom, and Jerusalem's judgment	13
A local banquet, the great banquet, and discipleship	14
The lost sheep, the lost coin, and the lost son	15
The unjust steward and the unjust rich man	16
Sin, faith, 10 lepers, the end times	17
Prayer, humility, children, riches, the cross, Bartimaeus	18
Zacchaeus meets the Savior; the 10 minas	19:1-27
E. The Savior's Last Days in Jerusalem	**19:28–23:56**
He rides in triumph into Jerusalem and cleanses the temple.	19:28-48
Four questions between Jesus and the Jewish leaders	20
He teaches on the end times from the Mount of Olives.	21
The Last Supper	22:1-38
From Gethsemane to Calvary	22:39–23:56
F. From the Savior's Resurrection to His Ascension	**24**
The Resurrection	24:1-12
The Post-Resurrection appearances	24:13-43
The Savior's final instructions	24:44-53

Figure 2.15 Outline of Luke

Q 21 *Fill in Figure 2.16.*

Gospel	Readers	Purpose and theme

Figure 2.16 Practice chart on the Synoptic Gospels

D. Only in Luke

Q 22 *What are 5 passages found only in Luke that emphasize his theme of Jesus our Savior?*

Only in Luke	Luke
Songs of Elizabeth, Mary, Zechariah, and Simeon	1:39-80
The shepherds and the angels	2:8-20
Jesus presented in the temple; Anna and Simeon	2:21-40
The boy Jesus in the temple	2:41-52
Jesus raises a widow's son	7:11-17
Samaritan opposition	9:51-56
Plow illustration on following Jesus	9:61-62
Jesus sends out the seventy-two	10:1-12
Return and report of the seventy-two	10:17-20
Parable of the Good Samaritan	10:25-37
At the home of Mary and Martha	10:38-42
Parable of the persistent friend	11:5-10
Parable of the rich fool	12:13-21
Repent or perish	13:1-5
Parable of the fruitless fig tree	13:6-9
A crippled woman healed on the Sabbath	13:10-17
Jesus' sorrow for Jerusalem	13:31-33

Continued on next page

Continued from previous page

Only in Luke	Luke
Jesus at a Pharisee's house	14:1-6
Parable about feasts and guests	14:7-14
Parable of the great banquet	14:15-24
Comparison: planning of the tower-builder	14:28-30
Further comparison: planning of king going to war	14:31-33
Parable of the lost coin	15:8-10
Parable of the lost son	15:11-32
Parable of the shrewd manager	16:1-15
The rich man and Lazarus	16:19-31
Illustration about duty	17:7-10
Ten healed of leprosy	17:11-19
The coming of the kingdom of God	17:20-21
Parable of the persistent widow	18:1-8
Parable of the Pharisee and the tax collector	18:9-14
Zacchaeus, the tax collector	19:1-10
Parable of the ten minas (pounds)	19:11-27
Jesus weeps over Jerusalem	19:41-44
Jesus heals Malchus' ear	22:51
The thief on the cross repents	23:32-43
On the road to Emmaus	24:13-35
Wait for the Holy Spirit baptism	24:49
The Ascension	24:50-53

Figure 2.17 More than 45 teachings and events found only in Luke

Lesson 7

Characteristics of the Synoptics

Goal A: *Summarize and apply 4 reasons Jesus taught in parables.*
Goal B: *Define the kingdom of God and explain its 2 phases.*
Goal C: *Explain why Jesus healed and did miracles. Apply this to today.*

A. Events in all three Gospels

Each Gospel is different in its main thought. However, there are six events of which all three Synoptic Gospels tell. This repetition helps us to know these six events well.

Q 23 *Name 6 events that are in all the Synoptic Gospels.*

B. Christ's unusual birth

Event or Teaching	Matthew	Mark	Luke
1. Announcement of the Savior by John the Baptist	3	1	3
2. Baptism of the Savior	3	1	3
3. Temptation of the Savior	4	1	4
4. Transfiguration of the Savior	17	9	9
5. Trial, death, and burial of the Savior	26–27	14–15	22–23
6. Resurrection of the Savior	28	16	24

Figure 2.18 Six events found in all three Synoptic Gospels

The birth of Christ was unusual. His virgin birth is essential to the Christian faith. Old Testament prophets told about it. Angels announced it to Joseph and Mary. And the Holy Spirit made it happen (Matt. 1–2; Luke 1–2). Thus our Savior was born of a virgin.

Years ago there was an old college teacher who believed in the virgin birth of Christ. Some other doubting professors ridiculed him because of this belief. One of them said, "Suppose a young woman entered the hospital near here today. If she had a baby boy and claimed that she was a virgin, would you believe her?" The old professor stroked his beard and was silent for a moment. Then he answered, "No, I probably wouldn't.

Q 24 *In what way was Christ's birth unique?*

Q 25 Why do you think Mark says nothing about the first 30 years of Christ's life?

However, if that baby boy grew up and became a man,

- and if he could open the eyes of the blind,
- and if he could enable cripples to walk,
- and if he could cleanse the lepers,
- and if he could raise the dead,
- and if he called a little group of followers and radically changed their lives,
- and if he died like a condemned criminal, but was raised from the dead,
- and if he changed the history of the world,
- and if, after 2,000 years, a third of earth's population called him Savior and Lord,
- and if all those people claimed that they knew His living presence in their hearts,

then I think I would listen to that woman's story a second time!" We believe in the virgin birth of Jesus because of His life and power.[6]

Parable or Similar Saying	Matthew	Mark	Luke
A lamp on a stand	5:14-16	4:21-23	8:16-18
The wise and foolish builders	7:24-27		6:46-49
New cloth on an old garment	9:16	2:21	5:36
New wine in old wineskins	9:17	2:22	5:37-39
The sower	13:3-23	4:2-20	8:4-15
The weeds	13:24-30		
The mustard seed	13:31-32	4:30-32	13:18-19
The yeast	13:33		13:20-21
The hidden treasure	13:44		
The pearl	13:45-46		
The net	13:47-50		
The house owner	13:51-52		
The lost sheep	18:12-14		15:3-7
The unmerciful servant	18:21-35		
The workers in the vineyard	20:1-16		
The two sons	21:28-32		
The tenants	21:33-45	12:1-12	20:9-19
The wedding banquet	22:1-14		
The fig tree	24:32-35	13:28-29	21:29-31
The ten virgins	25:1-13		
The talents	25:14-30		
The sheep and the goats	25:31-46		
The growing seed		4:26-29	
The day and hour unknown		13:34-37	
Two debtors			7:41-43
The Good Samaritan			10:25-37
The good gifts			11:5-13
The rich fool			12:16-21
Watchfulness			12:35-48
The fruitless fig tree			13:6-9
The great banquet			14:15-24
The lost coin			15:8-10
The lost son			15:11-32
The shrewd manager			16:1-13
The rich man and Lazarus			16:19-31
The master and the servant			17:7-10
The persistent widow			18:1-8
The Pharisee and the tax collector			18:9-14
The ten minas (pounds)			19:11-27

Figure 2.19 Parables and similar sayings of Jesus in the Synoptic Gospels

C. The parables of Christ

Christ taught often through parables. A parable is a short story or illustration with a spiritual meaning. Many cultures practice teaching through stories. Jesus taught in parables for several reasons. Parables were safe. The enemies of Jesus could not easily attack Him for telling a story. Also, parables illustrate and preserve truth. They are easy to remember. Again, a parable gets into a person's heart. Nathan told King David a parable (2 Sam. 12:1-4). It was about a rich man who sacrificed the only lamb of a poor man. The truth was in David's heart before he realized he was the rich man. Illustrations carry the truth past people's defenses.

Another reason Jesus used parables was to hide new truth from unfaithful people! Read Matthew 13:10-12. It says that God wanted the disciples to learn new truth. The disciples could not understand the parables. Therefore, Jesus explained them privately. However, God did not want the crowd to have new truth. Why? Because they had not been faithful with old truth. Whoever is faithful will be given more. Whoever is unfaithful will lose what he has (Matt. 13:12; 25:29). The parables were a form of judgment.

John recorded none of our Lord's parables. But the Synoptic Gospels contain at least 30 different parables. Among the best known of these are the parables of the Kingdom (Matt. 13) and the lost sheep, coin, and son

(Luke 15). The Synoptic Gospels also record many other short statements that are similar to parables.

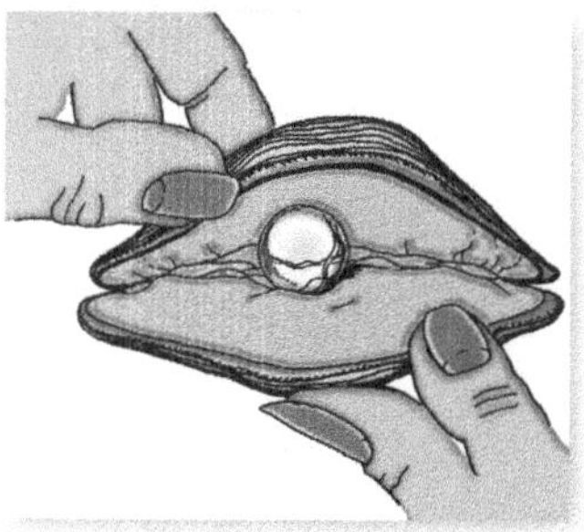

Figure 2.20 Jesus illustrated His teachings with common things, such as a pearl.

Some pastors went to a yearly meeting. There was a need to raise money to build a new building. The pastors agreed that all their church members should each give five shillings on the following Easter. Pastors at the meeting then began to argue about how the building should look. One elderly pastor said that it would be better to collect the money first. Later, they could decide the exact style of the building. To persuade others of his point, he told the following story.

Some farmers discovered that the wild pigs were eating their maize at night. Each farmer agreed to bring a spear. They would surround the pigs, kill them, and have a great feast. That night, the plan was going well. Slowly and silently, the farmers closed in on the pigs. They would taste so good. Then the farmers began to argue about who would get the best pigs. While the men were arguing, the pigs ran away. Nobody got anything.

Q 26 *Summarize 4 reasons Jesus taught in parables.*

Everyone at the meeting clapped. They agreed to stop arguing about the building details until after they got the money. The wise pastor had used an example which convinced the people. Wise preachers and teachers persuade many people through stories.

Q 27 *Do the best teachers and preachers you know use many stories? Explain.*

D. The Kingdom

Jesus taught much about the *kingdom of God.* The words *kingdom of heaven* and *kingdom of God* appear often. These are two different names for the same kingdom. His kingdom is everywhere He rules.

Q 28 *Explain the 2 phases of the kingdom of God.*

God's kingdom has two phases or time periods. *First,* there is the invisible phase. This phase of the Kingdom refers to God's spiritual rule. It is not an outward kingdom of land and buildings. "*The kingdom of God does not come with your careful observation, ...because the kingdom of God is within you*" (Luke 17:20b, 21b). The first phase of God's kingdom is in the hearts of believers. John the Baptist and Jesus announced this first phase of the Kingdom (Matt. 3:1-3; Mark 1:14-15). We cannot see it now. But we see some of the changes God's rule makes in people.

The *second* phase of the Kingdom will be visible. Then, we will see it on the earth. This will happen "*when the Son of Man comes in his glory, and...all the nations will be gathered before him*" (Matt. 25:31-32). The prophets often wrote about this (Isa. 11:1-10; Zech. 13:1-6; Mal. 4:1-3). He will separate the sheep from the goats. This is the mountaintop of judgment on the *"day of the Lord"* at the close of this age. The wicked will depart into everlasting torment. Perhaps we can liken hell to the King's dungeon or prison. After the judgment, the King will rule over all the earth. All things will be summed up in Christ. God will be all in all.

E. The miracles

Jesus showed that He was the Messiah, God's Servant, and our Savior through His miracles. Physical miracles proved that Jesus had power to meet people's spiritual needs.

Q 29 *Do you think that we still need healings and miracles today? Explain.*

A Muslim saw a large tent in his town of Mombasa, Kenya. Some followers of Jesus were having a meeting there each evening. Their religion was different from his. But he was attracted for one reason. He heard they were praying for the sick in the name of Jesus. This Muslim man's son, Muhammad, was 12 years old. The boy was a cripple and had never been able to walk. Each day Muhammad sat and watched the other children play. It seemed that there was no hope for him. But his father decided to give the Christian religion a test. One evening, he carried Muhammad to the big tent. The local pastor was preaching about the miracles of Jesus. Then, he made the claim that Jesus is the same yesterday, today, and forever (Heb. 13:8). At the end of the service, he invited people to come forward for prayer. Muhammad's father carried him forward. The pastor placed his hands upon him and prayed in the name of Jesus. Suddenly, Muhammad felt the power of God flowing into his weak and crippled legs. They straightened out. To his amazement, the boy found that he could walk. He took the first step of his life. People began to praise God all over the tent. Muhammad decided to become a follower of Jesus Christ. He wanted to serve the God who could meet his needs.

Healing or Miracle	Matthew	Mark	Luke
Man with leprosy	8:2-3	1:40-42	5:12-13
Roman centurion's servant	8:5-13		7:1-10
Peter's mother-in-law	8:14-15	1:30-31	4:38-39
Calming of the storm	8:23-27	4:37-41	8:22-25
Two men from Gadara	8:28-34	5:1-15	8:27-35
Paralyzed man	9:2-7	2:3-12	5:18-25
Raising Jairus' daughter	9:18-25	5:22-42	8:41-56
Woman with bleeding	9:20-22	5:25-29	8:43-48
Two blind men	9:27-31		
Man—dumb and possessed	9:32-33		
Man with a shriveled hand	12:10-13	3:1-5	6:6-10
Man—blind, dumb, and possessed	12:22		11:14
Feeding 5,000 people	14:15-21	6:35-44	9:12-17
Walking on water	14:25	6:48-51	
Canaanite woman's daughter	15:21-28	7:24-30	
Feeding 4,000 people	15:32-38	8:1-9	
Boy with epilepsy	17:14-18	9:17-29	9:38-43
Coin in fish's mouth	17:24-27		
Two blind men	20:29-34		
Fig tree withered	21:18-22	11:12-25	
Man—demon-possessed in synagogue		1:23-26	4:33-35
Deaf mute		7:31-37	
Blind man at Bethsaida		8:22-26	
Blind Bartimaeus		10:46-52	18:35-43
Catch of fish			5:1-11
Raising widow's son at Nain			7:11-15
Crippled woman			13:11-13
Man with *dropsy			14:1-4
Ten lepers			17:11-19
The high priest's servant			22:50-51

Figure 2.21 Healings and miracles of Jesus in the Synoptic Gospels

Test Yourself: Circle the letter by the ***best*** completion to each question or statement.

1. To fulfill his purpose, Matthew mainly used
a) a genealogy of Jesus Christ.
b) quotes from the Old Testament.
c) miracles that Jesus performed.
d) parables the Lord taught.

2. One of the five pillars in Matthew is
a) the genealogy in chapter 1.
b) the sermon in chapters 5–7.
c) the miracles in chapter 8.
d) the Resurrection in chapter 28.

3. Why did Matthew emphasize the kingdom of heaven?
a) To show that Jesus spoke often of the Kingdom
b) To emphasize the Lord's parables and teachings
c) To contrast it with the kingdom of God
d) To link the Kingdom with Jesus, the Messiah

4. A key word related to Mark's purpose is
a) immediately.
b) fulfill.
c) life.
d) kingdom.

5. What is the main way that Mark helped his readers?
a) He defined the locations of the main miracles of Jesus.
b) He explained Aramaic words and Hebrew customs.
c) He gave specific references for OT quotes.
d) He wrote in Hebrew so his readers would understand.

6. The parables of the lost coin and lost son are only in
a) Matthew.
b) Mark.
c) Luke.
d) John.

7. Luke emphasizes that Jesus came to be the Savior of
a) Romans.
b) Jews.
c) Greeks.
d) all.

8. Which phase of the kingdom of God are we in now?
a) The invisible phase
b) The national phase
c) The visible phase
d) The international phase

9. Jesus used parables to teach so that
a) everyone could understand what he taught.
b) people could interpret them in different ways.
c) his enemies would accept his teachings.
d) those who neglected truth would not get new truth.

10. Jesus proved he was the Messiah by
a) teaching in Jewish parables.
b) doing healings and miracles.
c) teaching in the temple at age 12.
d) riding into Jerusalem as a king.

Essay Test Topics: Write 50-100 words on each of these goals that you studied in this chapter.

The Gospel of Matthew

Goal: *Explain Matthew's purpose, and the main way he fulfilled it.*

Goal: *Identify and explain the 5 teaching pillars of Matthew (5–7, 10, 13, 18, and 24–25).*

Goal: *Explain why Matthew emphasized the Kingdom. State 3 ways he stressed it.*

The Gospel of Mark

Goal: *Explain Mark's purpose and how he fulfilled it.*

Goal: *Give 2 examples of how Mark helped Gentile readers.*

The Gospel of Luke

Goal: *Contrast the purposes of Matthew and Luke.*

Goal: *Identify 5 things found only in Luke that emphasize his theme of Jesus, the Savior of all.*

Characteristics of the Synoptics

Goal: *Summarize and apply 4 reasons Jesus taught in parables.*

Goal: *Define the kingdom of God and explain 2 phases.*

Goal: *Explain why Jesus healed and did miracles. Apply.*

Chapter 3:
The Gospel of John

Figure 3.1 John wrote to encourage his readers to believe in Christ.

Introduction

An African beggar named Ahmad began another long day. This cripple used his hands as feet to move his body along. His shriveled legs dragged in the dirt behind him like a ragged coat that was too long. It was a terrible sight. Yet for years he had stayed alive by begging from store to store. Friday was always his best day for begging. It is the day that Muslims give to the poor. Ahmad was the best known of the beggars because he was the worst to look at.

In 1988 a gospel video center opened. It was on the busiest street of Limbe, the largest city in Malawi. Many people came daily to watch the gospel preachers on the videos. James Kafotokoza and John Mpinga managed this center. At the end of each video, they invited people to come forward for prayer. During one of these invitations, Ahmad responded. Slowly, he slid forward on the floor to be prayed for. At the front of the room, James, John, and Pastor Kachinga of the Bangwe Assembly of God church waited. When Ahmad arrived, they placed their hands on him and began to pray. As they prayed they heard something like bones popping. Opening their eyes, they saw a miracle taking place. God was healing the legs of the beggar! Those present watched in amazement. Ahmad stood up and began praising the name of Jesus. In time, he walked out of the center with many who had witnessed this miracle.

Soon, Muslims began coming out of their stores to see the beggar who was healed. All were amazed and asked how this happened. Pastor Kachinga began to preach about the beggar that Jesus healed in Acts 3. More and more Muslims gathered to see the beggar who was healed in the name of Jesus. People said it was like the book of Acts happening again. News swept like fire through the Muslim community. Hundreds rejoiced that Jesus had healed their well-known beggar, Ahmad. As a result, many Muslims put their faith in Jesus.[1]

John tells us of the miracles Jesus did when He was on the earth. Likewise, He heals today through the faith and prayers of His followers (John 14:12-14).

Lessons:

Understanding John

8

Goal A: *Explain why John omitted many things that are in the Synoptics.*

Goal B: *Analyze the words signs, believe, and life in relation to John's purpose.*

The Structure of John

9

Goal A: *Analyze the introduction and conclusion of John.*

Goal B: *Identify the 5 parts of John's Gospel.*

The Teachings of Jesus in John

10

Goal A: *Analyze the relationship between the signs and teachings in John 5, 6, 9, and 11.*

Goal B: *Identify the 7 "I am" statements in John.*

Goal C: *Explain 3 lessons from people who talked with Jesus.*

Key Words

believe epilogue life prologue signs Word

Lesson 8 Understanding John

Goal A: *Explain why John omitted many things that are in the Synoptics.*

Goal B: *Analyze the words signs, believe, and life in relation to John's purpose.*

A. Author, date, and purpose

The author of the fourth Gospel was the apostle John. He was a fisherman, a son of Zebedee, and the brother of James. He may have been about 25 years old when Jesus called him. At that time, he may have been a follower of John the Baptist (John 1:40). John was one of the closest apostles to Jesus. Several times the fourth Gospel refers to him as *"the disciple whom Jesus loved"* (John 13:23; 19:26-27). The Lord's love changed John. In his early days Jesus named him a Son of Thunder (Mark 3:17). In those days, John wanted to call down fire from heaven to destroy the Samaritans (Luke 9:54). But the Lord's patient love for John changed him into a gentle apostle. As an elder, John was gentle (3 John).

Figure 3.2 A fisherman mending his net

The date John wrote was A.D. 80-95. This was probably at least 20 years after the writing of Matthew, Mark, and Luke. Note that this was 50-60 years after the resurrection of Christ. John wrote at least 20 years after Luke wrote Acts in A.D. 63. And John wrote at least 10 years after Titus destroyed Jerusalem in A.D. 70. The gospel was well known by then. The Lord's followers had preached it far and wide. So we see that John's Gospel was one of the last books of the New Testament. Only John's other letters came after his Gospel. Knowing the date of John's Gospel helps us discern his purpose.

Q 1 *Who was the author of John's Gospel? Explain.*

Q 2 *How does the date of John's Gospel relate to the dates of the Synoptics and Acts?*

The *purpose* of the fourth Gospel is clear in John 20:30-31. He wanted people to believe that Jesus is the Messiah, the Son of God, and thus receive eternal life by following Him.

John wrote after the life and teachings of Jesus were well known. So he did not need to repeat what the other Gospels had already taught. But false teachers were attacking the gospel. These denied that Jesus was the Son of God who came in the flesh. Matthew emphasized that Jesus was the Son of David. Luke emphasized that He was the Son of Man. But John emphasized that Jesus is the Son of God. In John, Jesus refers to God as *My Father* 35 times.[2] He claimed to be equal with God (John 5:18). John records no genealogy of Jesus and no birth. Instead, he stresses that Jesus was with God in the beginning (John 1:1). He does not record the Lord's boyhood, temptation, or transfiguration. John says nothing about the Lord's parables, ascension, or Great Commission. These were all well known when John wrote. But over and over John emphasized the deity of Jesus. He presented God's Son for unbelievers to receive and believers to follow.

Q 3 *Why did John omit many things that the Synoptics covered?*

It is helpful to think of John's Gospel as a house with a door on each side. We may identify four keys to help us unlock the riches of John.

Three important words help clarify John's purpose in John 20:30-31. These words are *signs, believe,* and *life.* Read John 20:30-31 again. Notice how he uses these three words. Now, let's look at each of the three.

Key	John	Verse
Front door	1:12-13	*[12]To all who received him, to those who believed in his name, he gave the right to become children of God—[13]children born not of natural descent, nor of human decision or a husband's will, but born of God.*
Left door	10:10	*"The thief comes only to steal and kill and destroy; I have come that they may have life, and have it to the full."*
Right door	16:28	*"I came from the Father and entered the world; now I am leaving the world and going back to the Father."*
Back door	20:30-31	*[30]Jesus did many other miraculous signs in the presence of his disciples, which are not recorded in this book. [31]But these are written that you may believe that Jesus is the Christ, the Son of God, and that by believing you may have life in his name.*

Figure 3.3 Four keys to John's Gospel

B. Signs

Q 4 For what purpose did John choose seven signs?

*Signs is John's word for Christ's miracles. Signs have a purpose. John's signs helped people know that Jesus was *"the Christ, the Son of God"* (John 20:31).

Sign	John
Changing water into wine	2:1-11
Healing the official's son	4:43-54
Healing the man at the pool	5:1-15
Feeding the five thousand	6:1-15
Walking on water	6:16-21
Healing the blind man	9:1-34
Raising Lazarus from the dead	11:1-44

Figure 3.4 The seven signs in John's Gospel

Jesus performed many signs. John chose seven to emphasize the deity of Christ. Later, we will study more about the spiritual truth related to each of the seven signs (See lesson 10, Figure 3.8).

Five of these seven signs are only in John. Feeding the five thousand and walking on the water are also in the other Gospels.

C. Believe

Q 5 Define the word "believe" in John.

Q 6 Name 5 words in John that help explain the word "believe."

John used the word **believe* at least 98 times in his Gospel. This is a word of action, showing that something is happening. How did John teach what it means to believe in Jesus? He taught through examples. *Believe* is the word that shows the response of people to Jesus. If they believed in Him, they became His followers. If they did not believe, they usually became His enemies. Jesus turned the water to wine. His disciples believed in Him and followed Him (John 2:11). The woman at the well believed in Jesus. This belief caused her to tell others about Him (John 4:28-42). The official and his household believed in Jesus (John 4:53). Many Jews began the journey of believing in Jesus. He told them they were really his students or followers if they continued and obeyed His teachings (John 8:31-32; compare 6:66). The man born blind believed in Jesus after being healed. His belief expressed itself through boldly testifying for Jesus and worshiping Him (John 9:30-38). All who met Jesus had to decide to believe or not to believe. They could not avoid making a decision.

Word	Explanation	John
receive	Believing in Jesus is like receiving a person to live in one's home.	1:12
drink	Believing in Jesus is like drinking refreshing water.	4:14
come to	Believing in Jesus is like coming to the source of food and water.	6:35
eat	Believing in Jesus is like daily eating food that satisfies.	6:51
follow	Believing in Jesus is like daily following Him on a path.	8:12
hold to; continue in	Believing in Jesus is like a student submitting to a teacher.	8:31-32; 6:66
enter through	Believing in Jesus is like entering through a door into safety.	10:7-9
listen to	Believing in Jesus is like listening to and obeying a shepherd.	10:26-27
obey	Believing in Jesus is like obeying a parent or a person in authority.	14:15, 23; 15:14
remain in	Believing in Jesus is like remaining in a bus until the end of a trip.	15:1-8

Figure 3.5 John used many words to explain what it means to *believe* in Jesus.

John used other words similar to *believe* to make his meaning clear. Figure 3.5 summarizes some words from John that explain what it means to believe. All of these words are common in daily life. But they have a richer meaning when we apply them to our relationship with Jesus.

D. Life

Life results from believing in Christ. People receive life when they receive Him. John also wrote this in another letter. He said, *"He who has the Son has life; he who does not have the Son of God does not have life"* (1 John 5:12). Some speak of eternal life as though it were a gift that comes by itself. Eternal life is free. But it is not a gift that comes alone.[3] Eternal life is the result of our relationship with Jesus. A hand is alive if it is connected to a living person. A fruit is alive if it is connected to a living tree or plant. Jesus is life (John 1:4; 14:6; Col. 3:4). Those who are connected to Him have eternal life. Those who are separated from Him will experience eternal death and punishment. Our *"life is hidden with Christ in God"* (Col. 3:3).

Q 7 What is "life" in John, and how do we get it?

Those who receive Jesus become God's spiritual children (John 1:12-13). They are born into the family of God. Jesus said to Nicodemus, *"You must be born again"* (John 3:7). At the new birth we experience life in relation to God. As sinners, we needed life because we were spiritually dead in our sins. Sin killed our relationship with the Heavenly Father (Eph. 2:1). Adam was alive toward God in the Garden of Eden. But he died spiritually on the day he disobeyed God (Gen. 3). Sin, when it is finished, brings forth spiritual death (James 1:15). But God gives us life through Christ (Eph. 2:4-5). This life is eternal (John 3:15). It is the opposite of perishing spiritually (John 3:16). Our eternal life begins when we receive Jesus as Savior and Lord. Our life continues as we follow, obey, and remain in Him. *"Whoever believes in the Son has eternal life, but whoever rejects* (disobeys) *the Son will not see life, for God's wrath remains on him"* (John 3:36).[4] When He returns, our life will appear (Col. 3:4). Then we will live with Him forever.

John's purpose for writing his Gospel is clear. He wanted to bring his readers face to face with the Person who called Himself *"God"* (John 1:1; 20:28). He wrote to encourage us to believe in Jesus. To believe in Jesus means to receive and come to Him. It means to eat, drink, follow, hold to, enter through, listen to, obey, and remain in Jesus.

Lesson 9 The Structure of John

Goal A: *Analyze the introduction and conclusion of John.*
Goal B: *Identify the 5 parts of John's Gospel.*

A. Introduction

John's introduction (John 1:1-18) is important. It contains the message of the entire Gospel. In it, John introduces three main themes of his Gospel.

- **The main Person** is *the* *Word. The Word is God, the Creator, the Giver of Life, and the One who came in flesh. Jesus is the Word who tells us about the Father (John 1:18).
- **The main words** are *life, light, darkness, witness, believe,* and *truth.*
- **The main action** is *conflict.* John used plain terms to describe battles. Light and darkness oppose each other. He used common words to show great spiritual conflict. He shows that Jesus becomes a friend to those who receive Him and walk in the light. But He becomes a judge and an enemy to those who refuse Him and remain in darkness. John contrasts the physical birth with spiritual birth. And he contrasts grace and law. Thus we see that John is a Gospel of conflicts and contrasts.

Q 8 *Summarize the 3 themes in John's introduction (John 1:1-18).*

Q 9 *Explain 4 examples of contrast in John's Gospel.*

These great conflicts continue throughout John until the final conflict. Then we see the conflict between the cross (death) and the resurrection (life). Hallelujah! Jesus arose as the conqueror of death.

B. Outline

Theme	John
Introduction *Prologue: The Presentation of the Son of God	**1:1-18**
A. The Public Ministry of the Son of God	**1:19–12:50**
Meeting people	1:19–4:54
Meeting the crowds	5:1–6:71
Problems with the crowds	7:1–11:53
The greatness of His public ministry	11:54–12:50
B. The Private Ministry of the Son of God	**13:1–17:26**
The Last Supper	13:1-30
The last sermon	13:31–16:33
The high priestly prayer	17:1-26
C. The Ministry in Death of the Son of God	**18:1–20:31**
His betrayal and trials	18:1–19:16
His crucifixion and burial	19:17-42
His resurrection	20:1-31
Conclusion (*Epilogue): The Final Call of the Son of God	**21:1-25**

Figure 3.6 Outline of John

Q 10 *Which chapters in John contain the introduction and conclusion?*

Q 11 *Which chapters in John deal with the Lord's private ministry?*

Q 12 *Which chapters in John deal with the week of the cross?*

Figure 3.7 Saving faith always comes with works of obedience.

C. Conclusion

The conclusion emphasizes the result of the gospel. Those who truly believe, like Peter, follow Jesus. Belief guides people to serve (John 21:19). Peter learned that believing in Jesus was more than confessing words. Belief in Jesus required Peter to give himself completely to Christ's service. All who believe in Jesus serve Him in some way.

An old man used a small boat with two oars to help people cross a river. One day a passenger noticed the word *faith* on one oar and the word *works* on the other. "Why have you carved a word on each oar?" asked the curious rider. "I'll show you," replied the old man. At first, he rowed only with the oar of faith. This caused the boat to go in a circle. Then, he rowed only with the oar of works. Again, the boat went in a circle, the other way. But when the elder rowed with the two oars of faith and works, the boat traveled straight ahead. "So it is in life," said the wise old man. Faith and works must pull together. One without the other is useless.[5]

Lesson 10

The Teachings of Jesus in John

Goal A: *Analyze the relationship between the signs and teachings in John 5, 6, 9, and 11.*

Goal B: *Identify the 7 "I am" statements in John.*

Goal C: *Explain 3 lessons from people who talked with Jesus.*

Q 13 *What did Jesus teach after the sign of feeding the 5,000?*

We have discussed the purpose, key words, and structure of John. Now, let's look at the teachings of Jesus in this fourth Gospel. What did He teach? How did He teach?

A. The relationship between the signs and teachings of Jesus

The signs gave Jesus an opportunity to teach. He healed the man beside the pool of Bethesda in Jerusalem (John 5:1-9). After this sign, the Jews questioned His right to heal on the Sabbath (John 5:16). This allowed Jesus to teach who He was. He taught that He was equal with God (John 5:17-18). Jesus claimed that He is the One who will raise the dead and judge them (John 5:21-30).

We are emphasizing the relationship between the signs and truth. In John 6, Jesus faced the problem of feeding more than 5,000 hungry people. Philip could not solve this problem. Andrew brought a boy to Jesus. This boy had five loaves and two fish (John 6:9). Jesus used these to feed the people and to meet their physical needs (John 6:12). The next day the large crowd returned. They were looking for another meal. The Lord told them not to work *"for food that spoils"* (John 6:27). Then He taught them about their spiritual need. This was when He told them, *"I am the bread of life"* (John 6:35). Thus we see the meaning of the sign.

John	Sign	Truth related to the sign	Jesus is Lord over[6]
2:1-11	Changing water into wine	This first miracle revealed His glory. That is, it showed that He was God in flesh. The miracle inspired His disciples to believe in Him.	quality
4:43-54	Healing the official's son	Those who reject Jesus miss God's blessings (John 4:44). But those who welcome Him receive good things (John 4:45, 47, 54).	distance
5:1-15	Healing the man at the pool	Jesus is equal with God in nature, power, and authority.	time
6:1-15	Feeding the five thousand people	*"I am the bread of life. He who comes to me will never go hungry, and he who believes in me will never be thirsty"* (John 6:35).	quantity
6:16-21	Walking on water	Jesus has power over circumstances. When He is with us, we have nothing to fear.	nature
9:1-34	Healing the blind man	[5]*"I am the light of the world...* [39]*For judgment I have come into this world, so that the blind will see and those who see will become blind"* (John 9:5, 39).	fate
11:1-44	Raising Lazarus from the dead	*"I am the resurrection and the life. He who believes in me will live, even though he dies"* (John 11:25).	death

Figure 3.8 The seven signs in John help us believe and are related to spiritual truths.

A long sermon followed the sign of feeding the five thousand. In it, Jesus showed the difference between *"the flesh"* and *"the spirit"* (John 6:63). The people did not understand spiritual truth. They came to Him only for physical bread. They had missed the true meaning of the sign. Jesus explained what it meant to eat *"living bread"* (John 6:51). But the people complained against this spiritual saying. They argued with one another about what Jesus meant (John 6:52). Finally, many of those following Him turned away (John 6:66). Those who follow Jesus only for earthly blessings will be disappointed.

Figure 3.9 Ruins of the Pool of Bethesda

Jesus healed a blind man in John 9. This sign illustrated His claim, *"I am the light of the world. Whoever follows me will never walk in darkness, but will have the light of life"* (John 8:12; 9:5). This miracle proved that Jesus can enable people to walk in the light. Notice the teachings that followed this sign. *"For judgment I have come into this world, so that the blind will see and those who see will become blind"* (John 9:5, 39). This is a proverb. It means that those who realize they are blind may ask Jesus for sight. Then, like the blind man, He will enable them to see the light. In contrast, some are like the Pharisees. They claimed to be able to see without any help from Jesus. Therefore, they remained guilty of sin and unable to see spiritual truth (John 9:40-41). Only the Savior can take away our sins. Only He can enable us to find our way back to God. John's Gospel enriches our lives. It enables us to see the relationships between the miracles and spiritual truth.

Q 14 *Explain the error of the multitude following Jesus.*

Q 15 *What did Jesus teach after healing the blind man?*

Jesus raised Lazarus from the dead (John 11). This illustrated His claim, *"I am the resurrection and the life. He who believes in me will live, even though he dies"* (John 11:25). Students should be able to identify the seven signs in John. And they should be able to explain the spiritual truth linked to each sign (Figure 3.8).

B. The seven *"I Am"* statements of Jesus

Jesus used the words *"I am"* to show people who He was. Figure 3.10 summarizes the claims of Christ in John's Gospel.

"I Am" Passages	John
"I am the bread of life."	6:35
"I am the light of the world."	8:12; 9:5
"I am the gate."	10:7, 9
"I am the good shepherd."	10:11
"I am the resurrection and the life."	11:25
"I am the way and the truth and the life."	14:6
"I am the true vine."	15:1

Figure 3.10 The seven *"I am"* statements of Jesus

The claims of Jesus are unique. No other religious leader has ever made claims like Jesus. Some have tried to help the hungry find bread. But Jesus said, *"I am the bread of life!"* The sun gives physical light to the world. But the Son of God is the only source of the world's spiritual light. What a big claim! Likewise, He claimed to be the only gate or door to the Heavenly Father. Consider this claim! No other religious leader ever claimed to be the only way to God. Again, He claimed that all who believe in Him will live forever. Who else ever claimed anything like that? Many have searched for truth. But Jesus said, *"I am the truth!"* He alone is the spiritual standard that shows what is true and false. And consider this. There are many vines on the earth. Vines bear various fruit, such as grapes, melons, and cucumbers. But Jesus claimed to be the true vine. He said that spiritual life comes only from abiding in Him. All who do not relate to Him as the vine will be cast into the fire. His claims are unique. They put Him in a class above all humans. His claims put Him at the level of God alone. Every student should know the seven *"I am"* statements of Jesus in John.

Q 16 *Learn to create Figure 3.10 from memory.*

I AM was the Old Testament name of God. It was the name God used to reveal Himself to Moses (Exod. 3:14). Our Bibles translate I AM as YAHWEH or Jehovah or the LORD. Jesus claimed to be that I AM. He told the Jews, *"I tell you the truth... before Abraham was born, I am"* (John 8:58). He gave himself the title of God—*"I AM"*—from the Old Testament Scriptures. This made the Jews so angry that they

Figure 3.11
***"If anyone eats of this bread, he will live forever"* (John 6:51).**

wanted to stone Him (John 8:59). Those who believe that Jesus spoke the truth believe that He is God.

Person and lesson related to belief	John
Andrew is an example of one who helped others believe in Jesus.	1:35-42; 6:8-9; 12:20-22
Simon Peter is an example of how Jesus changes our character as we believe in Him.	1:42; 6:68-69; 13:36-38; 18:15-18, 25-27; 21:15-22
Nicodemus shows us that we must be born again by believing in Jesus.	3:1; 7:50-51; 19:39-42
Philip shows us that we learn more as we believe in and follow Jesus.	1:43-46; 6:5-7; 14:8-14
The woman of Samaria shows that Jesus satisfies all who believe in Him.	4:1-42
The blind man teaches us that Jesus gives sight to those who receive Him.	9:1-39
Martha and Mary teach us that life's greatest priority is sitting at the feet of Jesus.	11:1-46
Thomas teaches us that Jesus will perfect our faith in Him.	11:16; 14:5-7; 20:24-28
Pilate is an example of unbelief.	18:28–19:16
Judas Iscariot is an example of one who started believing, but turned away.	6:70-71; 13:21-30; 18:1-5

Figure 3.12 The people who talked with Jesus teach us much about believing.

C. Lessons from conversations with Jesus

John used people to teach lessons about believing.

Through Andrew we learn that we should share our belief with others (John 1:35-42; 6:8-9; 12:20-22). We do not know Andrew as well as we know Simon Peter, his brother. However, Andrew was important. He believed in Jesus. Then he became a spiritual worker, helping others to believe. We always see him bringing someone to Jesus. *First*, he brought his brother, Simon. *Later*, he brought the boy with his lunch to Jesus. *Finally*, Andrew brought some Greek visitors in Jerusalem who wanted to meet Jesus.

Through Simon Peter we learn that Jesus changes those who believe (John 1:42; 6:68-69; 13:36-38; 18:15-18, 25-27; 21:15-22). When Simon met Jesus, the Lord prophesied about his new name, Peter. This change also meant a change in Simon's character. As Simon, he was unstable. The Lord could not depend on him. However, he became Cephas, "a rock."

Through Nicodemus we learn that believing is linked with being born again (John 3:1; also see John 7:50-51 and 19:39-42). Nicodemus had been trained to know the Old Testament truths. Still, he had not experienced the new birth. He did not know that Jesus was the Messiah. Jesus taught Nicodemus from the Old Testament. He compared Himself to the serpent that Moses lifted up in the wilderness. Our Lord came to be the Savior of all who believe in Him. Later events suggest that Nicodemus became a believer.

John taught a lot through people. Figure 3.12 summarizes people who talked with Jesus.

Q 17 *What do we learn about believing from Andrew, Peter, and Nicodemus?*

Q 18 *Summarize 2 main teachings from the sermon in the upper room.*

D. Final teachings and instructions in the upper room

Jesus gave an unusual sermon near the end of His life. It is recorded in John 13–16. People often call it the "upper room sermon." The details of the sermon are found only in John. Jesus had finished His public ministry at the end of John 12. He then met privately with His disciples. Jesus told them about two important things that would happen. *First*, He told them that He was leaving soon. He said that they could not go with Him. But He promised to return and take them to the Father's house.

Second, Jesus told His disciples that He would not leave them alone (John 14:18). He would send another Counselor to be with them. Our Lord promised to send the Holy Spirit to take His place. The Holy Spirit would live in them (John 14:17), teach them (John 14:26), and give them power to witness (John 15:26-27). And the Spirit would guide them into all of the truth (John 16:13).

John's Gospel enriches our lives. It presents the life and teachings of Jesus in a way that adds to the Synoptics. Together, the four Gospels give us a thorough understanding of Jesus—who He is, what He did, and what He taught.

Test Yourself: Circle the letter by the ***best*** completion to each question or statement.

1. John's main purpose was to
a) show how Christ fulfilled the Old Testament.
b) discuss the contrast between grace and the law.
c) persuade his readers to believe in Christ.
d) write a history of Jesus' life and ministry.

2. Why did John emphasize that Jesus is the Son of God?
a) To correct the errors of false teachers
b) To repeat the Synoptic teachings
c) To contrast Him with the Son of Man
d) To clarify the teachings of John the Baptist

3. In his Gospel, John used the word *believe* about
a) 10 times.
b) 30 times.
c) 70 times.
d) 100 times.

4. In John, a word that means the same as *believe* is
a) confess.
b) repent.
c) obey.
d) worship.

5. John's word for *miracles* is
a) healings.
b) signs.
c) wonders.
d) revelations.

6. In John's introduction, he contrasts
a) the beginning and end.
b) weakness and power.
c) poverty and wealth.
d) light and darkness.

7. Which of the following is an *"I am"* statement from John's Gospel?
a) "I am the Alpha and Omega."
b) "I am the Cornerstone."
c) "I am the Good Shepherd."
d) "I am the Son of Man."

8. To show the deity of Christ, John chose seven
a) signs.
b) conversations.
c) contrasts.
d) parables.

9. From Simon Peter, we learn that
a) Jesus changes our character as we believe in Him.
b) Jesus expects us to drink from His cup.
c) Jesus satisfies all who believe in Him.
d) Jesus knows our inner thoughts.

10. Who teaches us to bring people to Jesus?
a) Nicodemus
b) Andrew
c) Philip
d) Lazarus

Essay Test Topics: Write 50-100 words on each of these goals that you studied in this chapter.

Understanding John

Goal: *Explain why John omitted many things that are in the Synoptics.*

Goal: *Analyze the words signs, believe, and life in relation to John's purpose.*

The Structure of John

Goal: *Analyze the introduction and conclusion of John.*

Goal: *Identify the 5 parts of John's Gospel.*

Teachings of Jesus

Goal: *Analyze the relationship between the signs and teachings in John 5, 6, 9, and 11.*

Goal: *Identify the 7 "I am" statements in John.*

Goal: *Explain 3 lessons from people who talked with Jesus.*

Chapter 4:
The Book of Acts

Figure 4.1 The stoning of Stephen, as portrayed by Gustave Dorè

Introduction

J. W. Tucker was an Assemblies of God missionary to the nation now called the Democratic Republic of the Congo. The Simba Revolution began in Tucker's 11th year in the Congo. Simba is the Swahili word for "lion." This anti-foreign, anti-missionary group named themselves lions because they were fierce. They seized Tucker at his home, bound his hands behind his back, and took him to the central plaza. There they smashed a glass bottle in his face. When he fell on the pavement, they danced on his body until it would not move. Then they threw him into the nearby Bomokandi River. Crocodiles ate the body.

The world was shocked. It seemed like such a tragedy. How could this happen? Wasn't he in God's will? In that moment it was easy to question God's wisdom. But He had a purpose.

The Bomokandi River flowed through the land of the Mangbetu people. This tribe binds the heads of their babies to make their heads longer. To them, long heads are beautiful. Up to that time, they had never accepted the gospel. The Mangbetu had resisted missionary work. No church stood among them. Great missionaries like *C. T. Studd had worked there, but were unable to start anything that continued.

The government wanted peace. They sent an African policeman to calm the Mangbetu people. He was a big, husky man. Everyone called him the *Brigadier, a name for a top general in the British army. Just before J. W. Tucker died, he had led the Brigadier to Christ. The policeman had never preached a sermon and had no religious education. But he knew that Jesus had saved him.

Among the Mangbetu people, the Brigadier learned their customs. One of their sayings was, "We will always hear the words of anyone whose blood was shed in our river." Since Tucker's blood was in their river, the Brigadier shared Tucker's gospel with the chief. The good news spread among the tribe. Today, there are 40 Assemblies of God churches among the Mangbetu. God worked through persecution to lead many people to the Savior.[1] Likewise in Acts, persecution was a key to the spread of the gospel.

Lessons:

11 Understanding the Book of Acts

Goal A: *Analyze the title, author, and date of Acts.*

Goal B: *Summarize 5 purposes that Acts serves.*

12 Outlining the Book of Acts

Goal: *Divide Acts into 3 parts, giving the chapters for each part.*

13 Witnessing About Jesus

Goal: *Analyze 3 steps in which believers witnessed for Jesus from Jerusalem to Rome.*

Key Words

Jerusalem	Rome	Thessalonica	prejudice	Athens	Achaia
Theophilus	Galatia	Corinth	filled with the Holy Spirit	Antioch	Asia
		Philippi		Macedonia	

Lesson 11

Understanding the Book of Acts

Goal A: *Analyze the title, author, and date of Acts.*

Goal B: *Summarize 5 purposes that Acts serves.*

A. Title

When Luke first wrote Acts, it had no title. About A.D. 150, believers began to call Luke's book *The Acts of the Apostles.* Believers probably chose this title because the first chapter of Acts gives the names of the apostles (Acts 1:13). But as we read through Acts, we never see the names of most apostles again! After Acts 1, the only apostles called by name are Peter, John, James, and Paul.[2] Acts 1–12 focuses on Peter, and Acts 13–28 features Paul.

Figure 4.2 North end of Temple Mount with surrounding buildings. The ruins of the Fortress of Antonia are under this area.

In truth, the Holy Spirit is emphasized more than any of the apostles are. Luke introduces the Holy Spirit in the first verse of Acts. He shows us that even Jesus depended on the Holy Spirit (Acts 1:2). Then he reminds us that the apostles did not continue the ministry of Jesus without the power of the Spirit. Jesus commanded them not to leave Jerusalem until the Spirit filled them (Acts 1:4-5). Thus, from the beginning of Acts, Luke stresses that the Holy Spirit is the key to ministry. Jesus ascended to heaven. But He sent the Holy Spirit to live in and empower each believer. In Acts, Luke refers to the Spirit more than 50 times! Therefore, many agree that the best title for Acts is *The Acts of the Holy Spirit*![3]

Q 1 *What is the best title for Acts?*

B. Author

Most Bible teachers agree that Luke is the author of Acts. In humility, Luke does not place his name at the beginning of his Gospel or Acts. He was not an apostle, like Paul. But he wrote more words in the New Testament than Paul wrote.[4] We do not know if Luke ever preached a sermon or performed a miracle. His name was not known for power or authority. Therefore, there was no reason to place it at the beginning of his writings.

Figure 4.3
A ship like those of Paul's day

There are at least four reasons why we believe that Luke wrote Acts.

The writer of Acts traveled with Paul on some of his missionary trips. We know this from passages like Acts 16:10: *"After Paul had seen the vision, we got ready at once."* The word we shows us that the writer was with Paul. See passages such as Acts 20:5; 21:18; 27:1; and 28:16. Luke was a Gentile doctor who traveled some with Paul (Col. 4:14). This is one reason why we believe he wrote Acts.[5]

Whoever wrote Acts also wrote an earlier book. Acts 1:1 says, *"In my **former book**, *Theophilus, I wrote about all that Jesus began to do and to teach."* The Church has always believed that the *former book* mentioned in Acts 1:1 is Luke's Gospel. Both Luke and Acts are written to the same person, *Theophilus. Luke wrote these two volumes as an historical set. We understand them best together.

Q 2 *Summarize any 3 of the 4 reasons why we believe Luke wrote Acts.*

The writer of the Gospel of Luke was *not* an apostle. We know this from Luke 1:1-3. There, Luke says that others handed down the things that he wrote. He was not an eyewitness. Likewise, it appears that the writer of Acts was not an apostle. Luke fits this description. This adds to the evidence that he wrote Luke and Acts.

Believers from the early church to the present have accepted Luke as the author of our third Gospel and Acts. Fathers of the early church, such as Irenaeus and Clement of Alexandria, recognized Luke as the author. Likewise, the *Muratorian Canon (A.D. 170-210) names Luke as the author of Acts.

Q 3 ⛏ Acts was probably written between which two events (give dates)?

C. Date

Acts records the first time Paul was in prison in *Rome about A.D. 60-62. Therefore, Acts must have been written after this. Rome burned in A.D. 64. At that time a *Caesar named Nero blamed Christians for the fire. And he began to persecute them. The good relationship Paul had with the Roman government suggests that Acts was written before Rome burned. Also, Luke does not mention the destruction of Jerusalem. This took place in A.D. 70. So we think that Acts was written before this big event. Most Bible teachers think that Luke wrote Acts about A.D. 63.

D. Purposes

Date+ (A.D.)	Event	Acts	Letters Paul Wrote[8]
30	The ascension of Christ	1:9	
31-32	The conversion of Paul	9:1-19	
35	Paul's first visit to Jerusalem	9:26	
44	Paul's second visit to Jerusalem	11:30	
46-47	Paul's first missionary trip	13:4–14:28	Galatians (after first trip)
49	The first great Church Council	15:1-29	
49-53	Paul's second missionary trip	15:36–18:22	1 & 2 Thessalonians
53-57	Paul's third missionary trip	18:23–21:17	1 & 2 Corinthians, Romans
58	Paul's arrest in Jerusalem	21:17–23:35	
58-60	Paul's prison term in Caesarea	24–26	
60	Paul's trip to Rome	27:1–28:15	
60-62	Paul's first prison term in Rome	28:16-31	Ephesians, Philippians, Colossians, Philemon
63	The writing of Acts by Luke		
64	Rome burns		
63-65	Paul's ministry between prison terms in Rome	(After Acts)	1 Timothy, Titus
65-67	Paul's second prison term and death in Rome	(After Acts)	2 Timothy

Figure 4.4 Various dates related to Acts

There is a great danger in studying Acts. It is so full of action and stories that we can miss the big picture. A newspaper has many stories. These are often unrelated. In contrast, Luke chose a few stories for special reasons.

Q 4 ⛏ How many years passed from Christ's resurrection to Paul's imprisonment of Acts 28?

Acts gives us a history of the first 30 years of the Church.[6] Luke did not tell everything he knew. For example, he told us that Paul taught until midnight at Troas (Acts 20:7).[7] But Luke did not tell us anything Paul taught there. A book on the subjects Paul taught at Troas that one night would be longer than all of Acts! Imagine how many books it would take to tell all that happened in the Church during the first 30 years! Acts contains less than 1 percent of what happened in the early church. (Compare with John 20:30; 21:25.) Why did Luke leave most things out, but include only a few stories and events? Why did the Holy Spirit guide Luke to write about certain things? We can identify at least five purposes for which Luke wrote Acts.

Q 5 ⛏ How does Acts serve as a bridge between the Gospels and the Epistles?

1. Acts serves as a bridge between the Gospels and Paul's letters. In its early stage, the New Testament had only two parts. It included the Synoptic Gospels and the letters of Paul. So there were great gaps in the written history of the Church. Paul wrote letters to some churches. But many believers did not know how or when other churches started.

Review Figure 4.4. Notice that Luke wrote Acts after Paul wrote most of his letters. Acts 13–28 tell us about Paul's travels. In Acts we see how Paul started the churches in *Galatia, *Thessalonica, *Corinth, Ephesus, and *Philippi. Also, Acts introduces us to Timothy and Titus. Later in the New Testament we read Paul's letters to the churches and people that Acts introduced. Thus Acts gives us the background for Paul's letters. Acts has a special place in the New Testament. One of Luke's purposes was to give us a bridge between the Gospels and Paul's letters.

Figure 4.5 Acts is a bridge between the Gospels and the Epistles.

+ Bible teachers do not agree on the exact dates. These are approximate.

2. Acts traces the growth of the Church. Luke reveals that the Church grew in at least four ways.

Q 6 What are 4 types of church growth that Acts describes?

First, the Church grew in numbers. On the Day of Pentecost, the Church fit in one upper room. Then thousands of Jews were saved in Jerusalem (Acts 2:41, 47; 4:4). Acts 6:7 reveals that many more people accepted Christ, including many priests. Persecution scattered the believers. These witnessed and made converts everywhere they went (Acts 8:1, 4). Throughout Acts we see the number of believers increase.

Second, the Church grew *geographically, in new places. It started in Jerusalem. Acts explains how persecution scattered believers from Jerusalem to new locations (Acts 8:1). It also explains how Paul's journeys helped expand the Church. Still, the Church was in Rome before Paul arrived there (Acts 28:14-15). Acts 1 begins in Jerusalem and Acts 28 ends in Rome. Luke arranged his stories to show the growth of the Church.

Third, the Church grew socially. The early church was a Jewish church (Acts 1:1–7:60). How did the Church open up to other races? Acts 2 tells that Jews and Jewish converts from 15 different locations heard the gospel. Acts 6:1 reveals that the Church included two Jewish groups. One group spoke Greek and the other spoke Hebrew. Acts 8 tells us that Philip preached to Samaritans, and later, to an Ethiopian. Acts 10 tells us about Peter's vision related to Cornelius, a Roman centurion. This vision led to a change of attitude toward Gentiles. Even the Gentiles could be saved (Acts 11:18). This was amazing to Jewish believers! Thus the walls of *prejudice began to fall. Still, Acts 11:19-21 shows that the Church was limited by racial prejudice. A few Jews began to witness to Greeks! This was radical theology! But by Acts 13, we see Paul beginning to preach to the Gentiles after Jews reject the good news (Acts 13:43-46). Thus the Church grew to include those from all tribes, nations, languages, and cultures.

Fourth, the Church grew in its theology. In the early days the believers were Jewish. It took time for them to understand the relationship between law and grace. Acts 15 focuses on an important question. Do Gentiles need to be *circumcised and follow the law of Moses (Acts 15:5)? Peter's answer was "No!" (Acts 15:11). Still, the Jewish church leaders asked Gentile believers to follow some guidelines (Acts 15:19-21). Why? Partly so that there could be unity between Jewish and Gentile believers.[9] Thus Acts shows us how the theology of the Church grew to include all people. One of Luke's purposes was to show how the Church grew in numbers, new places, culture, and theology.

Q 7 How has your church grown in the 4 areas mentioned in Acts? Explain.

3. Acts explains and defends the Church.

- Acts explains and presents the Christian faith to all. Luke explains the background, growth, and beliefs of the Church. He does this in a way that invites people to receive and follow Jesus.
- Read Acts 4:8-12. Notice how it defends Christianity to Jews. Now read Acts 25:8-11. It defends the faith to Gentiles. The Spirit guides Luke to answer the religious questions of Jews and Gentiles.
- Acts also answers questions that government leaders would ask about Christianity. Acts shows that the Church is peaceful. Believers respect government leaders. In Acts, riots and civil problems are always caused by enemies of the Church.

Government Ruler	Explanation	Acts
1. The governor (proconsul) of Cyprus	This man, Sergius Paulus, believed when Paul and Barnabas came before him.	13:12
2. Rulers in Philippi	The Roman jailer was saved. The city rulers apologized for beating Paul, a Roman citizen.	16
3. Gallio, the governor of Achaia	Gallio refused to judge Paul. Why? As governor, he had no interest in problems of Jewish law.	18
4. Officials of Asia Minor and the town clerk of Ephesus	These officials were friends of Paul. The town clerk restored order. Thus he rescued Paul from harm.	19:31
5. Claudius Lysias	This Roman army captain guarded Paul when the Jews attacked the apostle in Jerusalem.	21–22
6. Governor Felix in Caesarea	Governor Felix listened to Paul talk to him about the gospel.	24
7. Governor Festus in Caesarea	Festus believed that Paul was innocent of charges brought by the Jews.	25

Figure 4.6 Acts gives seven examples to show that Christianity had a good relationship with the Roman government.

Luke probably wrote Acts while Paul was in prison in Rome. When Paul went to trial, Acts would support his defense. Likewise, Acts would help defend believers in other places. So we see that a third purpose of Acts was to defend the faith.

Q 8 Do you think that Acts should be used as a basis for doctrine? Explain.

4. Acts serves as a guide for faith and practice. Acts gives us guidance in what the Church should believe and do. Some argue that we should not use Acts as a guide because it is history. But recall that Luke did not write a complete history. He wrote a selective history. Paul used history for the purpose of teaching.[10] He referred to the historical book of Genesis. He reviewed the history of Abraham to teach that we are justified by faith (Rom. 4).[11] Likewise, Luke used history to teach certain themes.[12] He chose a few stories and events for special purposes. One of his purposes was to emphasize what the early church believed. Why is it helpful to know what the early church believed? Because the first believers were under the same covenant we are under! The Church in Acts teaches us to believe in the following:

- The Scriptures, prayer, sharing, and fellowship;
- The work of the Holy Spirit in glorifying Christ;
- Knowing and worshiping God;
- Witnessing, signs and wonders, being filled with the Spirit;
- Speaking in tongues, prophesying, and other spiritual gifts;
- Solving Church growth problems, evangelizing, and teaching new believers;
- God's power—He is working during persecution; He loves those in all nations.

Luke did not know how long the Church would remain on earth. But one of his purposes was to teach future believers. The power and principles of Acts are for the Church until Christ returns.[13]

Q 9 What is Luke's greatest purpose in Acts?

5. Acts emphasizes that being filled with the Spirit is the key to being witnesses for Jesus. The Gospel of Luke tells what Jesus began to do on earth, in a physical body. Acts tells us what Jesus continued to do from heaven. He did this through His spiritual body, the Church, by the Holy Spirit (Acts 1:1).[14]

Luke's greatest purpose is to emphasize the ministry of the Holy Spirit through believers. (See Figure 4.8.) In his Gospel, Luke stated that Jesus depended on the Spirit (Luke 4:1, 14, 18). Also, in his Gospel, Luke predicted that the Spirit would come to believers (Luke 11:13; 24:49). But in Acts, Luke mentions the Spirit 55 times! Use a concordance to review verses on the Holy Spirit in Acts. Luke emphasizes that the Holy Spirit is the source of all we do for Christ.

The fastest growing churches today emphasize the ministry of laypeople. Some of these growing churches have over 100 ministries that laypeople direct. Laypeople visit the sick, feed the poor, and teach people to read. They teach students who have problems with their studies. Laypeople help widows, adopt orphans, and counsel troubled youth. They paint schools in the community. They build buildings for young churches. They sew and cook to raise funds for the church. Laypeople tell Bible stories to children in their neighborhoods. They have Bible studies in their homes. They meet with those who are divorced, pregnant outside of marriage, depressed, or out of work. They fix people's broken bicycles or cars. Some doctors set up clinics in local churches. They provide free dental or medical care one or two evenings each week. Others pray with those in need. These are only a few of the things that laypeople can do. Pastors should encourage these types of ministries. As we are filled with the Spirit, He can lead us into many ministries. Every member of the body of Christ should have a ministry. Each believer should answer the question, "What am I doing to serve God and others?"[15]

Q 10 What would be missing in your life and church without the ministry of the Spirit?

The Holy Spirit wants to work through all believers today. His fullness gives us the boldness to serve and witness for Jesus. The early church had few of the things we value today. But the Church spread like a fire across the world. Many events and stories would be missing from Acts without the ministry of the Spirit. The Spirit is the key to helping each believer be a worker.

The last thing Jesus promised His disciples was, *"You will receive power when the Holy Spirit comes on you"* (Acts 1:8). We see that promise fulfilled in Acts. The Holy Spirit was the power for believers to witness and work for Christ. Acts records five times that various believers were first filled with the Spirit. Figure 4.7 summarizes these.

Q 11 Identify 5 chapters where believers were first filled with the Holy Spirit.

Acts often records that believers spoke in new languages as they were filled with the Spirit. Thus speaking in tongues was an outward evidence of an inward filling. The purpose of being filled with the Spirit is not speaking in tongues. The Spirit fills us so that we can witness about Jesus. We value speaking in tongues because the Bible teaches us that the early church valued it. Today there are more than 520 million believers who value speaking in tongues because the Bible teaches it.[16] For a thorough discussion of speaking in new languages, see the *Faith & Action* course titled *Acts of the Holy Spirit*.

#	Acts	Setting	Outward evidence of the inner filling
1.	2:1-4	The Day of Pentecost	All 120 spoke in new languages as soon as they were *filled with the Holy Spirit.
2.	8:14-19	Believers at Samaria	Something happened that caused Simon to offer money.
3.	9:17-19	The conversion and filling of Saul	We know that Paul often spoke privately in unknown languages (1 Cor. 14:18).
4.	10:44-46	The home of Cornelius	They spoke in new languages.
5.	19:1-7	Believers at Ephesus	They spoke in new languages and prophesied.

Figure 4.7 The five places in Acts where believers were first filled with the Holy Spirit

In Acts, notice that those filled were already believers. They had been born again. All believers receive the Spirit at conversion (Rom. 8:9). So why did these followers of Jesus need to be filled with the Spirit? So that they could be powerful servants of the Lord they loved.

It is good to know the reasons why Luke wrote Acts. *First*, Acts serves as a bridge between the Gospels and Paul's letters. *Second*, Acts tells how the Church grew in numbers, in new places, in culture, and in theology. *Third*, Acts explains and defends the Church. *Fourth*, Acts serves as a guide for faith and practice. But these are all small compared to Luke's *fifth* purpose. He emphasizes the power of the Holy Spirit. If we miss Luke's emphasis on the Holy Spirit, we miss his greatest purpose!

In our survey of the New Testament, it is helpful to realize that the emphases of writers vary. In his Gospel and in Acts, Luke emphasizes only one purpose of the Holy Spirit. He stresses that the Holy Spirit empowers believers to serve.[17] Specifically, Luke emphasizes that the Spirit empowers us to serve as witnesses for Jesus.

Luke, John, and Paul emphasize different ministries of the Holy Spirit. These three writers all emphasize that the Holy Spirit gives us power to serve. In Luke's Gospel, Jesus ministers because the Spirit is upon Him (Luke 4:18-19). But John goes a step beyond what Luke teaches about the Spirit. John adds the Spirit's role in salvation. John teaches us that it is the Spirit who draws sinners to the Savior. Luke does not write about this ministry of the Spirit. Luke describes only one role of the Spirit. But John explains two roles of the Spirit. Paul includes Luke's emphasis that the Spirit empowers us to serve. And Paul also includes John's emphasis that the Spirit has a part to play in salvation. Then, Paul adds a third role of the Spirit. He adds the Spirit's role in helping us live a holy life. Thus, Luke emphasizes one role of the Spirit, John emphasizes two roles of the Spirit, and Paul emphasizes three. Figure 4.8 summarizes what Luke, John, and Paul emphasize about the Holy Spirit.

Writer	Ministry of the Holy Spirit	Selected Scriptures
Luke	1) Service (The Spirit enables us to witness to the lost and help believers.)	1) Luke 1:15-17, 39-56, 67-80; 2:25-38; 3:21-22; 4:18-19; 11:5-13; 24:45-49; All references to the Spirit in Acts
John	1) Service 2) Salvation (The Spirit draws us to Christ and then helps us travel on the road to heaven.)	1) John 1:32; 7:37-39; 14:12-31; 15:26; 20:21-22 2) John 3:5-8; 16:8-11; 1 John 2:20
Paul	1) Service 2) Salvation 3) Sanctification (The Spirit enables us to live a holy life that pleases God.)	1) Rom. 15:19 2) Rom. 8:23; 1 Cor. 6:11, 12:13; 2 Cor. 1:22; Titus 3:5 3) Rom. 8:1-17; Gal. 5:22-23; 2 Thess. 2:13

Figure 4.8 The Spirit's ministry, according to Luke, John, and Paul

Luke emphasizes that the Holy Spirit enables us to serve.[18] In Acts, the focus of service is witnessing about Jesus. We will note the emphases of other New Testament writers as we survey the New Testament.

Q 12 Does Luke teach that the Holy Spirit draws sinners to Jesus? Explain.

Lesson 12

Outlining the Book of Acts

Goal: *Divide Acts into 3 parts, giving the chapters for each part.*

Background

Person(s)	Ministry	Acts
108 of the 120	Prayed and witnessed for Christ	1–2
Barnabas	Was generous; became a friend to Paul; ministered to and with Paul	4, 9, 11–15
The 7 deacons	Collected money and gave it to widows	6
Stephen	Served as a deacon; prayed for the sick; witnessed and taught for Jesus	6–7
Philip	Served as a deacon; took the gospel to Samaria	8, 21
Ananias	Prayed for and baptized Paul	9
Tabitha	Sewed clothes for widows	9
Simon the tanner	Provided housing for Peter	10
Cornelius	Gave alms; invited others to his home	10
Scattered believers	Told the gospel to Jews and Greeks	11
Mary, Mark's mother	Had a prayer meeting in her home	12
Unnamed believers	Prayed for Peter's release from prison	12
Silas	Traveled and ministered with Paul	15–18
John Mark	Traveled with and helped Paul and Barnabas	12–13, 15
Simeon, Lucius, Manaen	Prophesied and taught	13
Lydia	Provided housing for preachers	16
Philippian jailer	Fed Paul and Silas and washed their wounds	16
Timothy	Traveled with Paul and helped him	16–20
Jason	Provided housing for ministers	17
Unnamed believers	Escorted Paul to *Athens	17
Priscilla and Aquila	Gave housing and support to Paul	18
Apollos	Testified for Jesus at Ephesus and Corinth	18–19
Unnamed brothers	Encouraged and recommended Apollos	18
Sopater, Aristarchus, Secundus, Gaius, Timothy, Tychicus, Trophimus	Traveled with Paul; sometimes carried messages for him or other believers	20–21
Unnamed disciples	Gave 7 days' lodging to ministers	21
Unnamed disciples	Prophesied of trouble in Jerusalem	21
Philip's 4 daughters	Prophesied	21
Agabus	Prophesied of trouble in Jerusalem	21
Mnason	Provided housing for ministers	21
Paul's nephew	Warned Paul of a plot to kill him	23
Aristarchus	Sailed with Paul from Caesarea toward Rome	27
Luke	Wrote Acts and traveled with Paul	1, 20, 21, 27–28
Some brothers	Invited Paul and others to stay a week	28
The brothers	Walked out to meet Paul near Rome	28
Unnamed disciples	Paid Paul's rent for 2 years	28

Figure 4.10 People in Acts who were not apostles, but were used by the Holy Spirit

Outlining Acts reveals that it is organized mainly around the ministries of Peter and Paul. Still, Luke includes the ministries of many others. Acts teaches that the Spirit uses both apostles and others (Acts 2:17-18). For every apostle in the upper room, there were nine laypeople. Figure 4.10 shows that the Holy Spirit worked through many believers.

A. Two outlines of Acts

Place to witness for Jesus	Acts
1. *Jerusalem	1–7
2. *Judea and *Samaria	8–12
3. The ends of the earth	13–28

Figure 4.9
Acts 1:8 divides Acts into three parts.

The *first* outline is based on Acts 1:8. It gives us an outline of the book. The Lord Jesus described the future ministry of His followers. Their ministry would begin after the coming of the Holy Spirit. In Acts 1:8 Jesus told *who* would witness, and *where* they would witness. He said, *"you will be my witnesses."* This explained *who* would do the work. Then He explained *where* His followers would witness: *"in Jerusalem, and in all Judea and Samaria, and to the ends of the earth."*

A *second*, more detailed outline of Acts follows. It includes several people and their places of ministry.

Q 13 What is the most important verse of Acts? Explain.

Theme	Acts
A. Witnessing in Jerusalem	**1–7**
Peter's ministry began	1:12–5:42
Stephen's ministry	6:1–8:3
B. Witnessing in Judea and Samaria	**8–12**
Philip's ministry	8:4-40
Paul's conversion	9:1-31
Peter's ministry continued	9:32–12:19
Barnabas' ministry	11:19–12:25
C. Witnessing to the Ends of the Earth	**13–28**
Paul's three missionary trips	13:1–21:14
1. The first missionary journey	13:1–14:28
2. The Jerusalem Council	15:1-35
3. The second missionary journey	15:36–18:22
4. The third missionary journey	18:23–21:14
Paul's imprisonments and trip to Rome	21:15–28:31
1. Paul taken prisoner in Jerusalem	21:15–23:10
2. Paul as a prisoner in Caesarea	23:11–26:32
3. Paul as a prisoner in Rome	27:1–28:31[19]

Figure 4.11 Outline of Acts

Q 14 Create Figure 4.9 from memory.

Lesson 13

Witnessing About Jesus

Goal: *Analyze 3 steps in which believers witnessed for Jesus from Jerusalem to Rome.*

A. Witnessing in Jerusalem (Acts 1–7)

In the first part of Acts, we see Peter ministering in many different situations. He became the Church's leader after the Lord returned to heaven. Peter led the disciples to elect Matthias, who replaced Judas (Acts 1). Then, Peter preached on the Day of Pentecost. Three thousand people were added to the Church (Acts 2). Peter and John prayed, and God healed the lame man at the temple gate (Acts 3). After that, they had to defend their ministry and message before the Jewish Sanhedrin (Acts 4). Later, Peter condemned Ananias and Sapphira. They were lying to God and the Church (Acts 5). He also led the Church in choosing seven deacons (Acts 6). These assisted with offerings and food for the widows.

Q 15 Summarize 4 ways Peter led the early church.

The early church was united. Acts 1–5 gives many examples of the unity of believers.

- They often prayed together (Acts 1:14; 2:1; 4:23-31).
- They believed the same teachings (Acts 2:43-47; 4:23-35).
- They shared their possessions with those in need (Acts 2:44-45; 4:32-34).
- They ate together and worshiped together (Acts 2:46-47).

"All the believers were one in heart and mind" (Acts 4:32).

The main person in Acts 6–7 is Stephen. He was one of the first deacons. Stephen was a great, fearless defender of the faith. Filled with the Spirit, he did miracles and spoke with wisdom (Acts 6:8-10). Unbelieving Jews stoned him. Then a great persecution began against believers. This forced believers to flee from Jerusalem. *"Those who had been scattered preached the word wherever they went"* (Acts 8:4).

Q 16 What happened in Jerusalem after Stephen's death?

B. Witnessing in Judea and Samaria (Acts 8–12)

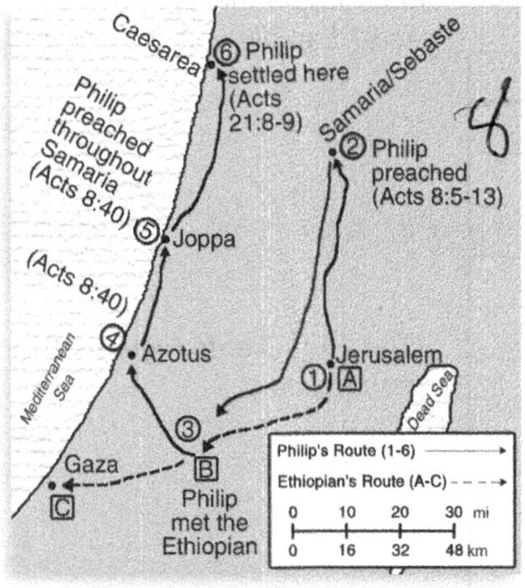

Figure 4.12 Map showing Phillip's journey to Samaria

The second part of Acts describes believers witnessing in Judea and Samaria. Philip, an evangelist, was one of the seven men chosen to serve as deacons (Acts 6). Persecution drove him to Samaria. There he preached and did miracles. Many believed his message about Christ. The church in Jerusalem heard this good report. They sent Peter and John to help the new believers in Samaria (Acts 8:15-17). These two apostles prayed for the new believers to be filled with the Spirit. Why? So the new believers would have power to serve Jesus. When the apostles prayed, the new believers were filled with the Spirit. Philip then left Samaria and went south. He led an Ethiopian official to Christ near Gaza.

Peter left Samaria and went south to Judea. There he preached in Lydda, Sharon, and Joppa. (See Figure 4.12.) A lame man in Lydda was healed. Dorcas was raised from the dead in Joppa. Many people accepted the Lord because of these two miracles. Likewise today, miracles are a great help in spreading the gospel.

Later, Peter went to the home of Cornelius. He was a Gentile and a Roman centurion in Caesarea (Acts 10). Peter had the joy of seeing Cornelius saved and baptized in water. After believing, the Gentiles in his house immediately received the baptism in the Holy Spirit. Peter knew they had been filled with the Spirit, *"for they heard them speaking in tongues"* (Acts 10:46).

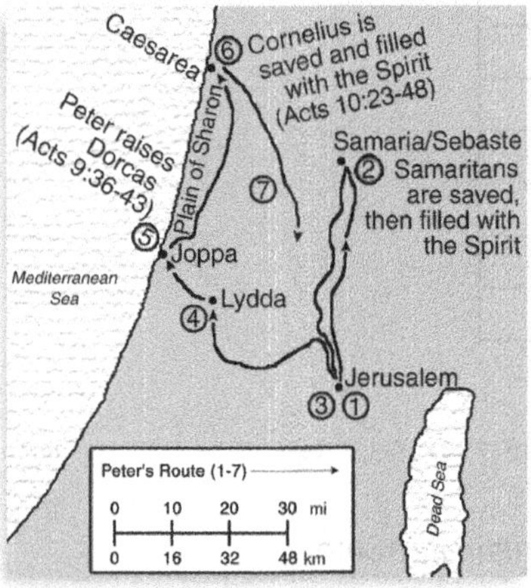

Figure 4.13 Map showing the ministry of Peter in Samaria, Judea, and Caesarea

Q 17 *What caused the gospel to spread to Samaria? Explain.*

Q 18 *How did miracles help spread the gospel in Judea?*

Q 19 *Do you think healings and miracles help spread the gospel today? Explain.*

During this time, Saul met Christ on the road to Damascus (Acts 9). Luke believed Saul's conversion was very important. He told about it three times (Acts 9, 22, 26). Saul, the great persecutor of the Church, became Paul, the most well-known preacher in the Church.

C. Witnessing in all the world (Acts 13–28)

In Acts 1–7 the Church witnessed to Jews in Jerusalem. In Acts 8–12 witnessing spread to Samaritans and Gentiles. The third part of Acts is the longest (Acts 13–28). It describes witnessing among the Gentiles. Paul led this ministry, with many co-workers. Acts 11:19 explains that persecution helped spread the gospel from Jerusalem to *Antioch in Syria. We do not know the names of those who witnessed for Jesus in Antioch. But we know that believers who are filled with the Spirit testify for Jesus. And this was the case in Antioch. As a result, many Greeks there welcomed Jesus into their lives. The church in Jerusalem sent Barnabas to teach the new believers in Antioch. This city became the center for sending missionaries to the Gentiles. Antioch is where believers were first called Christians (Acts 11:26).

After a time, Barnabas went from Antioch to Tarsus. He brought Paul to Antioch. These two men worked together in the Antioch church for a year. The church grew strong. Then Barnabas and Paul traveled to Jerusalem. Jewish believers were suffering because of a great famine in that area. Gentile believers in Antioch sent a gift to help the Jewish believers. Later, Paul and Barnabas returned to Antioch (Acts 11:27-30).

After this, the Holy Spirit called these two men to a new missions ministry. That was the beginning of Paul's three missionary journeys.

Paul's first missionary journey centered mainly on the province of Galatia (Acts 13–14). (See Figure 4.14).

Paul's second journey was through Galatia to the provinces of Macedonia and *Achaia (Acts 15:36–18:22). Notice that on the second trip, Paul visited most of the places where he went on the first trip. (See Figure 4.15).

Paul's third missionary trip took him many places (Acts 18:23–21:17). He visited the larger cities of Philippi, Thessalonica, and Corinth. Then, he spent over 2 years in the important city of Ephesus. (See Figure 4.16).

Paul ministered in many situations. Normally, he preached first to the Jews and then to the Gentiles. He preached often in Jewish synagogues. He used the Old Testament Scriptures as the basis for his message to Jewish people. Other times, Paul preached to Gentiles who did not know the Jewish Scriptures. He usually began his message to such people by describing something around them. It is always wise to begin talking to people about something they know. New truth must always be related to old ideas.

Paul's three missionary journeys happened during a ten-year period. He started many churches as he traveled. Later, Paul told the Roman Christians, *"From Jerusalem all the way around to Illyricum, I have fully proclaimed the gospel of Christ"* (Rom. 15:19).

Paul's third missionary journey ended with his last visit to Jerusalem. There the Jews tried to kill him. His life was saved when the Romans arrested and guarded him. As a result, Paul spent years in prison, both in Caesarea and Rome.

Figure 4.17 gives highlights of Paul's three missionary trips. All began in Antioch, Syria.

The last part of Acts is about Paul's experience as a prisoner. He first faced the Jewish leaders in Jerusalem (Acts 22–23). Later, he was on trial in Caesarea. There he stood before Felix, Festus, and Herod Agrippa II (Acts 24–26). After this, he was taken to Rome.

Paul faced many dangers while traveling to Rome, including a shipwreck (Acts 27–28). In Rome, he rented a house. He was always chained to a guard. Still, Paul was free to preach and teach. Even the house of Caesar heard and received the good news of salvation.

Thus Luke gives us the history of the first 30 years of the Church. We first see a few Jewish believers in an upper room in Jerusalem. Then the power of the Spirit enabled the Church to grow and spread. Acts closes when the gospel reaches Rome. By then, the Church has thousands of members. These include believers from many races and nations.

The spread of the gospel by the power of the Spirit continues today. On the Day of Pentecost 3,000 joined the Church. Today, more than 10,000 come to Christ each day.[21] This is due to revivals in Africa, Northeast *Asia, Latin America, and many other places. Each region of the world could add to the story as acts of the Holy Spirit continue.

Q 20 *Which city was the base of Paul's three missionary trips?*

Q 21 *On a map, circle 5 big cities in which Paul preached.*

Q 22 *Did Paul preach the same way to everyone? Explain.*

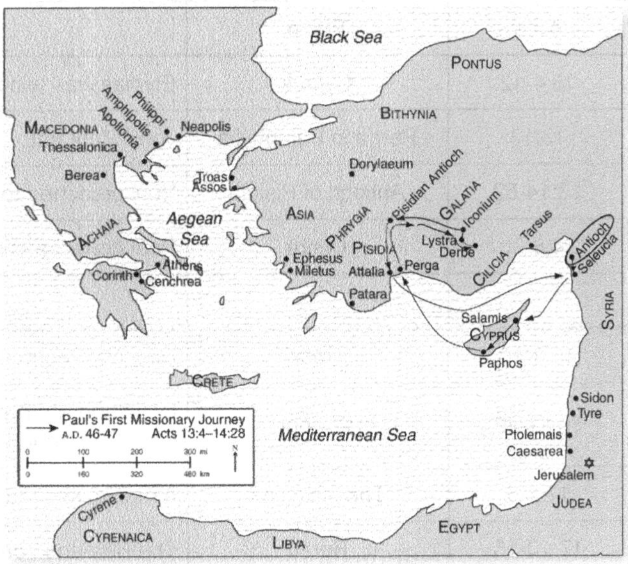

Figure 4.14 Paul's first missionary trip

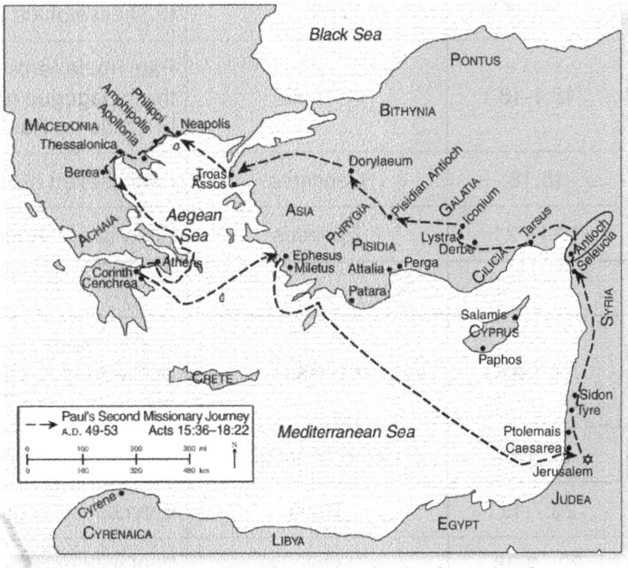

Figure 4.15 Paul's second missionary trip

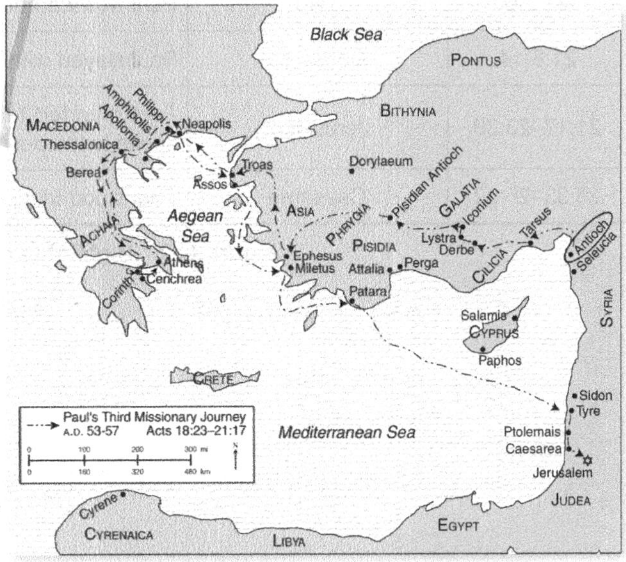

Figure 4.16 Paul's third missionary trip

Acts	Place	Highlights of Paul's First Missionary Trip
13:4-12	Cyprus	Elymas was blinded; Sergius Paulus, the proconsul, believed in Jesus.
13:13	Perga in Pamphylia	John Mark left.
13:14-52	Antioch of Pisidia	Paul preached to the Jews in the synagogue.
14:8-20	Lystra	Paul healed a cripple; Barnabas and Paul were worshiped; Paul was stoned.
		Highlights of Paul's Second Missionary Trip
16:8-10	Troas	Paul saw the man of Macedonia in a vision.
16:11-40	Philippi	Lydia and a jailer were saved. Paul and Silas delivered a demon-possessed girl and were imprisoned; an earthquake occurred at midnight.
17:1-9	Thessalonica	A mob assaulted the house of Jason, where Paul was staying.
17:10-15	Berea	The Bereans searched the Scriptures to verify Paul's message.
17:16-34	Athens	Paul preached on Mars' Hill. Timothy and Silas rejoined Paul. Paul sent Timothy back to Thessalonica and Silas elsewhere.
18:1-18	Corinth	Paul made tents with Priscilla and Aquila. Paul moved from the synagogue. Crispus, the synagogue ruler, was converted. In a vision Jesus told Paul to stay. Gallio refused to condemn Paul. Paul spent 18 months in Corinth.
18:18	Cenchrea	Paul shaved his head because of a vow.
18:19-21	Ephesus	Priscilla and Aquila accompanied Paul to Ephesus and stayed there.
		Highlights of Paul's Third Missionary Trip
19:1-41	Ephesus	Twelve men received the Spirit. Paul preached in the hall of Tyrannus. Seven sons of Sceva tried to cast out demons. Converts burned their magic books; Demetrius led a riot. Paul spent 2 years and 3 months in Ephesus.
20:1-6	Greece/Achaia	Jews plotted to kill Paul.
20:7-12	Troas	Eutychus fell out of a window during Paul's sermon.
20:13-38	Miletus	Paul said goodbye to the Ephesian elders.
21:3-6	Tyre	Paul was warned not to go to Jerusalem.
21:8-14	Caesarea	Paul stayed with Philip; Agabus warned Paul about going to Jerusalem.
21:17–23:30	Jerusalem	Paul reported to the church; took a Jewish vow; was rescued by Roman soldiers; spoke to the Jews and the Sanhedrin; was escorted to Caesarea.
23:33–26:32	Caesarea	Paul stood trial before Felix, Festus, and Agrippa, and appealed to Caesar.

Figure 4.17 Highlights of Paul's three missionary trips[20]

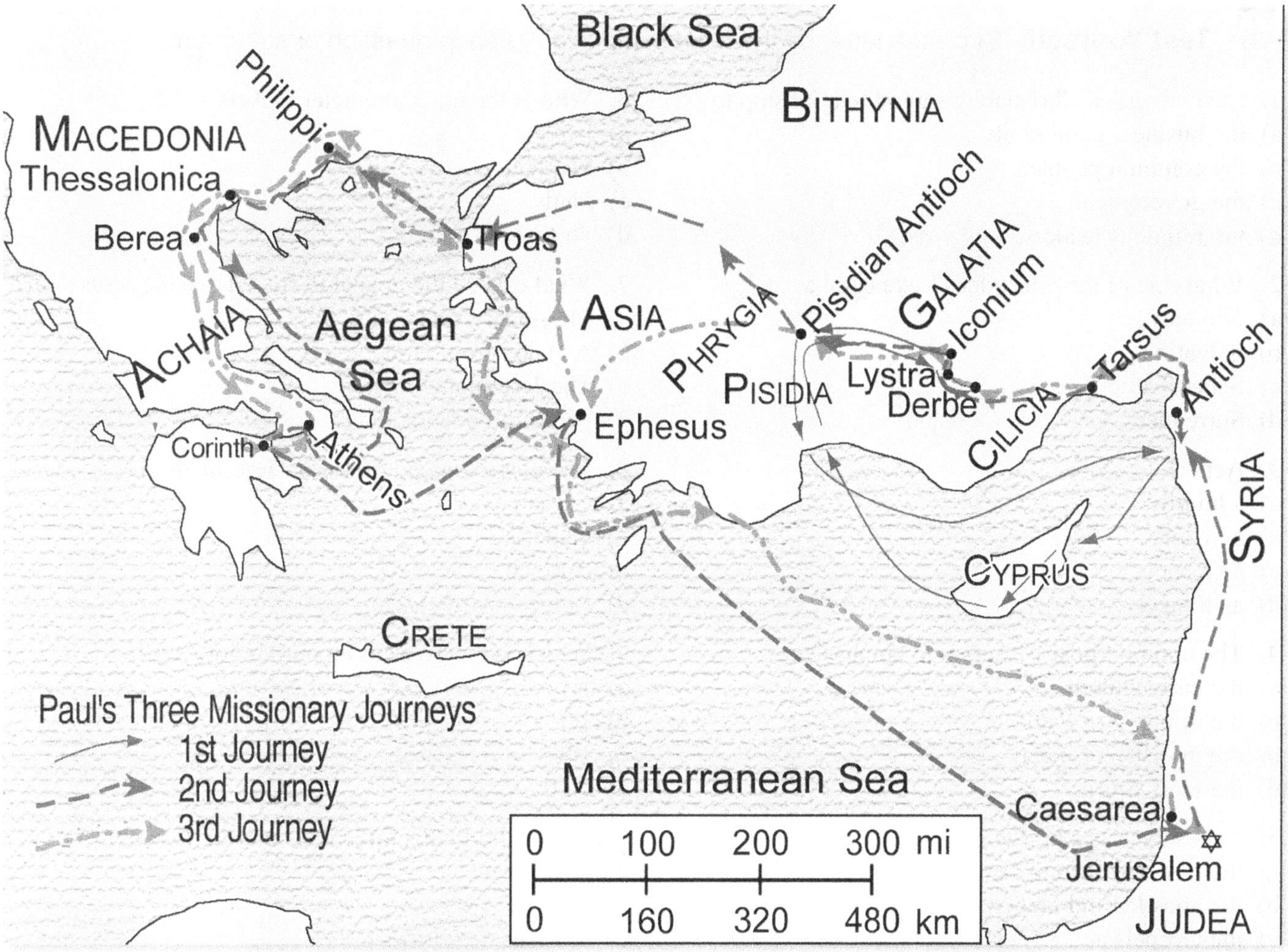

Figure 4.18 Comparison of Paul's three missionary journeys

Test Yourself: Circle the letter by the ***best*** completion to each question or statement.

1. Luke recorded Christianity's good relationship to
a) the business community.
b) the common people.
c) the government.
d) the religious leaders.

2. What role of the Spirit does Luke emphasize?
a) Service
b) Salvation
c) Sanctification
d) Surrender

3. Acts is
a) a homily.
b) a history.
c) a Gospel.
d) an allegory.

4. The main purpose of Acts is to emphasize
a) the early church.
b) the ministry of Paul.
c) the ministry of Peter.
d) the Holy Spirit.

5. Acts serves as a bridge between
a) the first and second centuries.
b) the apostles and laypeople.
c) the Gospels and Epistles.
d) the ministries of Peter and Paul.

6. Who is the main character in Acts 1–12?
a) Peter
b) Stephen
c) Paul
d) Philip

7. What caused the gospel to spread outside Jerusalem?
a) Missionary zeal
b) A vision from God
c) The Jerusalem Council
d) Persecution from Jews

8. The gospel spread first from Jerusalem to
a) Caesarea.
b) Samaria.
c) Antioch.
d) Rome.

9. Which verse gives us an outline for Acts?
a) 1:1
b) 1:3
c) 1:8
d) 1:10

10. Where did Paul's three missionary trips begin?
a) Jerusalem
b) Corinth
c) Ephesus
d) Antioch

Essay Test Topics: Write 50-100 words on each of these goals that you studied in this chapter.

Understanding the Book of Acts

Goal: *Analyze the title, author, and date of Acts.*

Goal: *Summarize 5 purposes of Acts.*

Outlining the Book of Acts

Goal: *Divide Acts into 3 parts, giving the chapters for each part.*

Witnessing About Jesus

Goal: *Analyze 3 steps in which believers witnessed for Jesus from Jerusalem to Rome.*

Unit 2:
13 Letters of Paul

Chapter 5 leads us through Romans and Galatians. These letters emphasize that we receive God's righteousness through grace. For the setting, we will look at Paul's background, conversion, and public ministry. We will divide his 13 letters into four groups. Also, you will learn to:

- *Relate righteousness to the five parts of Romans.*
- *Explain why Paul wrote to the Galatian churches.*
- *Summarize three reasons Paul gave the Galatians for believing the gospel.*

In Chapter 6 we study 1 and 2 Corinthians. These two letters, together with Romans and Galatians, are Paul's letters that focus on salvation. By the end of this chapter, you should be able to:

- *Describe the geographical, social, and religious setting of Corinth.*
- *Trace the history of the Corinthian church from its beginning to 1 Corinthians.*
- *Identify four problems and four questions of the Corinthians.*
- *Trace the flow of 2 Corinthians from Ephesus to Macedonia to Corinth.*
- *Contrast Paul with the false apostles in at least three ways.*

Chapter 7 includes all four of Paul's letters from prison: Ephesians, Philippians, Colossians, and Philemon. In this chapter we will teach you to:

- *Describe the background of Ephesus. Include its location, business, temple, and church.*
- *Analyze four relationships Paul wrote about in Ephesians.*
- *Analyze the Colossian heresy and Paul's teachings on it.*
- *Explain Paul's teaching about old and new clothes.*
- *Summarize the background of Paul's letter to the Philippians.*
- *Summarize what Philippians teaches about joy and unity.*
- *Analyze three people and two lessons in the letter to Philemon.*

Chapter 8 deals with Paul's letters about the future: 1 and 2 Thessalonians. Most believers want to learn all they can about what is ahead. We will teach you to:

- *Summarize the background of Paul's first letter to the Thessalonians.*
- *Identify the theme, purposes, and three main parts of 1 Thessalonians.*
- *Summarize and apply what 2 Thessalonians teaches about the Rapture, Antichrist, and Second Coming.*

Chapter 9 contains Paul's three letters for pastors: 1 Timothy, 2 Timothy, and Titus. These letters are both personal and practical. They will help you in your ministry. You will learn to:

- *Tell about Timothy's parents, conversion, and relationship to Paul.*
- *Identify at least three topics Paul wrote on in 1 Timothy.*
- *Compare Titus 1 and 1 Timothy 3 on qualifications for pastors.*
- *Summarize what Titus teaches about grace and the reputation of the gospel.*
- *Explain how a pastor is like: a soldier, an athlete, and a farmer.*
- *Summarize what Paul taught about the last days and the Scriptures.*

Chapter 5:
Letters About Law and Grace: Romans and Galatians

Figure 5.1 On the road to Damascus, the capital of Syria, Paul received grace that led to salvation (Acts 9:3-19). (Wood-cut art by Gustave Doré)

Introduction

In Lomé, Togo, there is an interesting market. The market is called the *Dead Yovo Market*. *Yovo* is the Ewe tribe's word for "white man." The market is filled with clothes from America. Many of the clothes there were given by family members of Americans who died. This is why the Ewe people call the market the *Dead Yovo Market!*

The market is a great blessing to the local people. Many get expensive clothes at a price they can pay. Shirts, skirts, pants, dresses, and suits sell at low prices. If the *Dead Yovo Market* did not exist, they would not be able to afford such nice garments.

The president of a Bible school in Lomé stood beside his office. He noticed two students walking across the campus. They were wearing beautiful, expensive suits. "Wow," he said. "Those students are dressed as well as the president!" Another student explained, "That is because they went to the *Dead Yovo Market*."

This story reminds us of what Jesus has done for us. He died on the cross to redeem us from sin. Now we are clothed with a righteousness that God gives us after a member of His family died (Rom. 10:3). By faith in Jesus we are clothed with a righteousness that is not our own (Phil. 3:9). The students who went to the *Dead Yovo Market* were dressed as well as the president. Because we've been to Calvary, we wear spiritual clothes that make us as righteous as God Himself.[1]

Lessons:

Paul

14

Goal A: *Summarize Paul's background, conversion, and public ministry.*

Goal B: *Identify the 4 groups of Paul's letters and the books in each.*

Romans

15

Goal: *Relate righteousness to the 5 parts of Romans.*

Galatians

16

Goal A: *Explain why Paul wrote to the Galatian churches.*

Goal B: *Summarize 3 reasons Paul gave the Galatians for believing the gospel.*

Key Words

conversion, Damascus, sanctification, salvation, soteriology, justification, righteousness, substitution, Judaizers

Lesson 14

Paul

Goal A: *Summarize Paul's background, conversion, and public ministry.*

Goal B: *Identify the 4 groups of Paul's letters and the books in each.*

A. Background

Paul was one of the greatest men in the history of the Church. His story is one of the most amazing accounts of mankind. The book of Acts describes how Paul met Jesus. The richest details about his life come from his letters to the Corinthians, Galatians, and Philippians.

Paul was a highly educated Jew from the city of Tarsus. For many years, he was called Saul of Tarsus. Let us consider several things about Paul's background.

As a youth, Paul learned to make tents (Acts 18:3). He often used this skill to support his ministry.

Q 1 *What languages did Paul speak?*

Perhaps Paul was also young when he began studying languages. Paul spoke Aramaic, which was the common language in Palestine at the time of Jesus. He also spoke Greek and Hebrew.

Q 2 *Is it important to speak the language of those to whom you witness? Explain.*

Q 3 *Describe Paul's teacher, religion, and tribe.*

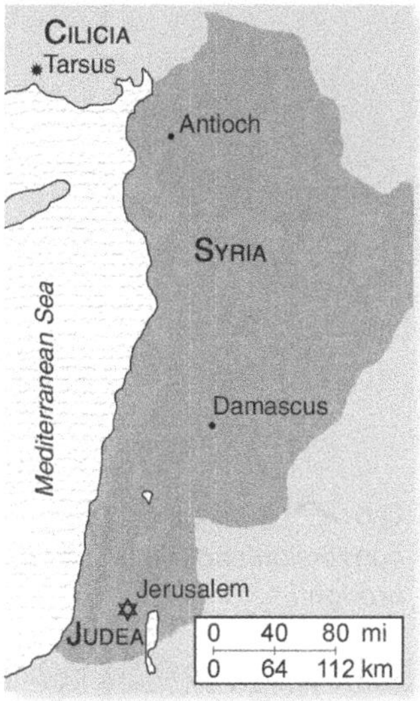

Figure 5.2 Map showing Tarsus, Paul's hometown

He studied the Law in Jerusalem under the great teacher Gamaliel (Acts 22:3). In Galatians 1:14, he said he was becoming a leader in the Jewish religion. In fact, he was more zealous for God and the Law than most other Jews. Saul tried hard to follow the traditions of the Jewish leaders. He became a Pharisee like his father (Acts 23:6).

Saul of Tarsus was from the tribe of Benjamin (Phil. 3:5). The Benjamites were fighters in Israel's history. Saul showed this fighting character, especially when he persecuted the Church (Gal. 1:13). Scripture tells about his evil effort to destroy the Church after Stephen was murdered (Acts 7:57–8:3).

Saul persecuted both men and women in Jerusalem. He had letters from the high priest. These gave him authority to arrest Christians outside of Jerusalem. With these letters, Saul continued his work in many other cities (Acts 26:10-11). He believed he was helping God get rid of false worshipers.

Then Saul met Jesus face to face on one of his trips to persecute believers. This meeting changed his life completely. Later, Saul became known as the apostle Paul.

Paul grew up in the Greek culture, even though he was a Jew. He understood Greek philosophy and knew many of the Greek writings (Acts 17:28; Titus 1:12). He also knew that the world was bigger than the place where he lived. Later, he could write, "*I have become all things to all men so that by all possible means I might save some*" (1 Cor. 9:22).

Qualification	Scripture(s)
1. He learned the Jewish language and culture well.	Acts 21:40; Phil. 3:5
2. He learned the Greek language and culture well.	Acts 17:22-31; Titus 1:12
3. He was a Roman citizen.	Acts 16:37; 22:23-29; 25:10-12
4. He was trained in Jewish theology.	Gal. 1:14
5. He learned to make tents to support himself.	Acts 18:3; 1 Cor. 9:14-18; 2 Cor. 11:7-11; 1 Thess. 2:9; 2 Thess. 3:8
6. He was called by God.	Acts 9:15-16; 22:14-15; 26:12-18; Rom. 1:1; 1 Cor. 1:1 (and others)
7. He was filled with the Spirit.	Acts 9:17
8. He was given great grace.	1 Cor. 3:10; 15:10; 2 Cor. 12:9
9. He was given a thorn in the flesh that kept him humble and dependent on Jesus.	2 Cor. 12:7-9
10. He had a great love for people.	Rom. 9:1-4; 2 Cor. 11:28-29; Phm. 12-19
11. He had the heart of a servant.	Acts 21:17-26; 1 Cor. 9:19-23; 2 Cor. 6:3-10; Gal. 2:2
12. He was diligent and persevered to run his race.	1 Cor. 9:24-27; 2 Cor. 11:23-33; Phil. 3:13-14

Figure 5.3 Twelve things that enabled Paul to be an effective missionary

Q 4 How did being a Roman citizen help Paul?

Paul was a Roman citizen. The Roman army captain in Jerusalem questioned Paul about this. Paul answered, "*I was born a citizen*" (Acts 22:28). Being a Roman citizen gave Paul some important rights. He used his citizenship in Philippi to gain respect from the local authorities (Acts 16:37-39). Paul had the right to a proper trial there. Instead, he was condemned and punished. As a Roman citizen, he could appeal to Caesar for justice (Acts 25:11-12). Also, Roman citizens had the right to be beheaded—not crucified—if sentenced to die.

B. *Conversion

Saul denied that Jesus was the Messiah, the Son of God. He did not believe that Jesus rose from the dead, as Stephen said. Saul heard Stephen say, "*I see heaven open and the Son of Man standing at the right hand of God*" (Acts 7:56). Then the mob began yelling. As they stoned Stephen, Saul stood by and agreed to his death.

Then one day, something Saul never imagined suddenly took place! The Lord Jesus Himself appeared to Saul on the road to *Damascus. Then Saul knew that Stephen had been right. Jesus was alive! He was the Son of God. Soon afterward, Saul began to preach Christ as Savior.

Q 5 Summarize Saul's conversion and the results it brought.

Saul met Jesus. Suddenly, things were different. The change in him lasted the rest of his life. It was a great change for the persecutor of the Church.

Q 6 Do you know anyone whose life was changed as much as Saul's? Explain.

Paul described his new relationship with Christ (Gal. 2:20; Phil. 3:7; 2 Cor. 5:14-19). Jesus changed his entire life. What he used to hate, he loved. Afterward he stayed in Arabia for a time before his first visit to Jerusalem (Gal. 1:16-19). Then Paul went back to his home in Tarsus for eight to ten years. The Bible says very little about his life during this time. Little by little he grew to become a great apostle.

Q 7 How did Paul get started as a missionary?

Paul clearly said that Jesus appointed him to be an apostle. Jesus also revealed the gospel to Paul so that he could preach it to the Gentiles (Gal. 1:1-20).

Q 8 In Figure 5.4, circle the names of 4 provinces in which Paul preached.

C. Paul's public ministry

The church in Jerusalem sent Barnabas to teach believers in Antioch, Syria. Later, Barnabas went to Tarsus to get Paul. They taught together for an entire year in Antioch (Acts 11:25-26). Paul continued to study and teach. One day Paul, Barnabas, and others were worshiping and fasting. The Holy Spirit spoke through one of the group. The Spirit said, "*Set apart for me Barnabas and Saul for the work to which I have called them*" (Acts 13:2). Barnabas and Saul must have already had an inner witness about this work. The group fasted and prayed some more. Then, it became clear to all that the Spirit was calling Barnabas and Saul to be missionaries. The group placed their hands on the two as they prayed for them. Then they sent them off as the first missionaries from the Antioch church. From the earliest days of the Church, the Holy Spirit directed believers as they worshiped and fasted. Likewise today, He directs us as we take the time to worship, fast, and pray.

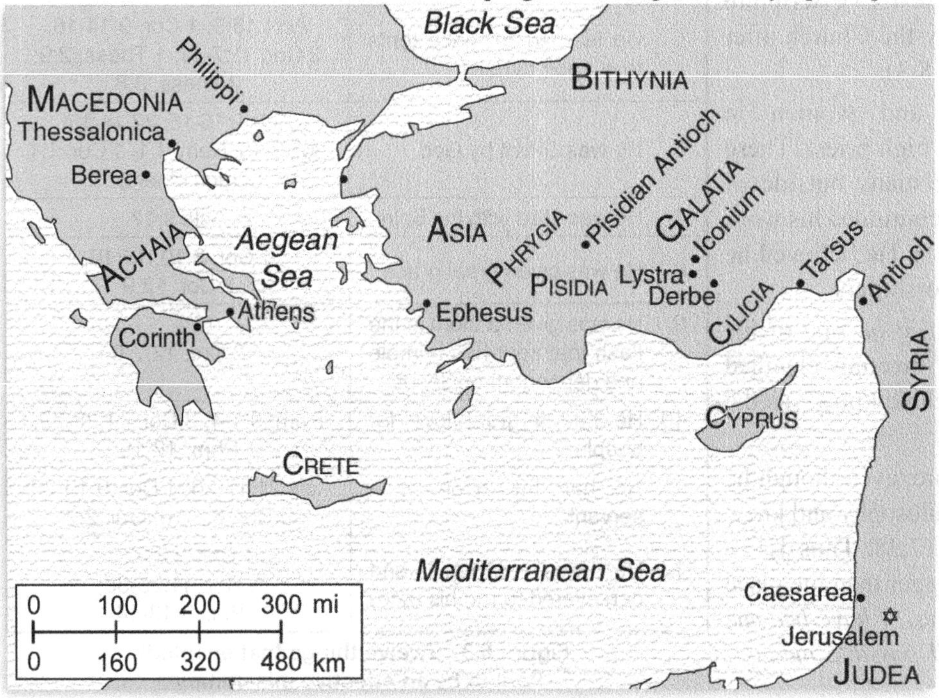

Figure 5.4 Provinces and cities of Paul's missionary trips

Acts 13–14 describes events that happened about A.D. 46-48.[2] This was about 16-18 years after the Resurrection. Paul had probably been a believer for at least 10 years. Consider this. He was called to be an apostle from his mother's womb (Gal. 1:15). But he was probably over 40 when he made his first missionary trip! It takes time for believers to mature. Paul spent a number of years growing in knowledge and in relation to others. He spent time studying the Scriptures. He spent time in Tarsus and in Antioch. Step by step he became the apostle God called him to be. Even apostles grow slowly![3]

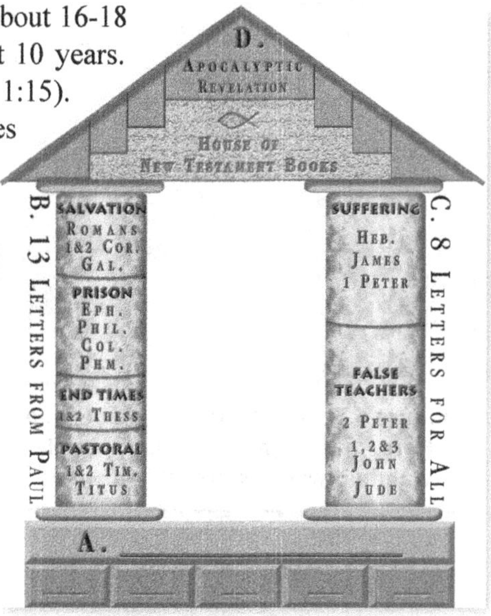

Figure 5.5 Practice house of New Testament books

Paul had a great ministry to Jews and Gentiles during the next 20 years. He evangelized the provinces of Galatia, Macedonia, Achaia, and Asia. He started churches in all those areas and strengthened them.

Problems developed between the Jews and the Gentiles. Paul worked with Barnabas, Peter, James, and other Church leaders to correct these problems (Acts 15:1-35; Gal. 2:1-10). He wanted the gospel to reach the entire world. This helped him see beyond the traditions of people. Paul believed his Lord, who said the gospel should reach all nations.

D. Paul's letters

Paul wrote many letters to individuals and churches. At least 13 of these letters are in the Bible.+ They vary in content and style. We can, however, put them into four groups according to their main thoughts or themes. Let us look briefly at each group.

Q 9 *Learn to complete Figure 5.5 from memory.*

Group 1: Letters about salvation: Romans, Galatians, and 1 and 2 Corinthians. Paul wrote these letters between A.D. 49-57. They contain many teachings about salvation. The Greek word for salvation is *soteria*. So the study of salvation is sometimes called *soteriology*. The Corinthian letters apply salvation to daily living. Romans and Galatians teach about *justification. These letters explain how believers relate to God, one another, and the world.

Group	Letters Paul Wrote	Date
4 letters about *salvation (*soteriology)	Romans, Galatians, 1 and 2 Corinthians	49-57
4 letters from prison (The Prison Epistles)	Ephesians, Philippians, Colossians, Philemon	62
2 letters about the future (eschatology)	1 and 2 Thessalonians	51-52
3 letters to pastors (The Pastoral Epistles)	1 and 2 Timothy, Titus	65-67

Figure 5.6 Paul's 13 letters are divided into four groups.

Group 2: Letters from prison: Ephesians, Philippians, Colossians, and Philemon. Paul wrote these letters about A.D. 62. He wrote them from prison, probably in Rome (Acts 28:30-31). These letters teach much about Jesus and His ministry (Eph. 1:7-12; Phil. 2:5-11; Col. 1:14-22; 2:3, 9-15; Phm. 15-20).

Group 3: Letters about the future: 1 and 2 Thessalonians. These early letters are dated about A.D. 51-52. They teach about the end times, especially the Second Coming of Christ. The Greek word *eschatos* means "last." So the study of the last days is called *eschatology*.

Group 4: Letters to pastors: 1 and 2 Timothy and Titus. Paul wrote these letters about A.D. 65-67. They teach many things about relationships in local churches. Also, they present the responsibilities of church leaders. The closing chapter of 2 Timothy tells about the last days of Paul's life.

Lesson 15

Romans

Goal: *Relate righteousness to the 5 parts of Romans.*

Romans is one of Paul's letters about salvation. The shepherds of Bethlehem received *good news of great joy*. The good news was that a Savior was born. The Savior came to

+ Some believe that Paul wrote Hebrews. However, Bible scholars do not agree on this.

Q 10 What is the theme of Romans?

make us righteous. That is, He came to bring us into the right relationship with God. Paul defines and explains *righteousness in Romans. Romans contains the most complete teaching on righteousness in the New Testament. The theme of Romans is *"the righteousness that comes by faith"* in Jesus (Rom. 4:13; 10:3).

Figure 5.7 The Colosseum in Rome. Here, in this great stadium, people watched wild beasts kill believers.

A. Background

Rome was the largest city of Paul's day. It was the capital and symbol of the Roman Empire. Rome was famous for its sin. Seneca said Rome was a *sewer of sin. The apostle John referred to Rome as a prostitute and the mother of all harlots (Rev. 17:1-18). Rome was also famous for its buildings. The Colosseum was completed by A.D. 80 (Figure 5.7). And Rome was the home of the Pantheon (Figure 5.8). To a Roman, Rome was the center of the world. Its roads and government went out into the entire world.[4]

Figure 5.8 The Pantheon was a famous temple in Rome.

For at least 3 years, Paul had wanted to reach Rome.[5] He arrived there about A.D. 60. But he had written to the Roman believers about A.D. 57.[6] Many think he wrote from Corinth on his third missionary trip. Figure 5.9 lists verses in Romans that refer to Paul's desire to visit Rome.

Q 11 How many passages in Romans show that Paul wrote to believers there before he went there?

Q 12 How did Paul finally get to Rome about A.D. 60?

Romans	Scripture
1:10	*I pray that now at last by God's will the way may be opened for me to come to you.*
1:11-12	*[11] I long to see you so that I may impart to you some spiritual gift to make you strong— [12] that is, that you and I may be mutually encouraged by each other's faith.*
1:13	*I planned many times to come to you (but have been prevented from doing so until now) in order that I might have a harvest among you, just as I have had among the other Gentiles.*
1:15	*That is why I am so eager to preach the gospel also to you who are at Rome.*
15:20-22	*[20] It has always been my ambition to preach the gospel where Christ was not known, ... [22] This is why I have often been hindered from coming to you.*
15:23-24	*[23] But now that there is no more place for me to work in these regions, and since I have been longing for many years to see you, [24] I plan to do so when I go to Spain. I hope to visit you while passing through and to have you assist me on my journey there, after I have enjoyed your company for a while.*
15:25-29	*[25] Now, however, I am on my way to Jerusalem in the service of the saints there. [26] For Macedonia and Achaia were pleased to make a contribution for the poor among the saints in Jerusalem... [28] I will go to Spain and visit you on the way. [29] I know that when I come to you, I will come in the full measure of the blessing of Christ.*
15:31-32	*[31] Pray that I may be rescued from the unbelievers in Judea and that my service in Jerusalem may be acceptable to the saints there, [32] so that by God's will I may come to you with joy and together with you be refreshed.*

Figure 5.9 Verses in Romans that tell of Paul's desire to visit Rome

Acts 28 tells us that Paul finally reached Rome, as a prisoner.

B. Outline

The *theme* of Romans is righteousness (Rom. 3:22-24). Paul explained five things about righteousness in this letter. They are clearly seen in the book's outline (Figure 5.10).

Romans	Sub-theme
1–3	Sin: The need for righteousness
4–5	Justification: The provision of righteousness
6–8	Sanctification: The result of righteousness
9–11	Rejection: The width of righteousness
12–15	Service: The fruit of righteousness

Figure 5.10 Five aspects of righteousness in Romans

Theme	Romans
Introduction	**1:1-17**
A. Sin: The Need for Righteousness	**1:18–3:20**
Gentile sin	1:18–2:16
Jewish sin	2:17–3:8
Everyone's sin	3:9-20
B. *Justification: The Provision of Righteousness	**3:21–5:21**
A summary of justification by faith	3:21-31
Abraham, an illustration of justification by faith	4:1-25
Blessings that come with justification by faith	5:1-11
Adam and Christ contrasted	5:12-21
C. *Sanctification: The Result of Righteousness	**6–8**
Our union with Christ	6:1-23
The conflict of our fleshly and spiritual natures	7:1-25
Our victory through walking in the Spirit	8:1-39
D. Rejection: The Width of Righteousness Includes Jews and Gentiles	**9–11**
Israel's past: God's judgment for sin	9:1-33
Israel's present: God's offer of salvation	10:1-21
Israel's future: God's promise of restoration	11:1-36
E. Service: The Fruit of Righteousness	**12–15**
The believer: a living sacrifice	12:1-2
The believer and others in the body	12:3-15
The believer and the government	13:1-7
The believer and the law of love	13:8–15:13
Conclusion and Greetings	**15:14–16:27**

Figure 5.11 Outline of Romans

Q 13 *What are the 5 topics in the outline that relate to righteousness?*

Q 14 *How does Romans 1–3 relate to the theme of righteousness?*

Q 15 *How does Romans 3–5 relate to justification?*

Q 16 *Which chapters in Romans deal with the rejection of redemption by the Jews?*

Q 17 *What is the theme of Romans 12–15?*

C. Explanations of the outline

We looked briefly at the outline of Romans. There we noted the introduction and five major points related to the theme of righteousness. Now, let us look more closely at these.

Introduction (Rom. 1:1-17). Paul's purpose in Romans is to teach about righteousness. The key verses in this book are Romans 1:16-17.

Q 18 *State Romans 1:16-17 in your own words.*

> [16]*I am not ashamed of the gospel, because it is the power of God for the salvation of everyone who believes: first for the Jew, then for the Gentile.* [17]*For in the gospel a righteousness from God is revealed, a righteousness that is by faith from first to last, just as it is written: "The righteous will live by faith"* (Rom. 1:16-17).

This verse emphasizes that we become righteous by believing the good news of Jesus Christ. Notice what verse 17 says about faith. Faith is the key to our relationship with God. In relating to Him we need faith from first to last. That is, from the beginning to the end of our journey to heaven. This faith expresses itself through trusting in and submitting to Jesus as Savior and Lord. Righteousness from God is the result of relating faithfully to Jesus.

Sin: The need for righteousness (Rom. 1:18–3:20). Romans covers righteousness from A to Z. It begins with our need for righteousness. The first major part of Romans describes our sinful condition (Rom. 1:18–3:20). It shows that everyone needs righteousness. All people have sinned and need salvation.

Q 19 *What is Paul's main purpose in Romans 1:18–3:20?*

- Men have turned away from God and have followed other gods (Rom. 1:21-23).
- God left men and let them go their own way (Rom. 1:24-28).
- Some judge others, but they are really judging themselves because they do the same things (Rom. 2:1-3).
- God will reward or punish each person for what he or she has done (Rom. 2:6).
- Gentiles, without the written Law of the Jews, know in their hearts what is right and wrong (Rom. 2:14-15).
- Jews have the Law, but don't obey all of it. Therefore, the Jews are also guilty of sin (Rom. 2:27).
- No one can be counted as righteous by following the Law (Rom. 3:20).
- All have sinned and fall short of the righteousness that God demands (Rom. 3:23).

Q 20 *Do you think Romans 3:23 summarizes Paul's main point of Romans 1:18–3:20? Explain.*

Justification: The provision of righteousness (Rom. 3:21–5:21). This section shows that faith in Jesus is the solution to the problem of sin. Salvation is *"through faith in Jesus Christ"* (Rom. 3:22). God justifies (counts righteous) those who relate to Jesus by faith.

Q 21 *Define justification. How is a believer justified?*

Our salvation is based on the great truth of *substitution. A substitute is one who changes places with another. We stood in the place of judgment. Because of sin, we deserved to be punished and separated from God. Jesus came to be our substitute. We deserved to be crucified. Jesus took our places on the cross. He bore our sins in his body on the cross (1 Pet. 2:24). In exchange for our sins, He offers us His righteousness. God justifies those who agree to receive Jesus as Savior and Lord. To *justify* means "to count righteous."

Q 22 *In what way was Jesus our substitute?*

Under the old covenant, they substituted animals for people. Once each year the high priest chose two goats. These were substitutes for the people in two ways. One goat was killed. This showed that the people deserved to die for their sins. Instead, the goat died and shed its blood. The other goat was sent out to wander in the desert. This showed that sin separates us from God (Lev. 16:6-10). Each year the high priest repeated what he did with the two goats. The problem was that goats were not equal to the value of humans. So the death of a goat, or the exile of a goat, could never take away the sins of people (Heb. 10:4, 11). God also required many other kinds of sacrifices. Each year, the death and punishment of these animals reminded people that their sins remained (Heb. 10:3). God accepted the sacrifice of animals because this was a picture of what Jesus would do for us. He allowed the people to sacrifice animals each year until Jesus could come and be our substitute. He gave His life and blood to free us.

Figure 5.12 Mt. Gerizim. This is where modern-day Samaritans sacrifice sheep for Passover.

Romans 3:21–5:21 contains several truths related to substitution, justification, and righteousness.

Q 23 *Did animal sacrifices cleanse the Jews from sin? Explain.*

- God remains righteous, yet makes sinners righteous through the substitution of Christ (Rom. 3:24-26).
- Abraham is an example of justification by faith. God counted him righteous because he trusted in God. Abraham lived long before the Law came. Therefore, he did not seek to be righteous by keeping the Law. He was counted righteous by faith alone (Rom. 4:10-13).
- When a sinner is justified, he or she receives blessings (Rom. 5:1-11). These blessings include peace with God, joy, and hope.
- Our righteousness is the result of Christ's death on Calvary (Rom. 5:12-21).

Q 24 *What is the key to defeating the old self each time it tries to rule?*

Q 25 *State another word or phrase for "sanctification."*

Sanctification: The result of righteousness (Rom. 6–8). Another word for sanctification is *holiness*. The Greek word for holy is *hagios*. It is often translated as *saints* in the New Testament. The word *holy* is used in relation to believers over 80 times in the New Testament.[7] Some would rather refer to believers as sinners. But those who have been saved from sin are never referred to as sinners. Paul never wrote any letters to the sinners in Ephesus, Corinth, Philippi, or anywhere else. Rather, he always wrote to those who are holy.

We are holy for two reasons: what Jesus did *for* us, and what He does *in* us. These two parts of holiness must never be divorced. Jesus died for us on the cross. He became our substitute. Our faith in what Jesus did *for* us is the basis for what He does *in* us. We believe in His death and resurrection. We turn from our sins to following Him. We receive Him into our lives by faith. Then a wonderful thing happens. Jesus begins to work in us. We are born again. We become God's children (John 1:12). We partake of, receive, and share the nature of God (2 Pet. 1:4). Eternal life from God flows into each new believer. God recreates a person through this spiritual birth. At the new birth we are "*created to be like God in true righteousness and holiness*" (Eph. 4:24). As new creations in Christ, we no longer follow the ways of the world (2 Cor. 5:17). Instead, we follow the leading of the Holy Spirit (1 Cor. 6:19-20). Day by day, we are being changed to be more like God in righteousness and holiness (2 Cor. 3:18).

God's children are those who are led by the Spirit, rather than by the flesh. The Greek word for flesh is *sarx* (Rom. 6:19; 7:5, 18, 25; 8:1, 3, 4, 5, 8, 9, 12, 13). Note that the New International Version translates the Greek word *sarx* as "*sinful nature*" (Rom. 8:13). This confuses some. So remember that the sinful nature is just another name for the flesh. And the desires of the sinful nature are just the desires of the flesh. Each believer still has sinful, fleshly desires. But Christ gives us the freedom to say "No" to the flesh. We live in a body of flesh, but we are no longer slaves of the flesh. As believers, we have the freedom to choose between the flesh and the Spirit. So we daily crucify, deny, and ignore the sinful desires of the flesh (Rom. 6:11-14; Gal. 5:24). As we follow the Spirit, we *"grow in grace"* (2 Pet. 3:18). God's holy ones are being perfected (Eph. 4:12). We are *"perfecting holiness out of reverence for God"* (2 Cor. 7:1). Our holiness is increasing. We are holy, and we are becoming holier (2 Cor. 3:18)!

Q 26 *Do believers have a sinful nature? Explain.*

There is a story about a man with two fighting dogs. One was black and the other white. The man traveled from town to town with the dogs. People came to watch the dogs fight each other. Sometimes they would bet or gamble on which dog would win. Sometimes the black dog was the victor. But other times, the white dog won. It was impossible for visitors to know which dog would defeat the other. But the owner always knew which dog would win. You see, he had a secret. For a few days before the fight, he fed only the dog he wanted to win! Likewise, whether the flesh or the Spirit wins depends on which one we feed.

Q 27 *Give 2 examples of "feeding the flesh" and 2 of "feeding the Spirit."*

In Romans 6:1–8:39 Paul describes the struggle between those under the Law and those under grace. He also describes the struggle between the flesh (sinful nature) and the spirit. The flesh is the same under the Law or under grace. Its desires do not change. Those under the Law are slaves to the desires of the flesh. The Law only condemns. It gives no power to do what is right. However, under grace, we receive the Holy Spirit of grace. He gives us power to live a holy life. Therefore, under grace we are no longer slaves of our fleshly desires. Paul writes about the difference between two kinds of slaves. We were once slaves of sin. Through the new birth we have become slaves of righteousness.

Q 28 *Does grace do away with the desires of the flesh? Explain.*

Slaves of sin serve sin, their master. Slaves of sin lack the freedom to do what is right. They are prisoners of the law of sin (Rom. 7:23). They are unspiritual, sold as slaves to sin (Rom. 7:14). Sin forces them to do evil things they don't want to do (Rom. 7:15). They cannot do the good things they want to do (Rom. 7:15). Paul writes about Jewish slaves of sin who were bound by the Law (Rom. 6:14; 7:6). The Law condemned them but gave them no power to do better (Rom. 8:3). These slaves yielded their bodies to obey sin, their master (Rom. 6:16). No slaves of sin can please God, for they are controlled by the flesh (Rom. 8:8). Slaves of sin are unspiritual (Gal. 6:1) and cannot inherit God's kingdom (Gal. 5:21). Paul was once an unspiritual person, a slave to sin (Rom. 7:14). Representing all slaves of sin he cried out, "*Who will rescue me from this body of death?*" (Rom. 7:24). We "*used to be slaves to sin*" (Rom. 6:17). Now we "*have been set free from sin and have become slaves to righteousness*" (Rom. 6:18). Figure 5.13 shows the contrast between slaves of sin and slaves of righteousness.

Q 29 *Will a slave of sin go to heaven? Explain.*

Rom. 7:5-6; 8:8	**Slaves of Sin (Living under the Law; controlled by the flesh)**	**Slaves of Righteousness (Living under grace; controlled by the Spirit)**	**Rom. 7:14-15; 6:14; 8:9**
5:21	Just as sin reigned in death,	so also grace might reign through righteousness...	5:21
6:1	*Shall we go on sinning* [as slaves of sin do]...?	[2]...*We died to sin; how can we live in it any longer?* [4]... *we too may live a new life!* [6]...*our old self was crucified with him...that we should no longer be slaves to sin...*	6:2, 4, 6
6:12-13	[12]*Therefore do not let sin reign in your mortal body so that you obey its evil desires* [as slaves of sin do]. [13]*Do not offer the parts of your body to sin, as instruments of wickedness* [as slaves of sin do]...	[11]...*Count yourselves dead to sin but alive to God in Christ Jesus.* [13]...*but rather offer yourselves to God, as those who have been brought from death to life; and offer the parts of your body to him as instruments of righteousness.* [14]*For sin shall not be your master, because you are not under law, but under grace.*	6:11-14
6:16	slaves to sin, which leads to death...	slaves to obedience, which leads to righteousness.	6:16
6:17	You used to be slaves to sin, ...	You have been set free from sin and have become slaves to righteousness.	6:18
6:20-21	[20]*When you were slaves of sin, ...* [21]...*Those things result in death!*	But now that you have been set free from sin and have become slaves to God, the benefit you reap leads to holiness, and the result is eternal life.	6:22
7:5	When we were controlled by the sinful nature, the sinful passions aroused by the law were at work in our bodies, so that we bore fruit for death.	*But now, by dying to what once bound us, we have been released from the law so that we serve in the new way of the Spirit, and not in the old way of the written code* [law].	7:6
7:8	Sin...produced in me every kind of covetous desire.	But now, by dying to what once bound us, we have been released from the law so that we serve in the new way of the Spirit, ...	7:6
7:14-15	[14]...*the law is spiritual; but I am unspiritual, sold as a slave to sin.* [15]...*what I want to do I do not do... what I hate I do.*	Through Christ Jesus the law of the Spirit of life set me free from the law of sin and death.	8:2
7:18-20, 23-24	[18]...*I have the desire to do what is good, but I cannot carry it out.* [19]...*The evil I do not want to do—this I keep on doing.* [20]...*sin living in me...does it.* [23]...[I am] *a prisoner of the law of sin...* [24]...*Who will rescue me from this body of death?*	[25]*Thanks be to God—through Jesus Christ our Lord!* [3]*For what the law was powerless to do...God did by sending his own Son...to be a sin offering...*[4]*in order that the righteous requirements of the law might be fully met in us, who do not live according to the sinful nature but according to the Spirit.*	7:25; 8:3-4
8:5, 8	[5]*Those who live according to the sinful nature have their minds set on what that nature desires;* ...[8][they] *cannot please God.*	but those who live in accordance with the Spirit have their minds set on what the Spirit desires.	8:5
8:8	Those controlled by the sinful nature cannot please God.	You, however, are controlled not by the sinful nature but by the Spirit, if the Spirit of God lives in you. And if anyone does not have the Spirit of Christ, he does not belong to Christ.	8:9
8:13	*For if you live according to the sinful nature, you will die* [eternally]...	[13]...*but if by the Spirit you put to death the misdeeds of the body, you will live* [eternally], [14]*because those who are led by the Spirit of God are sons of God.*	8:13-14

Figure 5.13 No one can serve two masters. We must be slaves of either sin or righteousness (Rom. 6–8).

Who will rescue us from being the slaves of sin? Jesus is the answer! *"Thanks be to God—through Jesus Christ our Lord"* we are free (Rom. 7:25)! *"Through Christ Jesus the law of the Spirit of life set me free from the law of sin and death"* (Rom. 8:2).

Romans 6:1-2 and 15-18 show that God's children are no longer slaves of sin. If a believer sins, those who are spiritual should seek to restore the sinner (Gal. 6:1).

Romans 7:7-24 describes Paul as an unsaved person living under the Law. Those under the Law are slaves of the flesh. The flesh causes them to commit many sins (Gal. 5:19-21). Slaves of the flesh or sinful nature will not inherit God's kingdom (Gal. 5:21).

Romans 8 describes a born-again person who is led by the Spirit (Rom. 8:1-17). Led by the Spirit, we are no longer powerless, like those who are under the Law (Gal. 5:18). And led by the Spirit, we do good deeds instead of evil acts (Gal. 5:19-26). The contrast in Romans 7 and 8 is the contrast between an unsaved person and a holy person. Once, Paul was an unspiritual person. He was a sinner living under the Law. But Jesus changed him to a spiritual, holy person living under grace. Led by the Spirit, Paul learned to bring every thought into captivity. He practiced making his thoughts bow before Christ (2 Cor. 10:5). Once he was born again, Paul was not a slave to the desires of his body. Rather, his body was his slave (1 Cor. 9:27).

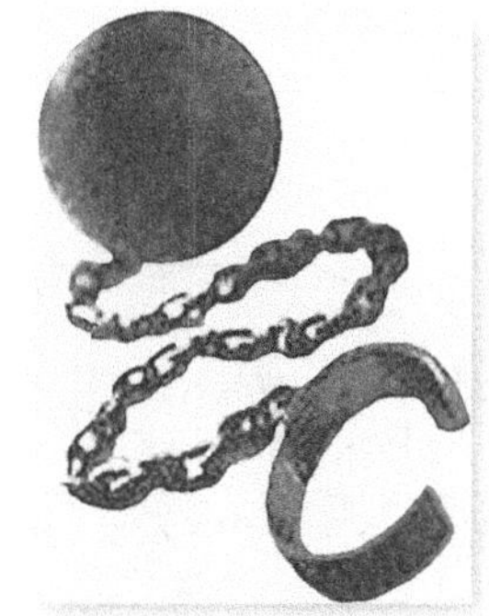

Figure 5.14 Those who become God's children are no longer slaves of sin (Rom. 6:1-2).

Rejection: The width of righteousness includes Jews and Gentiles (Rom. 9–11). In the next section, Paul showed that the gospel is for everyone. It is for both the Jew and the Gentile. The gospel went first to the Jews. Many of them rejected the Savior and Messiah God sent them.

Q 30 *Which verses say that all Israel will be saved?*

- God temporarily set aside His people Israel. But He has not thrown them out (Rom. 11:1).
- God is in control, working out His purpose of redemption (Rom. 9:19-32).
- Now, the gospel is for all. *"Everyone who calls on the name of the Lord will be saved"* (Rom. 10:13).
- A day of restoration and blessing for Israel will come (Rom. 11:25-32).

Q 31 *Practice completing Figure 5.15 until you can create it from memory.*

Romans	Sub-theme
1–3	
4–5	
6–8	
9–11	
12–15	

Figure 5.15 Practice chart on the outline of Romans

Service: The fruit of righteousness (Rom. 12–15). We are studying the five big parts of Romans on righteousness. We have reached the fifth part, which is service. Righteousness is like a tree that bears fruit. Those who are right with God

- dedicate themselves to the Lord. This is the way we worship Him (Rom. 12:1-2).
- humbly serve others (Rom. 12:3-8).
- have good relationships with others (Rom. 12:9-21).
- submit to and honor the government (Rom. 13:1-7).
- have the right attitude toward all other believers (Rom. 13:8–15:13).

Lesson 16 Galatians

Goal A: *Explain why Paul wrote to the Galatian churches.*
Goal B: *Summarize 3 reasons Paul gave the Galatians for believing the gospel.*

A. Background

In our Bibles, the order of Paul's letters is not based on the dates he wrote them. Rather, Paul's letters are listed from the longest to the shortest. In our Bibles, Romans is the first of Paul's letters because it is the longest, with 7,101 words. Likewise, Philemon is the last of Paul's letters because it is the shortest, with 335 words.[8] The exceptions to this are the Pastoral Epistles: 1 & 2 Timothy and Titus. These are the only letters of Paul that are not listed according to length.

Q 32 *When and to whom did Paul probably write Galatians? Explain.*

If we were studying Paul's letters according to dates, we would begin with Galatians. Most Bible teachers agree that it was the first letter Paul wrote.

Paul wrote Galatians to the churches in the province of Galatia. He went to Southern Galatia on his first missionary journey (Acts 13:4–14:28). Recall that he ministered in the Galatian towns of Pisidian Antioch, Derbe, Lystra, and Iconium. Many Bible teachers think Paul wrote Galatians to believers in Southern Galatia about A.D. 49. This would have been just before the big Church Council in Jerusalem about A.D. 49 (Acts 15). Recall that the Acts 15 Council was about the relationship between Jews and Gentiles.

The Council concluded that Gentiles are saved by faith in Christ. Therefore, Jewish believers did not require Gentiles to keep the Law of Moses. The main issue in Galatians is the one debated at the Jerusalem Council (Acts 15). The issue was: Are we saved by faith in Jesus alone, or must we obey some Old Testament laws?[9] It appears that Paul wrote to the Galatians before he went to Jerusalem. Then, the Church took an official position on salvation through Christ alone.

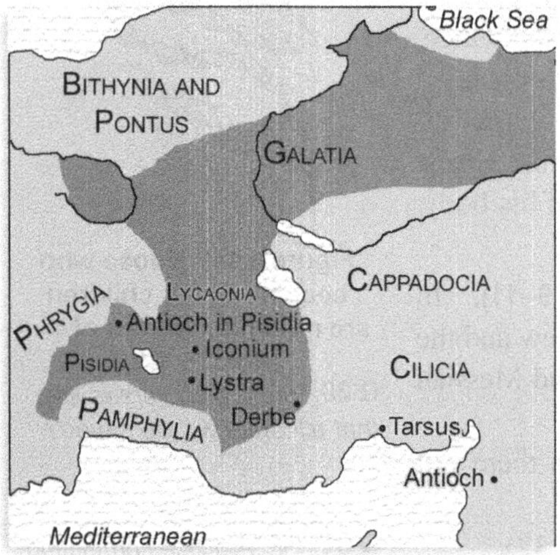

Figure 5.16 Map showing the Galatian churches of Derbe, Lystra, Iconium, and Pisidium Antioch

Galatians is a strong defense of justification by faith. In Galatians, Paul emphasized that "*a man is not justified by observing the law, but by faith in Jesus Christ*" (Gal. 2:16). The Galatians had received the gospel. They had been justified by faith in Christ. Afterward, however, Jewish teachers known as *Judaizers were leading some astray. These false teachers said that believers must follow Jesus and Moses.

Most of the first believers were Jewish. These early followers of Jesus continued their Jewish way of life. They attended the synagogues to worship and learn. They offered sacrifices in the temple. They celebrated the Jewish feasts. They obeyed the rules Moses gave them. So they circumcised their sons. And like all Jews, they lived socially distant from the Gentiles.

Then the Gentiles began to receive Christ. This forced the Jewish believers to face new questions. Should Gentiles be circumcised? Must Gentiles live like Jews to be saved? The Acts 15 meeting was about these questions.

Q 33 What problem did the believers in Galatia have?

Q 34 Do believers you know mix Old Testament laws and grace? Explain.

Judaizers taught that circumcision was necessary for salvation. But Paul reminded the Galatians of the basic truths of the gospel. We are saved by faith in Jesus, not by keeping the law of Moses. We have only one Savior, not two! Paul said that the Galatians had deserted Jesus and were following a useless gospel (Gal. 1:6-7). He said that those who were trying to keep the Law were under a curse (Gal. 3:10). He emphasized that salvation is by faith in Jesus alone. Under the new covenant, circumcision has no religious value (Gal. 5:6). In fact, Paul said that those who trusted in circumcision or laws had "*fallen away from grace*" (Gal. 5:4).

Q 35 Explain the greater and lesser purposes of Galatians.

B. Purpose

In Galatians, we see a greater purpose and a lesser purpose. After a short greeting, Paul stated the major problem. He marveled that these Galatians had so quickly deserted his gospel of grace. They had turned away from Christ to follow Moses. Paul condemned the false teachers among them (Gal. 1:6-7). In fact, he called down the curse of God upon them (Gal. 1:8-9). Then Paul focused on the source, message, and power of his gospel. His main purpose was to turn them away from the Judaizers and back to the truth. As Paul put it, "*I am again in the pains of childbirth until Christ is formed in you*" (Gal. 4:19).

Paul's greater and lesser purposes are closely related. The greater purpose of Galatians is to emphasize that we are saved by Jesus, not Moses. We are under grace, not Law. This brings us to Paul's lesser purpose. Even though we are not under Law, we must live holy lives. The basis of our salvation is faith, not works. Even so, God requires us to walk in the Spirit, and not the flesh. Paul emphasizes this lesser theme in Galatians 5:16–6:1. There he contrasts the acts of the flesh with the fruit of the Spirit. Those who fulfill the evil desires of the flesh will not inherit God's kingdom (Gal. 5:19-21). Grace teaches us to live godly, holy lives.

> 11 *For the grace of God that brings salvation has appeared to all men.* 12 *It teaches us to say "No" to ungodliness and worldly passions, and to live self-controlled, upright and godly lives in this present age,* 13 *while we wait for the blessed hope—the glorious appearing of our great God and Savior, Jesus Christ,* 14 *who gave himself for us to redeem us from all wickedness and to purify for himself a people that are his very own, eager to do what is good* (Titus 2:11-14).

C. Outline

Paul started with the problem (Gal. 1:1-10). Then he defended his belief that justification comes by faith, not by works. The key verse is Galatians 2:16.

> [15]*We who are Jews by birth and not 'Gentile sinners'* [16]*know that a man is not justified by observing the law, but by faith in Jesus Christ. So we, too, have put our faith in Christ Jesus that we may be justified by faith in Christ and not by observing the law, because by observing the law no one will be justified* (Gal. 2:15-16).

Galatians	Section
1–2	**Personal:** Paul's testimony—the gospel revealed
3–4	**Doctrinal:** The gospel explained
5–6	**Practical:** The gospel applied

Figure 5.17 There are three main parts in Galatians.

Q 36 *What contrast is in Galatians 2:16?*

D. Explanations of the outline

Paul gives the Galatians three reasons to believe the gospel. Notice that he uses two chapters to explain each reason.

The Personal Section (Gal. 1–2): Paul's gospel was from Christ. Paul received his gospel by revelation from the Lord (Gal. 1:11-12). Other apostles did not give it to him. They only agreed with his message and ministry (Gal. 1:16–2:10).

The Doctrinal Section (Gal. 3–4): The gospel message is not completely new. The Old Testament taught the truth of the gospel (Gal. 3:8). Abraham is the great example of justification by faith in God. Abraham lived long before the Law. Therefore, the Law did not justify him. In fact, the Law cannot justify *anyone* (Gal. 3:9-14). Paul explained this truth by showing the difference between an adopted child and a son (Gal. 3:23–4:7). He then used the story of Abraham's two sons to repeat his statement about the Law (Gal. 4:21-23).

Theme	Galatians
Introduction	**1:1-10**
A. Personal: Paul's Testimony—the Gospel Revealed	**1:11–2:21**
The revelation of the gospel came from God	1:11-24
The other apostles agreed with the gospel	2:1-10
The personal application of the gospel	2:11-21
B. Doctrinal: The Gospel Explained	**3:1–4:31**
The personal appeal	3:1-5
The experience of Abraham	3:6-14
The promise and the Law	3:15-22
The nature of the Son	3:23–4:7
The danger of turning away	4:8-20
The lesson from history	4:21-31
C. Practical: The Gospel Applied	**5:1–6:10**
Stand firm in freedom	5:1-12
Walk in the Spirit, not the flesh	5:13-26
Help one another	6:1-10
Conclusion	**6:11-18**

Figure 5.18 Outline of Galatians

The Practical Section (Gal. 5–6): The gospel works in personal experience. Those who accept the gospel receive freedom from the bondage of sin. But believers must stand firm in the truth. Paul warned the Galatians not to turn back to the Law. Some had already transferred their faith in Christ to faith in the Law. He said these had been separated from Christ. He said they had *"fallen from grace"* (Gal. 1:6-7; 5:4). They were like the branches that did not abide in Christ, the Vine (John 15:4-6). Such branches are burned. The New Testament often warns believers of the danger of turning away from Jesus and losing their salvation.

Q 37 *State 3 reasons the Galatians should believe Paul's gospel.*

Q 38 *To which Old Testament character does Galatians refer?*

Not all who begin following Jesus continue to do so. Some begin with joy, but don't put down roots (Matt. 13:20-21). Some, like Lot's wife, start the journey away from sin but turn back to the world (Luke 17:32; Gen. 19:26). Some, like Hymenaeus and Alexander, turn loose of the faith and blaspheme. Their faith ends up like a wrecked ship (1 Tim. 1:18-20). Others are on the journey to heaven until false teachers kill their faith (2 Tim. 2:18). Demons seduce some to depart from the faith (1 Tim. 4:1). Some, like the Galatians, fall from grace because they trust in rituals and rules (Gal. 5:4). Peter warns us about falling from our secure position (2 Pet. 3:17-18). Many in Sardis died spiritually because of sin (Rev. 3:4-5). For a thorough treatment of falling away from Christ, see the article by Don Stamps on Hebrews 3:12 in the *Full Life Study Bible*.[10] It is wise for believers to be aware of dangers. Then we can be alert and avoid them. Those

Q 39 *Who was the "child of promise" (Gal. 4:21-23)?*

Q 40 *What is the key to not sinning (Gal. 5:16)?*

Q 41 *Will those led by the flesh inherit heaven (Gal. 5:21)? Explain.*

unaware of danger often perish without a warning. Like Abner, they die as a fool dies (2 Sam. 3:33).

Also, Paul urged believers to follow the desires of the Spirit, and not the desires of the flesh.

Under the Law people had no inner power to do God's will. They were slaves of sin; captives of the desires of the flesh. But the Savior gives us victory over the flesh. Our new life in Christ gives us the ability to do good. The Holy Spirit gives us power to please God.

Also, notice Paul's teaching about a believer who sins. Paul contrasts spiritual believers with an unspiritual believer who is caught in a sin. *"Brothers, if someone is caught in a sin, you who are spiritual should restore him gently. But watch yourself, or you also may be tempted"* (Gal. 6:1).

Spiritual believers should gently and meekly try to restore a sinning believer. Our attitude should always be, "I would have the same problem, except for the grace of God." And remember, the source of self-control is not self. Self-control is a fruit of the Spirit. The secret of holy living is depending on the Holy Spirit.

"Since we live by the Spirit, let us keep in step with the Spirit" (Gal. 5:25).

Marcos was testifying to an old friend named José. Marcos was rejoicing. He praised the Lord for breaking the chains of sexual sins, alcohol, cursing, and smoking. José was annoyed and asked, "Are you saying you're better than I am?" "No," replied Marcos. "I'm not saying I'm better than you are. I'm just saying I'm better than I was!"

Jesus makes a difference in our lives. Paul reminded the Corinthians of their sinful way of life before they met the Savior (1 Cor. 6:9-11). As the angel told Joseph, "*You are to give him the name Jesus, because he will save his people from their sins*" (Matt. 1:21). Galatians emphasizes that we are free from the Law and the flesh, and led by the Spirit.

The acts of the sinful nature (flesh)	The fruit of the Spirit
[19]*The acts of the sinful nature are obvious: sexual immorality, impurity and debauchery;* [20]*idolatry and witchcraft; hatred, discord, jealousy, fits of rage, selfish ambition, dissensions, factions* [21]*and envy; drunkenness, orgies, and the like. I warn you, as I did before, that those who live like this will not inherit the kingdom of God* (Gal. 5:19-21).	[22]*But the fruit of the Spirit is love, joy, peace, patience, kindness, goodness, faithfulness,* [23]*gentleness and self-control. Against such things there is no law.* [24]*Those who belong to Christ Jesus have crucified the sinful nature with its passions and desires.* [25]*Since we live by the Spirit, let us keep in step with the Spirit* (Gal. 5:22-25).

Figure 5.19 In Galatians 5,
Paul contrasts the acts of the flesh with the fruit of the Spirit.

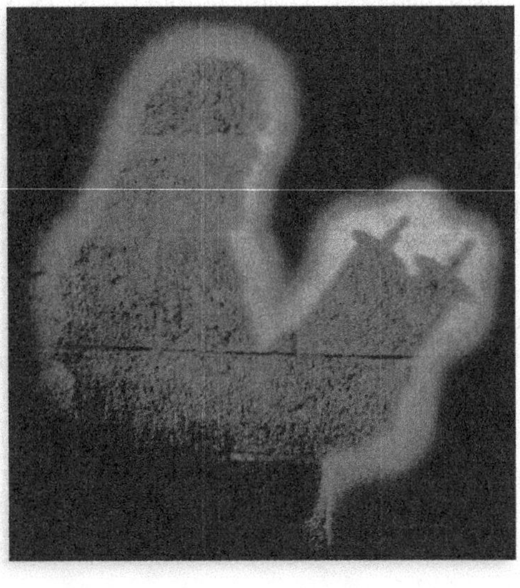

Figure 5.20
Galatians emphasizes that we are no longer slaves to the Law.

Test Yourself: Circle the letter by the ***best*** completion to each question or statement.

1. Of which group was Saul a member?
a) Pharisees
b) Sadducees
c) Essenes
d) Zealots

2. In which group of letters are Romans and Galatians?
a) Salvation Epistles
b) Prison Epistles
c) Pastoral Epistles
d) General Epistles

3. Which group includes 1 and 2 Timothy?
a) Letters about salvation
b) Letters from prison
c) Letters about the future
d) Letters for pastors

4. Romans 6–8 contrasts
a) Jews and Gentiles under God's judgment.
b) slaves of sin and slaves of righteousness.
c) the weak and the mature in Jesus Christ.
d) the young and the old under the Law.

5. Which word emphasizes that God counts us righteous?
a) Justification
b) Sanctification
c) Election
d) Predestination

6. Paul's great theme in Romans is
a) righteousness.
b) obedience.
c) sovereignty.
d) maturity.

7. Judaizers taught that salvation comes by obeying
a) Moses alone.
b) Jesus alone.
c) neither Jesus nor Moses.
d) both Jesus and Moses.

8. The Galatian churches were having problems
a) submitting to church leaders.
b) recognizing Jesus as the Messiah.
c) relating to other groups of believers.
d) trusting in grace alone to be saved.

9. An example of a Galatian church is
a) Iconium.
b) Philippi.
c) Ephesus.
d) Corinth.

10. Paul received the gospel from
a) Peter.
b) Christ.
c) Ananias.
d) an angel.

Essay Test Topics: Write 50-100 words on each of these goals that you studied in this chapter.

Paul

Goal: *Summarize Paul's background, conversion, and public ministry.*

Goal: *Identify the 4 groups of Paul's letters and the books in each.*

Romans

Goal: *Relate righteousness to the 5 parts of Romans.*

Galatians

Goal: *Explain why Paul wrote to the Galatian churches.*

Goal: *Summarize 3 reasons Paul gave the Galatians for believing the gospel.*

Chapter 6:
Letters About Church Problems: 1 and 2 Corinthians

Figure 6.1 Acrocorinth— at its peak was the temple of Venus (goddess of love). Many female prostitutes "served" there, providing the finances for maintaining the temple. On the back of their sandals were the words, "Follow me." (Ruins of Corinth in the front)

Introduction

Have you ever tried to find a perfect church? What would a perfect church look like? Can you find a perfect church in the Bible? Michael was unhappy with his church, so he decided to look for a perfect church. Before he went on his journey, he told his pastor what he was doing. "I'm going to find the perfect church," said Michael. "Get ready for a long trip," said Pastor Hekima with a smile. "And what will you do if you find a perfect church?" his pastor asked. "When I find the perfect church, I'll become a member," replied Michael. "Don't do that," his pastor said. "As soon as you join the perfect church, it won't be perfect anymore!"

Can you imagine a church with no problems? Such a church does not exist on earth. Churches are for people, and people are not perfect. Paul's letters to the church at Corinth remind us that all people have problems. Corinth was a church that was rich in spiritual gifts (1 Cor. 1:7). But even though the apostle Paul himself started the church, it had many problems. One of the biggest problems was division (1 Cor. 1–4). Other problems were sexual sins, believers fighting each other in court, and confusion during church services.

Studying Corinthians emphasizes a great lesson. No matter how bad the problems are in a church, God has a solution. Corinth was one of the darkest, most sinful cities of Paul's day. There, the gospel light shone brightly. And those who were saved learned to live at peace with other believers.

Lessons:

First Corinthians

17

Goal A: *Describe the geographical, social, and religious setting of Corinth.*
Goal B: *Trace the history of the Corinthian church from its beginning to 1 Corinthians.*
Goal C: *Identify 4 problems and 4 questions of the Corinthians.*

Second Corinthians

18

Goal A: *Trace the flow of 2 Corinthians from Ephesus to Macedonia to Corinth.*
Goal B: *Contrast Paul with the false apostles in at least 3 ways.*

Key Words

Corinth — Ephesus — Macedonia — Achaia — Gallio — reconciled — ambassadors

Lesson 17 First Corinthians

Goal A: *Describe the geographical, social, and religious setting of Corinth.*

Goal B: *Trace the history of the Corinthian church from its beginning to 1 Corinthians.*

Goal C: *Identify 4 problems and 4 questions of the Corinthians.*

Recall that it is easy to divide Paul's letters into four groups. Romans, Galatians, and 1 and 2 Corinthians are in the first group. These books focus on salvation (soteriology). Paul often uses the words *"in Christ."* These words emphasize our relationshi Savior and Lord.

Q 1 *Name Paul's 4 letters that discuss salvation.*

Paul wrote the letters to the Corinthians in A.D. 55-56 on his third missionary jo (Acts 18:23–21:17).[1] He wrote 1 Corinthians from *Ephesus (1 Cor. 16:7-9). H probably wrote 2 Corinthians from *Macedonia (2 Cor. 2:12-13; 7:5-7).

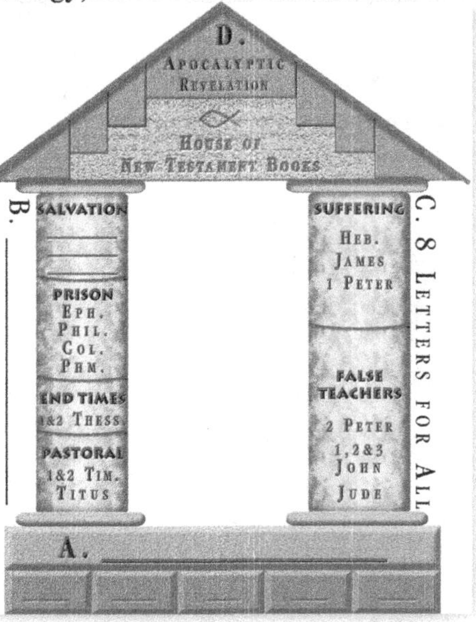

Figure 6.2 Practice house of New Testament books

Q 2 *Complete Figure 6.2.*

A. Corinth: the city and its people

*Corinth was famous for its sin. It was a city of the world and the flesh. To act like a Corinthian meant to commit sexual sins.[2] Behind the city was the Acrocorinth, or hill of Corinth. It stood like a tower, almost 1,500 feet (457 meters) above Corinth. On it was a temple to Aphrodite (Greek name) or Venus (Roman name). Venus was the goddess of love[3] and sex.[4] In this temple about 1,000 female slaves committed sexual sins with those who came to worship. At night, they walked the streets as prostitutes.[5] Paul reminds the Corinthians of their life before they met Jesus.

> [9]*Do you not know that the wicked will not inherit the kingdom of God? Do not be deceived: Neither the sexually immoral nor idolaters nor adulterers nor male prostitutes nor homosexual offenders* [10]*nor thieves nor the greedy nor drunkards nor slanderers nor swindlers will inherit the kingdom of God.* [11]*And that is what some of you were. But you were washed, you were sanctified, you were justified in the name of the Lord Jesus Christ and by the Spirit of our God* (1 Cor. 6:9-11).

Jesus made some big changes in people at Corinth.

Q 3 *What were the Corinthians like before Jesus changed them?*

Corinth was famous for business. Locate Corinth on the map. This huge city was 50 miles (80 km) west of Athens. Paul walked on a short neck of land from Athens to Corinth. Sailors dragged smaller ships four miles over this neck or *isthmus. It connected the Aegean and Adriatic Seas. Crossing these 4 miles over land saved them days of sailing 200 miles (322 km) around the southern part of *Achaia.[6] Ships from the East and the West came to Corinth. Sailors worked on the water and played in the temple.[7]

Q 4 *Did Athens and Corinth have the same number of people? Explain.*

Corinth was a big city. Athens may have had a population of less than 10,000.[8] But Corinth was much larger. Estimates range from 100,000 to several hundred thousand people.[9] Scholars of the NIV Study Bible think Corinth may have had 250,000 free people and as many as 400,000 slaves.[10] Most scholars agree that the most populated city of Paul's day was Rome, followed by Alexandria, and then Antioch. But cities like Ephesus, Philippi, and Corinth were also large. Large cities are more common today. Now, there are over 400 cities larger than a million.[11] Over half the world lives in big cities. But there have not always been so many large

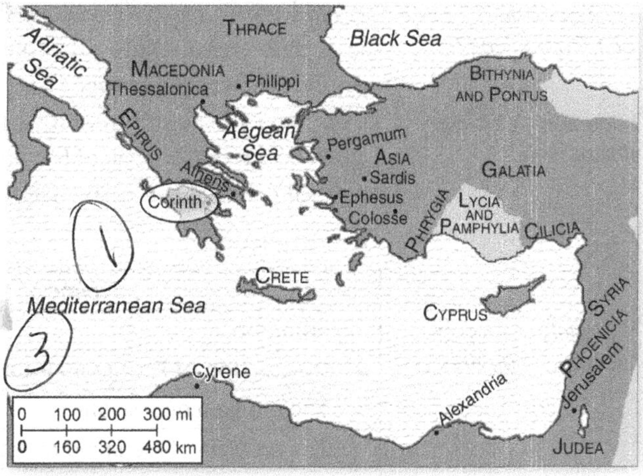

Figure 6.3 Corinth was located in a great place for business. It connected the Aegean and Adriatic Seas.

cities. In 1850, there were only four cities in the world with populations over one million.[12] Corinth was a big city in its day! And big cities were Paul's favorite targets for the gospel.

Q 5 *Which chapter in Acts describes Paul's visit to Corinth?*

Q 6 *How long did Paul stay in Corinth the first time he went there?*

Q 7 *Why did Gallio refuse to judge Paul's case in Corinth?*

B. Paul's ministry to the Corinthians

Paul first visited Corinth about A.D. 52 during his second journey (Acts 18:1-17). He was waiting for Silas and Timothy to come from Macedonia. In Corinth, Paul met Aquila and Priscilla. Like Paul, they were tentmakers. He lived with them while preaching in and around Corinth. They became close friends and ministers.

Silas and Timothy finally arrived. They told him about the conditions in Thessalonica and Berea. While in Corinth, Paul powerfully preached to the Jews "*that Jesus was the Christ*" (Acts 18:5). As usual, some Jews became upset with Paul's preaching. So he began to minister to the Gentiles (Acts 18:6). Many believed. Even Crispus, the ruler of the Jewish synagogue, believed in Christ. Paul ministered in Corinth for at least 18 months. 5

Figure 6.4 The Acrocorinth, or hill of Corinth, stood behind the city. A great temple to Venus stood on top of the mountain.

In Corinth, the Jews took Paul to *Gallio, the governor of Achaia. Achaia was a big and important province. So Gallio was an important Roman ruler. He was also the younger brother of Seneca, a famous philosopher. And Seneca was the tutor of Nero, who became the Emperor of Rome![13]

Gallio threw Paul's case out of the Roman court system in Corinth. This was a huge decision in favor of Christianity. The Roman government allowed Jews to worship God rather than Caesar. Gallio's decision meant that Christianity was protected under the umbrella of Judaism. Gallio ruled that following Jesus did not break Roman law. He said that followers of Jesus and Jewish leaders needed to settle their own disagreements. This prevented the unbelieving Jews from using Roman law against believers. What a great blessing! Gallio's decision helped believers in Achaia and probably many other places.

Q 8 *Did Paul write to the Romans and the Corinthians before he visited them? Explain.*

Q 9 *How did Paul know about problems in Corinth?*

Paul wrote to the Corinthians after he visited them. When he wrote 1 Corinthians, Paul was in Ephesus on his third journey (Acts 19:1-41). Someone from the house of Chloe reported that things were not well in Corinth (1 Cor. 1:11). Paul also received a letter from the Corinthian church elders. They asked questions about some issues and problems. Paul wrote to give them answers (1 Cor. 7:1; 8:1; 12:1; 15:12; 16:1). Paul wrote 1 Corinthians to respond to these and other matters.

Q 10 *What is the purpose of 1 Corinthians?*

Q 11 *Identify 4 problems in 1 Corinthians 1–6.*

C. Purpose

Paul wrote for two reasons. ***First,*** to correct the problems. Our outline shows that these problems include divisions, lawsuits, and sexual sins (1 Cor. 1–6). ***Second,*** Paul wrote to answer questions. Our outline shows that these questions were about marriage, head coverings, communion, spiritual gifts, the resurrection, and giving (1 Cor. 7–15). Let us take a closer look at the problems and questions at Corinth. Notice that Paul gives spiritual principles to solve each problem.[14]

Q 12 *Identify the topics of 4 questions the Corinthians asked.*

Q 13 *Which questions relate to believers you know?*

D. Outline

Theme	1 Corinthians
Introduction	1:1-9
A. Discussion of Problems Paul Knew	1–6
The problem of divisions	1:10–4:21
The problem of the immoral brother	5:1-13
The problem of lawsuits	6:1-11
The problem of sexual immorality	6:12-20

5

Continued on next page

Continued from previous page

B. Answer to the Letter From Corinth	**7–16**
Questions about marriage	7:1-40
Questions about conscience	8:1–10:33
Questions about head coverings	11:1-16
Questions about communion	11:17-34
Questions about spiritual gifts	12:1–14:40
Questions about the resurrection of the dead	15:1-58
Questions about giving	16:1-4
Conclusion	**16:5-24**

Figure 6.5 Outline of 1 Corinthians

Q 14 *Explain the 4 problems in 1 Corinthians 1–6.*

Q 15 *What types of divisions exist in the church today?*

Q 16 *Name 3 kinds of people who will not go to heaven (1 Cor. 6:12-20).*

E. Explanations of the outline

1 Cor.	Problem	Solution/Principle
1:10–4:21	Believers were divided into 4 groups. They followed Paul, Apollos, Peter, or Jesus.	• Live by God's wisdom, rather than worldly wisdom (1:18–2:16). • Become spiritually mature rather than fleshly (3:1-9). • Appreciate the ministry of all church leaders (3:5-22).
5:1-13	A member was sinning sexually with his father's wife.	• The church must discipline the sinning believer. • The purpose of discipline is to protect the church from sin and restore the sinner to Christ and the church.
6:1-11	Believers were accusing one another in court.	• The church must judge and settle such matters outside of the government courts. • Those living sinful lives will not inherit God's kingdom (6:9-11).
6:12-20	Believers may have been tempted to return to their old sexual sins with temple prostitutes.	• Believers must not be mastered by anything of the world. • Our bodies are the temple of the Holy Spirit. • We are not our own, but were bought with a price. Therefore, we must honor God with our bodies.

Figure 6.6 Problems and solutions in 1 Corinthians 1–6

We have noted that Paul received a letter with questions from Corinth (1 Cor. 1:11). He answers these questions in 1 Corinthians 7–16. Again, notice that Paul gives the Corinthians principles that apply to their questions.

1 Cor.	Question/Topic	Answer/Principles
7:1-40	**Marriage** Should believers marry?	• Because of our fleshly needs, it is good for each man to have a wife and each wife to have a husband (7:2). Ideally, the single life is the best (7:38). But it is better to marry than to live with lust (7:9). God has called some to marry and others to remain single. Each person should fulfill the role of God's calling (7:17).
8:1–10:33	**Conscience** Should believers eat food sacrificed to idols?	• Knowledge puffs up, but love builds up (8:1). • Sacrifice your freedom if it will cause a weak believer to stumble (8:9-13). • Paul gave up his rights and became all things to all people to win some (9:1-23). Paul made his body his slave (9:24-27). • If you think you are standing firm, be careful that you don't fall like the Israelites fell (10:1-12). • Nobody should seek his own good, but rather the good of others (10:24). • Do not cause anyone to stumble, whether Jews, Greeks, or the Church (10:32).
11:1-16	**Head coverings** Should women wear them?	• The head of every man is Christ, the head of woman is the man, and the head of Christ is God (11:3). • In Corinth, women showed submission by wearing a veil.

Q 17 *Did Paul encourage believers to marry? Explain.*

Q 18 *How do some believers cause others to stumble? Explain.*

Continued on next page

Q 19 *State 3 principles for using spiritual gifts.*

Q 20 *What is the theme of 1 Corinthians 15?*

Continued from previous page

1 Cor.	Question/Topic	Answer/Principles
11:1-16	**Head coverings** Should women wear them?	• The head of every man is Christ, the head of woman is the man, and the head of Christ is God (11:3). • In Corinth, women showed submission by wearing a veil.
11:17-34	**Communion** Why were death and sickness a problem at Corinth?	• The bread and juice represent the body and blood of Jesus. We take them to remember who He is and the new covenant He made with us (11:23-26). • Those who take communion should recognize that it represents the Lord. Taking it shows that we are in the right relationship with Him. Therefore, we should examine ourselves lest we sin against Christ and bring His judgment upon us. The Lord's discipline is to keep us from being condemned with the world (11:27-34).
12:1–14:40	**Spiritual gifts** How is the purpose of tongues unlike other gifts? Whom does prophecy edify? Why should most praying in tongues be done privately?	• There are different kinds of gifts, service, and work, but the same Spirit, Lord, and God. He is the source of all (12:4-6). • The Spirit gives gifts to each believer as He desires (12:11). • There are many parts, but one body (12:12-30). • Eagerly desire the greater gifts (12:31). • Love is the path to walk on as we minister our spiritual gifts to others (13:1). • Follow the way of love and eagerly desire spiritual gifts, especially prophecy (14:1). He who prays in tongues edifies himself. Like Paul, we should do this often, in private (14:4, 18). • In church, we should seek to prophesy, or speak in tongues and interpret, so that we edify others. Try to excel in gifts that build up the Church (14:1-25). • Be eager to prophesy, and do not forbid speaking in tongues, but do all in an orderly manner (14:39-40).
15:1-58	**Resurrection** Is there really a resurrection? What will the resurrection body be like? Will all believers die?	• We are saved by the gospel if we hold firmly to it. Otherwise, we believed in vain (15:2). • Jesus was raised from the dead on the third day. Many witnesses saw Him (15:3-8). • If there is no resurrection, Jesus is not raised, and our faith is useless (15:12-19). • But Christ has indeed been raised. He was first. Then when He comes, all who belong to Him will rise (15:20-28). • Do not be misled. Bad company corrupts good character. Come back to your senses and stop sinning (15:33-34). • The body that we put into the grave is like a seed. It will be raised as a glorious, spiritual body. As we have borne the image of the earthly Adam, we will be like the heavenly Adam (15:35-49). We will not all sleep, but we will all be changed—in a flash, at the last trumpet (15:51).
16:1-4	**Giving**	• Paul encouraged weekly giving in the church (16:1-2).

Figure 6.7 Questions and answers in 1 Corinthians 7–16

Lesson 18

Second Corinthians

Goal A: *Trace the flow of 2 Corinthians from Ephesus to Macedonia to Corinth.*

Goal B: *Contrast Paul with the false apostles in at least 3 ways.*

A. Background and purpose

Paul traveled to Corinth at least three times and wrote this church several letters.[15] Other books analyze these trips and letters.[16] For this study, it is enough to note three dates and events.[17]

Date (A.D.)	Event	Scriptures
52	Paul evangelized Corinth on his second missionary trip. Some Jews there accused him. Gallio threw Paul's case out of the Roman court.	Acts 18:1-17
Spring, 55-56	Paul traveled from Antioch, Syria, to Ephesus on his third missionary trip. He ministered in Ephesus for 3 years. During this time, he wrote 1 Corinthians. Timothy carried the letter to the church.[18]	Acts 18:23–21:26; 1 Cor. 16:5-8
Fall, 55-56	Paul traveled from Ephesus up to Troas after the Feast of Pentecost. Titus had agreed to meet him there, but was late with the report on Corinth.[19] So Paul continued to Macedonia on his third missionary trip. There he met Titus. Paul then wrote 2 Corinthians. Afterward, Paul went to see the Corinthians for the third time.	2 Cor. 2:13; 7:5-7; 12:14; 13:1

Figure 6.8 Dates and events related to 1 and 2 Corinthians

Paul ministered 3 years in Ephesus on his third missionary trip. From there, he sent the letter we call 1 Corinthians (Figure 6.8). This was not the first letter he ever sent the Corinthians.[20] First Corinthians 5:9 refers to an earlier letter. Paul may have sent many letters that we don't have.[21] Our Bibles contain two letters to the Corinthians. We call them First and Second Corinthians because of the order in which they appear in the New Testament. Our concern is for the letters God has given us, and not for letters we do not have. Our responsibility is always for what we have been given.

Q 21 *Did Paul write 1 and 2 Corinthians from the same place? Explain.*

Recall that 1 Corinthians called the church to repent. Paul insisted that they discipline the man sinning with his father's wife (1 Cor. 5:1-8). Some in the church repented because of Paul's letter (2 Cor. 2:1-11). Also, they disciplined the sinning believer.

Q 22 *Why did Paul write 2 Corinthians? Explain.*

Others, however, continued to cause problems. False teachers questioned Paul's character and authority. These said he was not a true apostle. They knew Paul had changed his plans to visit Corinth. He had first planned to sail from Ephesus to Corinth (2 Cor. 1:15-16). Later, he decided to travel by land up to Macedonia, and then down to Corinth. The false teachers used his change of plans to accuse Paul. They said believers could not trust his word. Also, they accused Paul of planning to steal the offering for the poor saints in Jerusalem. In response to these attacks, Paul wrote 2 Corinthians.

Paul's main purpose in 2 Corinthians was to defend his ministry. He exposed the false apostles. They were greedy. In contrast, Paul asked the Corinthians to remember his life among them. He urged them to consider the truth of his gospel. Paul reminded them to collect the offering for the poor at Jerusalem. He encouraged them to restore the sinner who repented. Finally, he warned that he would punish rebels soon, when he arrived.

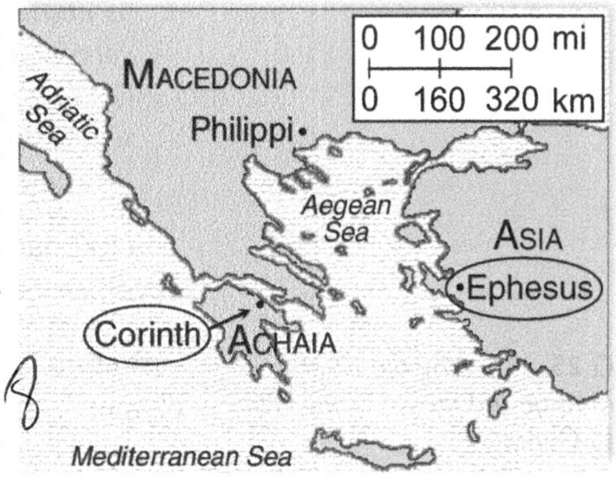

Figure 6.9 Map showing the relationship of Ephesus (in Asia), Philippi (in Macedonia), and Corinth (in Achaia)

B. Outline

Theme	2 Corinthians
A. Ephesus to Macedonia: Paul Defends His Apostolic Ministry	**1–7**
Greeting	1:1-2
Thanks for God's comfort	1:3-11

Continued on next page

Q 23 *In which 2 chapters of 2 Corinthians is Paul not defending his ministry or authority?*

Continued from previous page

Theme	2 Corinthians
The reason Paul changed his travel plans	1:12–2:4
Forgive the disciplined believer.	2:5-11
Ministers of the new covenant	2:12–3:6
The glory of the new covenant	3:7-18
Treasures in clay jars	4
Our heavenly dwelling	5:1-10
The ministry of reconciling the lost	5:11–6:10
A spiritual father's appeal to his children	6:11–7:4
The meeting with Titus	7:5-16
B. Macedonia's Example: The Collection for Poor Believers at Jerusalem	**8–9**
Paul encourages being generous.	8:1-15
Titus and others will care for the offering.	8:16–9:5
The results of sowing generously	9:6-15
C. Macedonia to Corinth: Paul Contrasts Himself With False Apostles	**10–13:10**
Paul defends his authority and mission.	10
Paul is forced into foolish boasting.	11–12
Final warnings	13:1-10
Conclusion	**13:11-14**

Figure 6.10 Outline of 2 Corinthians

Q 24 *Why did God allow Paul to suffer so much?*

C. Explanations of the outline

Paul begins with a greeting and thanksgiving for God's comfort. He does not explain his sufferings in Asia. But note what he says.

> 8*We do not want you to be uninformed, brothers, about the hardships we suffered in the province of Asia. We were under great pressure, far beyond our ability to endure, so that we despaired even of life.* 9*Indeed, in our hearts we felt the sentence of death. But this happened that we might not rely on ourselves but on God, who raises the dead.* 10*He has delivered us from such a deadly peril, and he will deliver us. On him we have set our hope that he will continue to deliver us,* 11*as you help us by your prayers* (2 Cor. 1:8-11).

God had delivered Paul from terrible suffering and deadly danger. After this brief introduction, Paul begins to defend himself.

Q 25 *Why did Paul change the timing of his visit to Corinth?*

Q 26 *Did Paul take the shortest way from Ephesus to Corinth on his third trip? Explain.*

Ephesus to Macedonia: Paul defends his apostolic ministry (2 Cor. 1–7). In these chapters, the readers move with Paul from Ephesus to Macedonia.[22] The false teachers accused Paul of changing his mind. It is true that Paul changed his travel plans to Corinth. Why? For the sake of the Corinthians. He had written to them about disciplining the believer committing a sexual sin (1 Cor. 5:4-5). This sinner was powerful. It appears that he was Paul's greatest enemy in the church at Corinth.[23] Some of the Corinthians had supported this sinner. The letter of 1 Corinthians called them to repent and discipline the man. The church needed some time to correct this problem. It would have been too painful for Paul to visit them when he planned (2 Cor. 2:1-2). So Paul delayed his coming. As he prayed, it seemed best to change his plans and visit them later. So he went to Macedonia first, instead of going straight to Corinth. All believers should allow the Holy Spirit to change their plans. We should walk softly before the Lord and not boast about what we will do tomorrow (James 4:13-17). Thus, it was foolish for the false apostles to accuse Paul for changing his plans (2 Cor. 1:12–2:4).

Explaining his trip from Ephesus to Macedonia, Paul mentions several great truths.

- The purpose of church discipline is to help and restore. Paul told the Corinthians to forgive and show love to the sinner who repented (1 Cor. 5:4-5; 2 Cor. 2:5-11). The goal of discipline should always be to help.
- The ministry of the new covenant is more glorious than the ministry of the old covenant. The face of Moses shined with glory. He covered his face with a veil. But the glory faded. In contrast, we, with unveiled faces, reflect the Lord's glory. We are being changed into His likeness with an increasing, unfading glory (2 Cor. 2:12–3:18).
- As ministers of the new covenant, we leave all secret and shameful ways behind us (2 Cor. 4:1-6).
- We have this treasure of God's Spirit in *"jars of clay."* This shows that the power is from God, not us (2 Cor. 4:7-12).
- Our light troubles are helping us gain eternal glory that is much heavier. So we focus our eyes on the invisible and the eternal (2 Cor. 4:17-18).
- We make it our goal to please Him. For we must all appear before the judgment seat of Christ to receive what is due us, whether good or bad (2 Cor. 5:9-10).
- God *reconciled us to Himself through Christ. God made Him who had no sin to become sin for us, so we could become righteous. All ministers, like Paul, are God's *ambassadors. We must be careful not to receive God's grace in vain, but to live to please Him (2 Cor. 5:11–6:2). Some of the Corinthian believers needed to be reconciled to God again, lest the grace they once received be in vain (2 Cor. 5:20; 6:1-2; 13:5).
- Like Paul, we should avoid blame in every way. Then we will not be stumbling blocks (2 Cor. 6:1-13).
- We are to perfect holiness. This means separating ourselves from sinful friends and sinful things (2 Cor. 6:14–7:1; 13:11).
- Godly sorrow brings repentance that leads to salvation (2 Cor. 7:8-13).

These are a lot of great truths on the short trip from Ephesus to Macedonia!

Q 27 What is the purpose of church discipline?

Q 28 What great danger did some Corinthian believers face?

Macedonia's example: The collection for poor believers at Jerusalem (2 Cor. 8–9). Now that we have reached Macedonia, Paul uses them for an example. Some of the churches in Macedonia were at Philippi, Thessalonica, and Berea. These believers were very poor, but very generous. They begged to give all they could. First, they gave themselves to the Lord. Then they gave all the money they could for the poor in Jerusalem. Paul urged the Corinthians to follow their example. He challenged them to excel in the grace of giving as they excelled in the grace of spiritual gifts (2 Cor. 8:1-7). Great truths in these two chapters include:

- Jesus was a model of grace for us. He became poor so that we could become spiritually rich (2 Cor. 8:8-9).
- Paul encouraged those with much to share with those who had little (2 Cor. 8:10-15).
- Paul encouraged those of Macedonia with the giving of those in Achaia. And He encouraged those in Achaia with the giving of the Macedonians (2 Cor. 9:1-5). Giving is *contagious. It spreads! When one believer gives, it encourages others to give.
- Those who sow sparingly will reap sparingly. Those who sow generously will reap generously (2 Cor. 9:6-14).
- Thanks be to God for His gift, Jesus Christ, that goes beyond our words to thank Him (2 Cor. 9:15).

Q 29 State the provinces that contained Ephesus, Philippi, and Corinth.

Q 30 Explain how we can relate 2 Corinthians to Ephesus, Macedonia, and Achaia.

Macedonia to Corinth: Paul contrasts himself with false apostles (2 Cor. 10–13). We are on the third part of the outline of 2 Corinthians. First, Paul told of his trip from Ephesus to Macedonia (2 Cor. 1–7). Then he told about the generosity of the Macedonians (2 Cor. 8–9). Finally, in 2 Corinthians 10–13, Paul focused on the problem at Corinth. The false apostles were leading some astray.

Q 31 *Contrast true and false apostles in at least 3 ways.*

Paul went to the root of the problem. The Corinthians were living by the wisdom and standards of the world (2 Cor. 11–13). Thus, they were looking only on the surface (2 Cor. 10:7). As Paul said earlier, they took pride in what is seen, rather than what is in the heart (2 Cor. 5:12). This was an old problem at Corinth. Remember the divisions in Corinth based on people like Paul, Apollos, and Peter (1 Cor. 1–4)? The Corinthian believers were young and immature. They had not yet learned to base their choices on spiritual principles. So Paul contrasts himself with the false apostles. Figure 6.11 contrasts the characteristics of true and false apostles.

Q 32 *Do you think there are apostles today?*

Thus Paul contrasted himself with false apostles in 2 Corinthians. He was very personal and opened his heart. He told about the many times he suffered for Jesus. In contrast, the false apostles lacked persecution, spiritual power, biblical teachings, and godly character.

False Apostles and Fleshly Leaders	True Apostles and Spiritual Leaders	2 Cor.
They act as if they were lords over others.	They humbly work with believers.	1:24
They rely on humans to recommend them.	Their fruits and results speak for them.	3:1-3
They depend on themselves.	They depend on God.	3:4-6; 4:7
They practice secret, shameful ways. They deceive people and distort God's Word.	They are honest and open before God and others. They speak the Word plainly.	4:2
They emphasize the seen and the temporal.	They focus on the unseen and the eternal.	4:18
They take pride in the outward appearance of ministry. They look only on the surface.	They take pride in what is in the heart.	5:13; 10:7
They cause many to stumble.	They are careful not to be a stumbling block.	6:3-10
They are known for wickedness, darkness, unbelief, Satan (Belial), idols, and uncleanness.	They are known for righteousness, light, Christ, belief, being the temple of God, and holiness.	6:14-18
They live by the standards of the world. They wage war as the world does. They look only on the surface of things.	They use spiritual weapons to fight. These include prayer, the Bible, and the fruit and gifts of the Spirit.	10:1-7
They commend themselves. They measure themselves by themselves and compare themselves with others.	They boast in the Lord, and are commended by Him.	10:8-18
They act like they are super-apostles, boasting about how well they speak. They are deceitful workers. They act like they are of Christ, but they are of Satan. These will one day be judged.	They fear that their converts will be deceived like Eve; be led astray; receive a different Jesus, a different gospel, and a different spirit. So they watch over young believers, often working with no pay.	11:1-15 (See 1 Cor. 4:18-21.)
They enslave, exploit, and take advantage of believers. They push themselves forward and "slap" believers in the face! They live a safe, easy life.	They may have suffered from prison, beatings, robbers, no sleep, no food, lack of clothes, and church problems. They live a hard, dangerous life.	11:16-33
They make up visions and teachings. They make up stories about miracles that never happened.	They have visions and revelations. They do signs, wonders, and miracles.	12:1-13
Their main concern is themselves.	Everything they do is to strengthen others.	12:19
They sin secretly. They slander true apostles and righteous leaders.	They judge sinning believers and false teachers in the church. They desire to use their authority to build up the Church.	12:19–13:10

Figure 6.11 Second Corinthians contrasts false and true apostles.

Test Yourself: Circle the letter by the ***best*** completion to each question or statement.

1. Which direction is Corinth from Jerusalem?
a) Northeast
b) Northwest
c) Southeast
d) Southwest

2. To *act like a Corinthian* meant to
a) speak in tongues.
b) read many books.
c) travel the world.
d) live in sin.

3. Which city had the most people?
a) Rome
b) Corinth
c) Athens
d) Antioch

4. On his second missionary trip, Paul went to Corinth and stayed for
a) 1 month.
b) 6 months.
c) 12 months.
d) 18 months.

5. First Corinthians 1–4 is about the problem of
a) divisions.
b) unbelief.
c) persecution.
d) Judaizers.

6. Paul wrote about ____ ____ in 1 Corinthians 12-14.
a) false teachers
b) spiritual gifts
c) good works
d) end times

7. First Corinthians 15 answers questions about
a) resurrection.
b) head coverings.
c) conscience.
d) marriage.

8. What was Paul's main purpose for writing 2 Corinthians?
a) To collect an offering
b) To confront false doctrine
c) To give comfort to believers
d) To defend his ministry

9. In 2 Corinthians 8–9, Paul said true apostles
a) have plenty of money.
b) expect others to serve them.
c) speak with powerful words.
d) are known for humility.

10. False apostles in Corinth
a) used spiritual weapons to fight.
b) made up stories about miracles.
c) were persecuted for their faith.
d) sacrificed their lives for the sheep.

Essay Test Topics: Write 50-100 words on each of these goals that you studied in this chapter.

First Corinthians

Goal: *Describe the geographical, social, and religious setting of Corinth.*

Goal: *Trace the history of the Corinthian church from its beginning to 1 Corinthians.*

Goal: *Identify 4 problems and 4 questions of the Corinthians..*

Second Corinthians

Goal: *Trace the flow of 2 Corinthians from Ephesus to Macedonia to Corinth.*

Goal: *Contrast Paul with the false apostles in at least 3 ways.*

Chapter 7:

Letters From Prison: Ephesians, Philippians, Colossians, and Philemon

Figure 7.1 At Ephesus, new believers burned magic scrolls worth enough money to pay 1,000 men for working 50 days. (by Gustave Doré)

Introduction

In 1873, a lawyer named Horatio Spafford planned a trip with his family to Europe. Business delayed him, but he sent his wife and four young daughters on ahead. Their ship, the Ville Du Havre, never made it to England. It sank into the cold grave of the Atlantic Ocean. Horatio's wife, Anna, was among the few who survived. His four daughters—Maggie, Tanetta, Annie, and Bessie—all drowned. He received the terrible news from his wife with only these two words: "saved alone." Spafford got on the next ship to go be with his grieving wife. On his way to meet her, he sailed near the place where his daughters had drowned. There, in the middle of his sorrow, the Spirit of God comforted him. He wrote the poem: It Is Well With My Soul. Later a songwriter wrote music for it. Today, believers around the world sing this great hymn of the church. It has brought comfort to millions of sad hearts.[1]

Likewise, in a prison, the Holy Spirit encouraged Paul. In chains, he wrote four of his most glorious letters. Spiritual giants of the church like John Bunyan, Dietrich Bonhoeffer, and Watchman Nee have also written from prison. Jesus promised that He would never leave or forsake us. And it is in our hardest times that this promise becomes the most precious to us.

Lessons:

Ephesians

19 **Goal A:** *Describe the background of Ephesus. Include its location, business, temple, and church.*

Goal B: *Analyze 4 relationships Paul wrote about in Ephesians.*

Colossians

20 **Goal A:** *Analyze the Colossian heresy and Paul's teachings on it.*

Goal B: *Explain Paul's teaching about old and new clothes.*

Philippians

21 **Goal A:** *Summarize the background of Paul's letter to the Philippians.*

Goal B: *Summarize what Philippians teaches about joy and unity.*

Philemon

22 **Goal:** *Analyze 3 people and 2 lessons in the letter to Philemon.*

Key Words

Prison Epistles, Philemon, Artemis, Priscilla, Apollos, predestined, Colossian heresy, supreme, firstborn, Gnosticism, Onesimus

Lesson 19

Ephesians

Goal A: *Describe the background of Ephesus. Include its location, business, temple, and church.*

Goal B: *Analyze 4 relationships Paul wrote about in Ephesians.*

What should we think of Paul's time in prison? Was it a problem or a blessing? Would it have been better for all if Paul had stayed free? Would the Church have grown faster if he continued to travel? Or was it God's will for Paul to be in prison? These are hard questions to answer. But we know that Paul's time in prison was a blessing to many (Acts 28:30-31). It gave Paul time to write his *Prison Epistles. These are Ephesians, Philippians, Colossians, and *Philemon.

Q 1 *Sing the song of New Testament books.*

Q 2 *Which 4 letters did Paul write from prison?*

Each of these four letters states that Paul wrote as a prisoner (Eph. 3:1; 4:1; 6:20; Phil. 1:12-13; Col. 1:24; 4:18; Phm. 9-10). Most Bible teachers believe he was a prisoner in Rome when he wrote these letters.

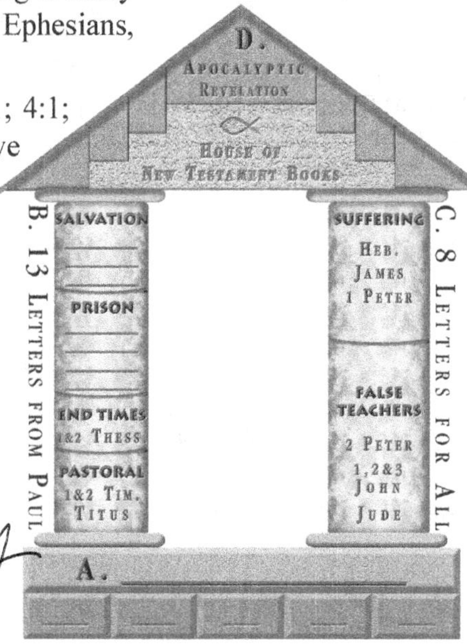

Figure 7.2 Practice house of New Testament books

A. Background

Pergamum was the capital of Asia, but Ephesus was the most important city there.[2] It was located on the eastern shore of the Aegean Sea. Some say 200,000[3] to a third of a million people[4] lived in Ephesus.[5] Others think the city had a population of half a million people.[6]

The biggest ships in the world came to Ephesus. Also, major roads ended in this city. Some researchers have dug up the main street of Ephesus. It was 36 feet (11 m) wide, 1,735 feet (529 m) long, and made of marble. The street ended at the sea. There were business shops all along the main street.

Ephesus was also famous for the temple of the Greek goddess *Artemis. It was four times bigger than the *Parthenon at Athens.[7] Her temple was one of the seven wonders of the Old World. In all the earth, there was no other Greek temple so great. It was 425 feet (130 m) long, 220 feet (67 m) wide, and had 120 stone pillars that were each 60 feet (18 m) high. People traveled to Ephesus from all over the Roman Empire. There they bowed down to the idol of Artemis.

Q 3 *Complete Figure 7.2.*

Some refer to Artemis by her Roman name, Diana.[8] People worshiped her as the goddess of the moon. She was also linked with childbirth. Local craftsmen made statues of the goddess. These statues had many breasts.[9] The Ephesians believed that men communicated with Artemis through the prostitutes in the temple.[10] Paul's preaching lessened the sale of idols. Recall the great riot in the city during Paul's ministry (Acts 19:23-41). Businessmen, like Demetrius, became angry when people began to turn from Artemis to Jesus. Opposition to the gospel was never greater than at Ephesus. Paul learned many things on his first two trips. No doubt this prepared him for the spiritual warfare in Ephesus on his third trip. Remember that even apostles grow in grace.

Q 4 *Why was Ephesus an important city for business?*

Q 5 *How did the gospel affect the worship of Artemis in Ephesus?*

The Bible contains much related to Ephesus.

- Paul left *Priscilla and *Aquila to minister in Ephesus near the end of his second trip (Acts 18:18-19). There they taught *Apollos, the great Jewish speaker (Acts 18:24-26).
- Later, Paul returned to Ephesus on his third trip. His greatest revival was there. Paul ministered 3 years in Ephesus; longer than in any other city (Acts 20:31). He preached the gospel in the synagogue, in the school of Tyrannus, in homes, and in the marketplaces (Acts 19).
- Twelve disciples were baptized in the Holy Spirit in Ephesus (Acts 19:1-7). Demons were cast out of others. The sons of Sceva had a race on the marble street (See Figure 7.3). In contrast, the anointing on Paul was so great that handkerchiefs from his body brought healing. Converts burned magic books worth enough money to pay 1,000 men for working 50 days. Did the smoke from these books fill the main street and enter the temple of Artemis?

Q 6 *Explain 3 things that happened in Ephesus on Paul's third trip.*

Q 7 Describe the location of 9 churches in relation to Ephesus.

- Timothy became the first pastor or overseer of Ephesus. Paul left him there and wrote to him later (1 Tim. 1:3).
- Ephesus was Paul's base of ministry for 3 years (Acts 19:8-10; 20:31). It was in the center of the churches that Paul planted. East of Ephesus were the Galatian churches of Pisidian Antioch, Iconium, Lystra, and Derbe. Northwest of Ephesus were the churches of Philippi, Thessalonica, and Berea. And straight west of Ephesus, across the Aegean Sea, were Athens and Corinth. Thus Ephesus was like the hub of a wheel. It was the center of God's strategy for a big area. *To Ephesus,* the churches sent messengers to Paul with questions or offerings. And *from Ephesus,* Paul sent letters to the churches he planted. Therefore, Ephesus became a new center for God's mission to the Gentiles. It was second only to Antioch, Syria, as a base for Gentile missions.[11]

Figure 7.3 This marble street at Ephesus led past businesses to the harbor of the Aegean Sea.

Figure 7.4 Ruins of the temple of Artemis (Diana) in Ephesus

Ephesus is truly one of the most important cities of the Bible. In Revelation, John wrote first to the Ephesians (Rev. 2:1-7). Paul's letter to the Ephesians is one of his most glorious letters.

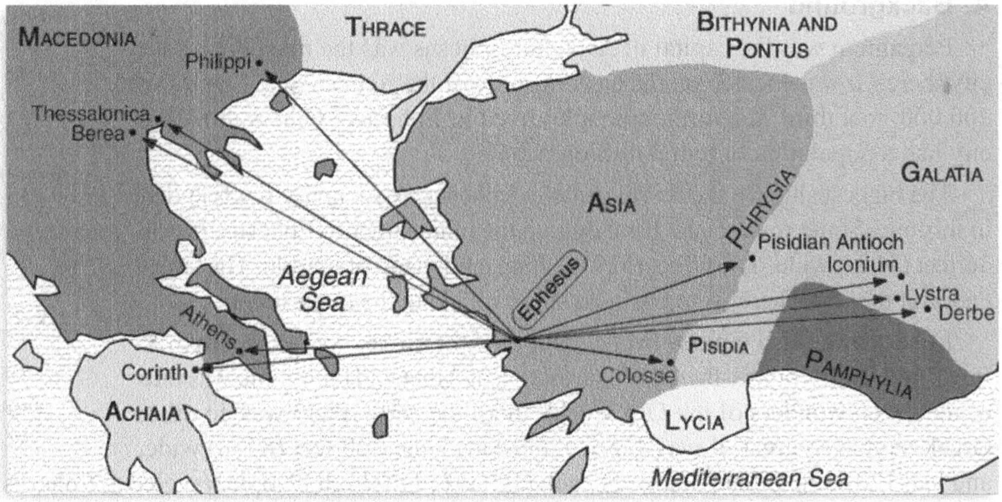

Figure 7.5 Ephesus was a strategic center for missions.

B. Outline

The theme of Ephesians is the Church as the body of Christ. Paul emphasized this theme throughout the book.

Figure 7.6 Statue of Artemis (Diana) at Ephesus

Q 8 What is the theme of Ephesians?

Q 9 Which chapters in Ephesians apply doctrine?

Theme	Ephesians
Greeting	**1:1-2**
A. Powerful Doctrine: The Believer's Redemption	**1–3**
The glory and greatness of Jesus	1:3-14
Prayer for believers to discern God's purpose	1:15-23
The results of redemption for Jews and Gentiles	2
God's revelation of His wisdom through the Church	3:1-13
Prayer for believers to fulfill God's purpose	3:14-21
B. Practical Teaching: The Believer's Daily Life	**4–6**
Unity	4:1-6
Maturity	4:7-16
Children of light	4:17–5:20
Wives and husbands	5:21-33
Children and parents	6:1-4
Slaves and masters	6:5-9
The armor of God	6:10-20
Conclusion	**6:21-24**

Figure 7.7 Outline of Ephesians

We can also outline Ephesians by relationships.

Ephesians	Relationship
1	Our relationship with God our Father
2–3	The relationship between Jews and Gentiles
4–6	Our relationships in the family of God
6	Our relationship to evil spirits

Figure 7.8 In Ephesians, Paul writes about four relationships.

C. Explanations of the outline

The letter is addressed to the "*saints*" and the "*faithful ones*." These two terms apply to all believers. They describe our place in Christ and our character.

Q 10 Did Paul write Ephesians to sinners? Explain.

Our relationship with God our Father (Eph. 1). Consider the spiritual blessings God has given us in Christ.

Q 11 What 5 things has God done for us (Eph. 1:3-14)?

- *"He chose us...to be holy and blameless"* (Eph. 1:4). We are holy for two reasons. *First,* because Jesus died for us on the cross. *Second,* because we faithfully obey the Word and the Spirit. Thus, we walk worthily (Eph. 4:1). As we walk in the light, the blood of Jesus cleanses us from all sins (1 John 1:7).
- He planned to adopt us as His children, through Christ (Eph. 1:5). God planned ahead or *predestined that some would believe. This does not mean that God chose who would be saved. God votes for all to be saved (1 Tim. 2:4). In contrast, Satan votes for all to be lost. The election depends on how each person votes.[12]
- He redeemed us through the blood of Jesus (Eph. 1:7). At the cross, God voted for all people to be saved. Jesus shed his blood to pay the penalty for everyone's sin (1 Tim. 4:10).
- He revealed His will to us (Eph. 1:9-10). Through the gospel, we understand God's will. He wants us to repent, receive Christ, and follow Him throughout life. Afterward, He wants to live with us eternally.
- He sealed us with the Holy Spirit (Eph. 1:13-14). All believers receive the Spirit when they are born again. This presence of God within assures us. He is the *down payment or deposit and guarantee of good things to come. The Spirit's presence in us shows that God owns us.

Q 12 Fill in the 8 letters, A-H, around Ephesus in Figure 7.9.

Read again the five things God has done for us. Take a few moments to pause and worship. Let your heart be filled with praise. Let your mind be filled with wonder that God loves us so much. Then note Paul's great prayer (Eph. 1:15-23). He continually asked God to help us know Him better (Eph. 1:17). How exciting! What an opportunity—to walk with God and know Him better day by day! How can it be that humans turn away from this invitation?

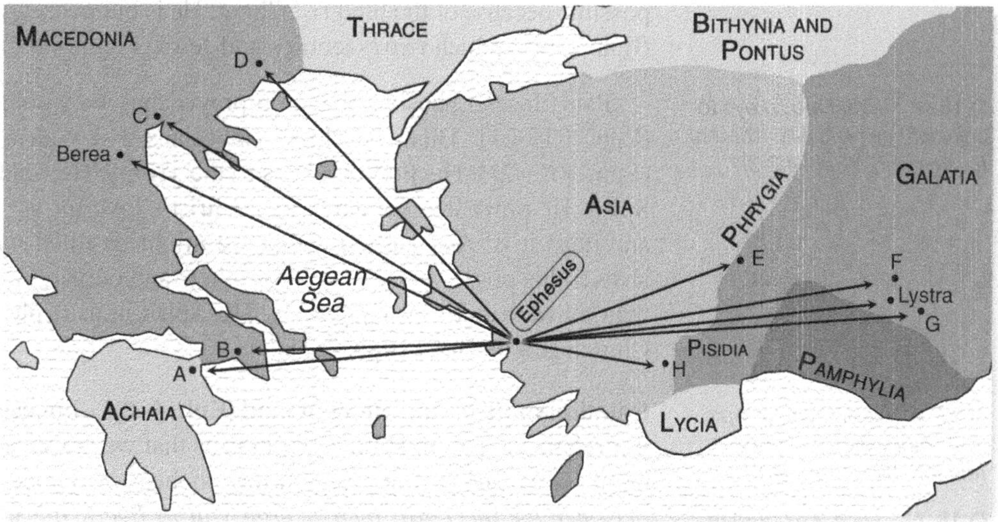

Figure 7.9 Practice map relating Ephesus to other cities and provinces

The relationship between Jews and Gentiles (Eph. 2–3). The big theme of Ephesians 2–3 is that in Christ, God unites Jews and Gentiles into one spiritual body. Jews and Gentiles come from different cultures. The principles that Paul teaches in these chapters can help believers everywhere relate better to each other.

Q 13 What is the relationship between Jews and Gentiles?

In the past, we Gentile believers were dead in sins (Eph. 2:1). At that time, we followed the ways of the world and the devil (Eph. 2:2). We were disobedient and were led by the desires of our flesh (Eph. 2:2-3). Back then, we were objects of God's wrath (Eph. 2:3). But by God's mercy we have been saved from sins, sinful living, and God's wrath (Eph. 2:4-5). Therefore, Paul tells us to remember the change that has taken place. Note the five terrible phrases that describe our past. We were:

Q 14 *What are 5 phrases that describe our past (Eph. 2:12)?*

Separate *from Christ,* ***excluded*** *from citizenship in Israel and* ***foreigners*** *to the covenants of the promise,* ***without*** *hope and* ***without*** *God in the world* (Eph. 2:12).

Scripture	Ephesians
[Christ] *made the two one . . .*	2:14
His purpose was to create in himself one new man out of the two . . .	2:15
And in this one body to reconcile both of them to God through the cross . . .	2:16
He came and preached peace to you [Gentiles] *who were far away and peace to those* [Jews] *who were near.*	2:17
For through him we both have access to the Father by one Spirit.	2:18
This mystery is that through the gospel the Gentiles are heirs together with Israel, members together of one body . . .	3:6
[Jews and Gentiles] *Make every effort to keep the unity of the Spirit . . .* [for] *There is one body and one Spirit . . . one hope . . . one Lord, one faith, one baptism; one God and Father of all . . .*	4:3-6

Figure 7.10
The theme of Ephesians 2–3 is that God unites Jews and Gentiles into one spiritual body.

Figure 7.11 A Roman soldier in full armor

Q 15 *Explain: The Gentiles were far, and the Jews were near (Eph. 2:17).*

But now we who were far (the Gentiles) have been brought near to God. This is possible because of the blood of Christ. He is our peace. And He has "*made the two one*" (Eph. 2:14). Which two? Gentiles and Jews (Figure 7.10).

Q 16 *What are 5 keys to unity for believers with different backgrounds (Eph. 4:2-3)?*

Paul closes Ephesians 1 with a prayer that we would continue to know God better (Eph. 1:15-23). Then, he closes Ephesians 2–3 with a prayer for the whole family (Eph. 3:14-21). His prayer relates to the Trinity. He wants us to be strengthened by the Spirit. He prays that we may grasp Christ's love for us—how wide and long and high and deep it is. And He prays that we might be filled with God's presence. May God answer this prayer as we pray it for others and ourselves. He is able to do so much more than all we can ask or imagine by His Spirit in us (Eph. 3:20). To Him be glory in the Church and in Christ (Eph. 3:21)!

Q 17 *Identify 4 groups that Paul writes to about relationships (Eph. 4–6).*

Q 18 *Give 3 examples that show what it means to live worthily.*

Relationships in the family of God (Eph. 4–6). Ephesians 1 emphasizes God's part in our relationship with Him. It reminds us that we are saved by grace. But Ephesians 4–6 emphasizes our part in the journey to heaven. Grace brings responsibilities. "*As a prisoner for the Lord, then, I urge you to live a life worthy of the calling you have received*" (Eph. 4:1).

Q 19 *Identify 3 types of people that will not go to heaven (Eph. 5:5).*

What does it mean to live a life worthy of our calling? Paul answers this question in Ephesians 4–6. There he discusses four types of family relationships. Both Ephesians and Colossians discuss these relationships in the family of God. Figure 7.12 compares Ephesians and Colossians on Paul's teachings about relationships.

Ephesians	Teaching on Family Relationships	Teaching on Family Relationships	Colossians
All Believers 4:1–5:3 5:19	*Be completely humble and gentle; be patient, bearing with one another in love. Make every effort to keep the unity of the Spirit through the bond of peace.* *Speak truthfully . . . for we are all* ***members*** *of one body. . . . Get rid of all bitterness, rage and anger, brawling and slander, along with every form of malice. Be kind and compassionate* ***to one another,*** *forgiving* ***each other,*** *just as in Christ God forgave you. Be imitators of God.* *But* ***among you*** *there must not be even a hint of sexual immorality, or of any kind of impurity, or of greed, because these are improper for* ***God's holy people.*** *Speak to* ***one another*** *with psalms, hymns and spiritual songs.*	*Put to death, therefore, whatever belongs to your earthly nature: sexual immorality, impurity, lust, evil desires and greed, which is idolatry.* *Rid* ***yourselves*** *of all such things as these: anger, rage, malice, slander, and filthy language from your lips. Do not lie to* ***each other*** *. . . as God's chosen people, holy and dearly loved, clothe yourselves with compassion, kindness, humility, gentleness and patience. Bear with* ***each other*** *and forgive whatever grievances you may have against* ***one another.*** *Forgive as the Lord forgave you. . . . Put on love, . . . teach and admonish* ***one another*** *with all wisdom, and as you sing psalms, hymns and spiritual songs . . .*	3:5, 8-9 3:12-14 3:16
Wives & Husbands 5:22-31	***Wives,*** *submit to your husbands.* ***Husbands,*** *love your wives, just as Christ loved the Church.*	***Wives,*** *submit to your husbands . . .* ***Husbands,*** *love your wives and do not be harsh with them.*	3:18 3:19
Children & Fathers 6:1-4	***Children,*** *obey your parents. This is God's command.* ***Fathers,*** *do not be too hard on your children.*	***Children,*** *obey your parents. This is the right thing to do.* ***Fathers,*** *do not be too hard on your children, or they will become discouraged.*	3:20 3:21
Servants & Masters 6:5-9	***Servants,*** *obey your masters as you obey Christ.* ***Masters,*** *do not show favoritism with your slaves, or threaten them, since you both have the same Master in heaven.*	***Servants,*** *obey your masters at all times. Work like you are serving Christ.* ***Masters,*** *be fair with your slaves because you have a Master in heaven.*	3:22-25 4:1

Figure 7.12 A comparison of Paul's teachings on family relationships in Ephesians and Colossians

Our relationship to evil spirits (Eph. 6). In closing, Paul discussed our relationship to evil spirits of darkness (Eph. 6:10-20). Believers are at war with Satan and evil spirits. Our protection in this warfare is the whole armor of God. If we use it, we will be able to overcome the attacks of the devil. Paul described six pieces of armor and the purpose of each.

Q 20 *Identify 6 pieces of spiritual armor (Eph. 6:10-17).*

Q 21 *What 2 things did Paul say to do with the armor of God (Eph. 6:18)?*

Lesson 20

Colossians

Goal A: *Analyze the Colossian heresy and Paul's teachings on it.*

Goal B: *Explain Paul's teaching about old and new clothes*

A. Background

Remember that we are studying the four letters Paul wrote from a prison. In Colossians, Paul mentions his sufferings and his bonds (Col. 1:24; 4:18).

Paul wrote two letters to churches he did not start: Romans and Colossians. He may have learned about the Colossian church from Epaphras. "*Epaphras, our dear fellow servant, who is a faithful minister of Christ on our behalf, and who also told us of your love in the Spirit*" (Col. 1:7-8; 4:12).

The city of Colosse was not as large or important as Ephesus. Unlike Ephesus, Colosse was not located beside a sea. However, Colosse was near the Lycus River. And it was on the major road between Rome and the East (Figure 7.14). Many people traveled this road. These travelers brought many false teachings. Paul wrote to correct these errors and to instruct the Colossians about holy living (Col. 2:8–3:4).

Q 22 *Who started the church at Colosse? Explain.*

Q 23 *What is the theme of Colossians?*

Figure 7.13 Map showing some churches in the province of Asia

The false teachings in Colosse were a mixture of Jewish and *Gnostic ideas. The word *Gnostic* comes from the Greek word *gnosis*, which means "knowledge." The Gnostic teachers claimed they had secret knowledge needed for salvation. Some Gnostic teachings were present in Colosse during the first century. They developed more in the second century.

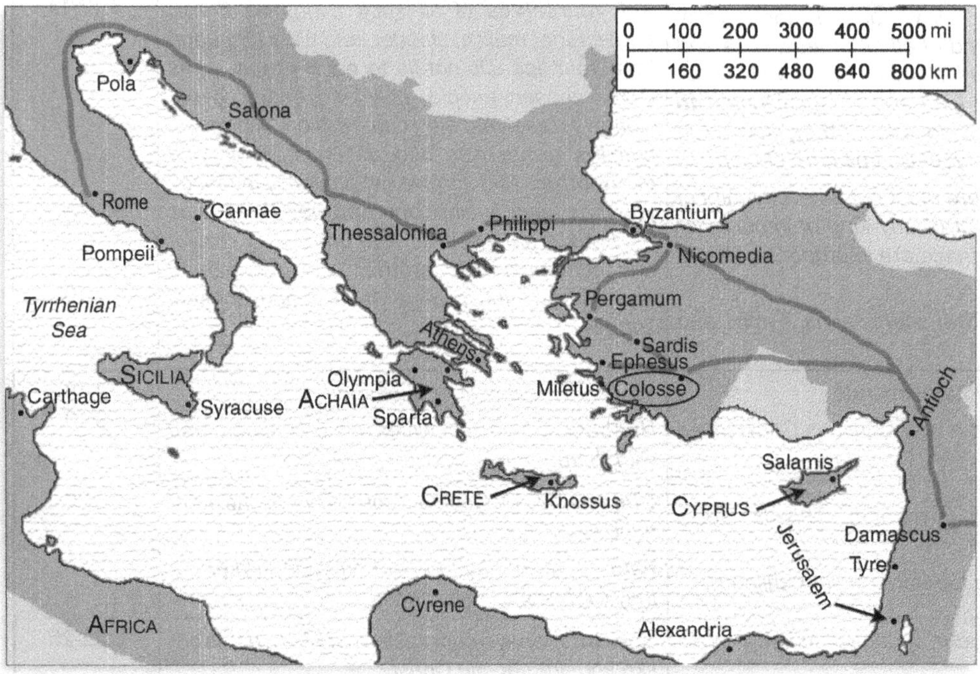

Figure 7.14 Colosse was on the main business road between Rome and the East.

The false teachings at Colosse are often called the **Colossian heresy*. The false teachers were taking away from the importance of Jesus. In contrast, Paul wrote that Jesus is *supreme and sufficient. He is the Head over every power and authority, and we are complete in Him (Col. 2:10). The main verse in Colossians is 1:18b: "*that in everything He* (Jesus) *might have the *supremacy.*"

Q 24 *Describe the Colossian heresy.*

B. Outline

It is helpful to divide Colossians into two parts (Figure 7.15). Paul often followed a pattern in his letters. He wrote about doctrine first. That is, he wrote about the theological basis of our salvation. Then, in the second part of his letters, Paul liked to answer the question, "Now what?" Thus, in the second part of his letters, Paul applied theology to daily living. All good teaching connects the *what* with the *so what?* or *now what?* All good teaching and preaching applies theology and doctrine to daily living. Colossians is an example of how Paul talked about theology first and then applied it.

Col.	Theme
1–2	Powerful doctrine: our supreme Savior
3–4	Practical teaching: guidelines for holy living

Figure 7.15 Colossians has a doctrinal part and a practical part.

Figure 7.16 is an expanded outline of Colossians.

Theme	Colossians
Introduction	**1:1-14**
Greeting	1:1-2
Thanksgiving	1:3-8
Prayer for the Colossian believers	1:9-14
A. Powerful Doctrine: Our *Supreme Savior	**1:15–2:23**
The supremacy of Christ	1:15-23
Paul's work for the Church	1:24–2:7
Warnings against false teachers	2:8-23
B. Practical Teaching: Guidelines for Holy Living	**3:1–4:6**
The old self and the new self	3:1-17
Rules for the family of God	3:18–4:1
More teachings	4:2-6
Conclusion	4:7-18

Figure 7.16 Outline of Colossians

C. Explanations of the outline

Q 25 *Which 2 chapters deal directly with the Colossian heresy?*

Q 26 *What is the theme of Colossians 3–4?*

The supremacy of Christ (Col. 1:15-23). Christ is supreme. That is, He is above everything and everyone. He is equal with God the Father. Note some of the things Paul tells us about Christ.

Q 27 *Explain: "Christ is supreme."*

- He is the (physical, visible) image of the invisible God (Col. 1:15).
- He is the firstborn over all creation. The firstborn had special rights and privileges. Jesus was never created. Rather, He created everything (John 1:3). Therefore, He is first in rank. Paul describes Him as firstborn to show that He is above all that He created (Col. 1:15-16).

- He is before all things, and in Him all things hold together (Col. 1:17).
- He is the head of the body, the Church (Col. 1:18).
- He is the beginning and the firstborn from among the dead, so that in everything He might have the supremacy (Col. 1:18).
- He is the One who changed us from being God's enemies into being God's children (Col. 1:21-22).

Warnings against false teachers (Col. 2:8-23). The false teachings in the Colossian church had five characteristics.

Q 28 *Explain 4 errors of the Colossian heresy.*

Characteristic	Explanation	Colossians
1. Rules	These strict rules were about eating, religious feasts, and circumcision. These rules were closely related to tradition.	2:4, 8, 11, 20; 3:11
2. Self-denial	*"Do not handle! Do not taste! Do not touch!"*	2:21, 23
3. Angel worship	Some taught that we should approach God through angels, rather than Jesus. These, like some Catholics, taught that God is too far above us, or too harsh to approach directly.	2:18
4. Lowering Christ	This is the main reason Paul emphasized that Jesus is above all. This is the biggest theme of Colossians.	1:15-20; 2:2-3, 9
5. Secret knowledge	These false teachers were like the *Gnostics,* a name based on the Greek word that means "knowledge." Teachers of **Gnosticism* claimed they had secret knowledge needed for salvation.	2:2-4, 18

Figure 7.17 The five characteristics of the Colossian heresy

The old self and the new self (Col. 3:1-17). Paul shows the meaning of his theology and doctrine. Christ demands a new way of living (Col. 3:5-17). Paul compares Christianity to taking off old clothes and putting on new ones. He says believers must get rid of evil actions that belong to our fleshly nature (Col. 3:5). Taking off our old clothes means putting away sexual sins, lust, evil desires, and greed. Taking off the old clothes means getting rid of anger, rage, malice, slander, and filthy language (Col. 3:5-8). Paul warns that God's wrath is coming on all who wear the *old clothes* (Col. 3:6).

Q 29 *Summarize Paul's teaching on old and new clothes.*

Q 30 *Identify 3 key words in the relationships of Colossians 3:18–4:1.*

In contrast, Paul insists that believers put on *new clothes*. Our new clothes include compassion, kindness, humility, gentleness, and patience (Col. 3:12). Over all these clothes we are to add the garment of love, which brings unity (Col. 3:14). These are impressive clothes! As we wear these new clothes, we forgive each other and put up with each other.

Figure 7.18 Ruins of an old water system at Laodicea, about 20 miles (30 km) from Colosse

Rules for the family of God (Col. 3:18–4:1). In Colossians, Paul gives special teachings for relationships in God's family. Paul's teachings about the family include:

- Wives—submit to your husbands (Col. 3:18).
- Husbands—love your wives (Col. 3:19).
- Children—obey your parents (Col. 3:20).
- Fathers—don't be too hard on your children (Col. 3:21).
- Servants—obey your masters (Col. 3:22–25).
- Masters—treat your servants fairly (Col. 4:1).

Christ must be the center of our beliefs. And He must direct how we live and act.

D. Comparison with Ephesians

Q 31 *How are the themes of Ephesians and Colossians different?*

Colossians is much like the letter to the Ephesians. Some people even call Colossians and Ephesians the "Twin Epistles" of the New Testament. They may be twins, but they are not identical twins! They are most alike in the way they describe Christ and His body, the Church. In Colossians, Paul emphasized that Christ is the "*head of the body*" (Col. 1:18). In Ephesians, he emphasized the Church as His body (Eph. 1:22-23). However, we do see a difference between these letters. Colossians emphasizes the supremacy of Christ. Ephesians emphasizes the nature of the Church and relationships in it. Figure 7.19 summarizes similar verses in the Twin Epistles.

Q 32 *State 3 topics that both Ephesians and Colossians cover.*

Overall, we may note three topics common to the Twin Epistles. Both teach about the relationship between Christ and His Church. Both letters describe the "*old man*" and the "*new man*" (Eph. 4:22-24; Col. 3:9-10). And both give instructions for the members of God's family (Eph. 5:22–6:9; Col. 3:18–4:1). Review Figure 7.12.

Eph. 1	Col.	Eph. 2	Col.	Eph. 3	Col.	Eph. 4	Col.	Eph. 5	Col.	Eph. 6	Col.
1:1	1:1	2:1, 12	1:21	3:1	1:24	4:15	2:19	5:3	3:5	6:1	3:20
1:2	1:2	2:5	2:13	3:2	1:25	4:19	3:1, 5	5:4	3:8	6:4	3:21
1:3	1:3	2:15	2:14	3:3	1:26	4:22	3:8	5:5	3:5	6:5	3:22
1:7	1:14	2:16	1:20	3:7	1:23, 25	4:25	3:8	5:6	3:6	6:9	4:1
1:10	1:18			3:8	1:27	4:29	3:8; 4:6	5:15	4:5	6:18	4:2
1:15-17	1:3-4					4:31	3:8	5:19	3:16	6:21	4:7
1:18	1:27					4:32	3:12	5:22	3:18		
1:21	1:16							5:25	3:19		
1:22	1:18										

Figure 7.19 Similar verses in Ephesians and Colossians[13]

Lesson 21

Philippians

Goal A: *Summarize the background of Paul's letter to the Philippians.*

Goal B: *Summarize what Philippians teaches about joy and unity.*

A. Background

In Europe, the gospel was first preached in Philippi. This city was named after King Philip II of Macedon. He was the father of Alexander the Great. Alexander died in 323 B.C.[14] Paul first visited Philippi around A.D 49-53. By then it was a Roman city with many citizens. Paul contrasted being a Roman citizen of Philippi with being a citizen of heaven (Phil. 3:20-21).

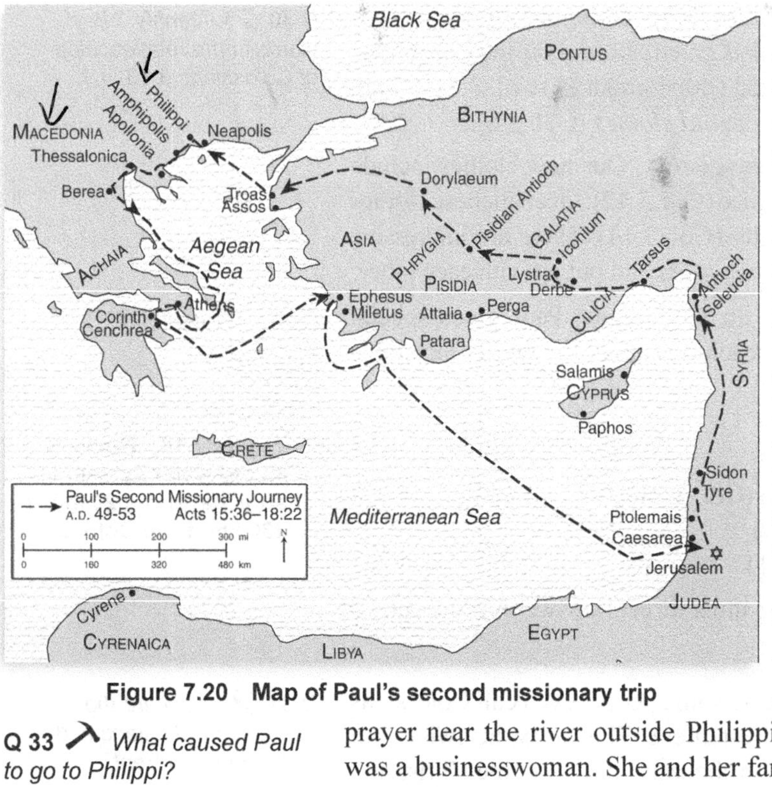

Figure 7.20 Map of Paul's second missionary trip

Acts tells us about Paul's ministry in Philippi. He sailed from Troas to Philippi on his second missionary trip. Find Philippi on the map in the province of Macedonia. It is about 8 miles north of Neapolis on the Aegean Sea. Paul went to Philippi after his vision (Acts 16:9). In the vision, a man from Macedonia asked Paul to come and help. The Spirit directed Paul and his friends to preach the gospel in Philippi (Acts 16:10). Likewise, we need the Spirit's guidance today. The Spirit knows every person. He can guide us to those who are seeking to know God.

Q 33 *What caused Paul to go to Philippi?*

In Philippi, Paul and his friends (Silas, Timothy, and Luke) first preached to a group of women. Perhaps this surprised them since they saw a man in the vision. These women met for prayer near the river outside Philippi (Acts 16:13-14). Among them was Lydia. She was a businesswoman. She and her family became an important part of the church Paul planted in the city.

Q 34 *Explain how the gospel affected Lydia, a slave girl, and a jailer.*

Trouble soon came, however. Paul and Silas cast out a demon in a slave girl. She had predicted the future by this demonic power. Her masters soon realized that she was no longer useful to them for profit (Acts 16:19). So they had Paul and Silas beaten and thrown into prison.

At night, God sent an earthquake to free His servants from prison. As a result, the Philippian jailer became a believer (Acts 16:34). The next day Paul appealed to his Roman citizenship. He and Silas were set free (See Acts 16:22-24, 38-40).

Years later, Paul was a prisoner again. Then, he wrote his letter to the Philippians. He was in prison because of false accusations by the Jews. Still, Paul was able to write with joy about the good news of Christ. This is a clear example of his testimony, *"For to me, to live is Christ..."* (Phil. 1:21).

"Rejoice in the Lord always. I will say it again: rejoice!" (Phil. 4:4). The theme of joy fills Philippians. We must understand Paul's great faith in God. Then we can learn the secret of having joy at all times.

B. Outline

Theme	Philippians
Introduction	**1:1-11**
Greeting	1:1-2
Thanksgiving and prayer for believers	1:3-11
A. Paul's Joy in Prison	**1:12-26**
B. Paul's Guidelines for Believers	**1:27–2:18**
Live a life worthy of the gospel	1:27-30
Follow the servant-example of Christ	2:1-18
C. Paul's Messengers to the Church at Philippi	**2:19-30**
Timothy	2:19-24
Epaphroditus	2:25-30
D. Paul's Warnings About False Teachers	**3:1–4:1**
The Judaizers: those who emphasized Moses too much	3:1-16
The worldly: those who emphasized the flesh too much	3:17–4:1
E. Paul's Final Counsel	**4:2-20**
Teachings about unity, joy, gentleness, and peace	4:2-9
Testimony and thanks to the Philippians	4:10-20
Conclusion	**4:21-23**

Figure 7.21 Outline of Philippians

Figure 7.22 The Gangetes River where Paul met Lydia

Q 35 *What are 2 reasons to rejoice that Paul found in prison?*

C. Explanations of the outline

Paul's joy in prison (Phil. 1:12-26). Paul worked at having a good attitude at all times. Even in prison, he found reasons to rejoice. Imagine this Spirit-filled apostle writing with a chain hanging from him.

- In prison, he prayed with joy for the Philippian believers (Phil. 1:3-11).
- In prison, he rejoiced that he could witness to the guards (Phil. 1:12-13).
- In prison, he rejoiced that his boldness in chains encouraged free believers to be bold (Phil. 1:14).
- In prison, he rejoiced that others preached Christ, whether they had good or bad motives (Phil. 1:15-18)!
- In prison, he rejoiced that the Philippians were praying for him (Phil. 1:19).
- In prison, he rejoiced that their joy would be full when he came to them (Phil. 1:20-26).

Figure 7.23 Paul and Silas prayed and sang in prison at Philippi (Acts 16:25).

Paul teaches us that we can always find reasons to rejoice. Prisons were not new to Paul. He was put in prison the first time he went to Philippi. Then, beaten and bound, he found a reason to sing praises to God. As David wrote, God gives songs in the

Q 36 *Have you learned to rejoice in the Lord always (Phil. 4:4)? Explain.*

night (Ps. 42:8). Complaining and worrying are like digging to get out of a pit. They do not help. But rejoicing is a ladder that will allow your spirit to climb above any circumstances. Review the illustration that opens this chapter.

Q 37 What is the key to unity (Phil. 2:1-11)?

Follow the servant example of Christ (Phil. 2:1-18). Paul wrote the Philippians about unity. Why? Because some believers were quarreling. Paul pleaded with two women, Euodia and Syntyche, to agree with each other (Phil. 4:2-3). Philippians was read to the entire church. Therefore, the disagreement between the two women must have been serious. Otherwise, Paul would not have mentioned it to other believers.

Christ showed us the way by His own example. The way up is down. Christ was equal with God (Phil. 2:6). Yet He made Himself nothing to redeem us on the cross (Phil. 2:7-8). So the Father raised His Son to the highest place. Christ now has a name greater than every other name. One day, every knee will bow before our Lord (Phil. 2:9-10). The key to unity is having the attitude that Jesus had (Phil. 2:1-18).

Q 38 In an argument between a husband and wife, who should show humility first?

John and his wife, Elizabeth, were arguing. He felt anger begin to rise within him. Soft as a whisper, John heard the Holy Spirit speak to him. "Humble yourself," said the Spirit. "Remember that the Scripture says a husband should never be harsh with his wife" (Eph. 5). In his heart, John did not want to be humble or gentle. Anger encouraged him to shout. Which voice would he obey, the voice of the flesh or the Spirit? For a few moments, he prayed in silence. During that short time, his anger cooled down a little. He found strength from the Spirit to be gentle. John and Elizabeth still talked about the problem. But the Spirit enabled him to be gentle. The husband is the head of the wife. He is the spiritual leader in the home. Thus, it is always his responsibility to lead the way in showing humility. In an argument, the husband should always humble himself first. A soft answer turns away wrath (Prov. 15:1).

Q 39 Why did Paul write Philippians 3:3-14? Explain.

Warnings against false Jewish teachers (Phil. 3:1–4:1). Philippians 3:3-14 contains a famous passage. It is about Paul's background as a Pharisee. He shows that he was very religious and zealous for the Law. Paul summarizes his past to teach that no one, not even himself, should trust in the Law. Rather, we should trust in Christ. He considered all of his education, good works, and religious past as trash (Phil. 3:8). Paul did not seek "*a righteousness of* (his) *own that comes from the law, but that which is through faith in Christ—*" (Phil. 3:9). Like a runner in a race, he focused on the goal ahead, not on his past (Phil. 3:12-14).

Q 40 Does circumcision have any religious value under the New Testament?

After summarizing his past, Paul warns about the false Jewish teachers. He called these *Judaizers "*enemies of the cross of Christ*" (Phil. 3:18). He refers to them as "*dogs*" and "*men who do evil*" (Phil. 3:2). These false teachers said salvation came by keeping parts of the Law. They taught that circumcision was necessary for salvation. Therefore, Paul referred to them as those who mutilate or cut the body (Phil. 3:2). Under the new covenant, we trust in Christ to save us, not in religious practices (Phil. 4:1).

Q 41 Summarize one of your favorite teachings from Philippians 4.

Paul's final counsel (Phil. 4:2-20). Philippians 4 is one of the favorite chapters in the Bible. It contains several famous teachings.

- *Rejoice in the Lord always. I will say it again: Rejoice!* (Phil. 4:4).
- *Do not be anxious about anything, but in everything, by prayer and petition, with thanksgiving, present your requests to God* (Phil. 4:6).
- [8]*Finally, brothers, whatever is true, whatever is noble, whatever is right, whatever is pure, whatever is lovely, whatever is admirable—if anything is excellent or praiseworthy—think about such things.* [9]*Whatever you have learned or received or heard from me, or seen in me—put it into practice. And the God of peace will be with you* (Phil. 4:8-9).
- *I can do everything through him who gives me strength* (Phil. 4:13).
- *And my God will meet all your needs according to His glorious riches in Christ Jesus* (Phil. 4:19).

Lesson 22

Philemon

Goal: *Analyze 3 people and 2 lessons in the letter to Philemon.*

A. Background

Q 42 *Who was Philemon, and where did he live?*

Paul wrote this short letter while he was in chains (Phm. 1, 9). He was probably a prisoner in Rome (Acts 28:16-31). The letter is to a believer named Philemon, who found Christ under Paul's ministry (Phm. 19).

Philemon lived in Colosse. We think this because the same people's names are in the letters to the Colossians and to Philemon (Phm. 1-2, 10, 23-24; Col. 4:9-10, 12, 14, 17). Paul sent the letter to the Colossians and the letter to Philemon together. It appears that Tychicus, a fellow worker of Paul, carried the two letters to Colosse (Col. 4:7-9).

Person	Explanation
1. Paul	God's apostle who was in prison
2. Philemon	A believer who lived in Colosse. He owned slaves (See Eph. 6:5; Phm. 15-16).
3. *Onesimus	A slave who ran away from Philemon. He was saved when he met Paul, probably in Rome.

Figure 7.24 There are three main people in Paul's letter to Philemon.

B. Outline

Theme	Philemon
A. Greeting	1-3
B. Thanksgiving and Prayer for Philemon	4-7
C. Request for Philemon to Restore Onesimus	8-21
D. Conclusion	22-25

Figure 7.25 Outline of Philemon

C. Explanations of the outline

Q 43 *How was Philemon related to the church at Colosse?*

Greeting (Phm. 1-3). A church in Colosse met in Philemon's home (Phm. 2). In those days, there were no church buildings like we have today. Therefore, believers met together in homes. If one home was too small for all the believers, they met in several homes.

Q 44 *What is the key to understanding our blessings in Christ?*

Thanksgiving and prayer for Philemon (Phm. 4-7). Paul thanked God for Philemon. Also, he prayed that Philemon would be active in fellowship. Having fellowship in the faith is a key to understanding our blessings in Christ (Phm. 6). We grow and value our faith more as we fellowship with others

Q 45 *What was the relationship between Philemon, Onesimus, and Paul?*

Request for Philemon to restore Onesimus (Phm. 8-21). Philemon was the master of Onesimus, a slave who had run away. Somehow, Onesimus met Paul in Rome. Like Philemon, Onesimus received Christ through Paul's preaching (Phm. 10). As a new believer, Onesimus was kind and helpful to Paul. Nevertheless, Paul sent Onesimus back to his master.

Roman law allowed Philemon to punish Onesimus or have him killed. But Paul asked Philemon to forgive him and receive him back. Paul wanted Philemon to accept Onesimus—not as a slave, but as a brother (Phm. 16). Perhaps Onesimus had stolen when he ran away. Paul offered to pay any debts Onesimus owed to Philemon (Phm. 18-19).

Q 46 *What 2 lessons does Philemon teach about the gospel in society?*

The letter to Philemon gives us two lessons. *First,* it shows how the gospel works in society. It gives believers the love needed to solve hard problems. Paul loved his converts enough to help pay their debts. Onesimus loved Paul enough to go back to his master. And Philemon loved Paul enough to forgive Onesimus. Paul asked Philemon to receive Onesimus as he would receive the apostle himself (Phm. 17). In Christ, apostles, masters, and workers are brothers who love each other. We love enough to forgive and do what is right.

Slavery is an issue we have seen three times in this chapter. Review these in the verses that follow.

> [5]*Slaves, obey your earthly masters with respect and fear, and with sincerity of heart, just as you would obey Christ.* [6]*Obey them not only to win their favor when their eye is on you, but like slaves of Christ, doing the will of God from your heart.*[7] *Serve wholeheartedly, as if you were serving the Lord, not men,* [8]*because you know that the Lord will reward everyone for whatever good he does, whether he is slave or free.* [9]*And masters, treat your slaves in the same way. Do not threaten them, since you know that he who is both their Master and yours is in heaven, and there is no favoritism with him* (Eph. 6:5-9).

> [22]*Slaves, obey your earthly masters in everything; and do it, not only when their eye is on you and to win their favor, but with sincerity of heart and reverence for the Lord.* [23]*Whatever you do, work at it with all your heart, as working for the Lord, not for men,* [24]*since you know that you will receive an inheritance from the Lord as a reward. It is the Lord Christ you are serving.* [25]*Anyone who does wrong will be repaid for his wrong, and there is no favoritism.* [1]*Masters, provide your slaves with what is right and fair, because you know that you also have a Master in heaven* (Col. 3:22–4:1).

> [12]*I am sending him—who is my very heart—back to you.* [13]*I would have liked to keep him with me so that he could take your place in helping me while I am in chains for the gospel.* [14]*But I did not want to do anything without your consent, so that any favor you do will be spontaneous and not forced.* [15]*Perhaps the reason he was separated from you for a little while was that you might have him back for good—* [16]*no longer as a slave, but better than a slave, as a dear brother. He is very dear to me but even dearer to you, both as a man and as a brother in the Lord* (Phm. 12-16).

Q 47 *How can the gospel help solve the problems in your social setting?*

The gospel brings change into society. But it does not bring change by force or rebellion. The gospel brings change by changing hearts, one at a time. It teaches believers to live by the golden rule (Matt. 7:12). It teaches us to love others as we love ourselves (Matt. 22:39). Those who obey the teachings of Christ become solutions to the problems of society.

Paul does not want the gospel to get a bad name. So he tells slaves to remain under their masters. This keeps the gospel from being slandered. Likewise, he tells wives not to rebel, but to obey sinful husbands. This fulfills God's will and ensures that the gospel will not be slandered (Titus 2:5).

A principle for Paul is that all should remain in the situation they are in when they become believers.

> *Nevertheless, each one should retain the place in life that the Lord assigned to him and to which God has called him. This is the rule I lay down in all the churches* (1 Cor. 7:17).

In religion, Gentiles should not seek to be circumcised for religious purposes. They should live as Gentiles and not try to become Jewish. In the home, wives should be subject to their husbands, and children should obey their parents. In society, slaves should not run away or rebel. And all believers should submit to the government (Rom. 13:1). The gospel does not cause confusion or disorder in society. Rather, it makes society a better place.

Second, accepting the gospel makes people better. The word *Onesimus* means "useful." As a slave who ran away, Onesimus was *useless* to Philemon. But because of the gospel, Onesimus became *useful*. He was useful to Paul as a helper (Phm. 11). And the gospel made Onesimus "*better than a slave*" (Phm. 16). God's love causes us to forgive others and treat them with love and respect. Accepting the gospel makes us better citizens.

Test Yourself: Circle the letter by the ***best*** completion to each question or statement.

1. Which was in the center of many churches Paul planted?
a) Jerusalem
b) Antioch
c) Ephesus
d) Corinth

2. Who was Artemis?
a) A famous poet
b) An early believer
c) A Greek goddess
d) The pastor at Ephesus

3. A big theme of Ephesians is
a) relationships.
b) false teachers.
c) end times.
d) suffering.

4. False teachers in Colosse claimed to have
a) power over demonic forces.
b) a new book of Scripture.
c) ability to predict the future.
d) secret knowledge for salvation.

5. In Colossians, *old clothes* represent
a) baptism.
b) poverty.
c) death.
d) sins.

6. What province includes Philippi?
a) Galatia
b) Macedonia
c) Achaia
d) Asia Minor

7. What is the theme of Philippians?
a) Grace
b) Joy
c) Mercy
d) Love

8. Having the same attitude as Christ is the key to
a) salvation.
b) rejoicing.
c) unity.
d) peace.

9. Who was the slave that Paul sent back to his master?
a) Philemon
b) Trophimus
c) Onesimus
d) Epaphras

10. What lesson does Philemon teach us?
a) The gospel supports the practice of slavery.
b) The gospel improves our standard of living.
c) The gospel changes the rules of society.
d) The gospel can make people better.

Essay Test Topics: Write 50-100 words on each of these goals that you studied in this chapter.

Ephesians

Goal: *Describe the background of Ephesus. Include its location, business, temple, and church.*

Goal: *Analyze 4 relationships Paul wrote about in Ephesians.*

Colossians

Goal: *Analyze the Colossian heresy and Paul's teachings on it.*

Goal: *Explain Paul's teaching on old and new clothes.*

Philippians

Goal: *Summarize the background of Paul's letter to the Philippians.*

Goal: *Summarize what Philippians teaches about joy and unity.*

Philemon

Goal: *Analyze 3 people and 2 lessons in the letter to Philemon.*

Chapter 8:

Letters About the Future: 1 and 2 Thessalonians

Figure 8.1 Paul preaching to the Thessalonians, as shown by Gustave Doré

Introduction

Abraham Lincoln was a great president. He led the United States to free all of its slaves. This was not easy. Many wanted to keep their slaves for financial reasons. The argument over slavery became so great that it divided the nation. For 4 years, from 1861-1865, the North fought against the South. During this war 500,000 soldiers died. People were criticizing President Lincoln from every side. Even at home his wife scolded him constantly.[1]

How did the President stand under such great pressures? His death revealed the secret. After the war, a political enemy shot and killed Lincoln. Thus he joined the many dead soldiers who died to free the slaves. Inside of Lincoln's coat was an old letter. The paper had turned a pale yellow. It was stained from the prints of fingers that had held it often. The letter was from a common person. It said some kind things about the President, and praised him for having the courage to stand for what was right. The letter was written only once. But Lincoln read it often. Encouragement is like a candle that chases away the darkness.

The apostle Paul wrote to encourage believers living in Thessalonica. They were facing fiery trials. Paul praised them for turning from idols to Jesus. He thanked them for standing firm in suffering. The apostle said they were a model to others. Then he encouraged them to remember that Jesus is coming back for believers. Paul only wrote two short letters to the Thessalonians. But his letters have encouraged millions of believers. Now, as we study these two Epistles, the Holy Spirit will encourage us. He will cause us to lift up our heads because our Redeemer is coming back for us. Criticism saddens. But encouragement always brings out the best in people.

Lessons:

First Thessalonians

23

Goal A: *Summarize the background of Paul's first letter to the Thessalonians.*

Goal B: *Identify the theme, purposes, and 3 main parts of 1 Thessalonians.*

Second Thessalonians

24

Goal: *Summarize and apply what 2 Thessalonians teaches about the Rapture, Antichrist, and Second Coming.*

Key Words

eschatology | coming of the Lord | Rapture | Day of the Lord | *Parousia* | apostasy

Lesson 23

First Thessalonians

Goal A: *Summarize the background of Paul's first letter to the Thessalonians.*

Goal B: *Identify the theme, purposes, and 3 main parts of 1 Thessalonians.*

Setting

We are making progress! Figure 8.2 gives a good summary of the 27 books in the New Testament. Recall that there are four groups of books. We illustrated this with the house drawing of New Testament books (Figure 1.14). We have studied the five historical books. These are the foundation in our house drawing. Now we are examining Paul's Epistles.

Paul's letters may be divided into four groups. We have studied his four letters on salvation and his four letters from prison. Now, we are studying 1 and 2 Thessalonians. These are his two letters about the future. Sometimes these two Epistles are called the Eschatological Epistles. The word **eschatology* is based on two Greek words. *Eschatos* means "last," and *logos* means "word." *Eschatology* is a word (a study) about last things. In 1 and 2 Thessalonians, Paul writes a lot about eschatology. The theme of these two letters is the Second Coming of Christ.

Q 1 *Which part of the house drawing represents Paul's Epistles?*

Q 2 *What is the theme of 1 and 2 Thessalonians?*

Q 3 *Sing the song of the New Testament books.*

Q 4 *Draw the house showing the books of the New Testament.*

Group	Book Title	Sub-group	Date+	Author
1. Historical Books (5)	Matthew	Synoptic Gospels	55-70	Matthew
	Mark		50-68	Mark
	Luke		60	Luke
	John		85-95	John
	Acts		62	Luke
2. Paul's Epistles (13)	Romans	Salvation Epistles	55-56	Paul
	1 Corinthians		55	
	2 Corinthians		56	
	Galatians		48-49	
	Ephesians	Prison Epistles	60-61	
	Philippians		61	
	Colossians		60-61	
	Philemon		60-61	
	1 Thessalonians	Epistles about the future	50-51	
	2 Thessalonians		51	
	1 Timothy	Pastoral Epistles	63	
	2 Timothy		67	
	Titus		65	
3. Hebrews and the General Epistles (8)	Hebrews	Epistles to suffering believers	65-70	Unknown
	James		45-49	James
	1 Peter		63-65	Peter
	2 Peter	Epistles to correct false teachings	65-67	Peter
	1 John		85-90	John
	2 John		85-90	John
	3 John		85-90	John
	Jude		67-80	Jude
4. Prophecy	Revelation		90-95	John

Figure 8.2 Groups, sub-groups, dates, and authors of New Testament books

---

+ Bible scholars differ on the exact dates of New Testament books.

Thessalonica was the capital of Macedonia. Some think its total population grew to about 200,000.[2] This great city was on the Egnatian Way, a road that stretched from Rome through Philippi.

Acts 17:1-9 gives us the background of Paul's first letter to the Thessalonians. Paul arrived there on his second missionary trip. Silas and Timothy were with him. Things went well for these missionaries until some of the Jews became jealous and angry. With loud voices, they accused Paul and his friends. "*They are all defying Caesar's decrees, saying that there is another king, one called Jesus*" (Acts 17:7). These bitter Jews forced Paul and his friends to leave Thessalonica.

Paul traveled from Thessalonica to Athens, and on to Corinth (Acts 18). After he left Thessalonica, the Jews persecuted believers there (1 Thess. 2:14). Later, Paul sent Timothy to Thessalonica to see how they were doing (1 Thess. 3:5). Timothy returned to Paul with good news about the Thessalonian believers. Timothy praised the Thessalonians for their faith and love (1 Thess. 3:6-10). Paul wanted to return to them, but he could not. So he wrote a letter from Corinth to encourage them.

Figure 8.3 The Egnatian Way was a road from Rome to the eastern part of the Empire.

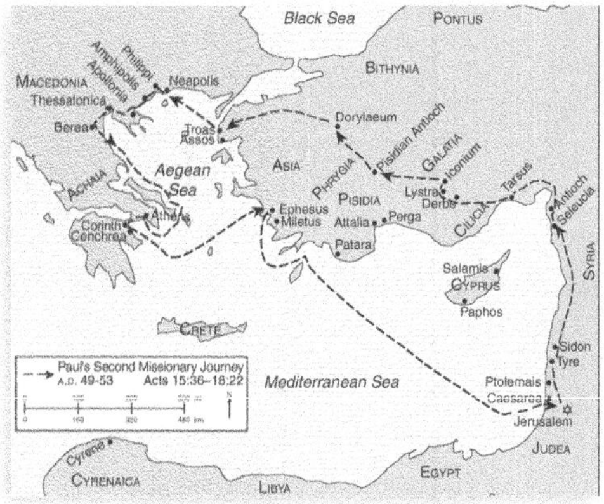

Figure 8.4 Map of Paul's second missionary trip

A. Outline

Theme	1 Thess.
A. Paul Gives Thanks to Encourage the Thessalonians	**1**
B. Paul Defends His Actions and Absence	**2–3**
Defense of Paul's actions	2:1-16
Defense of Paul's absence	2:17–3:10
Paul's prayer	3:11-13
C. Paul Instructs Believers	**4–5**
About sexual purity	4:1-8
About brotherly love	4:9-10
About honest work	4:11-12
About the coming of Christ	4:13–5:11
About respect for spiritual leaders	5:12-13
About Christian living	5:14-18
About spiritual discernment	5:19-22
Conclusion	**5:23-28**

Figure 8.5 Outline of 1 Thessalonians

B. Explanations of the outline

Q 5 Find Thessalonica in Figure 8.4. Describe its location.

Q 6 What are the 3 main parts of 1 Thessalonians?

Q 7 For what purpose did Paul praise the Thessalonians?

Q 8 Can you recall good things that people have said about you? Do you practice saying good things about others?

Paul gives thanks to encourage the Thessalonians (1 Thess. 1). The first letter to the Thessalonians begins with the names Paul, Silas, and Timothy. Paul wrote as a friend and spiritual counselor. The Thessalonian believers were his spiritual children. They had many problems and trials. They were discouraged. It was hard for these believers to understand why they were suffering.

Paul wrote to encourage these suffering believers. He began his encouragement by saying good things about them. Paul never used flattery (1 Thess. 2:5). But he did use praise. Praise, unlike flattery, is sincere. The things Paul said about the Thessalonians were true. And the reason he praised them was to encourage them. All of us feel better when people sincerely say good things about us. Praise brings out the best in us. Like a smile, it encourages us. Someone has said that a smile is a hug from a distance. Praise is a verbal pat on the back. Paul praised the Thessalonians for several things.

- He thanked God for the fruits of their faith, hope, and love (1 Thess. 1:3). Note that this was an indirect way of praising them.
- In spite of severe suffering, they followed the examples of Paul and the Lord (1 Thess. 1:6).
- They became a model for all believers in the provinces of Macedonia and Achaia (1 Thess. 1:7).
- Their testimony spread everywhere (1 Thess. 1:8).
- They turned from idols to serve the living God (1 Thess. 1:9).

Q 9 How does each chapter of 1 Thessalonians end?

After praising the Thessalonians, Paul adds another type of encouragement. He reminds them that they are waiting for Jesus to come again (1 Thess. 1:10). The Lord's return is a great encouragement to all believers. That is why we refer to it as the *Blessed Hope* (Titus 2:13). Every chapter in 1 Thessalonians closes with some teaching about the return of the Lord. This is the theme of the entire letter (Figure 8.6).

1 Thess.	Reference to the Second Coming of Christ
1:10	*Wait for His Son from heaven. . .*
2:19-20	*in the presence of our Lord Jesus when He comes. ...you are our glory and joy.*
3:13	*May He strengthen your hearts so that you will be blameless and holy in the presence of our God and Father when our Lord Jesus comes with all His holy ones.*
4:14-18	*God will bring with Jesus those who have fallen asleep in Him. ...we who are still alive, who are left till the *coming of the Lord, will certainly not precede those who have fallen asleep. For the Lord Himself will come down from heaven, ...Therefore encourage each other with these words.*
5:23	*May your whole spirit, soul and body be kept blameless at the coming of our Lord Jesus Christ.*

Figure 8.6 Each chapter of 1 Thessalonians closes with a reference to the return of Christ.

Paul defends his actions and absence (1 Thess. 2–3). In 1 Thessalonians 2:1-16 Paul defends his ministry. Perhaps some were slandering him. Or maybe the Thessalonians just needed to review the past. Paul emphasizes his actions and his absence. Let us look briefly at each of these.

First, Paul reviews his past actions (1 Thess. 2:1-16).

- He reminds the Thessalonians of his suffering in Philippi, before he came to them (1 Thess. 2:2).
- His motives were pure. He was not guilty of flattery or greed. He was not a financial burden to them. Rather, he worked night and day to support himself (1 Thess. 2:3-9).
- He was gentle, like a mother caring for her children (1 Thess. 2:6-7).
- He was holy, righteous, and blameless. He was like a father caring for his children (1 Thess. 2:10-12).
- His words were received as the Word of God (1 Thess. 2:13).

Q 10 What did Paul fear about the Thessalonians? Explain.

Second, Paul defends his absence (1 Thess. 2:17–3:10). Recall that Paul wrote from Corinth to the Thessalonians. He explains that he tried in every way to come to them. But Satan prevented him (1 Thess. 2:17-18). So Paul sent Timothy to encourage them. Timothy reminded them that trials come to all believers (1 Thess. 3:1-4). Paul was afraid that the Thessalonians would become discouraged and lose their faith. Then his ministry there would have been a waste of time (1 Thess. 3:5). But Timothy brought back a good report to Paul. Therefore, Paul gave thanks. And he prayed for God to strengthen the Thessalonians until Christ returned (1 Thess. 3:6-13).

Q 11 How do chapters 4–5 of 1 Thessalonians differ from chapters 1–3?

Paul instructs believers (1 Thess. 4–5). Look at the outline again. Note that 1 Thessalonians 1–3 deals with the past. In those chapters, Paul gave thanks for the Thessalonians. In chapters 4–5, Paul gives warnings and instructions about daily living.

Q 12 From the outline, name 3 practical topics Paul writes about (1 Thess. 4:1-12).

In 1 Thessalonians 4:13–5:11, Paul answers questions about the coming of the Lord. Some of the believers in Thessalonica had died after Paul left. Living believers were sorrowing. They were afraid that those who died would miss the coming of Christ. Their old pagan religion offered no hope for life after death (1 Thess. 1:9). Death was an experience filled with darkness and fear. Living believers wondered, "Will we ever see our dead loved ones again?" "Yes," wrote Paul. Read 1 Thessalonians 4:13-18 again. The *Rapture refers to the catching up of all believers to meet Jesus in the air. His coming is a great encouragement to believers.

Q 13 Explain what will happen at the Rapture (1 Thess. 4:16-17).

In 1 Thessalonians 5, Paul shifts from comfort to warning. He warns believers to watch for the Lord's return. Christ's coming will not surprise those who are alert. Those who do not watch for Jesus are in the group of the wicked. But the righteous watch for Jesus as they live holy lives.[3]

Q 14 Name 2 responsibilities that the return of Christ places upon all believers (1 Thess. 5).

The Rapture was a great comfort to suffering believers. But this future hope brought with it two responsibilities. All believers must be alert for His coming, and all must have self-control (1 Thess. 5:6).

Lesson 24 Second Thessalonians

Goal: *Summarize and apply what 2 Thessalonians teaches about the Rapture, Antichrist, and Second Coming.*

Setting

Q 15 What type of problems caused Paul to write 2 Thessalonians?

Paul wrote 2 Thessalonians from Corinth on his second missionary trip. He wrote it shortly after 1 Thessalonians. Why? Believers there were facing great persecution. This caused them to focus too much on the immediate return of Christ. Some had stopped working. They only sat watching the clouds—looking for Jesus to come back.

Q 16 Which chapter in 2 Thessalonians focuses on the Antichrist?

Also, someone claimed to have a prophecy, report, or letter from Paul (2 Thess. 2:1-2; 3:17). This false message claimed that Paul said Jesus had already returned. Perhaps some thought they were in the Great Tribulation after the Rapture. So Paul wrote 2 Thessalonians to correct these false beliefs about the second coming of Christ. He said 2 Thessalonians was the true letter from him.

Figure 8.7 In the second phase of His coming, Jesus returns to earth with His saints to judge His enemies.

A. Outline

Theme	2 Thess.
A. Paul Encourages Believers During Persecution	**1**
Greeting	1:1-2
He gives thanks for their progress during persecution.	1:3-4
He gives assurance of final rewards and judgment.	1:5-10
He prays for believers.	1:11-12
B. Paul Teaches Believers About the End Times	**2**
The *Day of the Lord has not yet come.	2:1-2
The man of lawlessness must first be revealed.	2:3-12
Believers are to stand firm in the truth.	2:13-15
Paul's prayer for believers	2:16-17
C. Paul Exhorts Believers About Daily Living	**3**
He urges them to pray for him and stand firm.	3:1-5
He urges each one to work hard.	3:6-13
He urges them to discipline the disobedient.	3:14-15
He prays for them and says farewell.	3:16-18

Figure 8.8 Outline of 2 Thessalonians

B. Explanations of the outline

Paul encourages believers during persecution (2 Thess. 1). Like he did in 1 Thessalonians, Paul begins his second letter with praise (2 Thess. 1:3-4). He compliments them for standing firm during persecution. However, the praise in 2 Thessalonians is briefer than it was in 1 Thessalonians.

Read 2 Thessalonians 1:6-10. There, Paul reminds believers that vengeance belongs to God.

> [6]*God is just: He will pay back trouble to those who trouble you* [7]*and give relief to you who are troubled, and to us as well. This will happen when the Lord Jesus is revealed from heaven in blazing fire with his powerful angels.* [8]*He will punish those who do not know God and do not obey the gospel of our Lord Jesus.* [9]*They will be punished with everlasting destruction and shut out from the presence of the Lord and from the majesty of his power* [10]*on the day he comes to be glorified in his holy people and to be marveled at among all those who have believed. This includes you, because you believed our testimony to you* (2 Thess. 1:6-10).

Q 17 Summarize 2 Thessalonians 1:6-10 in 2 sentences.

The future will be better for believers. This is encouraging during times of suffering.

Paul teaches believers about the end times (2 Thess. 2). Read 2 Thessalonians 2:1-12. There are six important theological phrases in these verses. Let us identify and define each of them.

Q 18 Can the Second Coming be an encouragement to believers you know? Explain.

- *The coming of our Lord* (2 Thess. 2:1), or *Second Coming,* is a broad phrase that includes two phases of the Lord's return. It includes His private and public coming. *First,* Jesus will come for His saints or holy ones. We refer to this event as the *Rapture.* This is a private or secret phase of His coming. At the Rapture, only the holy will see Him. Two will be in a bed. One will be taken and the other left behind (Luke 17:34). Left for what? Left for the 7 years of tribulation during the Antichrist's rule. The *second* phase of the Lord's coming is *with* His holy ones. We call this phase the public revelation of Christ. At that time, every eye will see Him (Jude 14; Rev. 1:7). In this public return, Jesus comes to judge His enemies. This happens after the seven years of Tribulation. The Greek word referring to the Lord's *coming* is **Parousia.* As explained above, we believe that the Second Coming or *Parousia* includes two phases. *First,* Jesus comes *for* believers to rapture them. *Second,* Jesus comes *with* believers to judge His enemies.

Q 19 Identify and define at least 3 key phrases in 2 Thessalonians 2:1-12.

- *Our being gathered to Him* (2 Thess. 2:1). This refers to the Rapture. In it, believers are caught up to meet Christ in the air (1 Thess. 4:16-17).
- *The day of the Lord* (2 Thess. 2:2). This refers to the period of time in which Christ will bring His judgments.[4]

Q 20 When do we believe that the Rapture will occur in relation to the Second Coming?

- *The rebellion* (2 Thess. 2:3). In the Greek, this word is *apostasia.* The related English word is **apostasy.* It refers to a "falling away" from Christ. This is a rebellion by those within the church. Jesus referred to this time, saying *"the love of most will grow cold"* (Matt. 24:12).[5]
- *The man of lawlessness* (2 Thess. 2:3). This refers to the Antichrist. He will rule the earth during the Tribulation. He is a world leader of wickedness and persecution in the last days.[6] Paul says this evil ruler exalts himself in God's temple. He claims to be God and demands to be worshiped (2 Thess. 2:4; Rev. 13). Jesus will destroy him with the breath of His mouth (2 Thess. 2:8; Rev. 19:11-21).
- *The one who now holds it back* (2 Thess. 2:7). The One who holds back lawlessness is the Holy Spirit. He works through the Church. When the Holy Spirit stops holding back evil, it will cover the earth like a

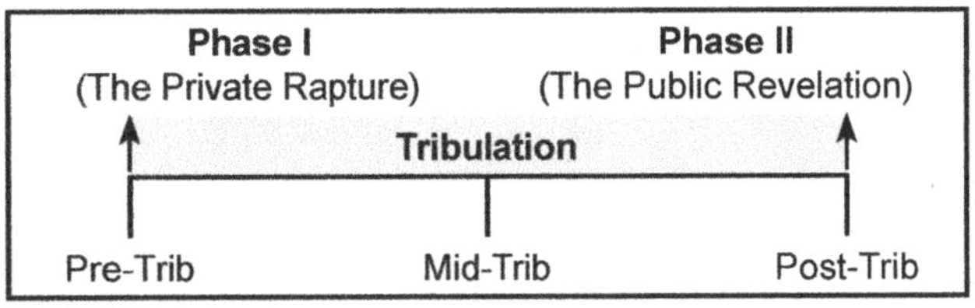

Figure 8.9 Two phases of our Lord's coming

flood. Many think this will begin just after the Rapture. Then, evil will have little to oppose it.

Some Thessalonian believers were confused. They were afraid that the Day of the Lord was past (2 Thess. 2:2). Paul assured them that God's judgments were still in the future. Before the final judgment, the Holy Spirit will stop holding back evil. The Church will be raptured. The man of lawlessness will rule the world. Then the Lord will return and destroy him in public. Therefore, the Thessalonians did not need to be afraid of missing the Day of the Lord. When these events happen, all on earth will know it!

#	Phase I (The Private Rapture)	Phase II (The Public Revelation)
1.	Jesus comes for His saints (1 Thess. 4:16-17).	Jesus comes with His saints (Rev. 19:8, 14; Zech. 14:1-5).
2.	*"Two people will be in one bed; one will be taken and the other left"* (Luke 17:34).	*Every eye will see him* (Rev. 1:7).
3.	Jesus promises to deliver us from the hour of trial (Rev. 3:10). He tells us to pray that we may be able to escape all these things (Luke 21:36).	Jesus resurrects those who died in the Tribulation. These were not delivered from the Tribulation. They did not escape it. They died in it (Rev. 20:4)!
4.	Believers are caught up to meet Jesus in the air before He comes to earth (1 Thess. 4:16-17).	Jesus returns to earth to rule (Rev. 19:1-21). Satan is thrown into the Abyss for 1,000 years (Rev. 20:1-3). Then those who died for Christ in the Tribulation are raised (Rev. 20:4).
5.	No signs show that the Rapture is near. We are only told to watch for the Lord (John 14:1-4; 1 Cor. 15:51-58; 1 Thess. 4:13-18).	Many signs show His coming. *"Even so, when you see all these things, you know that it is near, right at the door"* (Matt. 24:33).
6.	Trials are not mentioned in passages on the Rapture (John 14:1-4; 1 Cor. 15:51-58; 1 Thess. 4:13-18).	The Second Coming is in the midst of great tribulation (Zech. 14:1-2; Matt. 24:21; Rev. 6-18).
7.	Passages on the Rapture clearly teach that the saints will rise to meet Him (John 14:1-4; 1 Cor. 15:51-58; 1 Thess. 4:13-18).	None of the passages on the Second Coming clearly refer to a Rapture, since it occurred years earlier (Zech. 14:1-5; Matt. 24:26-31; Rev. 19:11-21).
8.	At the Rapture, those still alive will be changed (1 Cor. 15:51; 1 Thess. 4:17).	No passages on the Second Coming teach that living saints will be changed.
9.	Passages on the Rapture clearly show that the dead in Christ will be raised (1 Cor. 15:52; 1 Thess. 4:16).	Passages on the Second Coming do not clearly show the resurrection of the Church (Dan. 12:1-2; Rev. 20:4).
10.	No changes in the earth are linked with the Rapture.	Passages on the Second Coming teach changes in the earth. The Mount of Olives will split (Zech. 14:4). Ezekiel 40–48 assumes some changes in earth. (See Rev. 6:12-14.)

Figure 8.10 Ten differences in verses on the two phases of the Second Coming

Paul exhorts believers about daily living (2 Thess. 3). Finally, Paul urged the Thessalonians to do three things:

- He urged them to pray for him (2 Thess. 3:1-2). Paul reminded them that God is faithful. He knew the Lord would strengthen him and the Thessalonians.
- He urged them to work hard (2 Thess. 3:6-13). Believers cannot just sit and wait for the Lord to return. Those who do not work should not eat (2 Thess. 3:10)!
- He urged the church to discipline those who refused to obey his letter (2 Thess. 3:14-15). Discipline, in love, is necessary for every healthy church.

Q 21 *Why were some believers not working?*

Test Yourself: Circle the letter by the ***best*** completion to each question or statement.

1. Of what province was Thessalonica the capital?
a) Galatia
b) Achaia
c) Macedonia
d) Asia Minor

2. What is the theme of 1 and 2 Thessalonians?
a) Rejoicing in persecution
b) Freedom from the Law
c) The greatness of Christ
d) The Second Coming

3. One reason Paul wrote 1 Thessalonians was
a) to encourage suffering believers.
b) to request financial help.
c) to rebuke rebelling Christians.
d) to discuss speaking in tongues.

4. The three largest cities in Paul's day were
a) Jerusalem, Rome, and Athens.
b) Thessalonica, Rome, and Ephesus.
c) Rome, Alexandria, and Antioch.
d) Rome, Corinth, and Philippi.

5. *Eschatology* is the study of
a) church history.
b) false teachings.
c) end times.
d) salvation.

6. *Our being gathered to Him* refers to
a) the Rapture.
b) the Millennium.
c) the grave.
d) the Tribulation.

7. With what does every chapter in 1 Thessalonians end?
a) A warning against falling away
b) A prayer of thanksgiving
c) A statement of faith
d) A teaching on Christ's return

8. Which book comes the earliest in the New Testament?
a) James
b) 1 Thessalonians
c) Philippians
d) 2 Corinthians

9. The *man of lawlessness* refers to
a) the emperor.
b) the Antichrist.
c) the false prophet.
d) the devil.

10. The *Second Coming* refers to
a) Christ's coming after the Millennium.
b) only Christ's coming for His saints.
c) Christ's coming *for* and *with* His saints.
d) only Christ's coming to judge His enemies.

Essay Test Topics: Write 50-100 words on each of these goals that you studied in this chapter.

First Thessalonians

Goal: *Summarize the background of Paul's first letter to the Thessalonians.*

Goal: *Identify the theme, purposes, and 3 main parts of 1 Thessalonians.*

Second Thessalonians

Goal: *Summarize and apply what 2 Thessalonians teaches about the Rapture, Antichrist, and Second Coming.*

Chapter 9:
Letters for Pastors: 1 Timothy, 2 Timothy, and Titus

Figure 9.1 Ruins in Ephesus. Timothy was the pastor of the church in Ephesus.

Introduction

When Mark finished Bible school, He started a new church. First, He prayed a lot, asking God if this was His will. Mark also talked with a more experienced pastor in a nearby city. This other pastor prayed with Mark and encouraged him to start the church.

Mark owed a debt of gratitude to that other pastor. He not only encouraged Mark to start the church, he kept encouraging him for many years. The neighboring pastor took time to meet with Mark regularly. And he shared much of his wisdom in the ministry. He helped answer Mark's hard questions and helped him to understand what it means to be a pastor. Without the counsel of this other pastor, Mark would not have grown in the ministry as he did.

Paul encouraged Timothy and Titus. He helped them get started in the ministry. And he wrote letters to them to share his wisdom in the ministry. Almost all of Paul's other letters were written to churches. But the three Pastoral Epistles were written to individuals. In these letters, Paul tells Timothy and Titus how to be effective pastors and ministers of the gospel.

Lessons:

First Timothy

25 **Goal A:** *Summarize Timothy's parents, conversion, and relationship to Paul.*
Goal B: *Identify at least 3 topics Paul wrote about in 1 Timothy.*

Titus

26 **Goal A:** *Compare Titus 1 and 1 Timothy 3 on qualifications for pastors.*
Goal B: *Summarize what Titus teaches about grace and the reputation of the gospel.*

Second Timothy

27 **Goal A:** *Explain Paul's comparison of a pastor to a soldier, an athlete, and a farmer.*
Goal B: *Summarize what Paul taught about the last days and the Scriptures.*

Key Words

Timothy   Titus   overseer   deacon   Crete   Dalmatia   God-breathed

Lesson 25

First Timothy

Goal A: *Summarize Timothy's parents, conversion, and relationship to Paul.*
Goal B: *Identify at least 3 topics Paul wrote about in 1 Timothy.*

Setting

We have reached the last three of Paul's 13 letters. Recall that we divided his letters into four groups.

We call the last group of Paul's letters the *Pastoral Epistles*. They give instructions to pastors for both their home life and church work. Paul wrote these letters to *Timothy and *Titus, two men who had worked closely with him.

Q 1 *Sing the song on the books of the New Testament.*

Q 2 *Name 2 men Paul wrote letters to about pastoring.*

Q 3 *Describe Timothy's parents and conversion.*

Many Bible teachers think Paul was in prison twice in Rome. We know Paul wrote 1 Timothy after the events recorded in the end of Acts.[1] We think he wrote 1 Timothy and Titus after he was released the first time from Rome (2 Tim. 4:16-17). This was about A.D. 65. Then, he wrote 2 Timothy the second time he was in a Roman prison (A.D. 67).

Theme or Characteristic	Letters Paul Wrote
4 letters about salvation (*Soteriological Epistles)	Romans, Galatians, 1 and 2 Corinthians
4 letters from prison (Prison Epistles)	Ephesians, Philippians, Colossians, and Philemon
2 letters about the future (Eschatological Epistles)	1 and 2 Thessalonians
3 letters to pastors (Pastoral Epistles)	1 and 2 Timothy, Titus

Figure 9.2 Paul's 13 letters are divided into four groups.

A. Background

We first read about Timothy in Acts 16:1. Paul was in Lystra on his second missionary trip. The Bible calls Timothy a disciple. He probably became a Christian during Paul's first missionary trip to Galatia (Acts 14:8-20). Paul called Timothy *"my true son in the faith"* (1 Tim. 1:2) and *"my dear son"* (2 Tim. 1:2).

Timothy's father was a Greek, but his mother was a Jewess (Acts 16:1, 3). She had taught Timothy the Old Testament *Scriptures from the time he was a very small child (2 Tim. 3:14-15). The believers at Lystra and Iconium spoke well of him (Acts 16:2).

Q 4 *When did Timothy travel with Paul?*

Timothy traveled with Paul during the rest of his second missionary journey. And he was with Paul during the entire third journey. Later, Paul left Timothy in Ephesus to take care of church problems there (See 1 Tim. 1:3; 3:1-14; 4:6-16).

Q 5 *Where did Timothy pastor? What does this show us?*

We see from these letters that Timothy was a faithful, hard-working leader. He was close to Paul's heart (Phil. 2:19-20). Paul trusted him with the responsibility of the church at Ephesus. This was a large and important church. So we know that Paul had faith in Timothy's ability and faithfulness. However, at times Timothy needed encouragement from Paul (1 Tim. 4:12-16; 2 Tim. 1:6-7). Paul called him a *"man of God"* (1 Tim. 6:11). He told him to imitate the Lord, *"who while testifying before Pontius Pilate made the good confession"* (1 Tim. 6:13). And he warned Timothy: *"Guard what has been entrusted to your care"* (1 Tim. 6:20).

B. Outline

After Paul's release from prison in Rome and ministry further west, he commissioned Timothy to care for the church at Ephesus. Now in 1 Timothy Paul writes to instruct him

Theme	1 Tim.
A. Introduction	**1**
Greeting	1:1-2
Warning against false teachers	1:3-11
The Lord's grace to Paul	1:12-17
The purpose of the instructions to Timothy	1:18-20
B. Instructions on Public Worship	**2**
Prayer in public worship	2:1-8
Women in public worship	2:9-15
C. Instructions on Managing the Church	**3**
Qualifications for overseers	3:1-7
Qualifications for deacons	3:8-13
The purpose of the instructions to Timothy	3:14-16
D. Instructions on False Teachings	**4**
False teaching described	4:1-5
Methods of refuting false teaching	4:6-16
E. Instructions on Various People in the Church	**5–6**
The older and younger	5:1-2
Widows	5:3-16
Elders	5:17-25
Slaves	6:1-2
False teachers	6:3-10
The man of God	6:11-16
The rich	6:17-19
Conclusion	**6:20-21**

Figure 9.3 Outline of 1 Timothy

Q 6 *Which chapter in 1 Timothy is about pastors and deacons?*

Q 7 *What is the theme of 1 Timothy 4?*

Q 8 *State 2 reasons why Paul wrote 1 Timothy.*

about personal and church matters. These instructions clearly seen in the book's outline (Figure 9.3).

C. Explanations of the outline

Introduction (1 Tim. 1) Paul greets Timothy as his *"true son in the faith"* (1 Tim. 1:2). The apostle had *"no one else like him"* (Phil. 2:20).

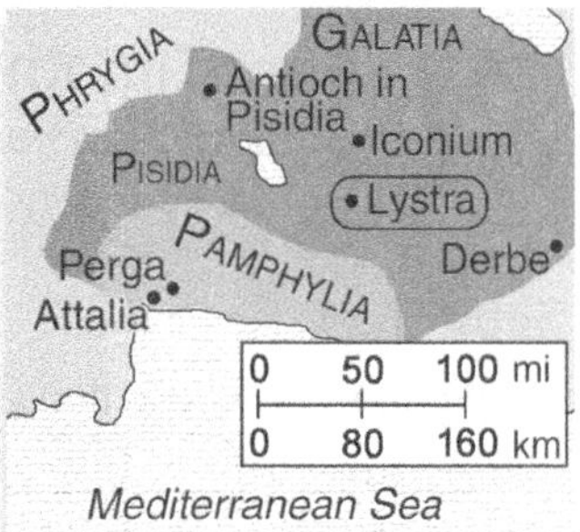

Figure 9.4 Timothy was from Lystra, a small city in Galatia.

Read 1 Timothy 1:3-11. Paul urges Timothy to rebuke false teachers. These false teachers emphasized the Law. Paul said that the Law is necessary for the lawless, not the righteous. Those who receive the gospel do what is right to please God.

Figure 9.5 Part of an old Roman amphitheater at Ephesus

Read 1 Timothy 1:12-17. Paul writes about his conversion and ministry. He was living proof that God could save the worst of sinners.

In 1 Timothy 1:18-20 Paul tells about his purpose for writing to Timothy. The elders had once prophesied over Timothy (1 Tim. 1:18; 4:14). It seems that the prophecies were about Timothy's role as a faithful church leader. Compare Acts 16:1-3. Paul wanted to help Timothy fight the good fight. So he wrote 1 Timothy for two reasons:

- To encourage Timothy as a person. Paul wanted him to continue to be a good example in his character.
- To enable Timothy to teach and manage the church properly.

Instructions on public worship (1 Tim. 2). Chapter 2 opens with a request for prayer. Paul urges believers to pray for everyone, especially government leaders. He gave three reasons for this.

Q 9 *Is God's will completely done on earth (1 Tim. 2:4)? Explain.*

Q 10 *Has Christianity affected the relationship of husbands and wives in your country? Explain.*

- God wants all to be saved (1 Tim. 2:4).
- God is able to save the worst of sinners. It is easiest to pray for family members and friends. But Paul urges believers to pray for everyone, including the most evil rulers and godless sinners. Recall Paul's testimony in 1 Timothy 1:12-17. How did Paul know that God could save the worst sinner? God had already done it!
- Jesus died for everyone (1 Tim. 2:6). So let us lift up holy hands and pray for everyone (1 Tim. 2:8).

Figure 9.6 Ruins of a Roman aqueduct in Asia Minor

The second half of chapter 2 is about Christian women (1 Tim. 2:9-15). Women should dress modestly, not calling attention to themselves. Also, they should be submissive to their husbands. Paul did not allow a woman to have authority over a man (1 Tim. 2:11). We know that he was not opposed to women helping in the ministry. Timothy knew that Paul worked closely with Aquila and Priscilla (Acts 18:1-28). Evidently, there were some unruly women in the Ephesian church. It appears that they were speaking out strongly in public. This reminds us of a similar problem at Corinth (1 Cor. 11). Some women there misunderstood their freedom in Christ. They thought that freedom meant that they did not need to submit to their husbands any longer. First Timothy 2:15 emphasizes the role of wives. God saves women in the same way he saves men. However, salvation does not often change a person's role in society. Saved women still continue to be mothers and submissive wives. The Bible commands husbands to treat their wives as they treat themselves, and not as slaves (Eph. 5:28)! Paul commands husbands never to be harsh with their wives (Col. 3:19). Wives, children, employees, and citizens do not resent submission when treated with love.

Instructions on managing the church (1 Tim. 3). Chapter 3 begins with the words, *"Here is a trustworthy saying."* In those days, this was a common way to introduce a Christian hymn or special teaching. The words *"Here is a trustworthy saying"* appear five times in the Pastoral Epistles (1 Tim. 1:15; 3:1; 4:9; 2 Tim. 2:11; Titus 3:8).[2] Paul uses these words to introduce the subject of qualifications for overseers. **Overseer* is the translation of the Greek word *episkopos*. It refers to one who supervises, such as a presbyter, bishop, or pastor. Figure 9.10 compares 1 Timothy and Titus on the twelve qualifications of a pastor. Notice that there are five characteristics to avoid, and seven to desire.

Q 11 Does your church require the same 12 qualifications that Paul did (Figure 9.10)? Explain.

A deacon is a person who helps an overseer. To please God, the church must choose pastors and deacons with biblical qualifications. Leaders in the church set an example for believers (1 Tim. 4:12).[3] (For a thorough study of these twelve qualifications, see the *Faith & Action* course on the Pastoral Epistles.)

First Timothy 3 closes by quoting an early Christian hymn or *creed. It traces the earthly life of Jesus, from appearing in a body to being taken up into glory.

Instructions on false teachings (1 Tim. 4). The Spirit warns that in the last days, some will abandon the faith. This type of warning shocks and saddens us. Not all who receive Christ continue to follow Him. Some are seduced away from Christ by deceiving spirits. These demons spread their teachings through false teachers. Paul says that it is a pastor's responsibility to point out false teachings (1 Tim. 4:1-6).

Q 12 Do all who come to Christ continue in the faith? Explain.

Q 13 Which false teachings trouble believers you know?

One of the best ways to teach the truth is to live it. Therefore, Paul commands Timothy to be *"an example for believers in speech, in life, in love, in faith, and in purity"* (1 Tim. 4:12).

Instructions on various people in the church (1 Tim. 5–6). First Timothy 5–6 is about pastoring church members. Paul gives practical advice about groups of people.

Q 14 Summarize what Paul said about old and young widows.

- *The older and younger* (1 Tim. 5:1-2). Men and women of any age should be treated like family members.
- *Widows* (1 Tim. 5:3-16). These should be supported by their families. Godly widows over 60 without families should receive help from the church. Younger widows should remarry to avoid an immoral lifestyle. Paul notes that some younger widows had already turned away from the faith to follow Satan.
- *Elders* (1 Tim. 5:17-25). Faithful elders who minister deserve financial support from the church. Accusations against elders must be made in the presence of two or more witnesses.
- *Slaves* (1 Tim. 6:1-2). The gospel does not free a slave from submitting to a master. But Philemon will teach us that the gospel turns slaves into brothers of believing masters.
- *False teachers* (1 Tim. 6:3-10). Paul says that false teachers are proud. Some of them think faith is a path to money. These have been robbed of the truth. God supplies our basic needs such as food and clothing. And those who learn to be content with the basic things of life are spiritually wealthy.
- *The man of God* (1 Tim. 6:11-16). Paul contrasts the pastor with false teachers who love money. Rather than running after riches, a pastor should seek righteousness, godliness, faith, love, endurance, and gentleness.
- *The rich* (1 Tim. 6:17-19). These should be humble and trust in God, not money. They should be generous in sharing with others. Then they will have treasure in heaven.

Q 15 Should the church help widows today? Explain.

Q 16 When is submission the easiest? Explain.

Q 17 Identify 2 characteristics that Paul mentioned about false teachers.

Lesson 26

Titus

Goal A: *Compare Titus 1 and 1 Timothy 3 on qualifications for pastors.*
Goal B: *Summarize what Titus teaches about grace and the reputation of the gospel.*

A. Background

Review Figure 9.7. How many letters did Paul write? Can you name the four groups of books in the Pauline Epistles?

Q 18 Practice filling in the left pillar in the house of New Testament books (Figure 9.7).

Q 19 Summarize the relationship of Titus to Paul.

Q 20 What type of ministry did Titus have?

It seems that Paul led both Titus and Timothy to Christ. The apostle called Titus *"my true son in our common faith"* (Titus 1:4). Titus was a Greek, probably from Antioch in Syria. He went with Paul and Barnabas when they traveled from Antioch to Jerusalem. There, with the leaders of the Jerusalem church, they discussed their ministry to the Gentiles (Gal. 2:1-3).

Titus was a Gentile. He became a follower of Christ without Jewish circumcision. Titus is an example of being saved through faith in Christ, rather than keeping the law of Moses.

> 15*We who are Jews by birth and not 'Gentile sinners'* 16*know that a man is not justified by observing the law, but by faith in Jesus Christ. So we, too, have put our faith in Christ Jesus that we may be justified by faith in Christ and not by observing the law, because by observing the law no one will be justified* (Gal. 2:15-16).

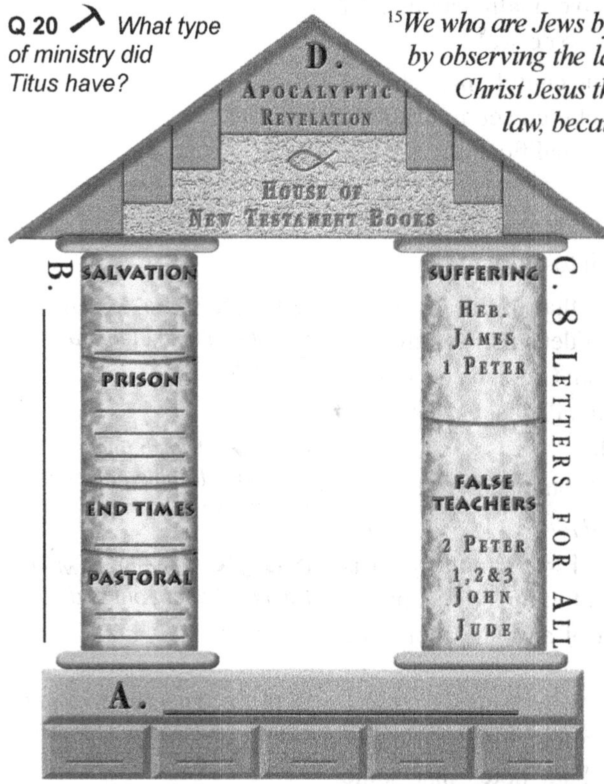

Figure 9.7 Practice house of New Testament books

Titus is not mentioned by name in the book of Acts. But his name appears 13 times in Paul's letters.[4] We know that he worked closely with Paul. Mechanics help people by solving car problems. Titus helped people by solving church problems. He was the kind of man Paul sent where there was a need in the church. Titus was on the island of *Crete when Paul wrote to him. He was there to *"straighten out what was left unfinished"* (Titus 1:5). His name also appears often in 2 Corinthians (2 Cor. 2:13; 7:6, 13-14; 8:6, 23). Paul sent him to various places to take care of church problems. Paul was happy when writing 2 Corinthians. Why? Titus had just returned from Corinth with a good report. Titus must have done well in taking care of the problems there (2 Cor. 7:6-10, 13-16). Titus had also checked on the offering that the Corinthians promised to send to Jerusalem believers. His name appears for the last time in 2 Timothy 4:10. There we learn that Titus had gone to *Dalmatia. (Today, this area is Yugoslavia, Bosnia and Herzegovina, and Croatia.) He probably went for ministry. Paul often sent others when he could not go himself.

The theme of the Epistle to Titus is good teaching (Titus 1:9; 2:1, 7-8). Healthy, biblical doctrine is a characteristic of all faithful ministers. It is like a badge that all faithful ministers wear.

Q 21 Locate 4 places where Titus traveled in ministry (Figure 9.8).

B. Outline

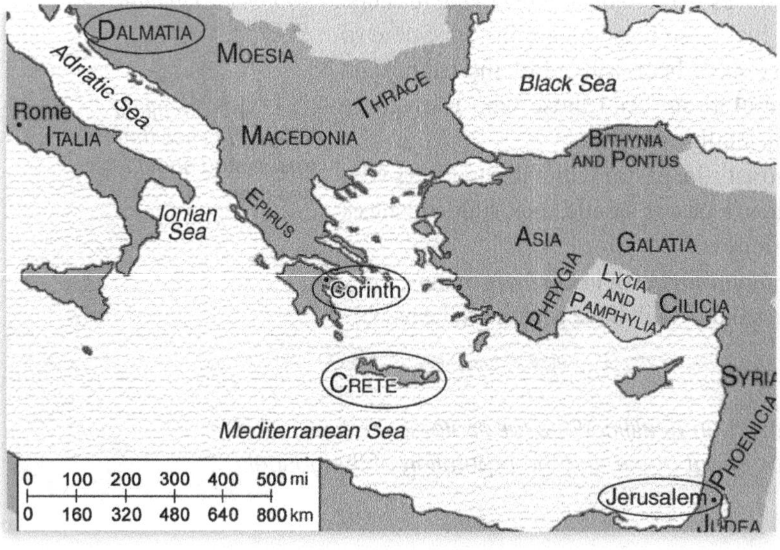

Figure 9.8 Map showing places where Titus ministered (Jerusalem, Crete, Corinth, Dalmatia)

Theme	Titus
Greeting	**1:1-4**
A. Instructions About Appointing Elders	**1:5-9**
B. Instructions About False Teachers	**1:10-16**
C. Instructions About Various Groups in the Churches	**2**
Teachings for each group	2:1-10
Lessons from grace	2:11-15
D. Instructions on Godly Living	**3**
Our relationship with all others	3:1-2
The reason for holy living	3:3-7
Discern between the profitable and unprofitable.	3:8-11
Conclusion	**3:12-15**

Figure 9.9 Outline of Titus

C. Explanations of the outline

1 Tim. 3:2	Titus 1:6-7	(-) Negative 5 Bad Characteristics to Avoid (Blameless: not guilty of 5 accusations)	(+) Positive 7 Good Characteristics to Have (Respected for 7 good reasons)	1 Tim. 3:2, 7	Titus 1:7
3:3	1:7	1. Not given to drunkenness	1. The husband of one wife	3:2	1:6
3:3	1:7	2. Not overbearing or quarrelsome	2. Gentle	3:3	
3:3	1:7	3. Not quick-tempered; Not violent	3. Temperate; self-controlled; disciplined	3:2	1:8
3:3	1:7	4. Not a lover of money; Not pursuing dishonest gain	4. Hospitable	3:2	1:8
3:6		5. Not a recent convert	5. One who loves what is good; upright and holy		1:8
			6. Able to teach; and holding firmly to sound doctrine	3:2	1:9
			7. A good manager of his own family	3:12	1:6

Figure 9.10 Twelve requirements for a pastor to be blameless and have a good reputation

Instructions about appointing elders (Titus 1:5-9). Teachings about appointing leaders are brief in Titus. In 1 Timothy, Paul wrote about appointing pastors and deacons. But the letter to Titus deals only with appointing pastors. Figure 9.10 summarizes the qualifications for pastors (1 Tim. 3; Titus 1). Church leaders must be godly and have proven character. They must succeed at home before leading in the church. The Cretans were known for being sinful (Titus 1:12-13). Therefore, the letter to Titus emphasizes that a pastor must be righteous and holy and love what is good (Titus 1:8).

Q 22 *Which qualities of a pastor are found in Titus, but not in 1 Timothy 3? Why?*

Q 23 *Which qualities of a pastor are hardest to find today? Explain.*

Instructions about false teachers (Titus 1:10-16). Titus was pastoring the church in Crete when Paul wrote this letter. The main problem in Crete was Jewish false teachers. Paul described the false teachers of his day:

- They are rebels. They refuse to cooperate (Titus 1:10).
- They are deceivers. They talk about worthless things like genealogies (relating salvation to dead ancestors; Titus 1:10; 3:9). Also, these false teachers teach myths and legends as truth (Titus 1:14).
- They are legalists (Judaizers). They teach that circumcision has religious value. Paul said that it had no Christian value (Titus 1:14).
- They have corrupt minds and consciences (Titus 1:15).
- They claim to know God, but their actions deny Him (Titus 1:16).
- They are disobedient and unfit for doing any good (Titus 1:16).

Q 24 *What type of cultural beliefs hinder believers you know? Explain.*

Q 25 *Can an entire family lose its salvation (Titus 1:11)? Explain.*

What was the result of these false teachers? Paul said that they ruined entire families (Titus 1:11)! And the main reason was to gain money (Titus 1:11)! Evil men once sold slaves for money. These false teachers were no better than the slave traders. Good teaching is important. False teachings destroy the faith of whole families! Paul urged Titus to give good teachings based on God's Word (Titus 1:3; 2:5, 10). We study these good teachings in Titus 2 and 3.

Q 26 *Why was Paul concerned about the actions of women, men, and slaves in the church?*

Instructions about various groups in the churches (Titus 2). Paul identifies several groups. We studied these in 1 Timothy 5:1–6:2. Therefore, we will not say much about them here. The groups Paul mentions include older and younger men and women and slaves.

Titus	Teaching on how believers should act	Why?
2:4-5	Younger women love your husbands; be self-controlled and pure; be busy at home; be kind; submit to your husbands.	So that no one will *malign or speak evil of the Word of God
2:6-8	Young men be self-controlled. Timothy, be an example for them in doing what is good. Teach with integrity that cannot be condemned.	So that those who oppose you may be ashamed because they have nothing bad to say about us
2:9-10	Slaves (workers) submit to your masters. Don't be rude. Don't steal from them. Be worthy of trust.	So that in every way they will make the teaching about God our Savior attractive

Figure 9.11 Paul taught that the actions of believers create the reputation of the gospel.

Notice one big theme in Paul's teachings to young women, young men, and slaves. He did not want the actions of anyone to be a stumbling block or to make the gospel look bad. Figure 9.11 shows the relationship between the actions of believers and the reputation of the gospel.

Titus 2:11-14 says that grace is a teacher. This is a very special passage on grace in the New Testament. It is a good passage for each student to memorize.

Q 27 *What 2 things does grace teach its students (Titus 2:12)?*

Q 28 *What is the Blessed Hope (Titus 2:13)?*

> [11]*For the grace of God that brings salvation has appeared to all men.* [12]*It teaches us to say "No" to ungodliness and worldly passions, and to live self-controlled, upright and godly lives in this present age,* [13]*while we wait for the blessed hope—the glorious appearing of our great God and Savior, Jesus Christ,* [14]*who gave himself for us to redeem us from all wickedness and to purify for himself a people that are his very own, eager to do what is good* (Titus 2:11-14).

Q 29 *Why do believers live differently than sinners (Titus 3:3-7)?*

Instructions on godly living (Titus 3). Paul states the reasons why believers can obey his teachings in Titus 3.

> [3]*At one time we too were foolish, disobedient, deceived and enslaved by all kinds of passions and pleasures. We lived in malice and envy, being hated and hating one another.* [4]*But when the kindness and love of God our Savior appeared,* [5]*he saved us, not because of righteous things we had done, but because of his mercy. He saved us through the washing of rebirth and renewal by the Holy Spirit,* [6]*whom he poured out on us generously through Jesus Christ our Savior,* [7]*so that, having been justified by his grace, we might become heirs having the hope of eternal life* (Titus 3:3-7).

Q 30 *What is Paul's advice about one causing division in the church (Titus 3:10-11)?*

Believers live holy and righteous lives because Jesus saved us! He has washed us and poured out His Spirit on us. So we live to please Him as we wait for His return. Then we will enjoy living with Him forever.

Lesson 27 Second Timothy

Goal A: *Explain Paul's comparison of a pastor to a soldier, an athlete, and a farmer.*
Goal B: *Summarize what Paul taught about the last days and the Scriptures.*

A. Background

Q 31 *Summarize Paul's circumstances when he wrote 2 Timothy.*

This is Paul's final letter. Nero, the Roman emperor, was persecuting believers in Rome. He was trying to stop the spread of Christianity. For the second time, Paul was Nero's prisoner (2 Tim. 1:16). All of his friends, except Luke, had deserted him (2 Tim. 1:15; 4:11). Paul knew that his ministry was over. He had run and won his race. Death was near (2 Tim. 4:6-8, 18).

Timothy was dear to Paul. The apostle called him *"my dear son"* and *"my fellow worker"* (2 Tim. 1:2; Rom. 16:21). Timothy had helped deliver six of Paul's letters. He was with Paul the first time the apostle was in the Roman prison (Phil. 1:1; Col. 1:1; Phm. 1). Paul wrote two personal letters to Timothy. So as the great apostle faced death, he wanted to see his son one more time. Twice in 2 Timothy, Paul requests that he come to the prison (2 Tim. 4:9, 21). We do not know if Timothy arrived before Paul was executed.[5]

Theme	2 Tim.
A. Paul's Fatherly Concern for Timothy	**1**
Greeting	1:1-2
Paul's encouraging words to his son	1:3-14
Paul's circumstances	1:15-18
B. Paul's Special Instructions to Timothy	**2**
Call to endure hardship	2:1-13
Warning about foolish questions	2:14-26
C. Paul's Warning About the Last Days	**3**
Terrible times are coming.	3:1-9
Continue to serve the Lord anyway.	3:10-17
D. Paul's Departing Words	**4**
Preach the Word.	4:1-5
His personal testimony	4:6-8
His personal words to Timothy	4:9-18
Conclusion	4:19-22

Figure 9.12 Outline of 2 Timothy

B. Outline

Paul's concern for both Timothy and the Ephesian church are seen in the outline of the book (Figure 9.12).

C. Explanations of the outline

Q 32 *Which of Paul's instructions in 2 Timothy are most needed today? Explain.*

Paul's fatherly concern for Timothy (2 Tim. 1) Second Timothy gives the last recorded words of Paul in the New Testament. It states Paul's thoughts as he came to the end of his life and ministry. He was alone, except for Luke (2 Tim. 4:11). His main concern was for Timothy and the success of his work in Ephesus. Paul gave Timothy some strict instructions. All of us should pay careful attention to these final commands of Paul. They are the most important part of 2 Timothy. Figure 9.13 summarizes these commands from 2 Timothy 1–4.

Paul's instructions to Timothy	2 Tim.
Fan into flame the gift of God, which is in you...	1:6
Do not be ashamed.... But join with me in suffering...	1:8
Keep... the pattern of sound teaching...	1:13
Guard the good deposit that was entrusted to you...	1:14
The things you have heard me say... entrust to reliable men...	2:2
Keep reminding them of these things.	2:14
Do your best to present yourself to God as one approved...	2:15
Flee the evil desires of youth...	2:22
Continue in what you have learned...	3:14
Preach the Word...	4:2

Figure 9.13 Paul's pastoral instructions to Timothy (2 Tim. 1–4)

Q 33 *Explain how a pastor is like a soldier, an athlete, and a farmer.*

Paul's special instructions to Timothy (2 Tim. 2). Paul used seven comparisons to describe the pastor (2 Tim. 2). These comparisons emphasize the responsibilities of a Christian leader.

Picture or Comparison	Explanation	2 Tim.
1. As a *son*	he is to be strong and active.	2:1-2
2. As a *soldier*	he is to suffer hardship and please his commander.	2:3-4
3. As an *athlete*	he is to obey the rules of the game.	2:5
4. As a *farmer*	he is to work hard. He should be the first to eat some of the food he grows.	2:6
5. As a *workman*	he is not to be ashamed. Rather, he should correctly handle the Word of God.	2:15
6. As an *instrument*	he is to be holy and useful for the Master.	2:21
7. As a *servant*	he is to be gentle and helpful.	2:24-25

Figure 9.14 Seven comparisons of a pastor in 2 Timothy 2

Q 34 *How does 2 Timothy 3:1-9 relate to today? Explain.*

Paul's warning about the last days (2 Tim. 3). Read 2 Timothy 3:1-9. Paul lists the characteristics of people in the last days. Which of these describe sinners in your area? Jannes and Jambres were probably two of Pharaoh's magicians (2 Tim. 3:8).[6] They opposed Moses. Likewise, false teachers today oppose God's leaders.

Q 35 *How did God give us the Scriptures (2 Tim. 3:16)? Why did He give them?*

Paul painted a dark picture of sinners in the last days. In contrast, he also painted a beautiful picture (2 Tim. 3:10-17). It was the picture of himself—the faithful, godly apostle. In the darkest times, it is good to focus on godly examples and imitate them. Paul left good footprints for Timothy to follow.

Second Timothy 3:14-17 describes a pastor's great weapon against evil. These verses explain the nature of the Scriptures. The Scriptures are *God-breathed. This means that God inspired those who wrote them. Therefore, they are truly God's Word. The Scriptures make one wise concerning salvation (2 Tim. 3:15). They equip pastors to teach, rebuke, correct, and train believers in the church (2 Tim. 3:17). The Bible is the sword of the Holy Spirit (Eph. 6:17). It is one of our main weapons for the work of the ministry. God will bless you for studying it in this course.

Q 36 *What contrast do you see in 2 Timothy 4:1-5?*

Paul's departing words (2 Tim. 4). Second Timothy 4:1-5 is a famous passage. All who are going into ministry should study these words.[7] Its main emphasis is on preaching the Word of God. The Bible is our main weapon against false teaching.

Second Timothy ends with some personal thoughts from Paul. These include his request for Timothy to come to him soon, before winter if possible (2 Tim. 4:9, 21). Paul wanted his coat for warmth and his books for study in prison. He was active and alert to the very end of his life.

Q 37 *Do you think Paul was about to die (2 Tim. 4:6-8)? Explain.*

> *[6]For I am already being poured out like a *drink offering, and the time has come for my departure. [7]I have fought the good fight, I have finished the race, I have kept the faith. [8]Now there is in store for me the crown of righteousness, which the Lord, the righteous Judge, will award to me on that day...* (2 Tim. 4:6-8).

Figure 9.15 Nero declared in public that he was number one among God's chief enemies.[8] He cut off Paul's head and crucified Peter.

Test Yourself: Circle the letter by the ***best*** completion to each question or statement.

1. Where did Timothy first learn the Scriptures?
a) At school
b) From Paul
c) At home
d) In a vision

2. Paul's relationship to Timothy was like a
a) brother to a brother.
b) father to a son.
c) teacher to a student.
d) pastor to a church member.

3. What is one topic Paul wrote about in 1 Timothy?
a) Managing the church
b) Spiritual gifts
c) The Resurrection
d) The Second Coming

4. Where did Timothy pastor?
a) Corinth
b) Philippi
c) Ephesus
d) Antioch

5. According to Titus, how does grace help believers?
a) It gives them power to witness.
b) It keeps them from sinning.
c) It helps them understand the Bible.
d) It teaches them to live godly lives.

6. In Titus, Paul teaches that the actions of believers affect
a) the growth of the church.
b) the character of believers.
c) the church's leadership.
d) the reputation of the gospel.

7. Paul teaches that a pastor must be
a) one with much education.
b) one with many talents.
c) one who welcomes visitors into his home.
d) one who speaks with great authority.

8. In 2 Timothy, Paul says a pastor is like an athlete
a) because he must train himself.
b) because he must run against others.
c) because he must obey the rules.
d) because he must finish the race.

9. In 2 Timothy, Paul compares people in the last days to
a) Euodia and Syntyche
b) Jannes and Jambres
c) Samson and Delilah
d) Nadab and Abihu

10. The Scriptures are *"God-breathed,"* means
a) God lives in and through the Scriptures.
b) God gave Scripture the breath of life.
c) God Himself wrote the Scripture.
d) God is the source of all Scripture.

Essay Test Topics: Write 50-100 words on each of these goals that you studied in this chapter.

First Timothy

Goal: *Summarize Timothy's parents, conversion, and relationship to Paul.*

Goal: *Identify at least 3 topics Paul wrote about in 1 Timothy.*

Titus

Goal: *Compare Titus 1 and 1 Timothy 3 on qualifications for pastors.*

Goal: *Summarize what Titus teaches about grace and the reputation of the gospel.*

Second Timothy

Goal: *Explain Paul's comparison of a pastor to a soldier, an athlete, and a farmer.*

Goal: *Summarize what Paul taught about the last days and the Scriptures.*

Unit 3:
8 Letters for All and the Apocalypse

Chapter 10 is made up of three letters to suffering believers: Hebrews, James, and 1 Peter. All believers face trials and suffering, so these letters are important to know. We will enable you to:

- *Analyze the author, date, first readers, and background of Hebrews. Explain six comparisons that show that Jesus is better. Summarize and apply the purpose of the seven warnings in Hebrews.*
- *Explain the name General Epistles and list the seven books in this group.*
- *Analyze the author, style, and purpose of James. Summarize and apply what James says about trials, the tongue, faith, and the wealthy.*
- *Explain four things that the Bible tells us about the author of 1 Peter. Summarize what 1 Peter teaches about suffering. Contrast the lifestyles of believers and unbelievers then and now.*

Chapter 11 is on two letters about false teaching: 2 Peter and 1 John. There are false teachers in every nation of the earth. In this chapter we will strengthen you to defend the faith. You will learn to:

- *Explain 2 Peter's contrasts between growing in grace and falling from grace.*
- *Summarize and apply what 2 Peter says about the Scriptures and false teachers.*
- *Explain how 1 John relates to the errors of the Gnostics.*
- *Summarize and apply what 1 John teaches about Jesus Christ, sin, knowledge, and love.*

Chapter 12 continues our study of letters about false teaching. In the General Epistles there are five letters on this subject. In the last chapter we looked at 2 Peter and 1 John. Now we will look at the other three books on false teaching: 2 and 3 John and Jude. We will help you to:

- *Identify three passages in 2 John that are similar to those in 1 John and the Gospel of John. Explain the relationship between love and truth in 2 John.*
- *Describe Gaius, Diotrephes, and Demetrius in 3 John.*
- *State the author and purpose of Jude.*
- *Summarize how we got the canons of the Old and New Testaments.*

Chapter 13 is the final part of this course. It is fitting that the New Testament ends with the book of Revelation. This is a hard book to understand, but step by step, we will teach you to:

- *Analyze the name, author, date, setting, and themes of Revelation.*
- *Evaluate four ways of interpreting Revelation.*
- *Divide Revelation into three parts based on Revelation 1:19. Note the chapters for each part.*
- *Summarize five descriptions of Jesus in Revelation.*
- *Explain how John uses symbols and characters in Revelation.*
- *Identify five contrasts in Revelation.*

Chapter 10:

Letters to Suffering Believers: Hebrews, James, and 1 Peter

Figure 10.1 Hebrew teaches that Jesus is better than Moses, who received the Law on Mt. Sinai.

Introduction

Dr. Mark Barclift has a beautiful picture on his desk. It reminds him that God is with us, even in our sufferings. The picture was made from small scraps of cloth. The cloth was torn from the dresses of women who were in prison during a war. One of these women was Kathryn, his mother's aunt.

Kathryn was a missionary to the country of Indonesia. She returned to the island of Sumatra knowing that she faced great danger. She also knew that God had called her. The man in the passport office said that missionaries were odd people. If she wanted to die, it was her choice.

After the war started, Kathryn was arrested and put into a prison camp. In that camp she and other ladies tore pieces of cloth from their dresses to make pictures. There was little food in the camp, but much disease. Hundreds of women and children died from hunger and sickness. Kathryn was near death when they released her.

But what did she remember best from this time of suffering? The Lord's help! She wrote, "Surely, if the Lord was ever sufficient, He was during this time. To know Him as I do now, I would be willing to endure it all again, if necessary." The light of His presence shines brightest in the darkest hours.

Suffering has always been a part of the Christian life. In this chapter, the letters to suffering believers show us that God is with us in the midst of trials.

Lessons:

Hebrews

28

Goal A: *Analyze the author, date, first readers, and background of Hebrews.*
Goal B: *Explain 6 comparisons that show that Jesus is better.*
Goal C: *Summarize and apply the purpose of the 7 warnings in Hebrews.*

James

29

Goal A: *Explain the name General Epistles and list the 7 books in this group.*
Goal B: *Analyze the author, style, and purpose of James.*
Goal C: *Summarize and apply what James says about trials, the tongue, faith, and the wealthy.*

First Peter

30

Goal A: *Explain 4 things that the Bible tells us about the author of 1 Peter.*
Goal B: *Summarize what 1 Peter teaches about suffering.*
Goal C: *Contrast the lifestyles of believers and unbelievers.*

Key Words

superior	mediator	sanctuary	High Priest	Diaspora	Babylon
	immaturity	perseverance	General Epistles	favoritism	

Lesson 28 Hebrews

Goal A: *Analyze the author, date, first readers, and background of Hebrews.*

Goal B: *Explain 6 comparisons that show that Jesus is better.*

Goal C: *Summarize and apply the purpose of the 7 warnings in Hebrews.*

A. Author and date

Group	Book Title	Common Characteristics	Date	Author
Hebrews and the General Epistles (8)	Hebrews	Epistles to suffering believers	67-69	Unknown
	James		45-49	James
	1 Peter		60-63	Peter
	2 Peter	Epistles to correct false teachings	66-68	Peter
	1 John		85-95	John
	2 John		85-95	John
	3 John		85-95	John
	Jude		70-80	Jude

Figure 10.2 Hebrews and the General Epistles

God did not choose to tell us who wrote the letter to the Hebrews (Jewish believers). However, the author knew his readers well. He asked them to pray that he would be restored to them soon (Heb. 13:18-19). So it is clear that he had a strong relationship with them. The words "*Those from Italy send you their greetings*" may give us a clue (Heb. 13:24). These words may show that the author was writing to those in Italy. If so, this means the author spent some time in Italy, and certainly in Rome, its capital.

Q 1 Try to sing the books of the New Testament in less than 30 seconds.

Some believe that Paul wrote Hebrews. Many do not agree with this for three reasons.

- Hebrews quotes mostly from the Septuagint. This is the Greek translation of the Old Testament. In contrast, Paul usually quotes from the Hebrew version of the Old Testament.
- The writer of Hebrews places himself among second-generation Christians. That is, he places himself in the group that was told the gospel by others who heard Christ (Heb. 2:3). In contrast, Paul claims to have heard the Lord directly (Gal. 1:11-12).
- The author's polished style and method is different from the style in letters that we know Paul wrote.

Q 2 Do you think Paul wrote Hebrews? Explain.

Many have tried to guess who wrote Hebrews. Some guess Barnabas. Others, like Luther, guess Apollos. But we agree with Origen, one of the early church fathers. He said, "Who it was that really wrote the epistle, only God knows."[1]

We are not sure who wrote Hebrews. But we are certain that the author wrote like an apostle filled with the Spirit. Throughout the centuries, the Church has recognized Hebrews to be inspired by God. More than any other book of the New Testament, Hebrews reveals Jesus as *better* than all who came before Him.

The destruction of the temple in Jerusalem marked the end of animal sacrifices in Judaism. Hebrews says much about the temple and priests. Yet it does not mention the destruction of the temple. Therefore, we assume that Hebrews was written before the temple was destroyed in A.D. 70. The letter to the Hebrews would surely have mentioned the temple's destruction if it had already occurred.[2]

Q 3 When was Hebrews written? Explain.

B. Background

There was a great difference between Gentile and Jewish believers. Gentile believers did not feel pressure from Judaism. Few Gentiles attended the temple. The past of the Gentiles did not include Jewish feasts, Jewish customs, the Law, or the temple. In contrast, Jewish believers faced many struggles with Judaism.[3] These Jewish believers trusted Jesus as Savior, but they held on to the Law. They kept the Sabbaths and attended the feasts. They circumcised their sons. They sacrificed animals in the temple. The book of Acts covers the first 30 years of church history. Acts reveals that most Jewish believers followed Jesus and the law of Moses (Acts 21:20; 22:12). It took many years for Jewish believers to realize that Jesus replaced animal sacrifices. It took time for Jewish believers to understand that we are saved by grace, not by keeping the Law.

Q 4 Did the first Jewish believers continue to sacrifice animals? Explain.

Q 5 Which 2 things pressured Jewish believers to turn from Jesus back to Judaism?

Jesus predicted that the temple would be destroyed. He said that one stone would not be left upon another. Every stone of the temple would be thrown down (Matt. 24:2). Thus, Jewish believers knew that the judgment of God was coming on Jews who rejected the Messiah. Still, they loved the Jewish Scriptures and the temple with its priests and sacrifices for sin. They were loyal to Moses and to God. Also, they loved their fellow Jews.

Unbelieving Jews were the greatest enemies of the Jews who followed Jesus. Recall how Paul, a Jew, breathed out hate and murder against Christians (Acts 9:1-2). He dragged men and women to prison. Everywhere he went, he tried to force believers to turn away from Jesus. Then Paul met the Lord himself and became His follower. At once the Jews sought to kill him (Acts 9:23). Over and over in Acts we read that Paul's greatest enemies on earth were the unbelieving Jews.

So we see that two things pressured believing Jews to turn from Christ back to Judaism. They were loyal to Moses and Jewish customs. And the persecution from unbelieving Jews was fierce. Following Jesus often cost believers their reputations, houses, lands, possessions, and freedom (Acts 8:1; Heb. 10:32-34). The temptation to turn back to Judaism was great.

C. Outline

Q 6 Which chapters in Hebrews show that Jesus is superior?

Notice how many times the word **superior* appears in the outline. *Superior* means "better, of more worth, more excellent, of higher quality, preferred, and above." The theme of Hebrews is that Jesus is superior to all humans and angels.

Figure 10.3 Hebrews teaches that Jesus is a superior High Priest.

Theme	Hebrews
A. Jesus Is a Superior Revealer and Leader	**1:1–4:13**
He is superior to the prophets.	1:1-3
He is superior to the angels.	1:4-14; 2:5-18
First warning: Neglect	2:1-4
He is superior to Moses.	3:1-6
Second warning: Unbelief	3:7-19
He is superior to Joshua.	4:2-10
Third warning: Unbelief	4:1, 11-13
B. Jesus Is a Superior *Mediator and Priest	**4:14–10:18**
He is superior to Aaron.	4:14–5:10
Fourth warning: *Immaturity	5:11–6:20
He is superior to the Levites.	7:1-28
His covenant is superior.	8
His *sanctuary is superior.	9:1-12
His sacrifice is superior.	9:13–10:18
C. Following Jesus Requires Faith	**10:19–13:21**
Faith is the key to *perseverance.	10:19-25
Fifth warning: The danger of not persevering to the end	10:26-31
Faith has always been the way people please God.	10:32–11:40
Faith helps us endure discipline.	12:1-13
Sixth warning: Turning away	12:14-17
Faith unites us with the Father, Jesus, and all in heaven.	12:18-24
Seventh warning: Refusal	12:25-29
Faith enables us to live holy, godly lives.	13:1-21
Conclusion and Greetings	**13:22-25**

Figure 10.4 Outline of Hebrews

D. Explanations of the outline

Jewish believers were persecuted and discouraged. Hebrews was written to strengthen the faith of Jewish believers and warn them of God's judgment on all who turned away from Christ.

Q 7 What was the purpose of Hebrews?

Q 8 Does Hebrews teach that the Old Testament was bad? Explain.

Q 9 What is the theme of Hebrews?

Jesus is a superior revealer and leader (Heb. 1:1–4:13). Hebrews is sometimes called, "The book of better things." The two Greek words for "better" occur 15 times in this letter.[4] Jesus is superior or better in many ways.

- *Jesus is superior to the prophets* (Heb. 1:1-3). He revealed God better than they did. The prophets brought a short word from God, from time to time. Each of them told a part of what God was like. But Jesus did not just tell us what God is like. He showed us! Jesus was God in flesh! He is greater than the prophets. He gave us a complete and final message of God (John 1:1).
- *Jesus is superior to the angels* (Heb. 1:4-14; 2:5-18). His name or title, the Son of God, is superior to theirs (Heb. 1:4-5). Angels worship Jesus (Heb. 1:6). They are messengers, but He is God (Heb. 1:7-9).
- *Jesus is superior to Moses* (Heb. 3:1-6). Moses was a servant over God's house, but Jesus built the house! And we are God's house if we hold on to our courage and hope (Heb. 3:6).
- *Jesus is superior to Joshua* (Heb. 4:2-10). The rest Jesus offers is better than the rest Joshua offered in Canaan. The Lord's rest is complete and eternal.

Descriptions of Jesus that show He is better	
1.	He is the One through whom God has spoken completely.
2.	He is the Son of God.
3.	He is the Heir of all things.
4.	He is the One through whom God created the universe.
5.	He is the One who shines God's glory.
6.	He is the exact representation of God the Father.
7.	He is the One who holds up all things by speaking.
8.	He is the One who provided cleansing for our sins.
9.	He is the One seated at the right hand of God the Father.

Figure 10.5 Descriptions of Jesus, God's complete and final message to mankind (Heb. 1:1-3)

Q 10 Complete the chart in Figure 10.6

Comparison	Hebrews
Jesus is better than	1:1-3
Jesus is better than	1:4-14; 2:5-18
Jesus is better than	3:1-6
Jesus is better than	4:2-10
Jesus is better than	4:14–5:10
Jesus is better than	7:1-28
His covenant is better than	8
His sanctuary is better than	9:1-12
His sacrifice is better than	9:13–10:18

Figure 10.6 Hebrews shows that Jesus is better in nine ways.

Jesus is a superior mediator and priest (Heb. 4:14–10:18).

- *As our *High Priest and Mediator, Jesus is better.* He is superior to Aaron and the Levites. Why? They were sinners, and they died. His life is sinless and endless.
- *His covenant is superior to the old covenant.* The old covenant promises were for life on earth. The new covenant promises are for eternity. And God, not man, built the city that we are seeking!
- *His heavenly sanctuary and sacrifice are superior to the temple and animal sacrifices.* The temple in heaven is better than the temple on earth. The blood of the Son of God is better than the blood of animals!

The theme of Hebrews is that Jesus is better than all who came before Him.

Q 11 Was faith necessary to please God under the old covenant? Explain.

Following Jesus requires faith (Heb. 10:19–13:21). Hebrews emphasizes that we must live by faith in Jesus to please God. Chapter 11 is a favorite chapter. It lists many heroes of faith. These Old Testament believers persevered by faith. They kept trusting in God, regardless of the circumstances. Believers are like runners in a stadium. Surrounding us as we run is "*a great cloud of witnesses*" (Heb. 12:1). They are witnesses that God is faithful.[5] If we continue in faith, we will be heirs together with the heroes of Hebrews 11 (Heb. 11:40). Only those who stay in the race receive a crown (Heb. 12:1; Phil. 3:12-14). We are running to get a crown that will last forever. Let us keep

Q 12 In what sense are those of Hebrews 11 witnesses?

1. Abel	7. Joseph	13. Samson
2. Enoch	8. Moses	14. Jephthah
3. Noah	9. The Israelites	15. David
4. Abraham	10. Rahab	16. Samuel
5. Isaac	11. Gideon	17. The prophets
6. Jacob	12. Barak	18. Many others

Figure 10.7 Hebrews 11 mentions many Old Testament examples of faith.

Q 13 How is the Christian life like running a race?

Q 14 Does Hebrews teach that believers can lose their salvation? Explain.

Q 15 With what does the author of Hebrews balance his warnings?

running by faith so that we won't be rejected or disqualified (1 Cor. 9:24-27)! Hebrews 11 teaches us that faith has always been the way people please God.

If we reject our faith, we will lose everything! Throughout the book, the author warns believers of the danger of losing their salvation. God will judge those who turn back. None who desert the faith will receive God's promises.

On the one hand, there are many warnings in Hebrews. On the other hand, there are many "*Let us*" passages. These encourage believers to persevere and keep living by faith.

"Let us" Passages	Heb.
Let us *be careful that none of you be found to have fallen short of it.*	4:1
Let us*, therefore, make every effort to enter that rest,. . .*	4:11
Let us *hold firmly to the faith we profess.*	4:14
Let us *then approach the throne of grace with confidence,. . .*	4:16
Let us *leave the elementary teachings about Christ and go on to maturity,. . .*	6:1
Let us *draw near to God with a sincere heart in full assurance of faith,. . .*	10:22
Let us *hold unswervingly to the hope we profess,. . .*	10:23
Let us *consider how we may spur one another on toward love and good deeds.*	10:24
Let us *not give up meeting together, as some are in the habit of doing,. . .*	10:25
Let us *encourage one another—and all the more as you see the Day approaching.*	10:25
Let us *throw off everything that hinders and the sin that so easily entangles,. . .*	12:1
Let us *run with perseverance the race marked out for us.*	12:1
Let us *fix our eyes on Jesus, the author and perfecter of our faith,. . .*	12:2
Let us *be thankful, and so worship God acceptably with reverence and awe,. . .*	12:28
Let us*, then, go to him outside the camp, bearing the disgrace he bore.*	13:13
Let us *continually offer to God a sacrifice of praise—. . .*	13:15

Figure 10.8 Hebrews uses 16 "*Let us*" passages to encourage believers to continue with faith in Christ.[6]

Lesson 29

James

Goal A: *Explain the name General Epistles and list the 7 books in this group.*
Goal B: *Analyze the author, style, and purpose of James.*
Goal C: *Summarize and apply what James says about trials, the tongue, faith, and the wealthy.*

A. Background and purpose

Figure 10.9 Practice house of New Testament books

The seven letters after Hebrews are commonly called the **General Epistles*. Another name for them is the **Catholic Epistles*. In this sense, the word *catholic* means "general, universal, or to all." These books include James, 1 and 2 Peter, 1-3 John, and Jude. All of these seven letters except for 2 and 3 John are general in nature. That is, they are written for all churches, rather than one local church. In contrast, Paul writes to the saints at Corinth, or the churches of Galatia, or to Timothy. Also, notice that, unlike Paul's letters, the General Epistles are named for their authors, as the Gospels are named.[7]

James was written "*To the twelve tribes scattered among the nations*" (James 1:1). This verse, along with James 2:21, suggests that the readers were Jewish believers. The Greek word for a scattering is **Diaspora*. It refers to Jews scattered outside their homeland of Palestine.[8] Some of these Jewish believers probably fled from Jerusalem. Recall that persecution arose after Stephen's death. Unbelieving Jews drove Jerusalem believers to escape into Judea and Samaria (Acts 8:1). Some of those scattered by the persecution traveled as far as Phoenicia (Lebanon), Cyprus, and Antioch of Syria. James was a leader of the Jerusalem church. So some of his readers were probably his scattered sheep.[9]

Recall that the readers of Hebrews, James, and 1 Peter were suffering.

[32]*Remember those earlier days after you had received the light, when you stood your ground in a great contest in the face of suffering.* [33]*Sometimes you were publicly exposed to insult and persecution; at other times you stood side by side with those who were so treated.* [34]*You sympathized with those in prison and joyfully accepted the confiscation (seizing) of your property, because you knew that you yourselves had better and lasting possessions* (Heb. 10:32-34).

Likewise today, believers in many places suffer from persecution. As we read Hebrews, James, and 1 Peter, we should remember to pray for our suffering brothers and sisters.

James wrote for three reasons:

- To encourage Jewish believers who were suffering for their faith;
- To correct false ideas about the nature of saving faith;
- To teach his readers how faith shows itself in righteous living and good deeds.

James has a lot to say about the fruit and footprints of faith. This Epistle is concerned mostly about faith in action!

Q 16 Fill in the blanks of the house of New Testament books in Figure 10.9.

Q 17 Explain the name General Epistles and list the 7 books in this group.

Q 18 Describe the early readers to whom James wrote.

Q 19 Summarize 3 reasons why James wrote his Epistle.

B. Author and date

The author is "*James, a servant of God and of the Lord Jesus Christ*" (James 1:1). Note that *James* is an English form of Jacob.[10] The New Testament mentions at least three men named James. So which one wrote the Epistle of James? The author was probably *not* the well-known apostle James. The apostle James was the brother of John and the son of Zebedee. Herod Agrippa I beheaded him before the year A.D. 44 (Acts 12:1-2). So the apostle James was probably not alive when the book of James was written about A.D. 45-49.[11] Nor does the author seem to be James the son of Alphaeus, who was also an apostle (Matt. 10:3). The Bible says little about him.

Q 20 Describe the author of the book of James.

Most Bible teachers agree that the author was James, the half-brother of Jesus (Gal. 1:19).[12] Catholics teach that Mary was always a virgin and had no other children. But the Scriptures teach that Jesus had several brothers and sisters (Matt. 13:55; Mark 6:3; John 2:12; 7:3, 10).[13] Jesus was their half-brother because Joseph was not His father.

[55]*"Isn't this the carpenter's son? Isn't his mother's name Mary, and aren't his brothers James, Joseph, Simon and Judas?* [56]*Aren't all his sisters with us?"* (Matt. 13:55-56).

The New Testament says much about James, the Lord's brother. He was one of the many sons of Mary. It is likely that he was the oldest of Jesus' brothers, since he is mentioned first in the list of Matthew 13:55.

- He was an unbeliever during Christ's earthly ministry (John 7:5). But later, he became a well-known leader.
- The Lord appeared to him after the Resurrection (1 Cor. 15:7).
- He was a pillar in the Jerusalem church (Gal. 2:9).
- After Paul was saved, he saw James in Jerusalem (Gal. 1:19).
- Years later, Paul saw James on his final visit to Jerusalem (Acts 21:18).
- When Peter was set free from prison, he sent word to James (Acts 12:17).
- James was a leader at the big Jerusalem Council (Acts 15).
- James was so well known that Jude refers to himself as *"Jude, the brother of James"* (Jude 1).

Josephus, the Jewish historian, says that James was stoned in Jerusalem about A.D. 62.[14]

C. Form and style of writing

James is like two kinds of Old Testament writings: prophecy and wisdom.[15] On the one hand, James writes like the prophets. At times, he is tender, like the prophet Jeremiah was when he wept. James calls his readers *"brothers"* and *"my dear brothers"* (James 1:2, 16, 19; 2:1, 5; 3:1, 10, 12; 4:11; 5:7, 9, 10, 12). At other times, James

Q 21 In what ways is James like Old Testament prophetic writings?

reminds us of the prophet Nathan. He rebuked King David face to face. Likewise, the words of James are strong and direct.

- *You foolish man, do you want evidence that faith without deeds is useless* (James 2:20)?
- *You adulterous people, don't you know that friendship with the world is hatred toward God? Anyone who chooses to be a friend of the world becomes an enemy of God* (James 4:4).
- [8]*Come near to God and he will come near to you. Wash your hands, you sinners, and purify your hearts, you double-minded.* [9]*Grieve, mourn and wail. Change your laughter to mourning and your joy to gloom* (James 4:8-9).

These strong words make us think that the face of James looked angry as he wrote! His words often remind us of John the Baptist or Jesus. Thus, we say that James wrote like a prophet. There are 108 verses in the 5 chapters of James. Of these verses, there are more than 50 direct commands![16]

Q 22 How is James like Proverbs?

On the other hand, the writing style of James reminds us of a wisdom book like Proverbs. He touches on a topic, and then goes on to another one. This style also reminds us of the way Jesus taught His Sermon on the Mount (Matt. 5–7). James moves quickly from thought to thought. Still, we see one theme throughout the book: *faith that works.*

Q 23 How many different topics do you see in the outline?

D. Outline

Theme	James
Greeting	**1:1**
A. Face Trials and Temptations	**1:2-18**
Recognize their purpose.	1:2-4
Pray for wisdom to face them.	1:5-8
Rejoice in their result.	1:9-12
Discern the source of temptation.	1:13-18
B. Hear the Word and Obey It	**1:19-27**
C. Be Impartial: Do Not Show *Favoritism	**2:1-13**
D. Prove Faith Through Deeds	**2:14-26**
E. Recognize and Avoid Sin	**3:1–5:6**
The tongue	3:1-12
Two kinds of wisdom: from below and from above	3:13-18
Two attitudes: loving the world and loving God	4:1-10
Slandering a brother	4:11-12
Boasting about tomorrow	4:13-17
Selfish wealth	5:1-6
F. Live by God's Standards	**5:7-20**
Be patient in suffering.	5:7-11
Be honest: Let yes mean yes.	5:12
Practice prayer for the sick.	5:13-18
Try to bring back those who wander from the faith.	5:19-20

Figure 10.10 Outline of James

Q 24 Name 2 kinds of trials or troubles mentioned in James.

Q 25 What is the purpose of trials (James 1:2-4)?

E. Explanations of the outline

Face trials and temptations (James 1:2-18). James often used the words *trials* and *temptations*. The word *trials* refers to troubles that come upon believers from the outside. In contrast, *temptations* come from within us (James 1:13-15). They arise from the lusts of our flesh.

James traces the complete life of sin (James 1:14-15).[17] Sin begins as small as a baby begins inside a mother. Little by little it grows. Then, when it is mature, it brings spiritual death. Sometimes we marvel at how quickly children grow. Likewise, sin grows faster and bigger than people expect. As one preacher said, "Sin will take you further than you want to go. It will keep you longer than you want to stay. And it will charge you more than you want to pay!"

Hear the Word and obey it (James 1:19-27).

> [23]*Anyone who listens to the word but does not do what it says is like a man who looks at his face in a mirror* [24]*and, after looking at himself, goes away and immediately forgets what he looks like* (James 1:23-24).

> [26]*"But everyone who hears these words of mine and does not put them into practice is like a foolish man who built his house on sand.* [27]*The rain came down, the streams rose, and the winds blew and beat against that house, and it fell with a great crash"* (Matt. 7:26-27).

Be impartial: Do not show *favoritism (James 2:1-13). James writes about poverty and wealth. Complete the chart that follows by writing what James says in your own words.

James	Summary of what James says about the poor and the rich
1:10-11	
2:1-4	
2:5	
2:6	
2:15-16	
5:1-6	

Figure 10.11 James teaches about the relationship between the rich and the poor.

Prove faith through deeds (James 2:14-26). In 1522 Martin Luther referred to James as an Epistle made of straw.[18] Straw is cheap and weak compared to wood (1 Cor. 3:12). In Luther's day, the Catholic Church taught that people are saved by works. They taught that most believers cannot go directly to heaven. Even today, the Catholic Church teaches that believers must suffer many years in *purgatory*. They say this is a place of torture between the grave and heaven. Catholics teach that by suffering in *purgatory* we pay for our sins, or work our way into heaven. False teachings like this subtract from the value of the blood of Jesus. Luther emphasized that we are saved by faith in Jesus Christ, not by our own good works. He thought that Romans and James contradicted each other. In fact, Luther said that if anyone could harmonize Romans 3:28 and James 2:17, 24, it would prove that he (Luther) was a fool.[20] When a man teaches that the Bible contradicts itself, we do not need more proof that he is being foolish! He has already proved his foolishness by criticizing the Bible. For certain, books like Romans have strong teachings on salvation by faith alone. Romans 3:28 says, "*a man is justified by faith apart from observing the law.*" But we believe that the Holy Spirit inspired James to emphasize the fruit and actions of faith. So we should respect the letter of James as much as Romans. James 2:20 sounds like it was written for men like Luther!

> [20]*You foolish man, do you want evidence that faith without deeds is useless?* [21]*Was not our ancestor Abraham considered righteous for what he did when he offered his son Isaac on the altar?* [22]*You see that his faith and his actions were working together, and his faith was made complete by what he did.* [23]*And the scripture was fulfilled that says, "Abraham believed God, and it was credited to him as righteousness," and he was called God's friend.* [24]*You see that a person is justified by what he does and not by faith alone* (James 2:20-24).

Faith that saves is more than just head-belief in God. *"You believe that there is one God. Good! Even the demons believe that—and shudder"* (James 2:19).

Q 26 *Trace the growth of sin from birth to death. Use an example like cheating, stealing, or a sexual sin.*

Q 27 *Do temptations come from demons (James 1:14)? Explain.*

Q 28 *One who hears but disobeys is like _______ (James 1:23-24).*

Q 29 *When you preach or teach, do you use comparisons like James and Jesus used? Explain.*

Q 30 *What example does James use to make his teaching come alive (James 2:2-4)?*

Q 31 *Complete Figure 10.11 in your own words.*

Q 32 *Are all the rich sinful, and are all the poor spiritual (Luke 12:21; 1 Tim. 6:18)? Explain.*

Q 33 *How would you harmonize Romans 3:28 and James 2:17, 24?*

Q 34 *Do you think that the book of James is like straw? Explain.*

Q 35 *Explain: "We are not saved by works, yet we cannot be saved without them."*

Figure 10.12 Martin Luther preferred Romans to James. A better view is to see the value of both Epistles![19]

We know that demons will not be saved. Likewise, those who claim to have faith, but have no good works, will not be saved. It is impossible to have fire without heat. And it is impossible to have saving faith without good deeds. As James says, faith without deeds is as dead as the body without the spirit (James 2:26).

Some say that James is the least doctrinal book in the New Testament.[21] But doctrine is just another word for teaching. And teachings for the tongue, the hands, and the feet are just as important as teachings for the head! For some, as in Luther's day, Romans has the most needed teachings. But for others, as in our day, James has the most needed teachings. Romans emphasizes that we are saved by faith in our hearts. James emphasizes that when faith is in the heart, we can see it in a person's hands and feet! And by the way, even Paul wrote that faith produces works (Eph. 2:10; 1 Thess. 1:3). Faith and works are two sides of the same coin.

Q 36 *Interpret and apply the parable about the bus ticket.*

Consider the following parable. A man stood waiting for a bus. He was holding a ticket that someone sold him. At last, the bus arrived. People ahead of him gave their tickets and got onto the bus. But a strange thing happened when he tried to step onto the bus. He was refused because his ticket was fake. He thought he had a real ticket, but he was mistaken. He had depended on a false assurance.

Recognize and avoid sin (James 3:1–5:6).

Q 37 *Complete Figure 10.13.*

Q 38 *In which chapter of Luke did Jesus use 3 illustrations to teach one truth?*

James	Topic	Summary, in your own words, of what James says
3:1-12		
3:13-18		
4:1-10		
4:11-12		
5:1-6		

Figure 10.13 James teaches us to recognize and avoid sin.

Q 39 *How can you relate James 5:19 to the purpose of James' letter?*

Live by God's standards (James 5:7-20). Have you noticed how many illustrations James uses? Like Jesus, James liked to teach through illustrations. James used one sentence to tell us to be patient (James 5:7). Then, he gave us three examples of being patient (James 5:7-11). The best teachers and preachers use many illustrations. Examples move truth from the head to the heart and to the hands.

Q 40 *Complete Figure 10.14.*

Jacob was a pastor from a *Reformed church. He needed God's help. His voice had been weak for several years. It was difficult for him to speak above a whisper. He took a year off, away from preaching, but his voice did not improve. Then, in the fall of 2001, Jacob visited James River Assembly of God church. Near the beginning of the service, there was prayer for the sick. He went forward and asked the elders to pray for him. They anointed him with oil and asked God to restore his voice. Jacob sensed the presence of God upon him. He returned to his seat and joined others in singing a song of praise to the Lord. Suddenly, he noticed that he was singing as loudly as others were. His voice was completely healed! Later, he sent Pastor John Lindell a letter about what the Lord had done for him. The prayer of faith still heals people today.

Verses to complete	James
A suffering believer should be as patient as	5:7-8
A suffering believer should be as patient as	5:10
A suffering believer should be as patient as	5:11
Those in trouble should	5:13
Those who are happy should	5:13
Those who are sick should	5:14-16+

Figure 10.14 Verses to complete from James 5

+ See the James 5:14-15 illustration about Frances in the *Faith & Action Series* book *The Life & Teachings of Christ* (chapter 4, Lesson 13B, 7th paragraph).

First Peter

Lesson 30

Goal A: *Explain 4 things that the Bible tells us about the author of 1 Peter.*
Goal B: *Summarize what 1 Peter teaches about suffering.*
Goal C: *Contrast the lifestyles of believers and unbelievers.*

A. Background

Q 41 *Did Peter write 1 Peter by himself? Explain.*

Recall that we are studying eight letters written to all believers. Seven of these letters are called the General Epistles.

The first book of the General Epistles was James. Now we turn our attention to 1 Peter. This is the first of two letters Peter wrote in the New Testament (1 Pet. 1:1; 2 Pet. 1:1). He testifies that a scribe named Silas helped him write this first letter (1 Pet. 5:12). Silas wrote very good Greek. In contrast, Peter probably wrote the second letter without help. Its Greek is less polished and more common.

Themes common to 1 Peter and Acts[22]	Peter's Sermons in Acts[23]	First Peter
1. Jesus, the prophesied Messiah, has come. A new age has dawned.	2:14-16; 3:13; 4:11; 10:34-43	1:3, 10-12; 4:7
2. Salvation is possible through the life, death, and resurrection of Christ.	2:20-31; 3:13-14; 10:43	1:20-21; 2:21-25
3. By the Resurrection, Jesus is exalted to the right hand of God. He is the Head of the New Israel.	2:22-26; 3:13; 4:11; 5:30-31; 10:39-42	1:21; 2:7; 2:24; 3:22
4. Christ will soon come again to judge the living and the dead.	3:19-23; 10:42	1:5, 7, 13; 4:5, 13, 17-18; 5:1, 4
5. All should repent of their sins and accept forgiveness, eternal life, and the Holy Spirit.	2:38-39; 3:19; 5:31; 10:42	1:13-25; 2:1-3; 4:1-5

Figure 10.15 The book of 1 Peter has five themes in common with Peter's sermons in Acts.

First Peter refers to several truths that Peter preached about in Acts.

Peter wrote his first letter to the "*strangers in the world, scattered throughout Pontus, Galatia, Cappadocia, Asia, and Bithynia*" (1 Pet. 1:1). We studied about scattered Jewish believers when we looked at the background of James. This scattering was called the *Diaspora*. It resulted from persecution after Stephen's death. Peter wrote to those who were scattered. Also, some of his readers may have been saved on the Day of Pentecost. On that day, Jews had come to Jerusalem from at least 15 different places (Acts 2:8-11). Peter referred to believers as "*strangers and aliens*" or foreigners (1 Pet. 1:1; 2:11). In this way, he reminded them that their true home was heaven.

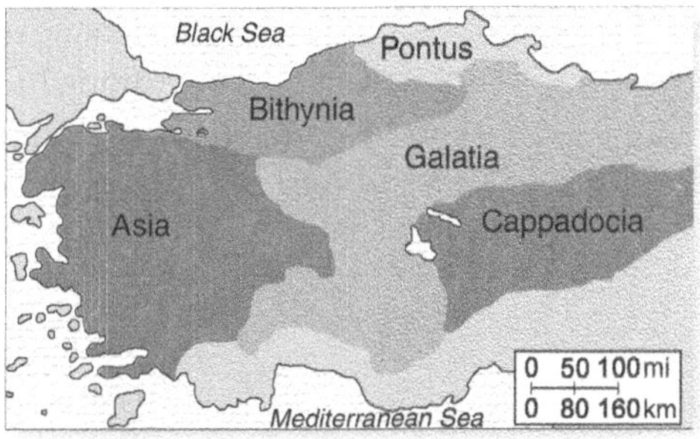

Figure 10.16 Map showing the five provinces of scattered believers (1 Pet. 1:1)

B. Author, date, and purpose

Q 42 *Did Peter and James write to the same believers? Explain.*

Peter identifies himself as the author of 1 and 2 Peter (1 Pet. 1:1; 2 Pet. 1:1, 16, 18). We think he wrote this letter about A.D. 60-63. The New Testament refers to him more than 150 times.[24] Therefore, we know a lot about Peter.

- He and his brother, Andrew, were fishermen. They grew up in Bethsaida, a little town on the northern coast of the Sea of Galilee (John 1:44).
- Peter was brought to Jesus by Andrew, his brother (John 1:40-42).
- Peter's original name was Simon. Jesus changed his name to Peter. Both *Peter* (Greek) and *Cephas* (Aramaic) mean "rock."[25] In his early years as a disciple of Jesus, Peter was unstable. He trusted in himself (Matt. 26:32-35). But little by little, Jesus changed him into a rock and pillar of the Church (Gal. 2:9). Jesus sees in each of us what we can become by His grace!

  There was once a famous woodcarver. He could take a part of a plain tree and carve it into the likeness of a beautiful person. Someone asked him how he did it. "It is easy," replied the woodcarver. "First, I look into the wood and discover the image of the person in it. Then, I just chip away what doesn't need to be there." Likewise, Jesus sees in us the beautiful people we can become. In sinners like Matthew and Peter, He saw future apostles!

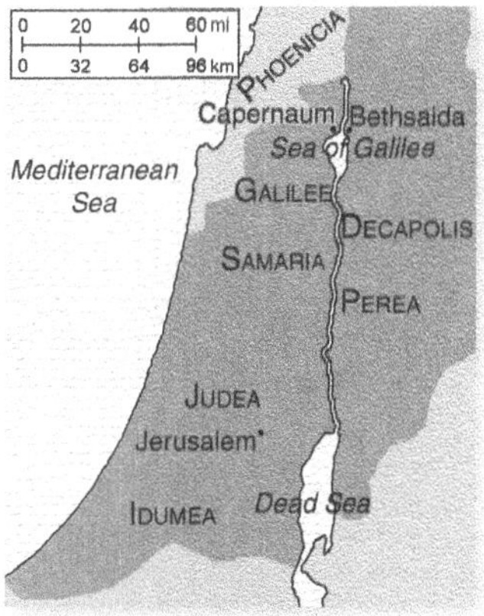

Figure 10.17 Map showing the Sea of Galilee in relation to Palestine

Q 43 How do the changes Jesus made in Peter encourage you?

- Later, Jesus called Peter to follow Him and learn to catch men (Mark 1:16-18). Peter became one of the twelve apostles when Jesus chose him (Mark 3:13-16). In fact, Peter was one of the three apostles closest to Jesus (Mark 5:37; 9:2).

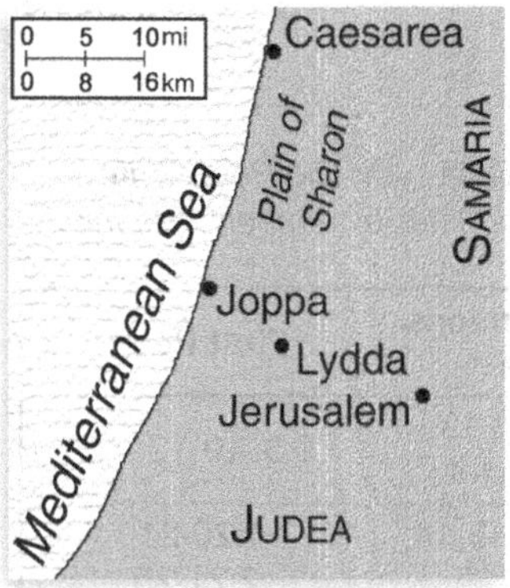

Figure 10.18 Map showing Lydda, the Plain of Sharon, Joppa, and Caesarea

- Peter was a man of great courage. He was quick to speak and act! Peter was the only apostle who dared to walk on the water to Jesus (Matt. 14:25-33). Again, it was Peter who declared that Jesus was the Son of God (Matt. 16:16). Yet, at times he trusted in himself too much. He rebuked Jesus when the Master said death on the cross was near (Matt. 16:22). And he denied Jesus after the Lord would not allow Peter to fight for Him (Matt. 26:69-75).
- At Pentecost, we see a great change take place in Peter. He received a new spiritual power. Jesus promised this spiritual power to all of us. We receive it when we are filled with the Spirit. We call this spiritual experience the *baptism in the Holy Spirit*. This filling takes place after a person is saved. Like Peter and all the apostles, those filled with the Spirit speak in new languages (Acts 2:4). This is an outward sign of new boldness inside. The Spirit brings us boldness to speak about Jesus. Before Pentecost, Peter denied Jesus in the presence of a few people by a fire. After Pentecost, this fisherman spoke boldly to a great crowd in Jerusalem. As a result of his new spiritual power, 3,000 were saved in one day (Acts 2:14-41)! Apostles and common believers need to be baptized in the Holy Spirit (Matt. 3:11; Luke 24:49; Acts 1:8; 8:14-17; 10:44-46; 19:1-7).

Q 44 What is the theme of 1 Peter?

- Full of the Spirit, Peter did miracles in Jesus' name. He healed a crippled beggar in Jerusalem (Acts 3:11-16). The Spirit-filled apostles healed many. But Peter was a leader of the Jerusalem church (Acts 5:12). People laid the sick in the street. They hoped that even Peter's shadow would touch them (Acts 5:15). Later, in the town of Lydda, Peter healed a cripple named Aeneas. As a result, all in Joppa and Sharon turned to Christ (Acts 9:32-35). Likewise, in Joppa, Peter raised Dorcas from the dead. This helped many believe in Jesus (Acts 9:36-42). The Spirit that enabled Peter has not changed. He still gives believers today power to do miracles. However, as Peter emphasized, the power is in the name of Jesus, not in the name of humans (Acts 4:8-12). Likewise, Paul reminded those at Lystra that we are only humans. Power to heal comes from the living God (Acts 14:14-15).
- Peter also helped lead the Jerusalem church in missions. He prayed for the new believers in Samaria to be filled with the Spirit (Acts 8:14-17). Returning to Jerusalem, Peter preached to many Samaritans (Acts 8:25). Later, through a vision, God led him to Cornelius. Peter preached to this Roman centurion in Caesarea. Cornelius and all his household were saved and filled with the Spirit (Acts 10:44-46). So Peter is a good example of witnessing to those of other cultures.

Q 45 Fill in province names for 1–5 in Figure 10.19.

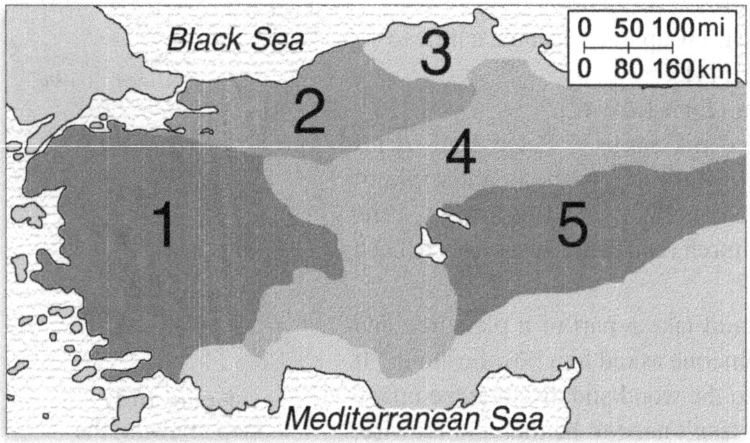

Figure 10.19 Practice map of the five provinces of scattered believers (1 Peter 1:1)

- Throughout his life, Peter suffered from persecution (Acts 5:17-18, 33, 41; 12:1-5). Jesus prophesied that Peter would die a cruel death (John 21:18-19). The Roman emperor, Nero, ordered him to be crucified. The great apostle felt unworthy to die like Jesus. So he asked to be crucified with his feet up and his head down. Nero agreed and crucified him upside down![26] As an old man, Peter wrote about suffering. He told believers to rejoice in sharing the sufferings of Christ (1 Pet. 4:13). Suffering as Jesus did is the great theme of 1 Peter.

C. Outline

Theme	1 Pet.
Greeting	**1:1-2**
A. The Believer's Relationship to God	**1:3–2:10**
Our suffering proves that our faith is real as we wait for Jesus to return.	1:3-12
We live holy lives because He is holy.	1:13–2:3
We are living stones, built into a spiritual temple for God.	2:4-10
B. The Believer's Relationship to Others	**2:11–3:12**
All should submit to rulers, even if this brings suffering.	2:11-17
Slaves should submit to masters, even if this brings suffering.	2:18-20
All should follow Christ's example of suffering.	2:21-25
Wives should submit to their husbands.	3:1-6
Husbands should be kind to their wives.	3:7
All should be loving and humble.	3:8-12
C. The Believer's Relationship to Suffering	**3:13–4:19**
Suffering should result from doing good following Christ's example.	3:13-22
Suffering kills our desire for sin and helps us live for God.	4:1-11
Suffering may be God's will for us.	4:12-19
D. The Relationship Between the Young and the Old	**5:1-11**
Conclusion	**5:12-14**

Figure 10.20 Outline of 1 Peter

D. Explanations of the outline

We noted that James wrote like a prophet. About half of the verses in James are commands. Likewise, Peter uses many commands as you will see in Figures 10.21 and 10.22.[27]

Q 46 *Complete Figure 10.21 on suffering.*

1 Peter	Topic	Summary of verse, in your own words
1:6	Length of suffering	
1:7	Purpose of suffering	
1:11	2 things the Spirit of Christ predicted	
2:19-20	Undeserved suffering	
2:21-25	The way Jesus, our Example, suffered	
3:14-16	Suffering for what is right	
3:17-18	Suffering like Christ	
4:1	An attitude for a weapon	
4:1-6	The result of suffering	
4:12	The painful trial of suffering	
4:13-14	The reason to rejoice in suffering	
4:15	4 sinful reasons some suffer	
4:16-19	Suffering as God's purifying judgment	
5:10	God's promise to those who suffer	

Figure 10.21 The theme of 1 Peter is suffering as Jesus suffered.

1 Peter	Commands to those who live like strangers in this world (1 Pet. 2:11)	Attitudes of those who live like this world is their home
1:13; 4:7; 5:8	Be ________, clear, watchful, and self-controlled (get your mind ready to work).	Relax; take it easy. Live like there is no ____ or __________.
1:15; 3:15	Be ____ as God is ____. Live like your holiness depends on what Jesus did for you, and what you _____ to let Him do in you.	Sin whenever you feel like it. Depend on ______ to cover every sin you want to commit. Live like your holiness is all God's responsibility.
1:17	Since you call on a Father who judges each man's work impartially, _______________ .	Enjoy yourself; live like you have ____________ of judgment.
1:22	Now that you have purified yourselves _______.	Hold grudges; refuse to _____________ others.
2:2	Like newborn babies _________________ .	Don't take time to read the Bible. Feed the ______ and starve the ________.
2:17; 5:5	Show __________ to others, rulers, and God.	Be rude; _________ only those whom you like.
2:18	Servants (employees), _____ to your masters.	Lie to, steal from, slander, and dishonor your boss.
3:1	Wives, __________ to your husbands.	_____ against your husband. Do what you want.
3:7	Husbands, be ___________ to your wives.	Treat your wife like she is your ________. Ignore her __________.
3:14	Don't worry; don't be _____; don't be afraid of things in this world.	Panic! Chew your nails in fear! Be afraid of all the _________ that can happen to you!
4:1, 12	Arm yourself with the attitude of _____ about suffering. Expect trials and be prepared.	Be amazed when trouble or persecution comes. Blame ________ for not being fair to you! Complain about trials!
5:5-6	Clothe yourselves with ______________ .	Be _________ and arrogant. Refuse to bend or ___________!
5:9	________ the devil.	Give in to temptations. Blame the devil, demons, or the flesh for your ___________!

Figure 10.22 Peter contrasts us (strangers in this world) with those living like the world is their home.

Q 47 *Complete both sides of Figure 10.22.*

Difficult verses in 1 Peter. First Peter contains two passages that are hard to interpret.

- **1 Peter 3:18-20**

[18]For Christ died for sins once for all, the righteous for the unrighteous, to bring you to God. He was put to death in the body but made alive by the Spirit, [19]through whom also he went and preached to the spirits in prison [20]who disobeyed long ago when God waited patiently in the days of Noah while the ark was being built. In it only a few people, eight in all, were saved through water.

Figure 10.24 James the brother of Jesus may have been buried in this ancient bone box, called an *ossuary*. The Aramaic words engraved on it read, "James, son of Joseph, brother of Jesus." Some scholars say that this "may be the most important find in the history of New Testament archeology."[30]

Verse 19 teaches that by the Spirit, Christ went and preached to the spirits in prison. Two questions arise. Who were the spirits in prison? And when did Christ preach to them? Believers have tried to answer these questions in many ways. Some think the spirits in prison were angels. But this view does not agree with the rest of the New Testament. The gospel is always preached to humans, not angels. In 1 Peter 1:12, Peter tells us that angels long to look into matters of salvation. But salvation is for humans, not

Figure 10.23
First Peter was probably written from Rome.

angels. Angels minister to humans who will inherit salvation (Heb. 1:14). Therefore, we believe that the spirits in prison were humans. Also, note that Peter tells us that these humans disobeyed long ago, in the days of Noah (1 Pet. 3:20).

This brings us to the second question: When did Christ preach to them by the Spirit? Some contradict the New Testament when they interpret this verse. These claim that Jesus preached to sinners in hell after He died. But the Bible teaches that our only chance for salvation is while we are alive on earth. Abraham told the rich man in torment that his chance was past (Luke 16:25-26). Likewise, Hebrews 9:27 teaches that what follows death is judgment. This thought brings tears to our eyes. But it is the truth of God's Word. The Scriptures offer no hope of a second chance after death. We must reach those we want to be saved in this life. The Bible sometimes refers to those who are dead. But the gospel is preached to people when they are alive on the earth (1 Pet. 4:6). "*Whether a tree falls to the south or the north, in the place where it falls, there it will lie*" (Eccles. 11:3).

Figure 10.25 The forum in Rome. First Peter was probably written from Rome.

So we conclude that the Spirit of Christ preached to sinners in Noah's time. This happened as the Spirit of Christ preached through Noah (Gen. 6:3, 5, 13-14). Peter refers to Noah as *"a preacher of righteousness"* (2 Pet. 2:5). Also, Peter says that the Spirit of Christ was speaking through the prophets (1 Pet. 1:10-11).

Q 48 *Can sinners be saved after death (1 Pet. 3:18-20)? Explain.*

Figure 10.26 Peter once denied Christ (John 18:25), but he repented and became a faithful leader. (by Gustave Doré)

Figure 10.27 Oval house structure on Palatine Hill in Rome. The emperors and aristocrats of ancient Rome lived on the Palatine Hill.

Figure 10.28 Temple of Athena in Rome

- **1 Peter 5:13**

"She who is in Babylon, chosen together with you, sends you her greetings, and so does my son Mark."

The question on this verse is about *Babylon. Does it refer to the Babylon mentioned in the Old Testament? Perhaps. In Peter's day, Babylon existed as a small city on the Euphrates River. The city had lost its former glory. But a large number of Jews lived there. Since Peter was an apostle to the Jews, he may have gone there and started a church (Gal. 2:7-8).[28] Others think that saying *Babylon* was Peter's way of referring to Rome. In Revelation, the apostle John referred to Rome as Babylon (Rev. 17–18). But this was 30 years after Peter wrote.

The Jews were captives in the foreign land of Babylon for 70 years. Peter's reference to Babylon reminds us that in the world we are strangers in a foreign country (1 Pet. 1:1, 17).

Figure 10.29 Temple of Venus in Rome with Colosseum in background

Test Yourself: Circle the letter by the ***best*** completion to each question or statement.

1. The author of Hebrews was
a) Paul.
b) Barnabas.
c) Apollos.
d) unknown.

2. What is the theme of Hebrews?
a) Jesus is sovereign.
b) Jesus is faithful.
c) Jesus is superior.
d) Jesus is righteous.

3. Hebrews teaches that Jesus is a better priest because
a) He gave a complete revelation.
b) He was faithful as God's Son.
c) He offers us an eternal rest.
d) He lived a sinless life on earth.

4. If believers keep ignoring God's warnings
a) they miss God's fullest blessings.
b) they lose rewards in heaven.
c) they spend time in purgatory.
d) they lose their salvation.

5. The *General Epistles* were written
a) from different places.
b) for all churches.
c) about various topics.
d) about the same time.

6. What does James teach about wealth?
a) Believers should not be wealthy.
b) Wealthy believers are more spiritual.
c) The wealthy will soon pass away.
d) Wealth is a measure of God's blessing.

7. According to James, temptations come from
a) demons.
b) the flesh.
c) the world.
d) the devil.

8. What does 1 Peter teach about suffering?
a) Trials purify our faith.
b) Trials reveal a lack of faith.
c) Trials are the result of sin.
d) Trials are caused by Satan.

9. A big theme in Hebrews, James, and 1 Peter is
a) unity.
b) witnessing.
c) suffering.
d) spiritual gifts.

10. The name *Peter* means
a) "fisherman."
b) "God is near."
c) "father."
d) "rock."

Essay Test Topics: Write 50-100 words on each of these goals that you studied in this chapter.

Hebrews

Goal: *Analyze the author, date, first readers, and background of Hebrews.*

Goal: *Explain 6 comparisons that show that Jesus is better.*

Goal: *Summarize and apply the purpose of the seven warnings in Hebrews.*

James

Goal: *Explain the name General Epistles and list the 7 books in this group.*

Goal: *Analyze the author, style, and purpose of James.*

Goal: *Summarize and apply what James says about trials, the tongue, faith, and the wealthy.*

First Peter

Goal: *Explain 4 things that the Bible tells us about the author of 1 Peter.*

Goal: *Summarize what 1 Peter teaches about suffering.*

Goal: *Contrast the lifestyles of believers and unbelievers.*

Chapter 11:

Letters About False Teaching—Part 1: 2 Peter and 1 John

Figure 11.1 Ruins of Pergamum (modern-day Bergama in Turkey). Some of the believers Peter wrote to lived in this area of Asia Minor.

Introduction

Several years ago, Dr. Mark Barclift ran a long race called a *marathon. The length of the race was 42 kilometers (26.2 miles). Most people who run a race like this have only one goal—to finish. Top runners want to finish first, or as quickly as possible. But for most, the goal is to cross the finish line. Mark was not a fast runner. His only goal was to finish the race.

The race ended in the town where Mark lived. Once, he was tempted to quit. But he encouraged himself by remembering that home was ahead. It helped to know that every step brought him closer to home.

Biblical writers compare the Christian life to running a race.

- [24]*Do you not know that in a race all the runners run, but only one gets the prize? Run in such a way as to get the prize.* [25]*Everyone who competes in the games goes into strict training. They do it to get a crown that will not last; but we do it to get a crown that will last forever.* [26]*Therefore I do not run like a man running aimlessly; I do not fight like a man beating the air.* [27]*No, I beat my body and make it my slave so that after I have preached to others, I myself will not be disqualified for the prize* (1 Cor. 9:24-27).
- [13]*Brothers, I do not consider myself yet to have taken hold of it. But one thing I do: Forgetting what is behind and straining toward what is ahead,* [14]*I press on toward the goal to win the prize for which God has called me heavenward in Christ Jesus* (Phil. 3:13-14).
- *Similarly, if anyone competes as an athlete, he does not receive the victor's crown unless he competes according to the rules* (2 Tim. 2:5).
- [7]*I have fought the good fight, I have finished the race, I have kept the faith.* [8]*Now there is in store for me the crown of righteousness, which the Lord, the righteous Judge, will award to me on that day—and not only to me, but also to all who have longed for his appearing* (2 Tim. 4:7-8).
- *Therefore, since we are surrounded by such a great cloud of witnesses, let us throw off everything that hinders and the sin that so easily entangles, and let us run with perseverance the race marked out for us* (Heb. 12:1).

The goal of the Christian life is to cross the finish line and win the crown of life. It is not enough to *begin* walking in the light of God. The Christian must *continue* walking in the light until the end. False teachers want believers to stop continuing in the light. They want them to quit before they cross the finish line. Second Peter and First John both warn against these false teachers. These letters encourage us to keep running the race.

Lessons:

Second Peter

31

Goal A: *Explain 2 Peter's contrasts between growing in grace and falling from grace.*

Goal B: *Summarize what 2 Peter says about the Scriptures and false teachers.*

First John

32

Goal A: *Explain how 1 John relates to the errors of the Gnostics.*

Goal B: *Summarize what 1 John teaches about Jesus Christ, sin, knowledge, and love.*

Key Words

effort divine nature God-breathed Gnostics sin

Lesson 31

Second Peter

Goal A: *Explain 2 Peter's contrasts between growing in grace and falling from grace.*

Goal B: *Summarize what 2 Peter says about the Scriptures and false teachers.*

A. Author and date

We are continuing our study of Hebrews and the General Epistles. We have studied Hebrews, James, and 1 Peter in this group. Now, we turn to the last five letters of the General Epistles. All of these books say a lot about false teachings.

The author of 2 Peter is "*Simon Peter, a servant and apostle of Jesus Christ*" (2 Pet. 1:1). *Simon* was his original name (John 1:42; Acts 15:14). Recall that Jesus changed his name to *Peter*, which means "rock." Review facts we studied about Peter in chapter 10, lesson 30. There, we noted that Peter was close to Jesus. Peter tells his readers that he was with Jesus when the Lord was glorified on a mountain (2 Pet. 1:16-18; Matt. 17:1-13).[1] This is the second letter Peter wrote to those who were scattered (2 Pet. 3:1).

Peter and Paul were brothers in Christ (2 Pet. 3:15). Earlier, we noted that Paul wrote 2 Timothy about A.D. 67. This was Paul's last letter, near the end of his life. Likewise, Peter wrote his second letter as an old man, about A.D. 66-68. He knew that he was standing near the door of death. The old apostle referred to the Lord's prophecy about Peter's last days (John 21:18-19).

*[13]I think it is right to refresh your memory as long as I live in the tent of this body, [14]because I know that I will soon put it aside, as our Lord Jesus Christ has made clear to me. [15]And I will make every *effort to see that after my departure you will always be able to remember these things* (2 Pet. 1:13-15).

Recall that Nero executed both Paul and Peter.

Q 1 *Try to sing the books of the New Testament in less than 30 seconds.*

Q 2 *Fill in the names in the house of New Testament books (Figure 11.2).*

Q 3 *Why do we refer to 1 Peter–Jude as "General Epistles"? (See Chapter 10, lesson 29.)*

Q 4 *What problem do 2 Peter, 1–3 John, and Jude all discuss?*

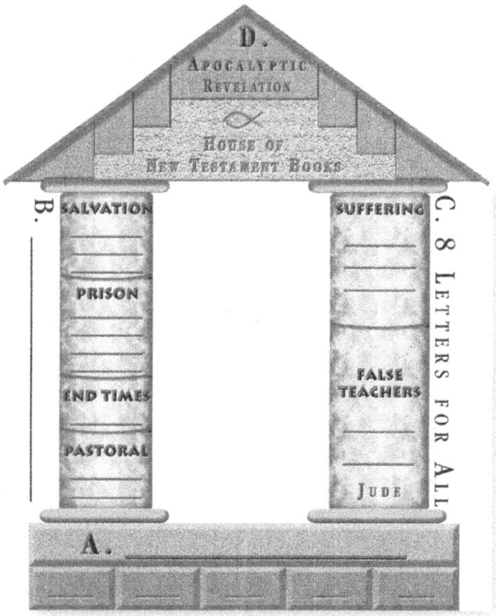

Figure 11.2 Practice House of the New Testament books

B. Outline

Theme	2 Pet.
Greeting	**1:1-2**
A. Take Steps to Grow in Grace	**1:3-11**
B. Pay Attention to the Scriptures	**1:12-21**
C. Be on Guard Against False Teachers	**2:1-22**
The characteristics of false teachers	2:1-19
The danger of being saved and then turning back to sin	2:20-22
D. Live a Holy Life Because the Lord Is Coming	**3:1-18**
Scoffers deny that Christ is coming again.	3:1-7
The return of Christ is certain.	3:8-10
Live ready for His coming.	3:11-18a
Closing prayer	**3:18b**

Figure 11.3 Outline of 2 Peter

Figure 11.4 Mount Tabor may be the place where Peter, James, and John saw Jesus glorified. This mountain is located near Caesarea Philippi, 12 miles (20 km) northwest of Capernaum.

C. Explanations of the outline

The outline of 2 Peter reveals four parts of Peter's purpose. Let us look at these one by one.

Take steps to grow in grace (2 Pet. 1:3-11). God's grace is a wonderful gift to us. By God's grace, He has given us great and precious promises (2 Pet. 1:3-4). Peter says that through these promises we "*participate in the divine nature and escape the corruption in the world caused by evil* *desires*" (2 Pet. 1:4). Another translation of 2 Peter 1:4 says that through God's promises we "*become partakers of the divine nature, having escaped the corruption that is in the world by lust*" (NASB). It is very important to understand 2 Peter 1:4. This verse is a key to understanding the Epistle. Peter will return to this thought when he talks about false teachers (2 Pet. 2:20). So we must ask ourselves some questions about this verse.

Q 5 *When do we partake of God's nature? Explain.*

What does it mean to participate, partake, or share in God's nature? When do we share in God's *divine nature? We share in God's nature when we are born again. At the new birth, eternal life from God Himself flows into us (John 3:16; 2 Pet. 1:4; 1 John 3:9). The moment we receive the Spirit of Christ by faith, God recreates us spiritually. At once, we become His children (John 1:12; Rom. 8:16-17; Gal. 3:26). As we partake of God's nature, we become new creations in Christ (2 Cor. 5:17; Col. 3:9-10). Through being born again we are "*created to be like God in true righteousness and holiness*" (Eph. 4:24). Thus we see that we begin to share in God's nature when we are born again. We grow in His likeness as we grow in grace. As Paul says, "*we. . . are being transformed into his likeness with ever-increasing glory, which comes from the Lord. . .*" (2 Cor. 3:18).

Q 6 *When do we escape the corruption and sinful bondage of the world (2 Pet. 1:4; 2:20)? Explain.*

Another question arises about 2 Peter 1:4. When do we escape the corruption or sin of the world caused by our lust? Peter answers this question clearly. He says believers "*escaped the corruption of the world by knowing our Lord and Savior Jesus Christ. . .*" (2 Pet. 2:20). This does not mean that we cannot return to the sin and bondage of the world. But every believer can testify of the change that takes place at the new birth. A man is a slave to whatever has mastered him (2 Pet. 2:19). But our Savior's name is called *Jesus* because He saves His people from their sins (Matt. 1:21). When Jesus saves us, He sets us free from the bondage of sin.

> 15 *What then? Shall we sin because we are not under law but under grace? By no means!* 16 *Don't you know that when you offer yourselves to someone to obey him as slaves, you are slaves to the one whom you obey—whether you are slaves to sin, which leads to death, or to obedience, which leads to righteousness?* 17 *But thanks be to God that, though you used to be slaves to sin, you wholeheartedly obeyed the form of teaching to which you were entrusted.* 18 *You have been set free from sin and have become slaves to righteousness* (Rom. 6:15-18).

A change takes place in our hearts when we are born again. We are freed from being slaves of sin. Sin loses its grip on us. We receive a spiritual desire to please God and obey Him. Thus we escape the sinful bondage of the world that enslaves people through lust (2 Pet. 1:4; 2:20). Everyone who practices sin is a slave to sin (John 8:34; 2 Pet. 2:19). But if the Son sets you free, you will be free indeed (John 8:36).

The process of sharing in God's nature is by grace from start to finish. Grace is the hand that extends the knowledge of God to us. And grace gives us the power to grow in Christ's image. Still, Peter tells believers to "*make every effort*" to grow in grace (2 Pet. 1:5; 3:14, 18). He says that to our faith we should add goodness, knowledge, self-control, perseverance, godliness, kindness, and love. The Bible lists goodness, self-control, kindness, and love as fruits of the Spirit (Gal. 5:22-23). We cannot add these spiritual fruits by our own efforts. The Spirit must produce this fruit in us. Still, Peter tells believers to "*make every effort*" to add these fruits (2 Pet. 1:5).

Q 7 *If salvation is by grace, why must we "make every effort" (2 Pet. 1:5; 3:14, 18)?*

So we find ourselves wrestling with a riddle. On the one hand, the Christian life is by grace. Salvation is by grace, not by our efforts. We do not deserve salvation. We cannot earn it; it is a gift. On the other hand, Peter tells us to "*make every effort*" to add the fruit that comes by grace (2 Pet. 1:5; 3:14)! Our efforts to please God show that we are thankful for the free gift. As God "*works in*" us (Phil. 2:13), we must "*work out*" our salvation (Phil. 2:12). Thus, we live in a manner that is worthy of God's grace (Eph. 4:1; Rev. 3:4). We *make every effort* to obey and please the Spirit of Grace. Likewise, Jesus said to "*make every effort*" to enter heaven through the narrow gate (Luke 13:24).

In contrast, some receive God's grace and then set it aside (Gal. 2:21). As a result, these fall from grace (Gal. 5:4). Others insult the Spirit of Grace (Heb. 10:29), or constantly resist Him (Acts 7:51). We must be careful not to put out the Spirit's fire (1 Thess. 5:19). Paul wrote about those who receive the grace of God in vain (2 Cor. 6:1).

Peter knew that believers usually grow in grace or fall from grace. No one stands still for long as a believer. We either move forward or backward.[2] So Peter commanded believers to "*make every effort*" to grow in grace so that they would not fall from grace (2 Pet. 1:5-10; 3:17-18; See also Heb. 12:14-15). Those who do not grow in grace live in great danger. They become like the believers of Hebrews 6. It was time for them to be teachers. Instead, they needed someone to re-teach them the basics of the faith (Heb. 5:11-13). Perhaps some had fallen away (Heb. 6:4-6). We lose what we refuse to use. Barnabas encouraged new believers *"to continue in the grace of God"* (Acts 13:43). Likewise, Peter urged believers to *"make every effort"* to grow in grace. He warned that the false teachers destroy the weak. They attack baby Christians "*who are just escaping from those who live in error*" (2 Pet. 2:18). In his lifetime, he had seen some grow and some fall away.

Figure 11.5 As a lion attacks a weak or young animal, false teachers may destroy baby believers (2 Pet. 2:18).

2 Pet.	Those who grow in grace	Those who fall from grace	2 Pet.
1:5-7	______________ to add to faith: _______, knowledge, ________, perseverance, _______, brotherly kindness, and _____.	Relax. Ignore their responsibilities. Thus, become near-sighted and ________. They forget that __________________.	1:9
1:8 (NASB)	Become ______ and ________ (John 15:5).	Become useless and _________ (John 15: 6).	1:8 (NASB)
1:10-11	Are _____ to make their calling and election _____. They will never _______ because ________. Rather, they will receive a rich _____ into the ______________.	Become lazy and fleshly. Follow and teach false doctrines. Refuse to let Jesus be Lord, even _____ the sovereign Lord who ____ them, bringing swift destruction on themselves.	2:1, 10
1:19	Pay attention to the Scriptures as to a ___________________.	They have _____ the straight way and ______ _______ to follow the way of Balaam.	2:15
3:11-12	Live ____ and ____ lives as they look forward to the ___ of God and speed its ________.	They have __________ the corruption of the world by ______ our Lord and Savior Jesus Christ and are again __________.	2:20
3:14	____________ to be found spotless, blameless, and at peace with Him.	It would have been ________ for them not to have ________ the way of ________, than to have ________ it and then to have _______ on the sacred command that was passed on to them.	2:21
3:17	Live on their guard to avoid __________ by the error of lawless men, and to avoid ____________.	Fulfill the proverbs: A dog ________ to its vomit: a sow that is ___________ goes back to her wallowing in the mud.	2:22

Figure 11.6 Peter contrasts those who grow in grace with those who fall from grace.

Grace is not something we usually receive as we lie in bed and sleep. Nor is grace something that forces itself upon us. We choose to receive or reject God's grace moment by moment. Paul says that we are stewards of God's grace (1 Cor. 3:10; 4:1-2). As stewards, we must be careful not to neglect God's grace. Neglect was the error of the lazy steward who wasted his talent. As a result, he was cast into outer darkness (Matt. 25:28-30; Heb. 2:1-4).

Q 8 *Fill in all of the blanks in Figure 11.6.*

Grace comes to us through the Spirit of Grace. So the key to growing in grace is walking in the Spirit. What are some keys to walking in the Spirit? *First,* believers should seek to be filled with the Spirit. Recall that believers were filled in Jerusalem, Samaria, Caesarea, and Ephesus (Acts 2:4; 8:17; 10:44; 19:6). Speaking in a new

Q 9 *Summarize 5 keys to obeying 2 Peter 1:5-7.*

Q 10 How does Peter say the Holy Spirit enabled those who spoke for God (2 Pet. 1:20-21)?

Q 11 Did early believers recognize that the apostles' letters were inspired (2 Pet. 3:2, 16)? Explain.

Q 12 Which 3 examples assure us that God will judge false teachers (2 Pet. 2:3-10)?

Q 13 Fill in the blanks in Figure 11.7.

language is the outward sign of this inner filling. *Second*, we should seek to be refilled with the Spirit day by day (Eph. 5:19). *Third*, other ways or means of receiving grace include:[3] praying (Heb. 4:16); fasting (Matt. 4:2; 6:16; Acts 13:2); worshiping (Acts 16:25); witnessing (Phm. 6); studying, meditating on and obeying Scripture (Matt. 4:4; 1 Pet. 2:2; 2 Pet. 1:12-21); singing spiritual songs (Col. 3:16); fellowship, church services, communion (Acts 2:42; 1 Cor. 11:23-26; Heb. 10:25); and resisting sin and serving God (Rom. 8:13-14; 2 Cor. 9:8).[4] We renew our physical strength daily by resting and eating. Likewise, we must renew our spiritual strength daily.

Pay attention to the Scriptures (2 Pet. 1:12-21). The Bible is the Word of God. The New Testament has two great passages on inspiration. Every student should memorize these two passages.

> *All Scripture is *God-breathed and is useful for teaching, rebuking, correcting and training in righteousness* (2 Tim. 3:16).

> 20 *Above all, you must understand that no prophecy of Scripture came about by the prophet's own interpretation.* 21 *For prophecy never had its origin in the will of man, but men spoke from God as they were carried along by the Holy Spirit* (2 Pet. 1:20-21).

Peter puts the words of Old Testament prophets and the words of New Testament apostles on the same level (2 Pet. 3:2). Also, Peter equates Paul's letters with *"other Scriptures."* This shows that Paul's letters were already seen as inspired (2 Pet. 3:16).[5]

Bible study helps us grow in grace as milk helps a new baby (1 Pet. 2:2). We do not live *"by bread alone."* Rather, we live *"on every word that comes from the mouth of God"* (Matt. 4:4).

> 20 *My son, pay attention to what I say; listen closely to my words.* 21 *Do not let them out of your sight, keep them within your heart;* 22 *for they are life to those who find them and health to a man's whole body* (Prov. 4:20-22).

Scripture is also a great weapon for fighting false teaching. Jesus defeated the devil using the words *"it is written"* (Matt. 4:4, 7, 10). The Bible is the sword of the Spirit (Eph. 6:17). God's Word is a lamp to our feet and a light for our path (Ps. 119:105). We should pay attention to Scripture *"as to a light shining in a dark place"* (2 Pet. 1:19).

Be on guard against false teachers (2 Pet. 2:1-22). Peter contrasts true prophecy (2 Pet. 1) with false teachers (2 Pet. 2).[6] False prophets are among believers as false prophets were among the Israelites (2 Pet. 2:1).

2 Pet. 2:	Characteristics of False Teachers
1	They will ________ introduce destructive heresies. These false teachings destroy the ________ of believers. As Paul said, they ruin the faith of entire ________ just for money (Titus 1:11).
1	They deny the sovereign Lord who ___________ them.
2	They lead many astray and give Christianity a bad ___________.
3	They create _______ to mislead and _________ people.
3-9, 12-13, 17	Their ________ is certain. God will judge them as he judged sinning _________, sinners of _________ day, and sinners of __________ and __________.
10	They follow the __________ of the flesh.
10	They despise ______________.
10	They are _________ and __________.
13-14	They never stop _____. They have eyes of ______. They are experts in _______.
15	They have _______ the straight way. They have ____ to follow the way of ______.
17-18	They are ________ without _________. They speak empty, boastful words.
18	They __________ weak or baby believers. How? By appealing to fleshly desires for wealth, success, and pleasure.
19	They promise ____________ while they themselves are _____________.
20-21	They may have once known the ________ and _______ from sin. But they became ______ of ______ again. Thus, they are worse off after they _______ than they were __________ they knew Christ.

Figure 11.7 Second Peter 2 describes the characteristics of false teachers.

Q 14 To what past judgment does Peter compare God's future judgment (2 Pet. 3:3-7)?

Live a holy life because the Lord is coming (2 Pet. 3:1-18).

> 10 *But the day of the Lord will come like a thief. The heavens will disappear with a roar; the elements will be destroyed by fire, and the earth and everything in it will*

be laid bare. [11]*Since everything will be destroyed in this way, what kind of people ought you to be? You ought to live holy and godly lives* [12]*as you look forward to the day of God and speed its coming* (2 Pet. 3:10-12).

Q 15 *Why does Peter say we should live holy and godly lives (2 Pet. 3:10-12)?*

Efforts we can make to be at peace with God when Christ returns	Scriptures
Remind ourselves that the Scriptures were ___________ by God. The Holy Spirit ___________ the writers along, protecting them from error.	2 Pet. 1:20-21; 2 Tim. 3:16
Make every effort to add the fruit of the Spirit to our faith. Be filled with the Sprit, and stay filled with the Spirit. Pray, fast, worship, study, meditate, obey, fellowship. ________ in grace so we won't _________ from our secure position.	2 Pet. 1:5-10; 3:17-18
Refuse to follow the _____ of our flesh. Rather, be led by the Spirit of _______. _______ what is right and _______ what is wrong.	2 Pet. 2:9-10; Heb. 1:9
Do not be a _________ to anything but righteousness.	2 Pet. 2:19; Rom. 6:15-18
Be on guard against ____________. Measure all _____________ by the Scriptures.	2 Pet. 2:1-22; 3:16-17
Be ___ like God is. A ____ years to us are like a ____ to our merciful Lord.	2 Pet. 3:8
Make decisions in light of _______. Live a life that is ______ and _______. God will bring a fiery _________ on all who disobey Him. But those who obey Him will inherit the _____________.	2 Pet. 3:10-13; 2 Thess. 1:6-10
____________ to be found spotless, blameless, and at peace with God. Be _____ as God is _____. Do not ______ to the ______ you had when you lived in ignorance. Live as _______ in your Babylon.	2 Pet. 3:14; 1 Pet. 1:14-15, 17; 5:13

Figure 11.8 Second Peter commands us to *"make every effort to be found spotless, blameless and at peace with God"* (2 Pet. 3:14).

Peter summarizes his purposes in the last two verses of his letter.

[17]*Therefore, dear friends, since you already know this, be on your guard so that you may not be carried away by the error of lawless men and fall from your secure position.* [18]*But grow in the grace and knowledge of our Lord and Savior Jesus Christ* (2 Pet. 3:17-18).

Q 16 *Complete the blanks in Figure 11.8.*

Q 17 *Summarize the purpose of 2 Peter based on 2 Peter 3:17-18.*

Lesson 32

First John

Goal A: *Explain how 1 John relates to the errors of the Gnostics.*

Goal B: *Summarize what 1 John teaches about Jesus Christ, sin, knowledge, and love.*

A. Author

The apostle John wrote five books in the New Testament. These are his Gospel, three letters, and Revelation. John does not state his name in 1 John. Still, there are several reasons why we believe he is the author.[7] We will note three types of evidence that show that the apostle John wrote 1 John.

- Early church fathers from the second century named the apostle John as the author. These witnesses include Irenaeus, Tertullian, Clement of Alexandria, and Origen.[8]
- The author of 1 John states that he had a close relationship with Jesus (1 John 1:1; 2:5-6, 24, 27-28). Likewise, we know that John was close to Jesus. He was *"the disciple whom Jesus loved."* He sat next to Jesus at the Last Supper (John 13:23).
- The style, words, and themes of 1 John and the Gospel of John are similar.

Q 18 *Summarize 3 reasons why we believe the apostle John wrote 1 John.*

Q 19 *Summarize what 1 John and the Gospel of John say about the Word, joy, light, the devil, and life.*

1 John	Verse	Verse	John
1:1	*That which was from the beginning, ...the Word of life.*	[1]*In the beginning was the Word, ...* [14]*The Word became flesh...*	1:1, 14
1:4	*We write this to make our joy complete.*	*"Ask and you will receive, and your joy will be complete."*	16:24
1:6-7	[6]*If we claim to have fellowship with him yet walk in the darkness, we lie...* [7]*But if we walk in the light, as he is in the light,. . .*	*"This is the verdict: Light has come into the world, but men loved darkness instead of light because their deeds were evil."*	3:19

Continued on next page

Continued from previous page

2:7	*Dear friends, I am not writing you a new command but an old one, ...*	[34]*"A new command I give you: ...As I have loved you, so you must love one another.* [35]*By this all men will know that you are my disciples, if you love one another."*	13:34-35
3:8	*He who does what is sinful is of the devil, ...*	*"You belong to your father, the devil, ..."*	8:44
3:14	*We know that we have passed from death to life, because we love our brothers.*	*"...whoever hears my word and believes...he has crossed over from death to life."*	5:24
4:6	*We are from God, and whoever knows God listens to us; ...*	*"He who belongs to God hears what God says."*	8:47
4:9	*This is how God showed his love among us: He sent his one and only Son into the world...*	*"For God so loved the world that he gave his one and only Son, ..."*	3:16; [1:14, 18]
5:9	*We accept man's testimony, but God's testimony is greater...about his Son.*	*"And the Father who sent me has himself testified concerning me."*	5:37
5:12	*He who has the Son has life; he who does not have the Son of God does not have life.*	*"Whoever believes in the Son has eternal life, but whoever rejects the Son will not see life."*	3:36

Figure 11.9 Similar verses in 1 John and the Gospel of John point back to one author for both books.

Q 20 *State at least 4 facts about the apostle John.*

Let us review some facts about John's personal life.

- John grew up in Galilee. His father, Zebedee, was a fisherman. John and his brother James were fishing with their father when Jesus called them (Matt. 4:21-22). John's mother, perhaps named Salome, was at times near Jesus (Matt. 20:20; 27:56; Mark 15:40; 16:1; John 19:25).
- John was a part of the *inner circle*. That is, he was one of the three apostles closest to Jesus. He was with Jesus at the raising of Jairus' daughter (Luke 8:51), on the mountain when Jesus was glorified (Luke 9:28), and in the Garden of Gethsemane (Mark 14:33). Also, recall that John leaned against Jesus at the Last Supper (John 13:25). He was present at the trial of Jesus (John 18:15-16). From the cross, Jesus guided John to care for Mary (John 19:26-27).
- John was one of the first to see the empty tomb (John 20:1-8). Also, he was one of the first to see the risen Lord. He saw Him in a locked room (John 20:19-28), and later in Galilee (John 21:1-24).[9]
- John was in Jerusalem when Paul and Barnabas went there about A.D. 45 (Gal. 2:6-10). Later, history records that John ministered in Ephesus. Near the end of his life, John was condemned to die on the island of Patmos. There, John suffered as Jesus had prophesied (Matt. 20:20-23). But the Lord did not forsake John. On Patmos, the old apostle received the visions he wrote about in Revelation (Rev. 1:9). We believe that John wrote Revelation about A.D. 95.[10] Likewise, we believe he wrote 1–3 John sometime during A.D. 85-95.

Figure 11.10 Illustration of the apostle John in exile on Patmos

B. Background

As we focus on 1 John, recall that it is one of the General Epistles. First John does not mention any people or cities. A letter like Romans was to a specific church. In contrast, the General Epistles were for several churches. John wrote Revelation to the seven churches in Asia. Likewise, the churches in Asia may have been the first readers of 1 John.

Q 21 *Why were some false teachers called Gnostics?*

False teachers caused great problems in the early church. One group of false teachers was called *Gnostics (pronounced Nos-tics). The religion of the Gnostics was Gnosticism. The word *Gnostics* is a form of the Greek word *gnosis*, meaning "knowledge." The Gnostics claimed to have secret knowledge. They said that everyone needed this knowledge to be saved.

All students should understand the five errors of the Gnostics.

Q 22 *Did the Gnostics believe that Jesus came as a man in flesh? Explain.*

Many of the verses in 1 John have new meaning when we understand what the Gnostics taught. John fought these false teachers by showing that Jesus Christ was both human and divine (1 John 1:1-3; 4:1-3). He wrote that Jesus is the Christ, the Son of God (1 John 2:22-23; 3:23; 4:15; 5:1, 5, 6-12, 20).

False Teachings of the Gnostics	Truth in 1 John
1. The spirit is good and the body is bad.	*That which was from the beginning, which we have heard, which we have seen with our eyes, which we have looked at and our hands have touched—this we proclaim concerning the Word of life* (1 John 1:1). *The Word became flesh, but remained sinless.* Therefore the body itself is not sinful or bad.
2. Salvation comes through secret knowledge, not the gospel.	[26]*I am writing these things to you about those who are trying to lead you astray.* [27]*As for you, the anointing you received from him remains in you, and you do not need anyone to teach you* (1 John 2:26-27). *He who has the Son of God has life; he who does not have the Son of God does not have life* (1 John 5:12).
3. Jesus was only a man. The divine Spirit of Christ joined Him at His baptism. The Spirit left Him before He died.	[2]*Every spirit that acknowledges that Jesus Christ has come in the flesh is from God,* [3]*but every spirit that does not acknowledge Jesus is not from God. This is the spirit of the antichrist, which you have heard is coming and even now is already in the world* (1 John 4:2-3). Notice that John stated *"Jesus Christ"* as one name (1 John 1:3; 2:1; 3:23; 4:2; 5:6, 20). In contrast, the Gnostics separated Jesus from the Christ.
4. The body should be treated harshly, since it is evil.	*If anyone has material possessions and sees his brother in need but has no pity on him, how can the love of God be in him?* (1 John 3:17).
5. Sinning with the body is not wrong, since only the spirit matters.	[7]*Dear children, do not let anyone lead you astray. He who does what is right is righteous, just as he is righteous.* [8]*He who does what is sinful is of the devil, because the devil has been sinning from the beginning. The reason the Son of God appeared was to destroy the devil's work* (1 John 3:7-8).

Figure 11.11 First John teaches the truth in contrast to the five errors of Gnosticism.

Group	Book Title	Book Sub-group	Date	Author
1. ________ Books (5)	______	________ Gospels	55-70	______
	______		50-68	______
	______		60	______
	______		85-95	______
	______		62	______
2. ________ Epistles (13)	______	________ Epistles	55-56	______
	______		55	
	______		56	
	______		48-49	
	______	________ Epistles	60-61	
	______		61	
	______		60-61	
	______		60-61	
	______	Epistles about the ________	50-51	
	______		51	
	______	________ Epistles	63	
	______		67	
	______		65	
3. ________ and the ________ Epistles (8)	______	Epistles to ________	65-70	______
	______		45-49	______
	______		63-65	______
	______	Epistles to correct ________	65-67	______
	______		85-90	______
	______		85-90	______
	______		85-90	______
	______		67-80	______
4. ________	______		90-95	______

Figure 11.12 Practice chart for groups, subgroups, and authors of New Testament books

Q 23 *Complete the chart on books of the New Testament. Recall the house drawing.*

Q 24 Why does 1 John emphasize that Jesus Christ came in the flesh (1 John 4:2-3)?

Q 25 Why did John refer to our Lord as "Jesus Christ," rather than Jesus?

Q 26 Are human bodies evil? Explain.

C. Purposes

John told his readers why he wrote. In his Gospel, he said he wrote so that we would believe and have eternal life (John 20:31). Likewise, in 1 John, the apostle referred eleven times to the reasons he wrote. From these verses, it is easy to see that John wrote for at least four purposes. We will study these four purposes as they appear in the outline below (I–IV). Still, students should realize that John's four purposes are not limited to parts of his letter. Rather, his four purposes are woven into the entire letter, like threads in a garment. John introduces a theme and moves on. Later, he returns to the theme again, as we return to the chorus of a song.[11] Let us look at the four purposes as they appear in the outline.

Theme	1 John
Introduction: We are sure that the Word became flesh	**1:1-4**
A. Children of God Fellowship With Him in the Light	**1:5–2:28**
Principles of fellowship with God	1:5–2:2
Evidence of fellowship with God	2:3-28
B. Children of God Know the Truth	**2:29–4:6**
Characteristics of God's children	2:29–3:18
Confidence of God's children	3:19-24
The Spirit and God's children	4:1-6
C. Children of God Love as God Loves	**4:7–5:3**
The source of love	4:7-16
The evidence of love	4:17–5:3
D. Children of God Have Assurance From Him	**5:4-20**
About life now and forever	5:4-12
About prayer and faith	5:13-20
Conclusion	**5:21**

Figure 11.13 Outline of 1 John

D. Outline

In 1 John we see how John gave believers assurance of salvation after he battled false teachers. See Figure 11.13.

E. Explanations of the outline

John wrote to complete our joy through fellowship with God (1 John 1:5–2:28). Our joy is complete as we have fellowship with the Father and His Son, Jesus Christ (1 John 1:3). John explained the conditions of fellowship with God.

Fellowship with God is possible only as we walk in the light. God is light. There is not any darkness in Him. So those who walk in the darkness cannot fellowship with God in the darkness. If we walk in the light, as He is in the light, we have fellowship with God and one another. His blood cleanses those who walk in the light (1 John 1:5-7).

Q 27 Does salvation depend on an experience or a relationship (1 John 5:12)? Explain.

Q 28 The Gnostics taught that _____, not Jesus, freed people.

Q 29 From the outline (A-D), state the 4 big truths about children of God.

Q 30 Can those who live in sin fellowship with God (1 John 1:6)? Explain.

Q 31 How does John define sin?

Q 32 Explain the difference between sins of commission and sins of omission.

Q 33 What sin of omission does John refer to in 1 John 3:17?

Q 34 Does John define sin as being less than perfect? Explain.

Fellowship with God is possible only as we turn away from *sin. Notice that the words *darkness* and *sin* mean the same thing to John. Walking in the darkness means walking in sin. Walking in the light means leaving the darkness of sin. What does John mean by sin? He says that *"sin is lawlessness"* (1 John 3:4). Sin is rebelling against God's Law. Also, John says sin is doing what is wrong (1 John 5:17). Sin is any act or attitude that is against God.[12] That is, sin is anti-God and anti-Christ.[13]

- *Sins of commission* refers to wrongs we commit. These sins may be actions or attitudes. We sin if we rebel against God by doing or meditating on what is wrong. Being tempted by an evil thought is not sin. Satan tempted Jesus with evil thoughts like bowing down to the devil. Jesus had these thoughts, but He did not sin.

Mental sin occurs when a person chooses to meditate on evil desires such as lust. One teacher explained that we sin in our thoughts if we turn sin over and over in our minds like we do a piece of candy in our mouths.[14]

- *Sins of omission* refers to the error of refusing to do the things that God commands us to do. It refers to things we omit or leave out through neglect or stubbornness. For example, it is a sin to refuse to be baptized, or to refuse to forgive. The Gnostics said that sinning did not matter. But John said that sin was darkness. One of his purposes was to remind us that darkness and light have no fellowship. *"My dear children, I write this to you so that you will not sin"* (1 John 2:1).

None of us will be perfect until we reach heaven. But the Bible does not define sin as "being less than perfect." We do NOT define *sin* as "being less than the best." Likewise, we do NOT define *holy* as "being better than the worst." Look at Figure 11.14.

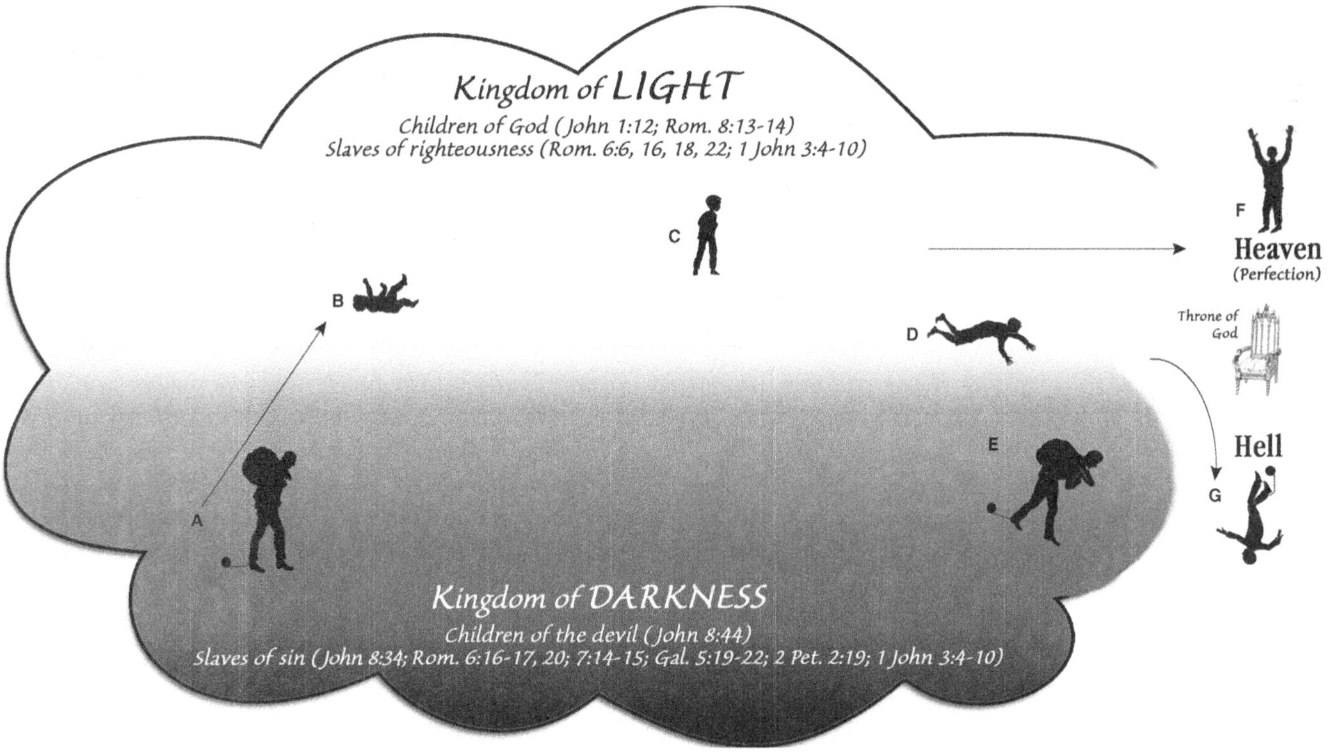

Explanations of A-G	Scriptures
A. All of us are born sinners. As sinners, we are slaves of sin, and children of the devil. As we serve sin, we add to the guilt we carry. As sin increases, the chains of sin grow stronger. All in this condition are bound for hell and need a Savior.	Rom. 3:23; Eph. 2:1; John 8:34-44; Rom. 6:16-17; 7:14-15; Gal. 5:19-22; 2 Pet. 2:19; 1 John 3:4-10
B. At conversion, we receive Jesus. He forgives us and frees us from the guilt and chains of sin. He rescuse us from the kingdom of darkness and brings us into the kingdom of light. Now, we are free to be servants or slaves of righteousness. Still, we are only babes in Christ and need to grow in grace.	John 1:12; Eph. 4:14; 5:8-11; Col. 1:12-14; Rom. 6:6, 16, 18, 22; 8:13-14; 1 Cor. 3:1-4; 1 John 3:4-10
C. We mature as we make every effort to grow in grace. This happens as we depend on the Spirit, obey Him, study the Bible, and become responsible members of His Church.	Eph. 4:14; 2 Pet. 1:5-8; 3:18; Heb. 5:11–6:3
D. Believers, especially the young and weak, may sin. If this happens, we must repent, turn away from sin, and receive the Lord's forgiveness. Those who abide in Christ will not practice sin, which is lawlessness and rebellion against God. Rather, instead of being led by the flesh (sinful nature), we will be led by the Spirit. This proves that we are the sons of God.	1 John 1:9; 3:4-10; Gal. 5:19-22; 1 Cor. 6:9-11; Rom. 8:13-14; Rev. 21:7-8
E. Some are born again, but turn back to become slaves of sin again. These forfeit their spiritual life, and lose their eternal inheritance. God is merciful and desires these to return to Him in the light. (See The Full Life Study Bible, Heb. 3:12, "Personal Apostasy.")	John 15:2, 6; Gal. 5:4; 1 Tim. 4:1; 2 Tim. 2:12; 4:3; Heb. 2:1-3; 3:6-8, 12-14; 6:4-5; 10:38; James 5:19-20; 2 Pet. 1:8-11; 3:17
F. Some persevere to the end. These live eternally and enter into the joys of heaven.	Matt. 24:12-13; 25:21-23; 2 Tim. 2:12; Heb. 10:36, 38-39; 1 Pet. 1:9; Rev. 1:9; 21:7
G. Those who reject Jesus as Savior and Lord will be eternally lost. They will be cast into the lake of fire, and tormented forever. God does not want anyone to perish, but all to repent.	Matt. 5:29-30; 8:12; John 5:28-29; 2 Pet. 3:9; Jude 7; Rev. 20:10; 21:8

Figure 11.14 Children of God in contrast to children of the devil (1 John 3:7-8)

Q 35 Describe a slave of sin (John 8:34-35; Rom. 6:16-17; 2 Pet. 2:19).

Q 36 How does a person move from the kingdom of darkness to the kingdom of light?

Q 37 What should a believer who sins do?

All of us have sinned in the past (1 John 1:8). We all rebelled against God's Law before He saved us. But Jesus "*appeared so that he might take away our sins. And in him is no sin* [darkness]" (1 John 3:5). Jesus gave us new desires when He saved us. He came to take away the roots and the branches of sin in us.[15] Now, we delight to please Him, rather than rebel against Him. Still, if we sin, John tells us not to remain in the darkness. Rather, he says we should confess our sins and repent. Then God will forgive our sins and purify us again from all unrighteousness (1 John 1:8; 2:1-2).

"*No one who lives* [abides] *in him keeps on sinning. No one who continues to sin has either seen him or known him*" (1 John 3:6). The Gnostics said doing wrong did not matter. They were trying to lead believers astray. So John wrote to correct this false teaching.

> [7]*Dear children, do not let anyone lead you astray. He who does what is right is righteous, just as he* [God] *is righteous.* [8]*He who does what is sinful is of the devil, because the devil has been sinning from the beginning. The reason the Son of God appeared was to destroy the devil's work.* [9]*No one who is born of God will continue to sin, because God's seed remains in him; he cannot go on sinning, because he has been born of God.* [10]*This is how we know who the children of God are and who the children of the devil are: Anyone who does not do what is right is not a child of God; nor is anyone who does not love his brother* (1 John 3:7-10).

Q 38 Must believers continue to sin? Explain.

Some teach that believers must continue to sin day by day. John did not teach this. He said that God's will is for us to abide in Christ, and thus avoid sinning (1 John 3:6). Do you believe it is possible to live an hour without sinning or doing wrong? Do you believe it is possible to live a day without rebelling against God? It is possible by God's grace! In fact, it is God's will for His children. He invites us to walk in His presence and in His Spirit throughout the day. He wants us to fellowship with Him in the light, moment by moment. None of us should be content to sin day by day. This was the teaching of the Gnostics! Our daily goal is to be led by the Spirit and not the flesh. Living without sinning can be a normal day for a believer. A day when we choose darkness and wrong should be unusual. The days that we obey God all day should be common. John encourages us to live without sinning. Remember that he defines sin as "being lawless or doing wrong" (1 John 3:4; 5:17).

Q 39 Do you think Don was telling the truth? Explain.

A believer named Don Stamps+ testified that he had not sinned that week. Some other believers at the meeting were surprised. Don claimed that he was not aware of rebelling against the Spirit that week. He said he did not know of any evil act he did or sinful attitude he had that week. Do you think Don was telling the truth? Do you think the apostle John lived day by day without rebelling against God? Do you think he often chose to do wrong instead of right? Do believers you know define sin the way 1 John defines it?

John says if we see a brother sin, we should pray. Why? So God will give life to the sinner (1 John 5:16). Sin causes spiritual death. It kills our relationship with God. It prevents us from having fellowship with Him. As Paul said, "*we were dead in our sins*" (Eph. 2:1). So we should pray for any brother we see sin. Turning a sinner from his error saves him from spiritual death (James 5:19-20).

Q 40 Do believers lose their salvation each time they sin? Explain.

Does one sin cause a believer to lose his or her salvation? This is a hard question. The answer is not the same in every case. On the one hand, Hebrews speaks of sinning believers who are still God's children. When we sin, God disciplines us because we are His children (Heb. 12:4-11). This shows us that we do not lose our salvation because of one sin. On the other hand, one sin can lead to the loss of salvation. Why? Because one sin often leads to another sin. Therefore, we should run from sin as from a deadly snake.

+ Donald Stamps was the main author of the notes in *The Full Life Study Bible*.

One sin caused Adam and Eve to lose Paradise (Gen. 3:23). One sin caused Achan and all of his family to lose their inheritance and their lives (Josh. 7). One sin caused Samson to lose his eyes and his relationship with God (Judg. 16:21). One sin caused Moses to lose his privilege of entering the promised land (Num. 20:1-13). One sin with Bathsheba caused David to lose his good name (2 Sam. 11). One sin of numbering the people caused 70,000 people to lose their lives (1 Chron. 21). One sin of Ananias and Sapphira resulted in their deaths (Acts 5). One sin has caused thousands to lose their marriages, reputations, and lives.

Q 41 *Do you know those who have lost much because of one sin? Give an example.*

How many sins does it take for a person to lose his or her salvation? Only one, if a person refuses to repent. God is merciful. He loves to forgive us. So why do we see people who refuse to repent? Because sin hardens a person's heart (Heb. 3:13). Water causes cement to become hard. Baking mud turns it into a brick. Likewise, sin can cause our hearts to become hard. Those with hard hearts refuse to repent. A dead tree cannot bend. Likewise, people can lose their ability to bow and repent. Therefore, believers who sin should quickly turn from sin and seek forgiveness. Let no one misjudge the danger of one sin!

Q 42 *Why do some believers refuse to repent?*

John's final word about sinning is near the end of his letter.

> *We know that anyone born of God does not continue to sin; the one who was born of God* [Jesus] *keeps him safe, and the evil one cannot harm him* (1 John 5:18).

Praise the Lord! Our Savior has delivered us from being slaves of sin (John 8:32, 34, 36). As His followers, may we be known for doing what is right. As Peter said, let none of us suffer as an evildoer (1 Pet. 4:15). Rather, let us enjoy fellowship with God, walking in the light as He is in the light. Let us abide in Christ. The Bible presents the redeemed, saved life as the complete opposite of sin.[16]

Two young people named Drew and Cara were talking. Drew claimed that he lived a life of victory over sin day by day. Cara asked, "Do you keep the great commandment? Do you love God with *all* your heart, soul, mind and strength" (Matt. 22:37)? Drew said, "To me, loving God with all my heart means two things. *First,* it means that my love for God must be number one. It must be the love in my life that reigns over all lesser loves. *Second,* my love for God must spread through my other loves as yeast spreads through dough. I do not shut my love for God out of any part of my heart. Rather, my love for Him guides my lesser loves. My love for God causes me to love myself, my neighbors, and even my enemies in ways that please Him. Also, my love for God governs how I have fun. When I choose a book, I let my love for God lead me, even if it is a book to read just for fun. When I watch television, I save a seat for Jesus beside me. If actors curse His name, I refuse to continue watching. How can I say I love God and be entertained by those who insult Him? Thus," said Drew, "I try to love God with all my heart. Most of the time, I believe I love God with all my heart. And it has been much easier since I was filled with the Holy Spirit. If the Spirit shows me an area of my heart in which I don't love God like I should, I do not respond as Cain. Rather, I repent. Then I ask Him to fill that part of my heart with His love." Cara smiled and nodded her head. She thought, "This kind of man would make a great husband and father! Submitting to him would be easy, as God intends."

Q 43 *What does the great command in Matthew 22:37 mean?*

John wrote to emphasize what God's children know (1 John 2:29–4:6). We noted above, under Background, that the Gnostics claimed to have secret knowledge. They said believers needed more knowledge to be saved. In contrast, 1 John emphasizes that we are already saved. We already know what we need to know about salvation. First John uses a form of the word *know* 33 times (Figure 11.15). John contrasted what we know with the secret knowledge that the Gnostics said we need.

Q 44 *Fill in the blanks in Figure 11.15.*

Q 45 *Why does 1 John emphasize the word "know"?*

1 John	Verses in 1 John that emphasize what WE KNOW
2:3	*We know that we have come to know him if ________________________.*
2:4	*The man who says, "I know him," but does not do what he commands is a _______,*
2:5-6	*This is how we know we are in him: whoever claims to live in him must ________.*
2:11	*But whoever hates his brother is in the darkness and walks around in the darkness; he does not know where he is going, because ________________.*
2:18	*Even now many ________ have come. This is how we know it is the last hour.*
2:20	*But you have ________ from the Holy One, and all of you know _________.*
2:21	*I do not write to you because you do not know the truth, but because you do know it and because __________.*
2:29	*If you know that he is righteous, you know that everyone who does ________________.*
3:1	*The reason the world does not know us is that ____________________.*
3:2	*Dear friends, now we are children of God, and what we will be has not yet been made known. But we know that when he appears, _________________.*
3:5	*But you know that he appeared so that ____________. And in him is no _________.*
3:10	*This is how we know who the _________ of God are and who the ________ of the devil are: Anyone who does not do __________ of God; nor is anyone who does not ________ brother.*
3:14	*We know ___________, because we love our brothers. Anyone who does not love remains in ________.*
3:15	*Anyone who hates his brother is a ________, and you know that no ________ has ________.*
3:16	*This is how we know what _______ is: Jesus Christ _______ for us. And we ought to _______ for our brothers.*
3:18-19	*Dear children, let us not love with ________ or ________, but with _______ and in _______. This then is how we know that we belong to the truth, and how we set our hearts at rest in his presence.*
3:24	*And this is how we know that he lives in us: We know it by _______________.*
4:8	*Whoever does not _______ does not know God, because ____________.*
4:13	*We know that we live in him and he in us, because _____________________.*
4:16	*And so we know and rely on _________. God is _________. Whoever lives in ____________.*
5:2	*This is how we know that we love the children of God: __________________.*
5:13	*I write these things to you who believe in the name of the Son of God so that _______________.*
5:15	*And if we know that he hears us—whatever we ask—we know that _________________.*
5:18	*We know that anyone born of God does not continue ________; the one who was born of God keeps him safe, and the evil one cannot harm him.*
5:19	*We know that we are children of God, and that the whole world is _________________.*
5:20	*We know also that the Son of God has come and has given us understanding, so that ______________.*

Figure 11.15
First John contrasts what *"we know"* with the "secret knowledge" of the Gnostics.

John wrote to remind us to love one another (1 John 4:7–5:3).

Q 46 *Fill in the blanks in Figure 11.16.*

1 John	Verses in 1 John that remind us to love one another
2:9	*Anyone who* ____________________ *is still in the darkness.*
2:10	*Whoever* __________ *lives in the light, and there is nothing in him to make him* __________.
3:12	*Do not be like* ______ *who belonged to* _______ *and* ______ *his brother.*
3:14	*We know that we have passed from death to life because* ______________.
3:16	*This is how we know what love is* ______________. *We ought to* ____ ____________.
3:17	*If anyone* __________________________, *how can the love of God be in him?*
3:18	*Dear children, let us not love with* ______ *or* _____ [only] *but with* ______ *and in* ______.
4:7	*Dear friends, let us love one another, for* _________. *Everyone who loves* ___________.
4:11	*Dear friends, since* ____________________, *we also ought to love one another.*
4:20	*Anyone who does not love his brother, whom he has seen, cannot* _______ ____________.
5:2	*This is how we know that we love the children of God:* ____________ __________.

Figure 11.16 Love one another.

Q 47 *How is loving one another related to setting our hearts at rest in God's presence (1 John 3:16-22)?*

Q 48 *What are 2 signs of being born again (1 John 4:7; 5:1)?*

John wrote to give us assurance from God (1 John 5:4-20). The Gnostics claimed that Jesus was only a man. They said that the Spirit of God came on Him at baptism and left before His death. In contrast, John says that Jesus Christ came through water and blood. That is, Jesus is the divine Christ who came through the waters of baptism. And, He came through the blood of the cross. Also, the Spirit bears witness in our hearts that Jesus died for us. Thus, John assures us that the Spirit, water, and blood testify about Jesus Christ.

Q 49 *Why does John emphasize water and blood (1 John 5:6, 8)?*

Q 50 *1 John 5:12 assures us of what?*

Q 51 *What assurance does John give in 1 John 5:14-17?*

Q 52 *What 3 things does 1 John 5:18-20 assure us that we know?*

Test Yourself: Circle the letter by the ***best*** completion to each question or statement.

1. Second Peter and First John both warn of
a) the Antichrist.
b) false teachers.
c) persecution.
d) a great famine.

2. Second Peter says the right attitude toward is
a) Relax and let God cause you to grow.
b) Make every effort to grow in grace.
c) Discern that all who are born again grow.
d) Depend on the church for growing in grace.

3. Peter contrasts those who grow in grace with
a) those who remain babies in Christ.
b) those who fall from God's grace.
c) those who depend on themselves.
d) those who use grace to cover sin.

4. Second Peter 1:21 includes the words
a) *"For prophecy never had its origin in the will of man"*
b) *"...you accepted it...as the word of God...*
c) *"All Scripture is God-breathed and is useful "*
d) *"His letters contain some things that are hard...*

5. Those who *fall from grace* (2 Pet. 3:17)
a) never knew God.
b) are secure in Christ.
c) lose rewards in heaven.
d) lose their salvation.

6. Second Peter says that false teachers follow
a) Adam.
b) Balaam.
c) Jezebel.
d) Achan.

7. John wrote his first Epistle to correct the errors of
a) Judaizers.
b) Herodians.
c) Gnostics.
d) Zealots.

8. First John stresses that
a) believers have secret knowledge.
b) Jesus Christ was God in flesh.
c) we cannot know if we are saved.
d) we should ignore needs of the body.

9. How does 1 John define *sin?*
a) Missing the mark
b) Not being perfect
c) Lawlessness
d) Making a mistake

10. John says we know we are God's children if
a) we pay our tithes.
b) we love our brother.
c) we do not feel guilty.
d) we confess our sins.

Essay Test Topics: Write 50-100 words on each of these goals that you studied in this chapter.

Second Peter

Goal: *Explain 2 Peter's contrasts between growing in grace and falling from grace.*

Goal: *Summarize what 2 Peter says about the Scriptures and false teachers.*

First John

Goal: *Explain how 1 John relates to the errors of the Gnostics.*

Goal: *Summarize what 1 John teaches about Jesus Christ, sin, knowledge, and love.*

Figure 11.17 John was probably very old when he wrote 1–3 John and Revelation.

Figure 11.18 A photo of the island of Patmos, where John wrote Revelation

Chapter 12:

Letters About False Teaching—Part 2: 2 and 3 John and Jude

Figure 12.1 In New Testament times, believers often met in homes. Also, teachers traveled and stayed a few days in the homes of faithful believers, like Gaius and Demetrius.

Introduction

In our world, writings and teachings increase faster than anyone could imagine. People produce magazines at an amazing rate. Likewise, new books appear every day. The largest bookstore in the world now has millions of different books. But not everything that people say or print is true.

Which spreads faster, truth or lies? People have debated this question for years. Some think that truth has stronger wings and flies faster and further than error. Others believe that for every tongue that spreads truth, there are two tongues that spread gossip and error.

The most important contest between truth and error is on the topic of religion. More religious books are printed today than ever before. And there are more preachers and teachers than ever before. False teachers claim to teach the truth of the Bible. But they twist and distort the Scriptures. Thus they destroy themselves and others (2 Pet. 3:16).

We find the truth, not by the mind alone, but also by the heart.[1] Some try to find truth using only the head or only the heart. Many of these are led astray. To find the truth we must use both the head and the heart. The Bible and the Spirit work together to guide us into all truth. The Bible is a bright light that shines in the darkness (2 Pet. 1:19-21). God's word is a lamp to our feet and a light for our paths (Ps. 119:105). Also, God's Spirit guides us into all truth (John 16:16; 1 John 2:20, 26-27). Second Peter and First John warn against false teachers. These brief letters in the Bible teach us that walking in truth means walking in love, holiness, and righteousness.

Lessons:

Second John

33 **Goal A:** *Identify 3 passages in 2 John that are similar to those in 1 John and the Gospel of John.*

Goal B: *Explain the relationship between love and truth in 2 John.*

Third John

34 **Goal:** *Describe Gaius, Diotrephes, and Demetrius in 3 John.*

Jude

35 **Goal A:** *State the author and purpose of Jude.*

Goal B: *Summarize how we got the canons of the Old and New Testaments.*

Key Words

chosen lady	Gaius	Demetrius	Enoch	Apocrypha	Jerome
Gnostics	Diotrephes	contend	Pseudepigrapha		

Lesson 33 Second John

Goal A: *Identify 3 passages in 2 John that are similar to those in 1 John and the Gospel of John.*

Goal B: *Explain the relationship between love and truth in 2 John.*

We are continuing our study of Hebrews and the seven General Epistles. What is the common theme of Hebrews, James, and 1 Peter? What is the theme of the five books, 2 Peter through Jude? Which three of the General Epistles have only one chapter each?

Q 1 *Try to sing the books of the New Testament in less than 30 seconds.*

A. Author and date

We have already noted that the apostle John wrote a Gospel, three letters, and Revelation. Take a moment to review some facts about John. We studied these at the beginning of lesson 29 in chapter 11. John was one of the closest apostles to Jesus.

Q 2 *Draw a house of New Testament books. Fill in the 27 names.*

We believe that the apostle John wrote all three of his Epistles between A.D. 85-95. Figure 12.2 shows similar verses in 2 John, 1 John, and the Gospel of John. These similarities suggest that one author wrote all three books.

Q 3 *Why do we think the same author wrote the Gospel of John and 1–2 John?*

2 John		1 John		Gospel of John	
5	*Dear lady, I am not writing you a new command…*	2:7	*Dear friends, I am not writing you a new command but an old one…*	13:34-35	*"A new command I give you: Love one another."*
6	*This is love: that we walk in obedience to his commands.*	5:3	*This is love for God: to obey his commands. And his commands are not [a burden].*	14:23	*"If anyone loves me, he will obey my teaching."*
7	*Many deceivers, who do not acknowledge Jesus Christ as coming in the flesh, have gone out into the world. Any such person is the deceiver and the antichrist.*	4:3	*Every spirit that does not acknowledge Jesus is not from God. This is the spirit of the antichrist…*	8:42	*"If God were your Father, you would love me, for I came from God…"*
12	*I hope to visit you and talk with you face to face, so that our joy may be complete.*	1:4	*We write this to make our joy complete.*	16:24	*"Ask and you will receive, and your joy will be complete."*

Figure 12.2 Similar verses in 2 John, 1 John, and John suggest the same author.

B. Outline

Q 4 *Why does 2 John emphasize the word "truth"?*

Theme	2 John
Greeting	**1-3**
To the *chosen lady	1
Because of the truth	2-3 [11 times]
A. Praise for Truth	**4**
B. Command to Love	**5-6**
C. Warning About False Teachers	**7-11**
Discern false teachers.	7
Beware, lest they deceive you.	8-9
Refuse to have them in your home.	10-11
Closing	**12-13**

Figure 12.3 Outline of 2 John

C. Explanations of the outline

Greeting (2 John 1-3). John the apostle was old when he wrote this letter. He refers to himself as *the elder*. This was probably a title of honor due to John's age. He was the last apostle to die.[2]

Q 5 *Who was the lady to whom John wrote? Explain.*

John wrote to the chosen or elect lady and her children. Some think that this lady was a widow John knew. This may be. However, there are three reasons why we think the words *elect lady* refer to a local church.

- In referring to the lady, John uses the word *you* in verses 5, 8, 10, and 12. In the Greek, the form of the word *you* is plural.[3] So, in writing to the *lady,* John is writing to a group of people. Thus, the lady is probably a church.
- Peter uses similar words. *"She who is in Babylon, chosen together with you, sends you her greetings"* (1 Pet. 5:13). Peter referred to the church as *she.* He sent greetings from the church in Babylon to other believers. Likewise John referred to the church as a *chosen lady.* The word *church* in Greek is *ekklesia.* This is a feminine word. It does not surprise us that the bride of Christ is called a *chosen lady.* Likewise, the *lady's children* probably refers to the church's members.
- John sends greetings from *"the children of your chosen sister"* (2 John 13). This likely refers to the church that John was pastoring.

Peter and John may have avoided the word *church* because of danger. The Caesars were persecuting believers. Thus, referring to the church as a *lady* gave safety.

Q 6 *How is Christian love related to truth? Explain.*

Notice that John links love and truth in verses 1 and 3.[4] The apostle says he "*loves*" the chosen lady and her children "*in the truth.*" And he says Jesus will be with us "*in truth and love*" (verse 3). Christian love is always in the realm of truth. The world uses the word *love* in lesser ways. To those of the world, love may refer to passion, desire, and lust that offend God. But Christian love is always righteous and true. Worldly love is often sick, soft, weak, and selfish. Sinners are in darkness, yet say they *love.* But biblical love is always in the light and in the truth. Christian love is strong. It does not close its eyes to error that leads to destruction. John's love caused him to warn believers. Think about how love is truthful as you read the 13 verses in 2 John.

Praise for truth (2 John 4). John had great joy because some of the lady's children were walking in truth. Every Christian parent and grandparent delights in righteous children. Still, John did not hide a sad fact. Not all of the church's members walk in truth. Some, like Ananias and Sapphira, are in the church, but not of the church. For now, the wheat and the weeds grow side by side. When Jesus returns, the angels will *"weed out of his kingdom everything that causes sin and all who do evil"* (Matt. 13:41).

Command to love (2 John 5-6). Love is a big theme in John's Gospel and in 1–3 John. Earlier, he wrote, *"Dear friends, since God so loved us, we also ought to love one another"* (1 John 4:11; John 13:34-35). Some people are harder to love than others. But God commands us to love other believers. How does love show itself? Love forgives others, as God forgave us. It shares with those in need, as the Good Samaritan did. Love visits those who are suffering. It prays for those who need God's help. Love reaches out a hand to those who need a friend. It listens when others speak. And as John emphasizes, love stands firmly for the truth.

Q 7 *Does loving others mean we must agree with their teachings? Explain.*

Warning about false teachers (2 John 7-11). Like 1 John, 2 John describes false teachers as those who deny that Jesus Christ came in the flesh. Recall that the *Gnostics said that Jesus was only a man. They claimed that God's Spirit came on Him at baptism, and left Him before the cross. John said these false teachers were antichrist (verse 7). In contrast, true teaching about Christ declares that He is God's Son (verse 3). The true gospel says that Jesus Christ is the Son of God who came in the flesh. God's Spirit was in Him in the womb and on the cross.

Q 8 *Who are those who "run ahead" (verse 9)?*

The Gnostics claimed to have new truth. They said that they had moved ahead of the gospel. Likewise, today, some claim to know more than apostles like Paul and John did. They say that the apostles were like children who needed to grow in knowledge. We recognize that those who *run ahead* of Scripture are false teachers. Have you heard any who claim to have truth that goes beyond and contradicts the Bible?

Believers must watch out for false teachers. We must reject all whose teaching rejects the Bible. Those who reject the teachings of Christ reject Christ.

Q 9 *Will God judge pastors who welcome false teachers? Explain.*

It is wrong to welcome false teachers to teach in our homes and churches. Recall that in John's time, many churches met in homes. Also, teachers traveled around. They needed a place to sleep and food to eat. So some welcomed these visiting teachers into their homes. There, the visitors would eat, sleep, and teach. Anyone who receives or helps a prophet in his work will receive a prophet's reward. And anyone who receives a righteous man because that man is righteous will receive a righteous man's reward (Matt. 10:40-41). But John warns that anyone who welcomes (supports) false teachers shares in their sin (2 John 11)! Love and truth must be united. Our love for God does not allow us to support false teachers.

Figure 12.4 The scene in New York just before terrorists guided the second plane to crash on September 11, 2001

September 11, 2001, was a sad day in the world. Two airplanes in America were taken over by a group of radical Muslim *terrorists. They crashed each of the planes into two tall buildings called the World Trade Center, in New York. As a result, thousands were killed. Some pastors and churches wanted to show that they still loved Muslims. So they invited Muslims to speak in their churches. It is good to love all people. But those who teach in our homes and churches should teach truth from the Bible.

Closing (2 John 12-13). Why was John's letter to the chosen lady so short?

I have much to write to you, but I do not want to use paper and ink. Instead, I hope to visit you and talk with you face to face, so that our joy may be complete (2 John 12).

Lesson 34

Third John

Goal: *Describe Gaius, Diotrephes, and Demetrius in 3 John.*

A. Author and date

John the apostle is the author of 3 John. Figure 12.6 shows similar words and phrases from 3 John and 2 John. Take a moment to look at these similarities. We believe that John wrote the three Epistles between A.D. 85-95.

3 John		2 John	
1	*The elder, To my dear friend Gaius, ...*	1	*The elder, To the chosen lady and her children, ...*
1	*whom I love in the truth.*	1	*whom I love in the truth—...*
4	*I have no greater joy than to hear that my children are walking in the truth.*	4	*It has given me great joy to find some of your children walking in the truth, ...*
13-14	*I have much to write you, but I do not want to do so with pen and ink. I hope to see you soon, and we will talk face to face.*	12	*I have much to write to you, but I do not want to use paper and ink. Instead, I hope to visit you and talk with you face to face, ...*

Figure 12.6 Similar verses in 3 John and 2 John point back to the same author.

B. Outline

Theme	3 John
Greeting	**1-2**
A. *Gaius: A Faithful Man	3-8
B. *Diotrephes: A Proud Man	9-11
C. *Demetrius: A Good Man	12
Conclusion	**13-14**

Figure 12.5 Outline of 3 John

C. Explanations of the outline

Greeting (3 John 1-2). John wrote his third letter to his dear friend, Gaius. In the Greek, the word *dear* is *agapetos*. This word means "dear, loved, or beloved." It appears ten times in John's three letters.

Gaius must have been known among the churches of Asia. John ministered in these churches during the last years of his life.

Q 10 *What are 3 ways in which 3 John and 2 John are alike?*

The name *Gaius* appears several times in the New Testament. We read about Gaius of Corinth (Rom. 16:23), Gaius of Macedonia (Acts 19:29), and Gaius of Derbe (Acts 20:4).

Q 11 Who was Gaius?

In verse 2, John prayed that Gaius would enjoy good health as his soul prospered. Jesus and the apostles cared about physical and spiritual needs. They recognized that people have bodies and souls.

Q 12 What is the greatest joy of a parent or pastor?

Gaius: a faithful man (3 John 3-8). In verses 3-4, John praises Gaius for walking in the truth. Truth is not only for the mind. It is also for the feet! The greatest joy of pastors, parents, or grandparents is to hear that their children are walking in the truth. The greatest joy of teachers is to hear that their students are walking in the truth. Truth is only helpful as it affects our feet.

Q 13 What is the big difference between 2 John and 3 John?

We see a big difference between 3 John and 2 John in verses 5-8. Earlier we noted how these two letters are alike. But there is one big difference between them. In 2 John, the apostle warned believers not to show hospitality to unworthy teachers. But in 3 John, he tells them to show hospitality to worthy teachers. Gaius was faithful to God by being kind to worthy preachers and teachers.

Recall that Jesus sent the apostles out in pairs to preach. He told them to stay in the homes of worthy people (Matt. 10:10-11). Likewise, in John's time, some continued to travel and preach. The elder praised Gaius for welcoming worthy preachers into his home. By helping God's workers, we are partners in truth (8).

Q 14 What error did Diotrephes make?

Diotrephes: a proud man (3 John 9-11). In contrast to Gaius, we see Diotrephes. Perhaps he was a local pastor or strong-willed elder. He was not kind to the visiting preachers. Why? John said that Diotrephes was proud. Like a king or dictator, he wanted to be the only leader. He rejected a letter from the apostle John (verse 9). Then he gossiped about John (verse 10). Diotrephes was not satisfied with refusing to help the visitors. He also stopped those who wanted to help them. And he put those out of the church who did welcome them. Thus we see that this proud leader was lacking in love and kindness. Leading and loving must go hand in hand.[5]

Q 15 What change did Jesus make in John over the years? Explain.

In passing, let us note John's love in dealing with this problem. John was a great and famous apostle. And he was the only living apostle of the Twelve. Yet a little leader like Diotrephes insulted this spiritual giant. As a young apostle, John might have tried to call down fire on Diotrephes. Recall what James and John did when the Samaritans rejected them? They wanted to call down fire to destroy them (Luke 9:54). That is why Jesus called James and John the Sons of Thunder. But Jesus changed John from an apostle of thunder to an apostle of love. As an elder, John wrote about Diotrephes with love. Yes, Diotrephes had rejected those working for Jesus. But John himself once made this same mistake. He rebuked one who was casting out demons in the name of Jesus (Mark 9:38). John had to correct Diotrephes, but he was gentle. The mistakes we make help us show love to others who make the same errors.

Demetrius: a good man (3 John 12). Demetrius had a good reputation. Perhaps he was the messenger who carried John's letter to Gaius. Or he may have been the pastor of a town near Gaius. Diotrephes had a bad reputation. But all spoke well of Demetrius.

Conclusion (3 John 13-14). As in 2 John, the elder says he hopes to visit them soon (verses 13-14). If so, he will call attention to the errors of Diotrephes (verse 10). Thus, John's letter gave Diotrephes time to repent.

Lesson 35 Jude

Goal A: *State the author and purpose of Jude.*

Goal B: *Summarize how we got the canons of the Old and New Testaments.*

Q 16 Which Jude wrote the Epistle of Jude? Explain.

Congratulations! You have come to the last of the General Epistles. Jude wrote to believers. These may have been Jews, Gentiles, or both. Jude is in the General Epistles because it was not written to a specific person or church.

As you begin to study Jude, take a few minutes to read through this short, fiery Epistle. Notice the many times Jude writes his thoughts in triplets (Figure 12.7).

A. Author and date

The author refers to himself in verse 1 as Jude (Judas in Greek). Was this the apostle Jude? Or was it the half-brother of Jesus? There are two reasons why we think the author is the Lord's half-brother.

- Jude says he is the brother of James. The Gospels mention only two brothers called Jude and James. These are the half-brothers of Jesus (Matt. 13:55; Mark 6:3). These same two brothers appear as believers in Acts 1:14. Therefore, it appears that the author of Jude is the half-brother of Jesus and full brother of James. We noted earlier that James was a leader in Jerusalem and the author of the book of James. Thus we believe that the two half-brothers of Jesus both wrote books in the General Epistles.
- Jude, the half-brother of Jesus, was not an apostle. And the writer of Jude seems to exclude himself from the apostles. He seems to refer to the apostles as a separate group (verse 17).

The date of Jude is linked to 2 Peter. Figure 12.8 shows similar verses in these two Epistles. But which came first, Jude or 2 Peter? Jude 17-18 seems to refer to 2 Peter 3:3. This suggests that Jude wrote after Peter. If so, Jude probably wrote in A.D. 70-80. During those years, believers faced false teachers like those Jude described.

Jude	Topic	Triplet or three-fold statement
1	The readers	*called … loved … kept*
2	Prayer	*Mercy, peace and love*
4	The false teachers	*Were written about … change grace … deny Christ*
5-7	Sinners God judged	*Israel in the wilderness, angels, Sodom*
8	The false teachers	*pollute … reject … slander*
11	3 sinners God judged	*Cain, Balaam, Korah*
12	False teachers	*rainless clouds … fruitless trees … twice dead*
14	The Lord is	*coming … to judge … to convict*
16	The false teachers	*Grumblers … faultfinders … followers of their own evil desires*
19	False teachers	*divide you … follow fleshly desires … do not have the Spirit*
20-21	Believers	*build yourselves up … pray … wait*
22-23	Helping weak believers	*be merciful … snatch … show mercy mixed with fear*
25	To God	*Glory … majesty … power and authority*
25	God's honor	*before all ages, now and forevermore!*

Figure 12.7 Three-fold statements in Jude[6]

B. Purpose

Jude wanted to write and rejoice about the blessings of salvation, but something was more important. There is a time when all leaders must teach against error. False teachers, like wolves, were among God's sheep. So Jude felt he must warn believers about these false teachers.

> *Dear friends, although I was very eager to write to you about the salvation we share, I felt I had to write and urge you to *contend* [fight, battle, struggle] *for the faith that was once for all entrusted to the saints* (Jude 3).

Q 17 What was Jude's purpose?

Godless men were using grace as an excuse or license to sin (verse 4). Jude said that the false teachers were denying Jesus Christ, our Sovereign and Lord. That is, these ungodly teachers refused to let Christ rule over them. Sin is anti-Christ. It is rebelling against the law or rule of Christ (1 John 3:4). Jude, like 2 Peter, rebukes those who say we can live in sin because we are covered by grace. Jude, like Paul, teaches that those who practice sin will not inherit heaven (Gal. 5:19-21).

Q 18 Are those who live in sin blameless because of grace? Explain.

Three words or phrases in Jude 3 deserve special attention.

Q 19 Explain the words "contend, faith, and once for all" in Jude 3.

- The *faith* refers to all the truth or true beliefs of the Church. The truth of Scripture is our weapon against error (Eph. 6:17; 2 Tim. 3:16). God gave us the truths of our faith through the apostles (verse 17).
- Jude urged believers to *contend,* wrestle, or fight for the faith. God gave the truth to the Church. It is the Church's responsibility to keep the truth pure and free from false doctrine (See Gal. 1:6-9; 1 Tim. 1:19; 6:3, 20-21; 2 Tim. 1:13-14). As believers, God expects us to resist, rebuke, and reject false teachers. This is why Jude urged all believers to *"contend"* or fight for the faith.

Q 20 Which is more important, unity or truth? Why?

- The faith or truth of the Bible was given *once for all.* That is, the truth of the gospel is final and unchanging. It is old, but ever new. As believers, we cannot allow false teachers to change the truth God gave us in Scripture.

The false teachers were enemies of God and the Bible. These Gnostics said that sin did not matter. Jude accused them of sexual sins (verses 4, 8, 16, 18). He said that they rebelled like Cain (verse 11). They were greedy like Balaam and rebellious like Korah (11). They were proud and deceitful (verses 8, 16). The false teachers were led by the flesh and caused divisions (verse 19).[7]

Q 21 *How are false teachers like "hidden reefs"?*

One translation says the false teachers were "*hidden reefs*" (Jude 12, NASB). A reef is a chain of rocks, *coral, or sand just under the surface of the water.[8] It can damage and even destroy ships that crash into it because they do not know it is there. Likewise, false teachers surprise young and weak believers and destroy their faith (1 Tim. 1:19; Titus 1:11).

Q 22 *What are 5 things that Jude and 2 Peter 2 both say about false teachers?*

Jude and 2 Peter 2 are much alike. Take time to compare the verses in Figure 12.8.

Jude		2 Peter 2	
6	*And the angels who did not keep their positions of authority but abandoned* [left] *their own home—these he has kept in darkness, bound with everlasting chains for judgment on the great Day.*	*For if God did not spare angels when they sinned, but sent them to hell, putting them into gloomy dungeons* [dark prisons] *to be held for judgment;*	4
7	*In a similar way, Sodom and Gomorrah and the surrounding towns gave themselves up to sexual immorality and perversion. They serve as an example of those who suffer the punishment of eternal fire.*	*if he condemned the cities of Sodom and Gomorrah by burning them to ashes, and made them an example of what is going to happen to the ungodly;*	6
8	*In the very same way, these dreamers pollute their own bodies, reject authority and slander celestial beings [evil angels].*	*This is especially true of those who follow the corrupt desire of the sinful nature and despise authority. Bold and arrogant [proud], these men are not afraid to slander celestial beings* [evil angels];	10
9	*But even the archangel Michael, when he was disputing with the devil about the body of Moses, did not dare to bring a slanderous accusation against him, but said, "The Lord rebuke you!"*	*yet even angels, although they are stronger and more powerful, do not bring slanderous accusations against such beings* [evil angels] *in the presence of the Lord.*	11
10	*Yet these men speak abusively against whatever they do not understand; and what things they do understand by instinct, like unreasoning animals* [that don't think]*—these are the very things that destroy them.*	*But these men blaspheme in matters they do not understand. They are like brute beasts, creatures of instinct, born only to be caught and destroyed, and like beasts they too will perish.*	12
12a	*These men are blemishes at your love feasts, eating with you without the slightest qualm* [without feeling guilty]*—shepherds who feed only themselves.*	*They will be paid back with harm for the harm they have done. Their idea of pleasure is to carouse in broad daylight. They are blots and blemishes* [spots], *reveling in* [enjoying] *their pleasures while they feast with you.*	13
12b-13	*They are clouds without rain, blown along by the wind; *autumn trees, without fruit and uprooted—twice dead. 13They are wild waves of the sea, foaming up their shame; wandering stars, for whom blackest darkness has been reserved forever.*	*These men are springs without water and mists driven by a storm. Blackest darkness is reserved for them.*	17
16	*These men are grumblers and faultfinders; they follow their own evil desires; they boast about themselves and flatter others for their own advantage.*	*For they mouth* [speak] *empty, boastful words and, by appealing to the lustful desires of sinful human nature, they entice people who are just escaping from those who live in error.*	18
17-18	*17But, dear friends, remember what the apostles of our Lord Jesus Christ foretold. 18They said to you, "In the last times there will be scoffers who will follow their own ungodly desires."*	*2I want you to recall the words spoken in the past by the holy prophets and the command given by our Lord and Savior through your apostles. 3First of all, you must understand that in the last days scoffers will come, scoffing and following their own evil desires.*	3:2-3

Figure 12.8 Jude and 2 Peter have similar verses about false teachers.[9]

C. Outline

Theme	Jude
Greeting	**1-2**
A. Purpose: Defense of the Faith	**3-4**
B. Warning About False Teachers	**5-16**
Their judgment illustrated	5-7
1. Israel	5
2. Angels who fell	6
3. Sodom and Gomorrah	7
Their condition described	8-16
1. Their speech	8-10
2. Their character	11-13
3. Their destruction	14-16
C. Counsel to Believers	**17-23**
Remember what the apostles warned	17-19
Build yourselves up by praying in the Spirit	20
Keep yourselves in God's love	21
Help others through mercy and fear	22-23
Prayer	**24-25**

Figure 12.9 Outline of Jude

Figure 12.10 Jude warns that God will judge false teachers as He judged Sodom and Gomorrah. (Doré)

Q 23 *What error were the false teachers of Jude's day teaching?*

D. Explanations of the outline

Warning about false teachers (Jude 5-16). Jude describes the condition of false teachers in verses 8-16. Look at Figure 12.8. It compares Jude with 2 Peter 2.

Q 24 *Complete Figure 12.12.*

Illustration	Principle	Jude
God destroyed the Israelites in the desert after He delivered them from Egypt.	Destruction can follow deliverance.	5
There are angels in darkness and chains.	Eternal judgment can come to those God has given a high position and privilege.	6
God destroyed Sodom and Gomorrah because of sexual sins.	Eternal fire will be the punishment of all who live sinful lives.	7

Figure 12.11 Principles of judgment based on Jude

Jude	Teaching
8-10	One teacher said that Satan is like a lion with no teeth or claws. Do you agree with this? ________________ ________________
11	Jude compares false teachers to ________, ________, and ________.
12-13	Explain how Jude compares false teachers to stains, shepherds, clouds, trees, waves, and stars. ________________ ________________ ________________

Figure 12.12 Jude describes the speech and character of false teachers (Jude 8-13).

Counsel to believers (Jude 17-23). Jude urges believers to do four things.

- **Remember what the apostles warned** (Jude 17-19). *"They said to you, 'In the last times there will be scoffers who will follow their own ungodly desires' "* (Jude 18).

Q 25 *How does Jude 18 relate to 2 Peter 3:3?*

- **Build yourselves up, praying in the Spirit** (verse 20). The best translation of Jude 20 from the Greek is: *"Building yourselves up in your most holy faith* [by] *praying in the Holy Spirit"* (Jude 20; See NASB). Notice that the word *and* is not in Jude 20. The NIV adds *and,* but the word *and* (*kai* in Greek) is not in any Greek text. What does *"praying in the Holy Spirit"* mean in Jude 20? The Spirit helps us pray in many ways. Paul wrote that we should *"pray in the Spirit on all occasions with all kinds of prayers and requests"* (Eph. 6:18).

Q 26 *What does Jude 20 mean*

But Jude 20 links praying in the Spirit to building ourselves up. Noting this link may help us understand what Jude 20 means. Jude was a Pentecostal believer. He was in the upper room with the apostles (Acts 1:14). So to Jude, praying in the Spirit had to include praying in tongues. *Praying in the Holy Spirit* reminds us of Paul's words in 1 Corinthians 14:4. There, Paul wrote that whoever speaks in tongues edifies or builds himself up. Paul prayed in tongues, by the Spirit, more than all the Corinthians (1 Cor. 14:18). Why? Because praying in tongues builds up the one praying. In a church service, we focus on building others up. Therefore, when we are with other believers, we seek to prophesy or speak in tongues and interpret. This edifies others. But much of private prayer is to build ourselves up. It is biblical to build ourselves up by praying in tongues as the Spirit leads us (1 Cor. 14:4; Jude 20).

Q 27 Explain the balance between God's part and our part in salvation (Jude 21).

Figure 12.13
Pentecost in the upper room by Doré. Jude spoke in tongues on the Day of Pentecost (Acts 2).

- **Keep yourselves in God's love** (v. 21). This shows us that we have a responsibility. We should not expect God to take care of us without our help. Near the start of his letter, Jude says we are *"loved by God the Father and kept by Jesus Christ"* (Jude 1). And near the end of his letter he gives glory to God *"who is able to keep you from falling"* (Jude 24). Thus, verses 1 and 24 of Jude focus on God's part in our salvation. But Jude reminds us to keep a balance between God's part and our part. So he says, *"keep yourselves in God's love."* Our part in salvation is small compared to God's part. But God does not save anyone who refuses to keep in step with the Spirit (Gal. 5:16). This is a big theme in Jude. The false teachers said that sinning did not matter. But Jude reminds us that our choices either keep us in God's love or eternally separate us from Him. He gives us the grace we need, but we must respond to it.
- **Help others through mercy and fear** (verses 22-23). Read these two verses in Jude. Jude writes as though he is speaking to a pastor or elder. He mentions three methods of dealing with the weak. We do not help everyone in the same way. It is important to be led by the Spirit in helping those who are weak or sinning. Note Jude's attitude of fear and hate toward sin. He compares sin to a bleeding sore that stains a person's clothes. Would you enjoy holding a shirt stained by blood and disease? No? Then have the same attitude toward the sins of those whom you help!

Q 28 To what does Jude compare sins? Explain.

Jude's closing prayer is like a mountaintop (verses 24-25). Some think that it is the most glorious prayer that closes a book of the New Testament.

E. The books in our Bible

Jude 14-15 refers to a prophecy made by *Enoch. How did Jude know about this prophecy? Perhaps by oral tradition handed down from parents to their children. Much truth is passed on this way from one generation to the next.

The prophecy Jude quotes is also found in the book of Enoch. This book claims that the Enoch of Genesis 5:18-24 was its author. But the book of Enoch did not appear until the first century. We do not know if it was written before or after the book of Jude. However, it may be that Jude and the writer of Enoch referred to the same oral source.[10]

Enoch was the seventh generation if we count Adam as the first (Gen. 5:18-24).

[14]Enoch, the seventh from Adam, prophesied about these men: "See, the Lord is coming with thousands upon thousands of his holy ones [15]to judge everyone, and

to convict all the ungodly of all the ungodly acts they have done in the ungodly way, and of all the harsh words ungodly sinners have spoken against him" (Jude 14-15).

The book of Enoch is not in any Bible. It is part of a group of books called the *Pseudepigrapha (Figure 12.14). The prefix *pseud* means "false." *Epigrapha* (plural) means "written" or "inscribed." Thus, *pseudepigrapha* are false writings. *Authors* who used false names wrote some of the books in the Pseudepigrapha. For example, the Enoch of Genesis did not write the book of Enoch, though many of the thoughts in the book may be his. So it is false to say that Enoch wrote the book. Books in the Pseudepigrapha contain some truth. But they also contain false statements. Therefore, they were not worthy to include in the Bible.

Books of the Pseudepigrapha		
1. 1 Enoch	7. Testament of Job	13. Life of Adam and Eve
2. 2 Enoch	8. Lives of the Prophets	14. Psalms of Solomon
3. 2 Baruch	9. Assumption of Moses	15. Letter of Aristeas
4. 3 Baruch	10.Martyrdom of Isaiah	16. 3 Maccabees
5. Sibylline Oracles	11.Paralipomena (Chronicles) of Jeremiah	17. 4 Maccabees
6. Testaments of the 12 Patriarchs	12. Jubilees	

Figure 12.14 Books in the Pseudepigrapha[12]

Why did biblical writers sometimes quote from a book that was not completely true? All truth is God's truth. Paul quoted Greek poets three times to illustrate his points (Acts 17:28; 1 Cor. 15:33; Titus 1:12).[11] This does not mean that everything those poets wrote was true. Using the poet's words fulfilled Paul's purposes. Likewise, Jesus referred to a local saying about the weather (Matt. 16:2-3). Another time He quoted a local proverb about a doctor (Luke 4:23). Again, the Lord referred to a tower that fell in Siloam and killed 18 people (Luke 13:4). There are thousands of sayings and events that are true. The Bible refers to some of these, whether they are found in local histories, poets, or other books. Similarly, all illustrations in sermons do not come from the Bible. Preachers refer to various truths and events outside of Scripture. Therefore, do not stumble if a biblical writer quotes from a book that is not in the Bible. All truth is God's truth. So biblical writers felt free to refer to truth wherever the Spirit led them. However, finding truth in some books is like eating fish. You must separate the meat from the bones. Many books contain some truth and some error. In contrast, the Bible contains no errors (2 Tim. 3:16; 2 Pet. 1:20-21).

Q 29 *Did the Enoch of Genesis write the book of Enoch? Explain.*

Q 30 *Why did Paul quote Greek poets?*

So how did the Protestants get the books in their Bible? Why are there books in the Catholic Bible that are not in the Protestant Bible? These types of questions are usually covered in a course on introduction to the Bible. We deal with questions like these in our course on the Bible, God, and angels. Still, we will note a few facts in passing.

- The first believers did not have New Testament Scriptures. They depended on the Jewish Scriptures, the oral teachings of Jesus, the teachings of the apostles, and the ministry of the Holy Spirit. Even after the apostles wrote, it took years for the whole church to have all of the New Testament writings.
- We refer to the books of our Bible as being in the *Canon. The word *canon* first meant "a standard used to measure." Today, the Canon refers to a *list* of books in our Bible. We consider these books to be inspired by God. Books were chosen to be in the New Testament because they met two standards. *First,* the authors were apostles or those who worked closely with apostles. These books showed signs that they came from the first century. *Second,* the message was the gospel truth of the apostles.[13]
- The 39 books of our Old Testament are the same books that the Jews accepted at the time of Jesus.[14] At the time of Jesus, the Jews of Jerusalem referred to their Scriptures as a fixed, well-known group of books. Quotes like *"It is written"* show that the Jewish Scriptures had the authority of God Himself (Matt. 4:10).

Q 31 *What does the word "canon" mean?*

Q 32 *How did we get the 39 books in the Old Testament?*

- The list of books in the Old Testament was an example for making a list of books in the New Testament. Under the old covenant, God's people referred to a list of inspired books. Therefore, we would expect God's people under the new covenant to refer to a list of inspired books.

Q 33 *How did the Holy Spirit help biblical writers (John 14:26)?*

- Jesus promised the apostles that the Holy Spirit would remind them of everything He had said (John 14:26). We believe that the Spirit guided the biblical writers to remember and record God's truth for us (2 Tim. 3:16; 2 Pet. 1:20-21).

Q 34 *When was the list of New Testament books completed?*

- The list of our 27 books of the New Testament formed over a period of three centuries. During those years, church leaders discussed the list many times. But they did not force the list on church members. Rather, the books that were really from God testified for themselves. The Spirit of God in believers testified about which writings were from God.[15] The list of our 27 books, as we know it today, was approved by A.D. 367.[16] But even before this, believers had already approved the books. The church councils merely stamped what the Church already believed. It is a matter of faith to believe that God guided the early church in choosing the books in our Bible.[17]

Q 35 *Why do we reject the books of the Apocrypha?*

- The Catholic Bible and some Eastern Orthodox Bibles contain some books that were not a part of the Hebrew Scriptures.18 We group these books into a class called the *Apocrypha. The word *Apocrypha* first meant "hidden books." Later, it came to mean "not in the Canon, or list."[19] The books in the Apocrypha contain some truth. But they also contain error.

Q 36 *When did the Catholic Church decide to accept some of the Apocryphal books?*

- The books in the Apocrypha did not meet the standards set for Scripture. The Catholics did not officially accept them until 1546, at the Council of Trent. (Trent is a city in Northern Italy.) Back then, during the time of Martin Luther, the Catholics accepted seven Apocryphal books: Tobit, Judith, Wisdom, Ecclesiasticus, Baruch, and 1 and 2 Maccabees. Also, they included minor additions to the books of Esther and Daniel.[20] These books were in the Septuagint.[21] But all of these books were rejected from the Hebrew Scriptures during Christ's time. Neither Jesus nor the apostles quote any of the Apocryphal books.[22]

Books of the Apocrypha Related to the Old Testament		
1. 1 Esdras (Ezra)	6. Wisdom of Solomon	11. Susanna
2. 2 Esdras (Apocalypse of Ezra)	7. Ecclesiasticus (Sirach)	12. Bel and the Dragon
3. Tobit	8. Baruch	13. Prayer of Manasseh
4. Judith	9. Letter of Jeremiah	14. 1 Maccabees
5. Additions to Esther	10. Prayer of Azariah & Song of the Three Young Men[23]	15. 2 Maccabees

Figure 12.15 *Jerome's list of books in the Apocrypha[24]

Test Yourself: Circle the letter by the ***best*** completion to each question or statement.

1. One evidence that the apostle John wrote John, 2 John, and 3 John is that
a) there are similar phrases in them.
b) all claim to be written by the apostle John.
c) Paul tells us that John wrote these books.
d) all three books refer to the antichrist.

2. 2 John, 3 John, and Jude are
a) letters written from prison.
b) letters to suffering believers.
c) letters written to pastors.
d) letters about false teaching.

3. According to 2 John, love is linked to
a) faith.
b) mercy.
c) truth.
d) justice.

4. What does John say about Demetrius?
a) He was a proud person.
b) He was spoken well of.
c) He did not walk in truth.
d) He was John's son in the faith.

5. John praised Gaius because he
a) suffered for Christ.
b) helped strangers.
c) was very intelligent.
d) had great faith.

6. What was true of Diotrephes?
a) He showed humility.
b) He was not a believer.
c) He loved to be first.
d) He walked in truth.

7. The author of Jude was
a) the brother of James the apostle.
b) the brother of Jesus.
c) the apostle Jude.
d) the son of Alphaeus.

8. Jude emphasized that believers should
a) love one another.
b) study the Scriptures.
c) rebuke the devil.
d) fight for the faith.

9. To what did the word *canon* first refer?
a) A gun
b) A council
c) A standard
d) A book

10. About when was the list of New Testament books approved?
a) A.D. 150
b) A.D. 250
c) A.D. 350
d) A.D. 450

Essay Test Topics: Write 50-100 words on each of these goals that you studied in this chapter.

Second John

Goal: *Identify 3 passages in 2 John that are similar to those in 1 John and the Gospel of John.*

Goal: *Explain the relationship between love and truth in 2 John.*

Third John

Goal: *Describe Gaius, Diotrephes, and Demetrius.*

Jude

Goal: *State the author and purpose of Jude.*

Goal: *Summarize how we got the canons of the Old and New Testaments*

Chapter 13:
The Book of Revelation

Figure 13.1 John saw Jesus returning as the KING OF KINGS AND LORD OF LORDS (Rev. 19:11-16).

Introduction

There was once a skit or drama for children. Its purpose was to teach about the armor of God in Ephesians 6:10-18. In the drama, one man was dressed like a Roman soldier. Besides his white clothes, he wore a helmet, a breastplate, a belt, and sandals. Also, he held a shield and a sword. The soldier in white represented a believer.

His enemy was dressed in black and represented the devil. In the skit, the two men pretended to fight each other. Finally, the warrior in white conquered the one in black.

When the drama was over, the leader asked some of the children to explain the meaning. What did it teach them? Some of the older children said the drama showed that it is important to wear the armor of God. Others said that the drama was about the need for truth or faith. But one small child spoke up and said, "This drama shows us that the man in white wins in the end."

The Book of Revelation is hard to understand in all of its details. But one message stands out above everything else. In the end, Jesus wins! John saw Him returning as a conqueror on a white horse. Those following Him were clothed in white and riding on white horses (Rev. 19:11-14). He will return as the King of kings and Lord of lords. Why? He comes to reward His holy ones and judge His enemies. The great theme of Revelation is that Jesus wins, and those who overcome evil will reign with Him.

Lessons:

36 **The Background of Revelation**

Goal: *Analyze the name, author, date, setting, and themes of Revelation.*

37 **Understanding Revelation**

Goal A: *Evaluate 4 ways of interpreting Revelation.*

Goal B: *Divide Revelation into 3 parts based on Revelation 1:19. Note the chapters for each part.*

Goal C: *Summarize 5 descriptions of Jesus in Revelation.*

38 **Symbols, Characters, and Contrasts in Revelation**

Goal A: *Explain how John uses symbols and characters in Revelation.*

Goal B: *Identify 5 contrasts in Revelation.*

Key Words

Revelation	Lamb	historist	Antichrist	beasts	false prophet
apocalyptic	preterist	idealist	futurist	harlot	Lord God
				bride	Almighty

Congratulations! You have made it to the last book of the New Testament. You are about to study God's final word to us in the New Testament. More than any other book in the Bible, *Revelation reveals Jesus. It gives over 70 descriptions of our Savior. The Gospels tell about Christ's first coming. Revelation tells about His second coming as the KING OF KINGS AND LORD OF LORDS. It unveils the ultimate victory of Christ over evil.

Q 1 Define apocalyptic, and give 2 examples of apocalyptic books.

Before beginning your study of Revelation, take a few minutes to study Figure 13.2. It will help you review what you have learned about each book of the New Testament.

Book	Author	Date+ (A.D.)	Place of writing	Theme
James	James, Jesus' half-brother	45-49	Jerusalem	Faith that works in suffering, in salvation, and in holy living
Galatians	Paul	49	Antioch in Syria	We are saved by faith in Christ, not by obeying the law of Moses.
1 Thessalonians	Paul	51	Corinth	The Second Coming of Christ
2 Thessalonians	Paul	51-52	Corinth	The Second Coming of Christ
1 Corinthians	Paul	55-56	Ephesus	Church questions and answers, problems and solutions
2 Corinthians	Paul	55-56	Macedonia	The apostle Paul in contrast with false apostles
Mark	Mark	55-65	Rome	Jesus, the Servant
Romans	Paul	57	Corinth	Righteousness that comes by faith in Jesus
Luke	Luke	60-63	Rome	Jesus, the divine Savior of all
1 Peter	Peter	60-63	Rome	Suffering as Jesus did
Matthew	Matthew	60-69	Antioch in Syria	Jesus, the Messiah and King of the Jews
Philemon	Paul	62	Rome	Love reconciles; it brings enemies together as friends.
Colossians	Paul	62	Rome	Jesus is Supreme, and the Head of the Church.
Ephesians	Paul	62	Rome	The Church is the body of Christ.
Philippians	Paul	62-63	Rome	Joy in living for Christ
Acts	Luke	63	Rome	The spread of the gospel from Jerusalem to Rome by the power of the Holy Spirit
1 Timothy	Paul	65	Macedonia	Teaching and managing the church; godly living
Titus	Paul	65-66	Nicopolis	Managing and teaching the church; godly living
2 Peter	Peter	66-68	Rome	Grow in grace; use the Scriptures against false teachers.
2 Timothy	Paul	67	Rome	Instructions to Timothy for the last days
Hebrews	Unknown	67-69	Unknown	Jesus is better.
Jude	Jude, Jesus' half-brother	70-80	Unknown	Fight for the faith; keep it pure from false teaching.
John	John	80-95	Ephesus	Believe in Jesus, the Son of God.
1 John	John	85-95	Ephesus	Children of God walk in light, know truth, and love others.
2 John	John	85-95	Ephesus	Love and truth
3 John	John	85-95	Ephesus	Being faithful to the truth and those who preach and teach it
Revelation	John	95	Patmos	Jesus will return to conquer evil and rule over His kingdom.

Figure 13.2 Chart of books in the New Testament, arranged by dates from the first book to the last

+ We are not sure of exact dates

Lesson 36

The Background of Revelation

Goal: *Analyze the name, author, date, setting, and themes of Revelation.*

Figure 13.3 Coin with image of Domitian, the emperor from A.D. 81–96

A. Name

**Revelation* comes from the Greek word *apokalupto*. This word means to "unveil" or "uncover" something that is hidden. Likewise, *apocalyptic books like Daniel and Revelation unveil the future.[1]

Revelation removes a veil in two ways. *First*, it lets us see Jesus in His glory. We will study pictures and descriptions of Jesus as we survey this book. *Second*, Revelation unveils future events like the return of Jesus to conquer evil. Do not try to divorce the person from the prophecy of the future.[2] Revelation unveils Jesus and His future victory.

Q 2 How do apocalyptic books tell their message?

Revelation is a blend of three types or forms of writing.

- The *first* form is *apocalyptic*. This final book of the Bible begins with the words *"The Revelation"* or *apokalupsis* (Rev. 1:1). This form of writing uses visions and symbols to unveil the future. Other examples of apocalyptic writings are Ezekiel, Daniel, and Zechariah.
- A *second* form of writing in Revelation is *prophetic*. John refers to *"the words of this prophecy"* (Rev. 1:3). Prophetic writings give the Word of God about the present and the future. The writings of the prophets usually have fewer visions and symbols than apocalyptic writings. The Major and Minor Prophets of the Old Testament are other examples of prophetic writings.
- A *third* form of writing in Revelation is *letter*. John wrote Revelation as a letter *"to the seven churches"* (Rev. 1:4). From the greeting through chapter 22, Revelation is a letter. Other examples of letters in the Bible are the letters of Paul and Peter.

B. Author and date

Q 3 Summarize 2 reasons why we believe that the apostle John wrote Revelation.

The Holy Spirit carried and inspired each biblical writer. We believe that the writer of Revelation was the apostle John, the son of Zebedee and brother of James. There are at least four reasons why we affirm that the apostle John was the author.

- The author refers to himself as John four times in Revelation (Rev. 1:1, 4, 9; 22:8). The book reveals that he was a Jew who knew the Scriptures well. It is also clear that he only needed to mention his name for the seven churches to recognize him. Thus most Bible teachers agree that this well-known, spiritual writer was John the apostle.
- The author was suffering and condemned to die. This matches what Jesus told John about suffering. Recall that the Lord promised James and John that they would both drink of His cup of suffering (Matt. 20:20-23). James was beheaded. John was probably the one condemned to die on the island of Patmos.
- The Holy Spirit inspired John to write his Gospel and three Epistles. There are phrases and subjects in Revelation that are the same as those in John's earlier writings. For example, John presents Jesus as *"the Word"* in John 1:1 and 14 and again in 1 John 1:1. Then in Revelation he also refers to Jesus as *"the Word of God"* (Rev. 19:13). No other New Testament writer refers to Jesus as *"the Word."* Another example is that John is the only Gospel writer who calls Jesus *"the *Lamb"* (John 1:29). The Lamb is a major emphasis in Revelation. This adds to the evidence that the apostle John wrote Revelation.
- The style and some of the words in Revelation are different from John's other books. However, we would expect this because the setting of Revelation is unusual. When John wrote his Gospel, he was younger and was calmly writing about earthly experiences. Revelation is a book filled with emotion. John was an old prisoner suffering on an island when he wrote it. Over and over he wrote what he saw in a

Figure 13.4 Looking from the mainland of Turkey to the island of Patmos

vision or heard an angel tell him. Thus we would expect the style and language of Revelation to be different from John's earlier books.

- Many of the early church fathers such as Irenaeus,[3] Tertullian,[4] Justin Martyr,[5] Hermas, and Origen believed that the apostle John was the author.[6]

The apostle John probably wrote Revelation[7] about A.D. 95.[8] This was the date that most of the early church fathers and historians agreed on.[9] The Roman ruler of that time was Domitian. He was a cruel Caesar who ruled from A.D. 81-96.

Q 4 Is it true that John wrote to Ephesus about 40 years after Paul was there? Explain.

C. Setting

John tells us that he was suffering on the island of Patmos when he wrote Revelation (Rev. 1:9). This island was in the Aegean Sea near the seven churches of Revelation 2–3. Patmos was a place where the Roman government sent criminals to die. Thus John was not alone on Patmos. The Roman ruler Domitian probably exiled John to Patmos for two reasons. He was punishing John for refusing to worship him, the Caesar, and for preaching that Jesus Christ is Lord.

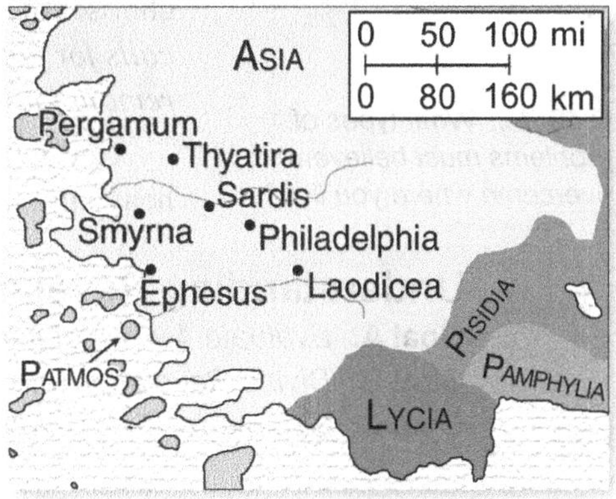

Figure 13.5 Map of the seven churches of Asia Minor and the island of Patmos (Rev. 1:9-11)

The books of the New Testament are for the entire Church. Still, they were written to certain people or churches. John wrote Revelation to the seven churches in Asia (Rev. 1:4). The message that the Holy Spirit inspired him to write is for believers of all times. But to interpret Revelation correctly, we need to understand as much as possible about the first readers.

Believers were facing persecution when John wrote Revelation. Domitian made a law that everyone had to bow and worship him as a god. But faithful Christians said that Jesus was Lord. They refused to worship the Roman Caesars. Refusing to worship Caesar could cause believers to lose their jobs, friends, families, and even their lives. Faithful Christians became known as enemies of the government. Thus, loyalty to Jesus brought persecution.

Q 5 Describe John's setting when he wrote Revelation.

Q 6 Which of the seven churches is the farthest north?

The demand to worship the Roman emperors was a major cause of persecution for Christians. But there were at least four other sources of suffering. *First,* the religions of the Greeks and Romans caused problems for believers. There were many temples, feasts, and public meetings related to these gods. Christians were persecuted when they refused to take part. *Second,* there were the local or native religions. Some of these emphasized fertility or fruitfulness. *Third,* the emphasis on Greek and Roman worldly wisdom was a cause of suffering. Also, there were many other false teachings. Believers were persecuted because they trusted in the wisdom from above, rather than human teachings. *Finally,* persecution came from the unbelieving Jews. The Roman government did not require Jews to worship Caesar. They were allowed to worship in their synagogues. But the unbelieving Jews often rejected Jews who accepted Jesus as the Messiah. Thus they were forced out of the synagogues. When this happened, the believing Jews were no longer protected from worshiping the Roman rulers. This led to great persecution. Thus, Satan used several forces to persecute believers. Discerning these forces of persecution will help us understand John's praises and rebukes to the seven churches. Persecution was causing some believers to compromise (Rev. 2:14-15, 20). They were bending their beliefs to avoid persecution.

Q 7 What were 4 sources of persecution for the first readers of Revelation?

Figure 13.6 Ruins of an old church in Philadelphia (Asia Minor)

D. Themes

The *first* theme of Revelation is the greatest. It is that Jesus will return to triumph over all evil.[10] John emphasizes that the time of Christ's return is near (Rev. 1:3; 22:12, 20). Then all will know that He is "*the ruler of the kings of the earth*" (Rev. 1:5). John summarizes this big theme in Revelation 1:7.

Q 8 What are the 2 themes of Revelation?

> *Look, he is coming with the clouds, and every eye will see him, even those who pierced him; and all the peoples of the earth will mourn because of him. So shall it be! Amen* (Rev. 1:7).

The final victory of Jesus Christ over all His enemies is certain.[11]

Q 9 *Does our spiritual inheritance depend only on Jesus? Explain.*

A *second* theme of Revelation is that only those who overcome evil in this life will inherit the Kingdom. The Lord inspired Revelation to encourage believers facing persecution. Satan was working through the Roman Caesars. Together, the devil and the Caesars were opposing God. They were trying to draw worship away from God and the Lamb.[12] John makes it plain that each person must choose between the Lamb and the beast. No one can love both the world and God (1 John 2:15-17). Each person who chooses the mark of the beast will be tormented forever (Rev. 14:9-11). Therefore, "*This calls for patient endurance on the part of the saints who obey God's commandments and remain faithful to Jesus*" (Rev. 14:12).

Q 10 *What types of problems must believers overcome where you live?*

God will give a crown of life to those who are faithful unto death (Rev. 2:10). The heavenly kingdom is only for those who overcome by God's grace.

Lesson 37

Understanding Revelation

Goal A: *Evaluate 4 ways of interpreting Revelation.*

Goal B: *Divide Revelation into 3 parts based on Revelation 1:19. Note the chapters for each part.*

Goal C: *Summarize 5 descriptions of Jesus in Revelation.*

A. Four views for interpreting Revelation

There are four main directions on a map. Likewise, there are four different ways that believers interpret Revelation.

Q 11 *What does the preterist view of Revelation teach?*

The *first* is the past or *preterist view. Those with this view say that Revelation 1–18 happened in the first century.[13] They say that the prophecies of Revelation were fulfilled as the first Christians struggled against Rome. Therefore, these people emphasize the past. They believe that Revelation says little about the future.

It is true that some of Revelation applied directly to the early church. The city of Rome was built on seven hills (Rev. 17:9). The Roman Caesars or emperors were cruel to Christians. But the preterist view seems to conflict with other Scriptures. It seems impossible to fit all of Revelation 1–18 into the first century. For example, none of the people on earth were ever forced to take a mark on the right hand or the forehead (Rev. 13:16-17).

Q 12 *How does the historist view of Revelation differ from the preterist view?*

The *second* view is the *historist or historical view. Christians with this view also face the past. But unlike those with the preterist view, they do not limit Revelation to the first 100 years of the Church. Instead, they try to match Revelation with events of history, from the early church to the present. Key things this view emphasizes include historical events like the rise of the Catholic Church and the Crusades. Those following the historical view do not see a Great Tribulation at the end of the age. Rather, they spread the Tribulation and other events over the history of the Church. The problem with this view is that each generation interprets Revelation in a different way![14]

Q 13 *Does the idealist view of Revelation teach that there will be an Antichrist? Explain.*

The *third* view is the spiritual or *idealist view. Unlike the first two views, this does not face the past. We could say that those with this view look up! They say that Revelation is about spiritual ideas, not real people or events. They believe that Revelation is like a parable. It did not happen and will not happen. They say that the book emphasizes spiritual warfare and God's triumph over evil. The problem with this view is that it contradicts other Scriptures. For example, Paul does not say that the *Antichrist is only an idea. He teaches that the Antichrist will be a real person (2 Thess. 2:3-12). We cannot accept any view like this one that does not agree with the rest of the Bible.

Q 14 *How does the futurist view of Revelation differ from the preterist view?*

The *fourth* view is the *futurist view. This is the view of multitudes of believers today. As futurists, we believe that Revelation 5–19 will take place during a period of about 7 years. This 7-year period of tribulation is based on Daniel 9:27. These 7 years of God's wrath and judgment will end with the return of Jesus Christ.[15] Then Revelation 20–22 will follow. Throughout this book, we view Revelation as mostly about the future. There are fewer problems with the futurist view than with the other three views.[16]

John saw the Roman Empire as a great beast that hated the Church. Still, in the last days, there will be another beast like the Roman Empire. This beast will persecute believers and rule during the final 7 years of tribulation. We must not forget that prophecy is often fulfilled in two ways. There may be an historical fulfillment, but also an end-time fulfillment. For example, in Matthew 24 Jesus prophesied many events. Some of these were fulfilled historically in A.D. 70. But the greatest fulfillment will come at the end of the age.[17]

B. The outline and structure of Revelation

Many Bible teachers like Revelation 1:19 as a natural outline of the book. "*Write, therefore, what you have seen, what is now and what will take place later.*" This verse suggests that there are three parts to the book of Revelation.

- *What you have seen* refers to the vision that John saw of Christ (Rev. 1).
- *What is now* refers to the seven churches in Asia Minor (Rev. 2–3).
- *What will take place later* refers to the future (Rev. 4–22).
- No other outline seems to be easier or clearer than this one.[18] Consider it as you study the chart that follows.

Q 15 *How does Revelation 1:19 serve as an outline of the book? (Give chapters in your answer.)*

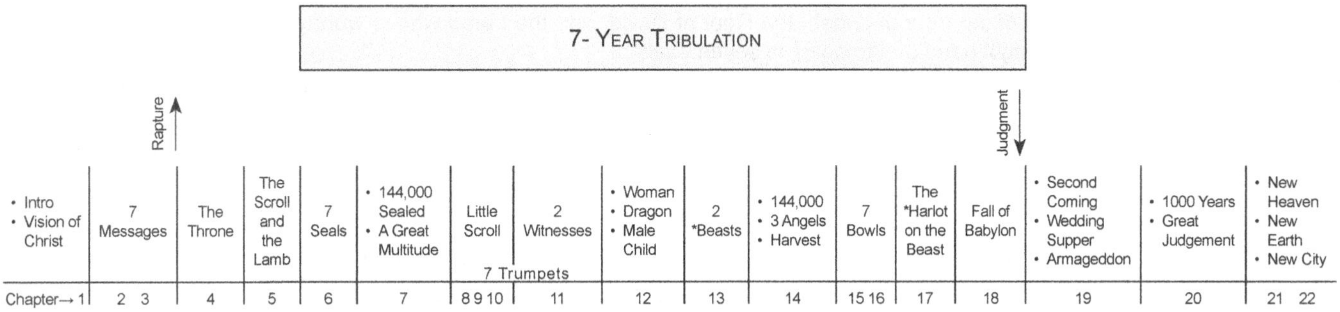

Figure 13.7 Overview chart of Revelation

C. The 7 seals, 7 trumpets, and 7 bowls

John writes about three groups of sevens: the seals, trumpets, and bowls. The judgments become worse and worse. The seals are less severe than the trumpets. And the trumpets are less frightening than the bowls.[19] Together, the seals, trumpets, and bowls stretch from Revelation 5–16.

How do the seals, trumpets and bowls relate to one another? Time is too short to answer that question in this study. For a thorough discussion, study *Revelation & Daniel* by Dr. Glen D. Cole in the *Faith & Action Series*.[20]

Figure 13.8 The first four seals: four horsemen (Rev. 6:1-8)

D. Pictures and descriptions of Jesus in Revelation

The greatest value of Revelation is not what it teaches about the dragon, the beast from the sea, or the beast from the earth. Nor is the highest value of Revelation in what it teaches about the new heaven, the new earth, and the New Jerusalem. The supreme value of Revelation is what the book teaches about Jesus. All of the treasures of wisdom and knowledge are hidden in Christ (Col. 2:3).

Revelation gives us insights about Jesus that no other book gives. The partial lists that follow show some of the things that Revelation reveals about Jesus. Enjoy these. Do not be in a hurry. This is a good time to worship.

Rev.	Revelation reveals Jesus as:
1:7	The One coming with clouds whom all the peoples of earth will see and mourn over
1:13-16	The One walking among the *lampstands with white hair, eyes like fire, feet like bronze, and a voice like rushing waters. The One with a sword flashing from His mouth and a face shining like the sun
2:2	The One who knows when believers work hard, do good deeds, persevere, do not tolerate wicked men, and expose false apostles
2:4	The first love of every believer

Continued on next page

Continued from previous page

Rev.	Revelation reveals Jesus as:
2:5, 16, 22; 3:3, 19	The One who calls the churches to repent
2:7, 11, 17, 29; 3:3, 6, 13, 22	The One who emphasizes that we should hear what the Spirit says to the churches
2:9	The One who knows the afflictions, poverty, and spiritual condition of believers
2:10	The One who tells us not to be afraid of what we will suffer. The One who promises to give those who are faithful to death a crown of life
3:5	The One who will not blot out the names of overcomers from the book of life, but will confess their names to the Father (2 Tim. 2:12)
3:8	The One who knows when a believer has only a little strength
3:10	The One who will keep patient believers from the hour of trial (this will come on the whole world to test them)
3:11	The One who is coming soon, and who warns believers not to lose their crowns
3:15-16	The One who will spit the lukewarm believer out of His mouth
3:19	The One who rebukes and disciplines those He loves
3:20	The One who knocks on the door of each lukewarm believer's heart, wanting to come in
5:5-9; 6:1-12; 8:1	The Lion of the tribe of Judah, the Root of David, and the Lamb who is worthy to take the scroll from the Father's right hand and to open its seven seals
5:9-10	The One who gave His life's blood to purchase men for God, and made them a kingdom and priests who will serve God as they reign on earth
5:11-14	The One whom the angels and every creature declare to be worthy to receive power, wisdom, strength, honor, glory, and praise
6:16-17	The One who, with the Father, will pour out wrath on the wicked of the earth
7:9-17	The One who is worshiped by the saints who come out of the Great Tribulation, and who will protect them forever
7:17	The Lamb at the center of the throne
7:17	The Shepherd of those who come out of the Great Tribulation
11:15	The One who will reign forever over the kingdom of the world
12:5; 19:15	Israel's Son who will rule the nations with an iron *scepter (rod)
13:8	The One who owns the book of life
14:14-16	The Son of Man, seated on a cloud, wearing a gold crown, holding a sharp sickle
17:14	The One who overcomes the ten kings
19:7	The Bridegroom who will come for His *bride
19:10	The theme of prophecy
19:11	The Rider who is called Faithful and True
19:13	The One whose name is the Word of God
19:14	The One who leads the armies of heaven
19:15, 19-21	The One who strikes down the nations with the sword of His mouth
19:15	The One who treads the winepress of the wrath of God Almighty
19:16	The King of Kings and Lord of Lords
20:4	The One who reigns a thousand years
21:22-23	The temple and the lamp of the Holy City, the New Jerusalem
22:4	The One who will show us His face and put His name on our foreheads
22:7, 12, 20	The One who is coming soon
22:7; (1:3)	The One who blesses those who keep the words of the prophecy of Revelation

Figure 13.9 Insights about Jesus in Revelation 1–22

Q 16 *Which 5 things that Revelation reveals about Jesus mean the most to you? Why?*

All else is poverty compared to the wealth of knowing Jesus Christ.

- It is good to study each of the seven seals on the scroll. But it is nothing compared to rejoicing over One in heaven worthy to open the scroll! Let us bow with the thousands of angels, the elders, the four living creatures, and all of creation to worship the Lamb (Rev. 5:6-14).

- It is interesting to study the seven trumpets one by one. But the trumpet that means the most to us is the one that will announce the return of our beloved Savior (1 Thess. 4:15-18).
- Likewise, we may tremble as we read about the seven bowls of God's wrath (Rev. 15–16). These bowls of wrath are poured out as the Antichrist reigns on seven hills. But what is all of this compared to the fact that God poured out His love for us on the hill of Calvary? May it never be the false christ on a white horse that captures the attention of the saints (Rev. 6:1-2). It is the true Christ returning on a white horse with His saints that lifts our spirits (Rev. 19:11-16). All that thrills our souls is Jesus!

Lesson 38

Symbols, Characters, and Contrasts in Revelation

Goal A: *Explain how John uses symbols and characters in Revelation.*

Goal B: *Identify 5 contrasts in Revelation.*

A. Symbols in Revelation

Earlier, we noted that apocalyptic writings speak through symbols. God may have inspired John to use symbols in order to protect Christians. Symbols are only discerned and understood by believers. The enemies of Jesus could not use His parables to condemn Him. Likewise, the enemies of believers could not use Revelation to condemn believers.

Q 17 *What are 2 examples that show that symbols give us powerful pictures?*

But there is a greater reason why John used symbols. Symbols give us word pictures that add emotion and value to truth. John could have said that Jesus walked among the seven churches. However, using the symbol of a lampstand instead of the word *church* gives us a picture. The lampstand reminds us that the churches are in the world to give light in the darkness. Likewise, John could have said that an evil leader would rise to rule the world. But he used the symbol of a beast instead of the words *evil leader*. The symbol of a beast emphasizes the kind of leader that the Antichrist will be. Again, John contrasted the symbols of a pure bride and a harlot instead of just contrasting the Church with a worldly system.[21] Symbols communicate truth in a powerful, emotional way.

It is important to allow Revelation to explain its own symbols when

Rev.	Symbol	Rev.	Meaning
1:12-13	7 lampstands	1:20	7 churches
1:16	7 stars	1:20	7 messengers or pastors
2:28	the morning star	22:16	Jesus
3:7	key of David	3:7-8	power to open and close doors
4:5	7 lamps	4:5	7-fold Spirit of God; the Holy Spirit
5:6	the Lamb	17:14	Jesus, Lord of lords and King of kings
5:6	7 eyes	5:6	7-fold Spirit of God; the Holy Spirit
5:8	golden bowls full of incense	5:8	prayers of the saints
6:1-8	4 horses and riders	6:1-8	conquest, war, famine, and death
9:1	fallen star	9:1	an angel
12:1-2, 5	woman and child	12:5	Israel and Christ
12:3; 20:2	red dragon, old serpent	12:9; 20:2	Satan, the devil
12:4	1/3 of the stars of heaven	12:7-9	fallen angels
12:14	a time, times and ½ a time	12:6	1,260 days = 3½ years
13:1-10; 17:8-12	the beast out of the sea, with 7 heads and 10 horns	17:11	the Antichrist who is the 8th king, and his kingdom
13:1; 17:3, 7	7 heads of the beast	17:9-10	7 hills and 7 kings
13:1; 17:3, 7	10 horns of the beast	17:12-13, 16-17	10 kings with the beast who is the Antichrist
13:11-17	the beast out of the earth	19:20	the false prophet
17:1-7	the great harlot, Babylon the Great, who sits on a beast with 7 heads and 10 horns	17:9, 18	the great city that sits on 7 hills and rules over the kings of the earth
17:1	the waters on which the woman sits	17:15	the peoples of the world
19:8	fine linen	19:8	righteous deeds of the saints
19:11-16	the rider of the white horse	19:16	Christ, King of kings and Lord of lords
22:16	the Root of David	22:16	Jesus

Figure 13.10 Symbols and their meanings in Revelation[22]

Q 18 *What do the following symbols mean: lampstands, dragon, fine linen, 10 horns?*

Q 19 *Give 2 examples of powerful symbols in your country.*

Q 20 *Name at least 6 characters in Revelation.*

possible. The parables that we understand best today are the ones that Jesus explained. Likewise, the symbols we understand best in Revelation are the ones John explained to us. The chart that follows lists many of the symbols in Revelation. The left column gives the symbol and the reference. The right column gives the place in Revelation where John interprets the meaning of symbols. Read Figure 13.10.

B. Characters in the story or drama of Revelation

We have already noted many of the characters in Revelation. Figure 13.11 summarizes most of them.

Character	Explanation in Revelation
1. Jesus Christ	The book reveals Him in such ways as: One like a *Son of Man* (1:13; 14:14), the *Lamb* (6:5-6), the *Lion* (5:5), a *Male Child* (12:5), the *Rider* on the white horse (19:11), and the One on the great white throne (20:11).
2. God the Father	He is seated on the throne (4:1-11), and referred to throughout the story.
3. The Holy Spirit	He is referred to as the 7-fold Spirit of God (1:4; 4:5; 5:6). John was in the Spirit on the Lord's Day (1:10). The Spirit speaks to the seven churches (2:1–3:22), and is active throughout the story.
4. The apostle John	He sees the visions and narrates or tells the story to us (1:9-19). Also, he often shares his feelings and responses to the visions.
5. The 7 churches	Jesus speaks to these in chapters 1–3. They remain in the background the rest of the book. All of Revelation was written for these churches and the churches that they represent.
6. Satan	He is the main enemy in Revelation, and is referred to as the devil, Satan, and the Dragon (12:3–13:1; 20:1-10).
7. The 4 creatures	These may represent all of creation. They appear often (4:6, 8; 5:6, 8, 14; 6:1, 6; 7:11; 14:3; 15:7; 19:4).
8. The 24 elders	These may represent all whom God has redeemed (4:4, 10; 5:8; 11:16; 19:4).
9. The angels	These are active throughout the book. An angel brought the revelation to John (1:1). They worship God and the Lamb (4–5), declare judgment (10:1-20), and fight in heavenly warfare (12). They blow the seven trumpets (8:2), and pour out the seven bowls and seven plagues (15–16). An angel, perhaps the one of Rev. 1:1, showed John many things (22:8).
10. The 2 witnesses	These dress in black clothes and call sinners to repent. Likewise, they prophesy and declare God's judgment (11).
11. The Antichrist and beast	The Antichrist is the ruler of the beast, which is his kingdom. Sometimes John refers to the Antichrist as the beast. This is because a king and his kingdom are one. The beast has seven heads and ten horns (13). Five of these heads were in the past (17:10). We believe that these represent the world kingdoms of Egypt, Assyria, Babylon, Medo-Persia, and Greece. The sixth head of the beast was present in John's day. That head was Rome. We believe that the seventh head is a revised form of the Roman Empire. The Antichrist is the horn that arises to rule over it. The ten horns on the head of the seventh beast are ten kings. They reign a short time with the Antichrist.[23]
12. The *false prophet	This person represents the Antichrist as the Holy Spirit represents Christ. Satan, the Antichrist, and the false prophet form an unholy trinity.
13. The harlot	John tells us that the harlot is the capital city of the Antichrist (17:18). This great city represents the world and its values. In John's day this capital city was Rome. John referred to it as Babylon to protect believers. Caesar was considered to be the Antichrist in John's day. But we believe there will be a final Antichrist who will rule the world from a great city.
14. The bride	The bride is the Church, the body of Christ (19:7-8). The bride includes those who go up in the Rapture (1 Thess. 4:13-18), and all those saved during the Great Tribulation (7:9-17). The bride is united with Christ when He comes to conquer evil.
15. Others	There are many more characters in Revelation. These include Jezebel (2:20-23), the riders on horses (6:5-8), the woman (12), the martyrs, kings, merchants, sailors, followers of the beast, faithful witnesses of the Lord, slaves, rich and poor people, the 144,000, a great multitude in white robes, all the dead who came to life, and people on thrones. Likewise, we meet things and creatures who act like humans. An eagle cries with a loud voice (8:13). The earth opens its mouth (12:16). An altar responds to God (16:7). The new Jerusalem comes as a bride (21:9-10). Finally, death and Hades are judged like God's other enemies. Thus Revelation has a great and varied list of characters. These all play a part in the story of God's final victory over evil.

Figure 13.11 Characters in the story or drama of Revelation

C. Contrasts in Revelation

A	Rev.	B	Rev.
The *dependable* One: who was, is, and is to come	1:4, 8; 4:8	The *undependable* one: who was, now is not, and will come	17:8, 11
The *holy* Trinity: the Father, the Son, and the sevenfold Spirit	1:4-5	The *evil* trinity: the devil, the Antichrist, and the false prophet	20:10
The description of *Christ*	1:12-16	The description of the *Antichrist*	13:1-3
The *rebukes* Christ gave 5 of the 7 churches	2–3	The *lack of rebuke* to Smyrna and Philadelphia	2–3
The *good things* He said to 6 of the 7 churches	2–3	The *absence of any praise* to Laodicean believers	3:14-22
Those *who have ears* to hear what the Spirit says	2–3	Those *who do not have ears* to hear what the Spirit says	
Promises to overcomers in all 7 churches	2–3	*Warnings* to those who are overcome	2–3
The **Lord God Almighty* on His throne in heaven	4:2-3	*Earthly rulers* on earthly thrones	
Our God who is *holy* and *eternal*	4:8	The beast who is *evil* and *temporary*	13:5
The *Creator*	4:11	All *created things*	4:11
He who *was*, and *is*, and *is to come*	4:8	The beast who *once was, now is not*, and *is going to destruction*	17:11
The Lamb who alone is *worthy* to open the scroll	5:7-10	All in heaven, on earth, and under the earth who are *not worthy* to open the scroll	5:3

Figure 13.12 Contrasts in Revelation 1–5

A	Rev.	B	Rev.
The white-horse rider with one temporary *stephanos* crown	6:2	The white-horse rider with many permanent *diadem* crowns	19:11-12
The fifth seal: martyrs resting in heaven, praying, *"Avenge us!"*	6:9-11	The sixth seal: sinners trembling on earth, saying, *"Hide us!"*	6:12-17
The *silence* before the scroll is opened	8:1	The *roar* of great multitudes in heaven shouting, *"Hallelujah!"*	19:1-6
3½ years of *hell* on earth with the Antichrist	11:2-3; 12:6, 14	1,000 years of *peace* on earth with Christ	20:2-6
The *anger of the nations*	11:18	The *wrath of God*	11:18
Rewarding the prophets, saints, and those who respect God	11:18	*Judging* the dead and destroying those who destroy the earth	11:18
The woman *out* of the serpent's reach	12:14	The woman's children *within* the dragon's reach	12:17
Those with the name or *mark of the beast* on their foreheads	13:16-17	Those with the *name of God* on their foreheads	14:1; 22:4
The *lost who never find rest,* tormented in the lake of fire	14:10-11	The *saved who find eternal rest* in the presence of God	14:13
The *vile* dress of the harlot of the Antichrist	17:3-4	The *pure* dress of the bride of Christ	19:7-8
The city of *Babylon* in ruins	18:2	The city of the *New Jerusalem*	21:2
The *sinful* citizens of Babylon	18:4-5	The *holy* citizens of the New Jerusalem	22:14-15
Mourning of kings, merchants, and sailors over Babylon's fall	18:9-19	*Rejoicing* of saints, apostles, and prophets over Babylon's fall	18:20

Figure 13.13 Contrasts in Revelation based on the Tribulation (Rev. 6–18)

Q 21 *Explain 3 contrasts in Revelation 1–5.*

Q 22 *What are your favorite 3 contrasts in Revelation 6–8? Why?*

Figure 13.14 The emerald throne scene in heaven (Rev. 4:1-8)

Figure 13.15 Casting crowns before the throne (Rev. 4:9-11)

Q 23 *Describe any 4 contrasts in Revelation 19–22.*

A	Rev.	B	Rev.
The *Wedding Supper* of the Lamb	19:9	The *great supper* of God	19:17-18
The *first* resurrection	20:5-6	The *second* resurrection	20:12-13
Overcomers, children of God who *inherit the New Jerusalem*	21:7	Cowards, unbelievers, the vile, murderers, the sexually immoral, those who practice magic, idolaters, and liars who *inherit the lake of fire*	21:8
Those who do shameful or deceitful deeds	21:27	Those whose names are written in the *Lamb's book of life	21:27
Those who are *vile* and *do wrong*	22:11	Those who are *holy* and *do right*	22:11
Come	22:17	Depart	20:15

Figure 13.16
Contrasts in Revelation based on Christ's return and reign (Rev. 19–22)

Figure 13.17
The New Jerusalem
(Rev. 21:1-21)

Figure 13.18 The books are opened, and also the book of life (Rev. 20:12-13).

Q 24 *Complete the House of New Testament Books.*

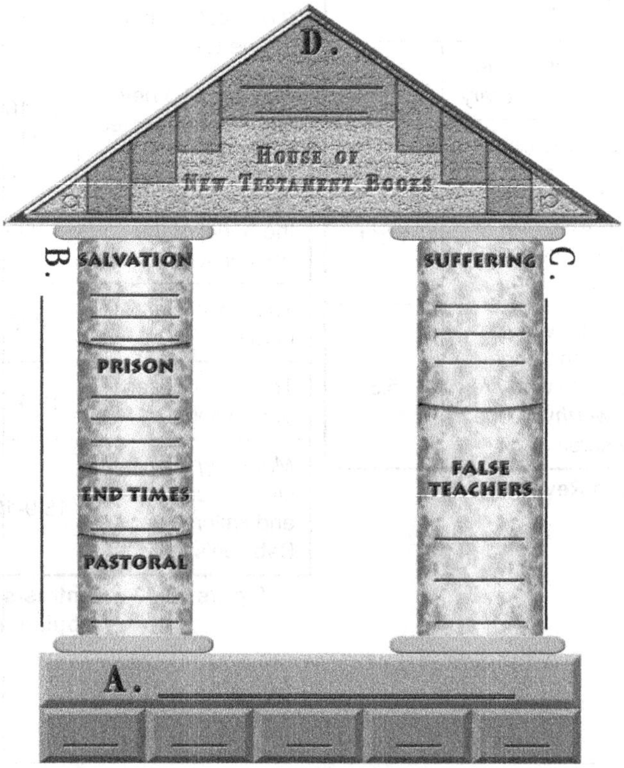

Figure 13.19 Final practice chart on the house of New Testament books

Test Yourself: Circle the letter by the ***best*** completion to each question or statement.

1. The Greek word *apokalupto* means
a) "to cover."
b) "to prophesy."
c) "to unveil."
d) "to deceive."

2. When was Revelation probably written?
a) A.D. 65
b) A.D. 75
c) A.D. 85
d) A.D. 95

3. The author of Revelation wrote from the island of
a) Malta.
b) Patmos.
c) Cyprus.
d) Crete.

4. We think the apostle John wrote Revelation since
a) the author says that he is the apostle John.
b) Revelation was addressed to John's home church.
c) the author was suffering and condemned to die.
d) Revelation opens with the same words as 2 John.

5. To whom was Revelation written?
a) Churches in Galatia
b) Churches in Asia
c) Churches in Cilicia
d) Churches in Achaia

6. What is the MAIN theme of Revelation?
a) Only overcomers will inherit the Kingdom.
b) God will judge people according to their deeds.
c) Believers should watch for the Antichrist.
d) Jesus will return to triumph over all evil.

7. Which chapters describe *"things that are now"?*
a) 2–3
b) 4–5
c) 6–7
d) 8–9

8. Which view of Revelation does this course emphasize?
a) Preterist
b) Historist
c) Idealist
d) Futurist

9. John wrote Revelation in symbols
a) to hide the revelation from some believers
b) to add emotion to the truth he was teaching
c) to make the truth plain for all to understand
d) to represent ideas, not real people and events

10. A great contrast in Revelation is between
a) the harlot and the bride of Christ.
b) the dragon and the angel Gabriel.
c) the cities of Babylon and Nineveh.
d) the second and third resurrections.

Essay Test Topics: Write 50-100 words on each of these goals that you studied in this chapter.

The Background of Revelation

Goal: *Analyze the name, author, date, setting, and theme of Revelation.*

Understanding Revelation

Goal: *Evaluate 4 ways of interpreting Revelation.*

Goal: *Divide Revelation into 3 parts based on Revelation 1:19. Note the chapters for each part.*

Goal: *Summarize 5 descriptions of Jesus in Revelation.*

Symbols, Characters, and Contrasts in Revelation

Goal: *Explain how John uses symbols and characters in Revelation.*

Goal: *Identify 5 contrasts in Revelation.*

Who Said It?

This is a good game for two or more students to play. A student or teacher can read a quote to a student or a class, without mentioning a Scripture reference. Then, the listener can try to answer 3 questions:

1) Who said it? **2)** To Whom? **3)** Why?

If the listener cannot identify the quote, the reader can give the Scripture reference that goes with it. These quotes are a great way to review the New Testament. Even students who cannot identify the quotes the first time will soon come to know them well.

Chapter 2—Review of the Synoptic Gospels (Matthew through Luke):

Who Said it? To Whom? Why?

"Give him the name Jesus, because..." (Matt. 1:21).

"As soon as you find him, report to me" (Matt. 2:8).

"Every tree that does not produce good fruit will be cut down..." (Matt. 3:10).

"He will baptize you with the Holy Spirit" (Matt. 3:11).

"Let it be so now; it is proper for us to do this to fulfill all righteousness" (Matt. 3:15).

"'Man does not live on bread alone'" (Matt. 4:4).

"Repent, for the kingdom of heaven is near" (Matt. 4:17).

"Come, follow me... and I will make you fishers of men" (Matt. 4:19).

"You are the light of the world" (Matt. 5:14).

"You have heard that it was said..." (Matt. 5:43).

"Do not worry about your life" (Matt. 6:25).

"I am willing" (Matt. 8:3).

"Just say the word, and my servant will be healed" (Matt. 8:8).

"He took up our infirmities and carried our diseases" (Matt. 8:17).

"Follow me, and let the dead bury their own dead" (Matt. 8:22).

"You of little faith, why are you so afraid?" (Matt. 8:26).

"What do you want with us, Son of God?" (Matt. 8:29).

"Which is easier?" (Matt. 9:5).

"It is not the healthy who need a doctor, but the sick" (Matt. 9:12).

"No one sews a patch of unshrunk cloth on an old garment" (Matt. 9:16).

"If I only touch his cloak, I will be healed" (Matt. 9:21).

"It is by the prince of demons that he drives out demons" (Matt. 9:34).

"A man's enemies will be the members of his own household" (Matt. 10:36).

"Those who wear fine clothes are in kings' palaces" (Matt. 11:8).

"We played the flute for you, and you did not dance" (Matt. 11:17).

"Your disciples are doing what is unlawful on the Sabbath" (Matt. 12:2).

"In his name the nations will put their hope" (Matt. 12:21).

"Could this be the Son of David?" (Matt. 12:23).

"'I will return to the house I left'" (Matt. 12:44).

"Here are my mother and my brothers" (Matt. 12:49).

"Why do you speak to the people in parables?" (Matt. 13:10).

"Give me here on a platter the head of John the Baptist" (Matt. 14:8).

"Send the crowds away" (Matt. 14:15).

"Lord, save me!" (Matt. 14:30).

"What goes into a man's mouth does not make him 'unclean'" (Matt. 15:11).

"But even the dogs eat the crumbs that fall from their masters' table" (Matt. 15:27).

"How many loaves do you have?" (Matt. 15:34).

"You cannot interpret the signs of the times" (Matt. 16:3).

"Some say... Jeremiah or one of the prophets" (Matt. 16:14).

"This shall never happen to you!" (Matt. 16:22).

"If you wish, I will put up three shelters" (Matt. 17:4).

"Why couldn't we drive it out?" (Matt. 17:19).

"Yes, he does" (Matt. 17:25).

"How many times shall I forgive my brother?" (Matt. 18:21).

"Not everyone can accept this word" (Matt. 19:11).

"Let the little children come to me" (Matt. 19:14).

"What do I still lack?" (Matt. 19:20).

"What then will there be for us?" (Matt. 19:27).

"The last will be first, and the first will be last" (Matt. 20:16).

"What do you want me to do for you?" (Matt. 20:32).

"Blessed is he who comes in the name of the Lord!" (Matt. 21:9).

"By what authority are you doing these things?" (Matt. 21:23).

"I will, sir" (Matt. 21:30).

"This is the heir" (Matt. 21:38).

"How did you get in here without wedding clothes?" (Matt. 22:12).

"Is it right to pay taxes to Caesar or not?" (Matt. 22:17).

"At the resurrection, whose wife will she be... ?" (Matt. 22:28).

"Whose son is he?" (Matt. 22:42).

"You strain out a gnat but swallow a camel" (Matt. 23:24).

"When will this happen?" (Matt. 24:3).

"There may not be enough for both us and you" (Matt. 25:9).

"'Here is what belongs to you'" (Matt. 25:25).

"'Lord, when did we see you hungry or thirsty?'" (Matt. 25:44).

"Why this waste?" (Matt. 26:8).

"What are you willing to give me... ?" (Matt. 26:15).

"This is my blood of the covenant" (Matt. 26:28).

"Could you not keep watch for one hour?" (Mark 14:37).

"Tell us if you are the Christ, the Son of God" (Matt. 26:63).

"You also were with Jesus of Galilee" (Matt. 26:69).

"What is that to us? ... That's your responsibility" (Matt. 27:4).

"Which of the two do you want me to release to you?" (Matt. 27:21).

"Let his blood be on us and on our children!" (Matt. 27:25).

"Surely he was the Son of God!" (Matt. 27:54).

"Go, make the tomb as secure as you know how" (Matt. 27:65).

"He is not here; he has risen, just as he said" (Matt. 28:6).

"Therefore go and make disciples of all nations" (Matt. 28:19).

"How can I be sure of this?" (Luke 1:18).

"My spirit rejoices in God my Savior" (Luke 1:47).

"You will find a baby wrapped in cloths and lying in a manger" (Luke 2:12).

"This child is destined to cause..." (Luke 2:34).

"Why have you treated us like this?" (Luke 2:48).

"Don't cry" (Luke 7:13).

"If this man were a prophet, ..." (Luke 7:39).

"Which of these three do you think was a neighbor?" (Luke 10:36).

"'Take life easy; eat, drink and be merry'" (Luke 12:19).

"'I am no longer worthy to be called your son'" (Luke 15:21).

"'I'm not strong enough to dig'" (Luke 16:3).

"Where are the other nine?" (Luke 17:17).

"'Grant me justice...'" (Luke 18:3).

"I must stay at your house today" (Luke 19:5).

"'To everyone who has, more will be given'" (Luke 19:26).

"Stay in the city until you have..." (Luke 24:49).

Chapter 3—Review of the Gospel of John:
Who Said it? To Whom? Why?

"'He who comes after me has surpassed me because he was before me'" (John 1:15).

"Look, the Lamb of God, who takes away the sin of the world!" (John 1:29).

"Nazareth! Can anything good come from there?" (John 1:46).

"Do whatever he tells you" (John 2:5).

"Destroy this temple, and I will raise it again in three days" (John 2:19).

"A man can receive only what is given him from heaven" (John 3:27).

"He must become greater; I must become less" (John 3:30).

"Come, see a man who told me everything I ever did" (John 4:29).

"I have food to eat that you know nothing about" (John 4:32).

"Sir, come down before my child dies" (John 4:49).

"Do you want to get well?" (John 5:6).

"Stop sinning or something worse may happen to you" (John 5:14).

"All who are in their graves will hear his voice and come out" (John 5:28-29).

"Rabbi, when did you get here?" (John 6:25).

"From now on give us this bread" (John 6:34).

"'They will all be taught by God'" (John 6:45).

"Lord, to whom shall we go? You have the words of eternal life" (John 6:68).

"No one who wants to become a public figure acts in secret" (John 7:4).

"How did this man get such learning without having studied?" (John 7:15).

"When the Christ comes, will he do more miraculous signs than this man?" (John 7:31).

"If anyone is thirsty, let him come to me and drink" (John 7:37).

"No one ever spoke the way this man does" (John 7:46).

"Does our law condemn anyone without first hearing him?" (John 7:51).

"Go now and leave your life of sin" (John 8:11).

"The only Father we have is God himself" (John 8:41).

"Who do you think you are?" (John 8:53).

"Who sinned, this man or his parents, that he was born blind?" (John 9:2).

"Ask him. He is of age; he will speak for himself" (John 9:21).

"What? Are we blind too?" (John 9:40).

"My sheep listen to my voice; I know them, and they follow me" (John 10:27).

"Let us also go, that we may die with him" (John 11:16).

"Lord, if you had been here, my brother would not have died" (John 11:21, 32).

"It is better for you that one man die for the people than that the whole nation perish" (John 11:50).

"Leave her alone" (John 12:7).

"Unless a kernel of wheat falls to the ground and dies, it remains only a single seed" (John 12:24).

"You shall never wash my feet" (John 13:8).

"I will lay down my life for you" (John 13:37).

"Lord, we don't know where you are going, so how can we know the way?" (John 14:5).

"You believe at last!" (John 16:31).

"Is that your own idea... or did others talk to you about me?" (John 18:34).

"What is truth?" (John 18:38).

JESUS OF NAZARETH, THE KING OF THE JEWS (John 19:19).

"It is finished" (John 19:30).

"I have seen the Lord!" (John 20:18).

"My Lord and my God!" (John 20:28).

"If I want him to remain alive until I return, what is that to you?" (John 21:22).

Chapter 4—Review of Acts:
Who said It? To Whom? Why?

"In my former book, Theophilus, ..." (Acts 1:1).

"Do not leave Jerusalem, but wait for the gift my Father promised" (Acts 1:4).

"You will receive power when the Holy Spirit comes on you; and you will be my witnesses" (Acts 1:8).

"This same Jesus, who has been taken from you into heaven, will come back..." (Acts 1:11).

"For one of these must become a witness with us of his resurrection" (Acts 1:22).

"All of them were filled with the Holy Spirit and began to speak in other tongues" (Acts 2:4).

"What does this mean?" (Acts 2:12).

"The gift of the Holy Spirit... is for you and your children and for all..." (Acts 2:38-39).

"Silver or gold I do not have, but what I have I give you" (Acts 3:6).

"Salvation is found in no one else, for there is no other name under heaven given to men by which we must be saved" (Acts 4:12).

"Yes... that is the price" (Acts 5:8).

"We gave you strict orders not to teach in this name" (Acts 5:28).

"'Who made you ruler and judge over us?'" (Acts 7:27).

"Lord, do not hold this sin against them" (Acts 7:60).

"Give me also this ability" (Acts 8:19).

"How can I... unless someone explains it to me?" (Acts 8:31).

"Who are you, Lord?" (Acts 9:5).

"Brother Saul, the Lord... has sent me so that you may see again and be filled with the Holy Spirit" (Acts 9:17).

"Get up and take care of your mat" (Acts 9:34).

"Tabitha, get up" (Acts 9:40).

"Your prayers and gifts to the poor have come up as a memorial offering before God" (Acts 10:4).

"Do not call anything impure that God has made clean" (Acts 10:15).

"God anointed Jesus of Nazareth with the Holy Spirit and power" (Acts 10:38).

"They have received the Holy Spirit just as we have" (Acts 10:47).

"It must be his angel" (Acts 12:15).

"This is the voice of a god, not of a man" (Acts 12:22).

"Set apart for me Barnabas and Saul for the work to which I have called them" (Acts 13:2).

"You are a child of the devil and an enemy of everything that is right!" (Acts 13:10).

"Since you reject it and do not consider yourselves worthy of eternal life..." (Acts 13:46).

"The disciples were filled with joy and with the Holy Spirit" (Acts 13:52).

"The gods have come down to us in human form!" (Acts 14:11).

"*...putting on the necks of the disciples a yoke that neither we nor our fathers have been able to bear?*" (Acts 15:10).

"*We should not make it difficult for the Gentiles who are turning to God*" (Acts 15:19).

"*Come over to Macedonia and help us*" (Acts 16:9).

"*If you consider me a believer in the Lord... come and stay at my house*" (Acts 16:15).

"*These men are servants of the Most High God, who are telling you the way to be saved*" (Acts 16:17).

"*Sirs, what must I do to be saved?*" (Acts 16:30).

"*What is this babbler trying to say?*" (Acts 17:18).

"'*For in him we live and move and have our being*'" (Acts 17:28).

"*Do not be afraid; keep on speaking, do not be silent*" (Acts 18:9).

"*Settle the matter yourselves. I will not be a judge of such things*" (Acts 18:15).

"*Did you receive the Holy Spirit when you believed?*" (Acts 19:2).

"*In the name of Jesus, whom Paul preaches, I command you to come out*" (Acts 19:13).

"*Man-made gods are no gods at all*" (Acts 19:26).

"*Don't be alarmed... He's alive!*" (Acts 20:10).

"*Be shepherds of the church of God, which he bought with his own blood*" (Acts 20:28).

"'*It is more blessed to give than to receive*'" (Acts 20:35).

"'*In this way the Jews of Jerusalem will bind the owner of this belt and will...* '" (Acts 21:11).

"*Thousands of Jews have believed, and all of them are zealous for the law*" (Acts 21:20).

"*Tell me, are you a Roman citizen?*" (Acts 22:27).

"*My brothers, I am a Pharisee, the son of a Pharisee*" (Acts 23:6).

"*As you have testified about me in Jerusalem, so you must also testify in Rome*" (Acts 23:11).

"*That's enough for now! You may leave. When I find it convenient, I will send for you*" (Acts 24:25).

"*You have appealed to Caesar. To Caesar you will go!*" (Acts 25:12).

"*Do you think that in such a short time you can persuade me to be a Christian?*" (Acts 26:28).

"*I have faith in God that it will happen just as he told me*" (Acts 27:25).

"*We want to hear what your views are*" (Acts 28:22).

Chapters 5–6—Review of the Salvation Epistles (Romans through Galatians):

Who said it? To whom? Why?

No, in all these things we are more than conquerors through him who loved us (Rom. 8:37).

You, however, are controlled not by the sinful nature but by the Spirit (Rom. 8:9).

Against all hope, Abraham in hope believed and so became the father of many nations (Rom. 4:18).

All Israel will be saved (Rom. 11:26).

"*All nations will be blessed through you*" (Gal. 3:8).

Don't you know that all of us who were baptized into Christ Jesus were baptized into his death? (Rom. 6:3).

All things are yours, whether Paul or Apollos or Cephas or the world or life or death or the present or the future— (1 Cor. 3:21-22).

All who rely on observing the law are under a curse (Gal. 3:10).

And now these three remain: faith, hope and love. But the greatest of these is love (1 Cor. 13:13).

Be eager to prophesy, and do not forbid speaking in tongues (1 Cor. 14:39).

Before certain men came from James, he used to eat with the Gentiles (Gal. 2:12).

Brothers, I could not address you as spiritual but as worldly—mere infants in Christ (1 Cor. 3:1).

God will give to each person according to what he has done (Rom. 2:6).

Brothers, if someone is caught in a sin, you who are spiritual should restore him gently (Gal. 6:1).

All who sin apart from the law will also perish apart from the law (Rom. 2:12).

But if we judged ourselves, we would not come under judgment (1 Cor. 11:31).

But thanks be to God, who always leads us in triumphal procession in Christ (2 Cor. 2:14).

Christ is the end of the law (Rom. 10:4).

Circumcision is circumcision of the heart, by the Spirit, not by the written code (Rom. 2:29).

Did God reject his people? By no means! (Rom. 11:1).

"*Abraham believed God, and it was credited to him as righteousness*" (Rom. 4:3).

Do not be deceived: God cannot be mocked. A man reaps what he sows (Gal. 6:7).

Do not be yoked together with unbelievers. For what do righteousness and wickedness have in common? (2 Cor. 6:14).

Do you not know that the wicked will not inherit the kingdom of God? (1 Cor. 6:9).

Do you not know that your body is a temple of the Holy Spirit, who is in you... ? (1 Cor. 6:19).

Don't you know that a little yeast works through the whole batch of dough? (1 Cor. 5:6).

Each man should have his own wife, and each woman her own husband (1 Cor. 7:2).

Everyone must submit himself to the governing authorities (Rom. 13:1).

Faith comes from hearing the message (Rom. 10:17).

Five times I received from the Jews the forty lashes minus one (2 Cor. 11:24).

Follow the way of love and eagerly desire spiritual gifts, especially the gift of prophecy (1 Cor. 14:1).

Therefore do not let sin reign in your mortal body so that you obey its evil desires (Rom. 6:12).

For all have sinned and fall short of the glory of God (Rom. 3:23).

For you know the grace of our Lord Jesus Christ, that though he was rich, yet for your sakes he became poor (2 Cor. 8:9).

God is faithful; he will not let you be tempted beyond what you can bear (1 Cor. 10:13).

How unsearchable his judgments, and his paths beyond tracing out! (Rom. 11:33).

I am astonished that you are so quickly deserting the one who called you by the grace of Christ (Gal. 1:6).

I am not ashamed of the gospel, because it is the power of God for the salvation of everyone who believes (Rom. 1:16).

I am obligated both to Greeks and non-Greeks, both to the wise and the foolish (Rom. 1:14).

I could wish that I myself were cursed and cut off from Christ for the sake of my brothers (Rom. 9:3).

I have become all things to all men so that by all possible means I might save some (1 Cor. 9:22).

I thank God that I speak in tongues more than all of you (1 Cor. 14:18).

"I will call her 'my loved one' who is not my loved one" (Rom. 9:25).

If anyone is in Christ, he is a new creation; the old has gone, the new has come! (2 Cor. 5:17).

If God is for us, who can be against us? (Rom. 8:31).

If we or an angel from heaven should preach a gospel other than the one we preached to you, let him be eternally condemned! (Gal. 1:8).

If you forgive anyone, I also forgive him (2 Cor. 2:10).

Is God the God of Jews only? Is he not the God of Gentiles too? (Rom. 3:29).

It is better not to... do anything else that will cause your brother to fall (Rom. 14:21).

Since we have been justified through faith, we have peace with God through our Lord Jesus Christ (Rom. 5:1).

Knowledge puffs up, but love builds up (1 Cor. 8:1).

"Let him who boasts boast in the Lord" (1 Cor. 1:31).

Let no debt remain outstanding, except the continuing debt to love one another (Rom. 13:8).

Listen, I tell you a mystery: We will not all sleep, but we will all be changed— (1 Cor. 15:51).

Live by the Spirit, and you will not gratify the desires of the sinful nature (Gal. 5:16).

May the grace of the Lord Jesus Christ, and the love of God, and the fellowship of the Holy Spirit be with you all (2 Cor. 13:14).

"My grace is sufficient for you, for my power is made perfect in weakness" (2 Cor. 12:9).

Offer your bodies as living sacrifices, holy and pleasing to God— (Rom. 12:1).

Sin entered the world through one man, and death through sin (Rom. 5:12).

So the law was put in charge to lead us to Christ that we might be justified by faith (Gal. 3:24).

Some from Chloe's household have informed me that there are quarrels among you (1 Cor. 1:11).

The letter kills, but the Spirit gives life (2 Cor. 3:6).

The weapons we fight with are not the weapons of the world (2 Cor. 10:4).

There are different kinds of gifts, but the same Spirit (1 Cor. 12:4).

Therefore you do not lack any spiritual gift as you eagerly wait for our Lord Jesus Christ to be revealed (1 Cor. 1:7).

Those who are led by the Spirit of God are sons of God (Rom. 8:14).

We can comfort those in any trouble with the comfort we ourselves have received from God (2 Cor. 1:4).

We have this treasure in jars of clay to show that this all-surpassing power is from God and not from us (2 Cor. 4:7).

Whoever sows sparingly will also reap sparingly, and whoever sows generously will also reap generously (2 Cor. 9:6).

Woman is not independent of man, nor is man independent of woman (1 Cor. 11:11).

You have fallen away from grace (Gal. 5:4).

You who preach against stealing, do you steal? (Rom. 2:21).

Chapter 7—Review of the Prison Epistles (Ephesians through Colossians and Philemon): Who said it? To whom? Why?

—An old man and now also a prisoner of Jesus—I appeal to you for my son Onesimus (Philem. 9-10).

As a prisoner for the Lord... I urge you to live a life worthy of the calling you have received (Eph. 4:1).

As for you, you were dead in your transgressions and sins (Eph. 2:1).

As God's chosen people, holy and dearly loved, clothe yourselves with compassion, kindness, humility, gentleness and patience (Col. 3:12).

Be imitators of God, therefore, as dearly loved children (Eph. 5:1).

But I think it is necessary to send back to you Epaphroditus (Phil. 2:25).

But one thing I do: Forgetting what is behind and straining toward what is ahead, ... (Phil. 3:13).

Do not be anxious about anything, but in everything, by prayer and petition, with thanksgiving, present your requests to God (Phil. 4:6).

For God was pleased to have all his fullness dwell in him (Col. 1:19).

For he himself is our peace, who has made the two one (Eph. 2:14).

For in Christ all the fullness of the Deity lives in bodily form (Col. 2:9).

For of this you can be sure: No immoral, impure or greedy person... has any inheritance in the kingdom of Christ and of God (Eph. 5:5).

God placed all things under his feet and appointed him to be head over everything for the church (Eph. 1:22).

He is the image of the invisible God, the firstborn over all creation (Col. 1:15).

Husbands, love your wives, just as Christ loved the church and gave himself up for her (Eph. 5:25).

I am sending him—who is my very heart—back to you (Philem. 12).

I can do everything through him who gives me strength (Phil. 4:13).

If he has done you any wrong or owes you anything, charge it to me (Philem. 18).

In him we have redemption through his blood, the forgiveness of sins (Eph. 1:7).

"In your anger do not sin": Do not let the sun go down while you are still angry (Eph. 4:26).

It has been granted to you on behalf of Christ not only to believe on him, but also to suffer for him (Phil. 1:29).

It was he who gave some to be apostles, some to be prophets, some to be evangelists, and some to be pastors and teachers (Eph. 4:11).

Let the word of Christ dwell in you richly... as you sing psalms, hymns and spiritual songs (Col. 3:16).

My God will meet all your needs according to his glorious riches in Christ Jesus (Phil. 4:19).

No longer as a slave, but better than a slave, as a dear brother (Philem. 16).

Pray in the Spirit on all occasions with all kinds of prayers and requests (Eph. 6:18).

Put on the full armor of God so that you can take your stand against the devil's schemes (Eph. 6:11).

Put to death, therefore, whatever belongs to your earthly nature: sexual immorality, impurity, lust, evil desires and greed, which is idolatry (Col. 3:5).

Remember my chains. Grace be with you (Col. 4:18).

Since, then, you have been raised with Christ, set your hearts on things above (Col. 3:1).

The important thing is that in every way, whether from false motives or true, Christ is preached (Phil. 1:18).

This is my prayer: that your love may abound more and more in knowledge and depth of insight, so that you may be able to discern what is best (Phil. 1:9-10).

This mystery is that through the gospel the Gentiles are heirs together with Israel (Eph. 3:6).

To him who is able to do immeasurably more than all we ask or imagine... (Eph. 3:20).

Watch out for those dogs, those men who do evil, those mutilators of the flesh (Phil. 3:2).

Whatever is true, whatever is noble, whatever is right, ... think about such things (Phil. 4:8).

Your attitude should be the same as that of Christ Jesus (Phil. 2:5).

Chapters 8–9—Review of 1 Thessalonians through Titus: Who said it? To whom? Why?

Do your best to present yourself to God as one approved, a workman who does not need to be ashamed (2 Tim. 2:15).

For the grace of God... teaches us to say "No" to ungodliness and worldly passions (Titus 2:11-12).

For the Lord himself will come down from heaven, with a loud command (1 Thess. 4:16).

For the love of money is a root of all kinds of evil (1 Tim. 6:10).

God is just: He will pay back trouble to those who trouble you and give relief to you who are troubled (2 Thess. 1:6-7).

This is good, and pleases God our Savior, who wants all men to be saved and to come to a knowledge of the truth (1 Tim. 2:3-4).

If we endure, we will also reign with him. If we disown him, he will also disown us (2 Tim. 2:12).

People will be lovers of themselves, lovers of money, boastful, proud, abusive... (2 Tim. 3:2).

Preach the Word; be prepared in season and out of season (2 Tim. 4:2).

That day will not come until the rebellion occurs and the man of lawlessness is revealed (2 Thess. 2:3).

The day of the Lord will come like a thief in the night (1 Thess. 5:2).

The overseer must be above reproach, the husband of but one wife, temperate,... (1 Tim. 3:2).

The reason I left you in Crete was that you might straighten out what was left unfinished... (Titus 1:5).

The Spirit clearly says that in later times some will abandon the faith (1 Tim. 4:1).

To the King eternal, immortal, invisible, the only God, be honor and glory for ever and ever (1 Tim. 1:17).

You became a model to all the believers in Macedonia and Achaia (1 Thess. 1:7).

You know what is holding him back, so that he may be revealed at the proper time (2 Thess. 2:6).

Your sincere faith, which first lived in your grandmother Lois and in your mother Eunice... (2 Tim. 1:5).

Chapter 10–12—Review of Hebrews and the General Epistles (James through Jude):

Who said it? To Whom? Why?

...To the chosen lady and her children, whom I love in the truth— (2 John 1).

"A dog returns to its vomit," and, "A sow that is washed goes back to her wallowing in the mud" (2 Pet. 2:22).

As the body without the spirit is dead, so faith without deeds is dead (James 2:26).

Be on your guard so that you may not... fall from your secure position. But grow in the grace and knowledge of our Lord (2 Pet. 3:17-18).

Be self-controlled and alert. Your enemy the devil prowls around like a roaring lion (1 Pet. 5:8).

Consider it pure joy, my brothers, whenever you face trials of many kinds (James 1:2).

Contend for the faith that was once for all entrusted to the saints (Judg. 3).

Every good and perfect gift is from above, coming down from the Father of the heavenly lights (James 1:17).

For the word of God is living and active. Sharper than any double-edged sword, ... (Heb. 4:12).

For to which of the angels did God ever say, "You are my Son?" (Heb. 1:5).

He himself bore our sins in his body on the tree, so that we might die to sins and live for righteousness (1 Pet. 2:24).

He was faithful to the one who appointed him, just as Moses was faithful in all God's house (Heb. 3:2).

He who has the Son has life; he who does not have the Son of God does not have life (1 John 5:12).

How great is the love the Father has lavished on us, that we should be called children of God! (1 John 3:1).

I pray that you may enjoy good health and that all may go well with you, even as your soul is getting along well (3 John 2).

If anyone loves the world, the love of the Father is not in him (1 John 2:15).

If we confess our sins, he is faithful and just and will forgive us our sins and purify us (1 John 1:9).

In the past God spoke to our forefathers through the prophets (Heb. 1:1).

Is any one of you sick? He should call the elders of the church to pray over him and anoint him with oil... (James 5:14).

It is written: "Be holy, because I am holy" (1 Pet. 1:16).

Jesus Christ is the same yesterday and today and forever (Heb. 13:8).

Just as man is destined to die once, and after that to face judgment (Heb. 9:27).

Land that produces thorns and thistles is worthless... In the end it will be burned (Heb. 6:8).

Let us throw off everything that hinders and the sin that so easily entangles, and let us run... (Heb. 12:1).

Likewise the tongue is a small part of the body, but it makes great boasts (James 3:5).

Men spoke from God as they were carried along by the Holy Spirit (2 Pet. 1:21).

Now faith is being sure of what we hope for and certain of what we do not see (Heb. 11:1).

Submit yourselves, then, to God. Resist the devil, and he will flee from you (James 4:7).

The one who is in you is greater than the one who is in the world (1 John 4:4).

This Melchizedek was king of Salem and priest of God Most High (Heb. 7:1).

Treat them with respect as the weaker partner and as heirs with you of the gracious gift of life (1 Pet. 3:7).

We must pay more careful attention, therefore, to what we have heard, so that we do not drift away (Heb. 2:1).

With the Lord a day is like a thousand years, and a thousand years are like a day (2 Pet. 3:8).

You may participate in the divine nature and escape the corruption in the world caused by evil desires (2 Pet. 1:4).

Chapter 13—Review of Revelation:

Who is it? (Who is the verse talking about?)

In his right hand he held seven stars, and out of his mouth came a sharp double-edged sword (Rev. 1:16).

"You have forsaken your first love" (Rev. 2:4).

"I know your afflictions and your poverty—yet you are rich!" (Rev. 2:9).

"You have people there who hold to the teaching of Balaam" (Rev. 2:14).

"You tolerate that woman Jezebel, who calls herself a prophetess" (Rev. 2:20).

"You have a reputation of being alive, but you are dead" (Rev. 3:1).

"I have placed before you an open door that no one can shut" (Rev. 3:8).

"You are neither cold nor hot. I wish you were either one or the other!" (Rev. 3:15).

Day and night they never stop saying: "Holy, holy, holy is the Lord God Almighty, who was, and is, and is to come" (Rev. 4:8).

"Worthy is the Lamb, who was slain, to receive power and wealth and wisdom and strength and honor and glory and praise!" (Rev. 5:12).

Each of them was given a white robe, and they were told to wait a little longer (Rev. 6:11).

...a great multitude that no one could count, from every nation, tribe, people and language (Rev. 7:9).

In their tails they had power to torment people for five months (Rev. 9:10).

He was robed in a cloud, with a rainbow above his head; his face was like the sun, and his legs were like fiery pillars (Rev. 10:1).

These men have power to shut up the sky so that it will not rain... (Rev. 11:6).

A woman clothed with the sun, with the moon under her feet and a crown of twelve stars on her head (Rev. 12:1).

An enormous red dragon with seven heads and ten horns and seven crowns on his heads (Rev. 12:3).

He was given power to make war against the saints and to conquer them (Rev. 13:7).

He forced everyone, small and great, rich and poor, free and slave, to receive a mark (Rev. 13:16).

These... did not defile themselves with women, for they kept themselves pure (Rev. 14:4).

She held a golden cup in her hand, filled with abominable things and the filth of her adulteries (Rev. 17:4).

"She has become a home for demons and a haunt for every evil spirit" (Rev. 18:2).

A white horse, whose rider is called Faithful and True (Rev. 19:11).

I saw thrones on which were seated those who had been given authority to judge (Rev. 20:4).

When the thousand years are over, ____ will be released from his prison (Rev. 20:7).

He was thrown into the lake of fire (Rev. 20:15).

"Behold, I am coming soon!" (Rev. 22:7).

"I am the Root and the Offspring of David, and the bright Morning Star" (Rev. 22:16).

Definitions

The right-hand column lists the chapter in the textbook in which the word is used.	**Chapter**
Achaia—a Roman province in Greece. It included cities like Athens and Corinth. Paul went to Achaia on his second missionary trip. There, Gallio threw Paul's case out of court.	4, 6
ambassador—a person who represents another person or nation. We are called *ambassadors of Christ* because we tell people His message.	6
Antichrist—*against* or *in place* of Christ. Refers to the person who will fight against and imitate Christ in the Tribulation. He is an evil ruler who will come out of the Abyss to reign on earth for 7 years (Rev. 17:8). Paul refers to him as the *"man of lawlessness"* (2 Thess. 2:8).	13
Antioch—a large Syrian city that was about 300 miles (485 km) north of Jerusalem. It was the second largest city in the Roman Empire. Antioch became a key center for ministry to the Gentiles and was the base of Paul's three missionary trips.	4
apocalyptic—a type of book like Revelation or Daniel that unveils the future through visions and symbols	13
Apocrypha—first meant "hidden" [books]. This group of books was not part of the Hebrew Scriptures. Some people, like Catholics, include it in their Bible.	12
Apollos—an educated, fervent disciple from Alexandria. This Jew became a powerful evangelist after Priscilla and Aquila helped him. Then he realized that there was much beyond John's baptism.	7
apostasy—*a falling away.* Jesus said that in the end times, many people would turn from God, and most people's love would grow cold.	8
Aquila—husband of Priscilla. These two were faithful laypeople. They made tents and helped Paul. They also guided Apollos to be filled with the Spirit.	7
Aramaic—the common language of Jewish people in Jesus' time. It was the language of Babylon. Jewish prisoners learned it there. Sometimes Aramaic is called "Hebrew" because it was the language of the Jews. Jesus probably spoke Aramaic.	2
Artemis—the Greek goddess of the moon. Her Roman name was Diana. She was associated with becoming pregnant. Her statues had many breasts.	7
Asia—in biblical times, this referred to the province whose capital was Pergamum. John wrote to the seven churches of Asia (Rev. 2–3).	4
Assyria—a strong nation northeast of Israel. Its capital was Nineveh. Assyria took the ten Northern Tribes (Israel) into exile in 722 B.C. Babylon conquered Assyria in 612 B.C.	1
Athens—a city of about 10,000 in the province of Achaia. Athens was famous for its philosophy and its university. It was the intellectual capital of the Greek world.	4
autumn trees—autumn is the season between summer and winter. In Israel, autumn fruit trees should have been full of fruit.	12
Babylon—the kingdom north of the Euphrates River that ruled the world from 612-539 B.C. It was the head of gold in Daniel 2 and the lion in Daniel 7. Its first ruler was Nebuchadnezzar. Also, Babylon is a name used to represent Rome. It stands for all who love the world (See 1 John 2:15-17).	1, 10
beasts—symbols that represent the Antichrist and the false prophet of the Antichrist	13
believe—in John, this is an action word. Belief is shown by obedience.	3
bride—in Revelation, this refers to the Church. John contrasts the pure bride of Christ with the harlot of the Antichrist.	13
brigadier—a top general or leader in the British army	4
C. T. Studd—an English missionary in the early 1900s. He served in China, India, and Africa. His motto was: "If Jesus Christ is God and died for me, then no sacrifice can be too great for me to make for Him."	4

Caesar—the top ruler of the Roman Empire	1, 4
Calvary—the Latin word for Golgotha, which is Aramaic for *the place of the skull.* The hill where they crucified Jesus looked like a skull.	2
canon—first meant "standard." Refers to the lists of books in the Old and New Testaments.	12
Catholic Epistles—the seven letters after Hebrews. These are also called *General Epistles.* In this sense, *catholic* means "general, universal, to all."	10
chosen lady—refers to the church. John may have used this term because believers were being persecuted.	12
circumcise—to cut a piece of skin off of the male sex organ. Jewish people circumcised their sons on the 8th day after their birth. This sign of the covenant showed that God ruled over a person's sexual desire. The New Testament emphasizes circumcision of the heart.	4
Colossian heresy—the false teachings of Gnostics in Colosse. These teachings were on rules, self-denial, worshiping angels, lowering Christ, and claims of secret knowledge.	7
coming of the Lord—also called the *Second Coming.* It is used to refer to either Christ's private return (the Rapture) or His public return.	8
contagious—easily spread. (For example, the flu is very *contagious.*)	6
contend—to fight, wrestle, confront, or battle	12
conversion—turning from sin to follow Christ. As this happens, a person is born again.	5
coral—a hard red, pink, or white chalky substance discharged by certain sea creatures to make their place to live and to support themselves	12
Corinth—a large city in Greece known for its sin. Paul spent 18 months there on his second trip.	4, 6
creed—a summary or statement explaining a church's beliefs	9
Crete—an island southeast of Corinth in the Mediterranean Sea. Titus was the pastor there.	9
Dalmatia—a Roman province northwest of Macedonia. Today, this area includes Yugoslavia, Bosnia and Herzegovina, and Croatia.	9
Damascus—the capital city of Syria. It is about 150 miles (242 km) north of Jerusalem. It is about halfway between Jerusalem and Tarsus. Damascus was famous for business.	5
Day of the Lord—refers to the period of time in which Christ will bring His judgments	8
deacon—from the Greek word that meant "minister;" a person who helps an overseer	9
Demetrius—a man of whom everyone spoke well	12
Diaspora—*a scattering;* refers to the scattering of Jews outside their homeland of Palestine because of persecution	10
Diotrephes—a proud man who loved to be first. Diotrephes did not welcome visitors.	12
divine nature—humans begin to share in God's divine nature at the new birth. At that time believers receive the Spirit of Christ and eternal life. His plan for us is to grow daily in His likeness, in holiness and righteousness.	11
down payment—a deposit; in business, money given as a pledge (usually of full payment in the future)	7
drink offering—a sacrifice that was offered with the burnt offering and the fellowship offering, together with a grain offering (flour mixed with oil). The drink offering was usually about a liter (a quart) of wine.	9
dropsy—a medical term for a build-up of water in an unusual part of the body. This can be a symptom of several diseases. Only Luke uses this term.	2
dynasty—a kingdom where one family rules for several generations	1
effort—an attempt; a try; something you do to reach a goal	11
Enoch—a man who lived between Adam and Noah. There is also a book of the Pseudepigrapha with the same name, but this Enoch did not write it.	12

Ephesus—the leading city of Asia. Paul ministered there for 3 years. It was in the center of some churches that Paul planted. 6

epilogue—the concluding section of a letter, play, or piece of music 3

eschatology—the study of the end times. From the Greek words *eschatos,* or "last," and *logos,* "word" or "study." 8

---

false prophet—a title for the one who will assist the Antichrist. John refers to him as the beast that rose out of the land. 13

favoritism—treating one person better than you treat someone else 10

filled with the Holy Spirit—also called "baptized with the Spirit." This happens after conversion. The outward, biblical evidence of this experience is speaking in a new language. 4

firstborn—the person had special rights and privileges because of birth order. Jesus is called the Firstborn because He is first in rank. He is above all that He created. 7

futurist—a view that focuses mostly on the future to interpret Revelation. It teaches that Revelation 4–22 will happen in the future. 13

Gaius—a man who walked in the truth and welcomed strangers. Third John was written to him. 12

Galatia—a province that included churches like Pisidian Antioch, Iconium, Lystra, and Derbe. Paul founded these on his first trip and visited them on his second and third trips. He wrote the letter of Galatians to them between his first and second missionary trips. 4

Gallio—the proconsul (governor) of Achaia. He threw Paul's case out of court. 6

genealogy—a list of descendants covering several generations 2

General Epistles—the seven letters after Hebrews that are named for their authors. All of them except 2 and 3 John are written to *the* Church. That is, they are not written to a specific church. 1, 10

geographically—geography is the study of the earth's surface. We say the church grew *geographically* because its physical location expanded. 4

Gnostic—from the Greek word *gnosis,* or "knowledge." These false teachers claimed to have secret knowledge for salvation. They taught that the body and all matter were evil. 7

Gnosticism—the teachings of the Gnostics 7

God-breathed—in regard to Scripture, this means that God breathed His Spirit into those who wrote the Bible. Thus we are sure that the Scriptures are inspired, true, and without error. 9

Greeks—a people who, under Alexander the Great and his generals, ruled from 330-166 B.C. They spread their language and culture across the world 1

---

harlot—a prostitute. In Revelation, it is a symbol of Rome and the people with her values. The harlot represents all who love the world (See 1 John 2:15-17). 13

Hellenistic—the Greek word for a Greek person is *Hellene*. Therefore, Greek ideas and culture are referred to as *Hellenistic*. Antioch was a major center of Hellenism, that is, Greek ideas and culture. 1

High Priest—the most important religious leader of Israel. He entered the inner part of the temple once a year to make a sacrifice for the nation's sin. 10

historist—a view that focuses on the past and present to interpret Revelation. It matches Revelation with events of history, from the early church to the present. 13

---

idealist—a view that says that Revelation is about spiritual ideas, not real people or events. It interprets Revelation like a parable that did not happen and will not happen. 13

immaturity—not being or acting fully-grown; having to depend on someone else to give you what you need to live and grow, like a baby 10

isthmus—a narrow strip of land, with water on both sides, that connects two larger areas of land 6

Jerome—a Catholic Church leader who made a list of books in the Apocrypha. He also translated the Bible into Latin. This famous translation is called the Vulgate. 12

Jerusalem—the capital city of Jews in New Testament times. The final part of the word, *salem* (shalom), means "peace." David was the first of Israel to conquer the city, sometimes referred to as *Zion* (See 2 Sam. 5:6-8). It became his capital. Later, Solomon built the temple there. 4

Jews—those from the 12 tribes of Israel. A person who is not a Jew is called a *Gentile.* 1

Judaizers—born-again Jewish believers who were Pharisees. They accepted Jesus, but still taught that all believers must obey the law of Moses. Thus they emphasized circumcision for Gentiles. 5, 7

Judea—the southern part or region of ancient Palestine. It was just north of the region of Idumea. 4

justification—being counted as righteous by God 5

---

kingdom of heaven—the place where the King reigns. On earth, this is in the hearts of believers. The kingdom of heaven has an invisible and a visible phase. 2

Lamb—a title of Jesus emphasizing that He became the sacrifice to take away our sins 13

Lamb's book of life—a book Christ has of all who love God and make peace with Him through Jesus 13

lampstands—seven different stands; each held up or supported a lamp. 13

life—as used in John, *eternal* life. Life results from believing in Christ. 3

Lord God Almighty—*Lord*—the One in heaven who rules over all; *God*—in contrast to humans, angels, and evil spirits; *Almighty*—the One with all power 13

Maccabean Period (also called Hasmonean)—a time between the Old and New Testaments (166-63 B.C.) during which a family of Jewish priests led a revolt against Greek and Syrian leaders with pagan religions. *Maccabeus* means "hammer." This was a nickname given to Judas, who was one of these leaders. He was the son of a priest named Mattathias. 1

Macedonia—a province in northern Greece. The capital was Thessalonica, but it also included the important city of Philippi. 4, 6

malign—to accuse, insult, or slander someone 9

marathon—long-distance running race, usually 26 miles 385 yards (42.195 km) 11

mediator—someone who goes between two people or groups of people 10

Messiah—a Hebrew word for *anointed one.* The Greek word is *Christ.* The Jewish people believed that God would send a Messiah to deliver them. John shows in his Gospel that Jesus is the Messiah. 2

monotheism—belief in one God; from Greek, *mono* (one) and *theos* (God) 1

Muratorian Canon—an ancient list of New Testament books. It is named after its first editor, Ludivico Muratori. This list or canon is dated about A.D. 170-210. 4

Onesimus—the slave that Paul sent back to his master, Philemon. *Onesimus* means "useful." 7

overseer—the translation of the Greek word *episkopos*. It refers to one who supervises, such as a presbyter, bishop, or pastor. 9

Palestine—the area occupied by the 12 tribes of Israel. Roughly, Canaan plus some land east of the Jordan. It is defined by some mountains and a river on the north, the Mediterranean on the west, the Negev (desert) on the south, and the Syrian desert on the east. 1

parable—a short story or illustration with a spiritual meaning 2

Parousia—a Greek word that refers to the coming of Christ at the end of this age 8

Parthenon—a temple to the goddess Athena in Athens. It was built in the 5th century. 7

Passion Week—refers to the week before Jesus' death. It is called this because in Latin, *passio* means "suffering." 2

Passover, Feast of—a Jewish feast remembering how God saved His people from the last plague in Egypt. The angel of death was to kill every firstborn male in a house. But if a family killed a lamb, and put its blood on their doorframe, the angel would *pass over* that house. This showed how Jesus would die on Passover as a sacrifice for our sin, and we would not die spiritually if we would accept Him. 1

Pentecost, Feast of—a Jewish feast celebrating the barley harvest and the giving of the Ten Commandments on Mt. Sinai. It took place 50 days after the Passover Feast (*pentecost* means "fiftieth day" in Greek). The Holy Spirit was given on the Day of Pentecost in Acts 2. Also called "Feast of Weeks." 1

persevere—not to give up; to continue in spite of hard situations 10

Pharisees—*the separate people.* They were members of a Jewish group. These strictly followed the law of Moses and Jewish religious customs. Many did not like Jesus because He did not follow all of their rules. 1

Philemon—Paul's friend who was the master of Onesimus (See above) 7

Philippi—a city in Macedonia that Paul visited on his second missionary trip. He saw a vision of a man from Macedonia, and went to Philippi to preach Christ. 4

predestine—to plan ahead; to choose in advance 7

prejudice—hatred toward someone that is different from you (usually because they have a different skin color or religion) 4

preterist—a view that focuses on the past to interpret Revelation. It teaches that Revelation 1–18 happened in the first century. 13

Priscilla—wife of Aquila. This husband and wife team made tents. They helped Paul and others, like Apollos. Priscilla seems to be the leading teacher of the team. 7

Prison Epistles—Ephesians, Philippians, Colossians, and Philemon. Paul probably wrote these letters from the Mamertine Prison in Rome. 7

prologue—the opening section of a letter, play, or piece of music (like an introduction) 3

Pseudepigrapha—a group of books with false authors written in between the Old and New Testaments 12

Rapture—the event in which believers will be caught up to meet Jesus in the air (1 Thess. 4:17) 8

reconcile—to bring into agreement; to settle differences 6

Reformation—a religious movement in the 16th century. Many churches split off of the Roman Catholic Church. These churches (such as Lutheran and Methodist) are called *Protestant* because they protested. They teach that we are justified by faith and that the Bible is a higher authority than tradition or the pope.

Reformed Church—a group of churches that follow teachings of John Calvin. They split off of the Catholic Church during the Reformation (See above). They believe that we do not have a free will. God has chosen some people for heaven, and some for hell. This is not based on works or on willful faith. Those whom God has chosen to go to heaven cannot resist His grace. The Presbyterian church is a Reformed church. 10

Revelation—a translation of the Greek word *apokalupto,* which means "unveil." 13

righteousness—being right with God and doing what is right. Righteousness is a gift of God and is based on Christ's death. 5

Romans—people who conquered the Greeks and ruled from 63 B.C. to A.D. 486. They ruled from the western end of the Mediterranean Sea to the Euphrates River in the East. 1

Rome—the capital city of the Roman Empire, where the Caesar lived. Rome was very sinful. 4

Sadducees—a group of powerful Jewish leaders. The high priest and the leading officials of the Sanhedrin were Sadducees. They did not believe in the resurrection, angels, or spirits. 1

salvation—being rescued from sin and death by trusting in Jesus 5

Samaria—the biblical area between Galilee and Judea. (There was also a city called Samaria that was in this region.) Samaritans, the people who lived there, were only partly Jewish. The Jews and the Samaritans hated each other. 4

sanctification—holiness that results from what Jesus did for us and what He does in us 5

sanctuary—a holy or sacred place; usually refers to a place of worship 10

Sanhedrin—the highest Jewish court. It was made up of 70 elders and the High Priest. 1

scepter—a short rod used as a symbol of authority. It is held by a king or ruler. 13

Scriptures—means "writings." This first referred to the Old Testament, but can refer to the whole Bible. 1, 9

Septuagint—the Greek translation of the Hebrew Old Testament. From a Latin word meaning "seventy," because there were about seventy scholars who worked on it. 1

sewer—a place that is polluted with human bodily waste 5

sign—John's word for miracle. Refers to a miracle that shows that Jesus is the Messiah. These signs were done so that people would believe in Christ. 3

sin—lawlessness; rebellion against God 11

Son of Man—a name that Jesus called Himself. This title emphasizes that Jesus was both God and man at the same time. 2

soteriological—having to do with salvation 9

soteriology—the study of salvation. From the Greek word *soteria,* which means salvation. 5

substitution—one thing or person being replaced by another 5

superior—better, more excellent 10

supreme—highest in rank or quality 7

synagogues—buildings where Jewish people met to learn Scripture, worhsip and pray, and study 1

Synoptic Gospels—the first three Gospels—Matthew, Mark, and Luke. They are called *Synoptic* because they tell similar stories about the life of Christ. 2

Tabernacles, Feast of—also called *Feast of Booths.* A Jewish feast that remember how God took care of His people when they left Egypt and lived in tents in the desert. People made tents and lived in them for a week while they celebrated this feast. 1

temple—a building where people worship God. Usually refers to the temple in Jerusalem, where Jews came to make sacrifices and celebrate feasts 1

terrorist—a person who uses violent methods or threats to forcefully persuade a government or com 12

Theophilus—a common Greek name that means "lover of God." Both Luke and Acts were addressed to a Theophilus 4

Thessalonica—the capital of Macedonia. Paul started a church at Thessalonica on his second missionary trip. 4

Timothy—one of Paul's close friends and helpers. He has a Jewish mother and a Greek father, and knew the Scriptures from when he was young 9

Titus—a Greek man who was one of Paul's friends and helpers. Titus helped solve church problems. (There was also a famous Roman general named Titus, who conquered Jerusalem in A.D. 70.) 9

Torah—refers to the first five books of the Bible. From a Hebrew word meaning "instruction" or "law." 1

Triumphal Entry—the time when Jesus rode into Jerusalem on a donkey during the week before His death. The crowd was very excited, and treated Him like a king. They thought that Jesus was going to overthrow the Roman government. 2

Word—a title John uses for Jesus. *The Word* is God, the Creator, the Giver of Life, and the One who came in flesh. Jesus is the Word who tells us about the Father. 3

Scripture List

Bibliography

Barclay, William. *The Letters to James and Peter*. Philadelphia, Pennsylvania: The Westminster Press, 1976.

_____. *The Letters to John and Jude*. Philadelphia, Pennsylvania: The Westminster Press, 1976.

Barker, Kenneth, gen. ed. *The NIV Study Bible*. Grand Rapids, Michigan: Zondervan Publishing House, 1985.

Barrett, C. K. *The Second Epistle to the Corinthians*. London: Adam and Charles Black, 1976.

Barrett, David. *International Bulletin of Missionary Research*, Fall 2000.

Bruce, F. F. *The Book of Acts*. Grand Rapids, Michigan: Wm. B. Eerdmans Publishing Co., 1974.

Carnegie, Dale. *How to Win Friends and Influence People*. London, Great Britain: Cedar, 1981.

Carson, D. A., Douglas J. Moo, and Leon Morris. *An Introduction to the New Testament*. Grand Rapids, Michigan: Zondervan Publishing House, 1992.

Cole, Glen D. "Waiting for the Promise," *Cassette Series on Acts*, Sermon Number One. Sacramento, California: Capital Christian Center.

_____, and Quentin R. McGhee. *Revelation & Daniel*. 3rd ed. Springfield, Missouri: Resource & Development Ministries, 2005.

Cooley, Robert E. "The Apocalypse: 7 Letters to the Church," *The Pentecostal Evangel*, April 11, 1999.

deSilva, David A. *Exegesis of the Apocalypse: Graduate Study Guide*. Irving, Texas: ICI University Press, 1997.

Douglas, J. D., ed. *The New Bible Dictionary*. Grand Rapids, Michigan: Wm. B. Eerdmans Publishing Co., 1978.

Drane, John. *Introducing the New Testament*. Minneapolis, Minnesota: Fortress Press, 2001.

Dunnet, Walter M. *New Testament Survey, Matthew–Revelation, Broadening Your Biblical Horizons*. Wheaton, Illinois: Evangelical Training Association, 1963.

Eadie, John. *A Commentary on the Greek Text of the Epistle of Paul to the Ephesians*. Grand Rapids, Michigan: Baker Book House, 1979.

Elwell, Walter A., and Robert W. Yarbrough. *Encountering the New Testament*. Grand Rapids, Michigan: Baker Book House, 1998.

Geisler, Norman. *A Popular Survey of the Old Testament*. Grand Rapids, Michigan: Baker Book House, 1982.

Geldenhuys, Norval. *The New International Commentary on the New Testament: Commentary on the Gospel of Luke*. Grand Rapids, Michigan: Wm. B. Eerdmans Publishing Co., 1977.

Gibbs, Carl. *Acts of the Apostles*, The Barnabas Series—A Faculty Enrichment Packet. November, 1999.

Gillespie, G. K. *Englishman's Greek Concordance of the New Testament*. Grand Rapids, Michigan: Zondervan Publishing House, 1970.

Gundry, Robert H. *A Survey of the New Testament*. Grand Rapids, Michigan: Zondervan Publishing House, 1994.

Harding, Joe. *Don't Blame Mary*, printed sermon. Richland, Washington: Central United Protestant Church, 1984.

Harris, Laird. *The Inspiration and Canonicity of Scripture*. Grand Rapids, Michigan: Zondervan Publishing House, 1975.

Harris, Ralph W., ed. *The Complete Biblical Library: The New Testament Study Bible, Matthew*. Vol. 1. Springfield, Missouri: World Library Press, Inc., 1989.

_____, ed. *The Complete Biblical Library: The New Testament Study Bible, Romans–Corinthians*. Vol. 7. Springfield, Missouri: World Library Press, Inc., 1989.

_____, ed. *The Complete Biblical Library: The New Testament Study Bible, Galatians–Philemon*. Vol. 8. Springfield, Missouri: World Library Press, Inc., 1995.

_____, ed. *The Complete Biblical Library: The New Testament Study Bible, Hebrews–Jude*, Vol. 9. Springfield, Missouri: World Library Press, Inc., 1986.

Hewett, James S., ed. *Illustrations Unlimited.* Wheaton, Illinois: Tyndale House Publishers, Inc., 1988.

Horton, Stanley M. *The Book of Acts*. Springfield, Missouri: Gospel Publishing House, 1994.

_____. *The Ultimate Victory, An Exposition of the Book of Revelation*. Springfield, Missouri: Gospel Publishing House, 1991.

Hughes, Philip E. *The Second Epistle to the Corinthians*. Grand Rapids, Michigan: Wm. B. Eerdmans Publishing Co., 1977.

Hybels, Bill. *Live Wisely: James*. Grand Rapids, Michigan: Zondervan Publishing House, 1999.

Hymns of Faith & Inspiration. Nashville, Tennessee: Ideals Publications Incorporated, 1990.

Klein, William W., Craig L. Blomberg, and Robert L. Hubbard, Jr. *Introduction to Biblical Interpretation*. Dallas, Texas: Word Publishers, 1993.

Kraybill, J. Nelson. "Apocalypse Now," *Christianity Today*, Volume 43, No. 12, October 25, 1999.

Leaney, A. R. C. *The Cambridge Bible Commentary on the New English Bible: The Letters of Peter and Jude.* London: Cambridge University Press, 1967.

Lemair, André. "Evidence of Jesus Written in Stone," *Biblical Archaeology Review* (online), Nov./Dec. 2002, http://www.bib-arch.org/bswb_BAR/bswbbar2806f1.html. Accessed 11/12/02.

McGee, Gary B. *Initial Evidence*. Peabody, Massachusetts: Hendrickson Publishers, 1991.

Mears, Henrietta. *What the Bible Is All About*. Ventura, California: Regal Books, 1983.

Menzies, William W., and Robert P. Menzies. *Spirit and Power*. Grand Rapids, Michigan: Zondervan Publishing House, 2000.

Merriam Webster's Collegiate Dictionary, 10th ed. Springfield, Massachusetts: Merriam-Webster, Inc., 1993.

Metzger, Bruce. *The Oxford Annotated Apocrypha*. New York: Oxford University Press, 1977.

Morris, Leon. *New International Commentary on the New Testament: The Gospel According to John.* Grand Rapids, Michigan: Wm. B. Eerdmans Publishing Co., 1971.

Mounce, Robert H. *New International Commentary on the New Testament: The Book of Revelation.* Grand Rapids, Michigan: Wm. B. Eerdmans Publishing Co., 1977.

_____. *New International Commentary on the New Testament: The Book of Revelation.* rev. ed. Grand Rapids, Michigan: Wm. B. Eerdmans Publishing Co., 1998.

The New English Bible with the Apocrypha. Great Britain, Oxford University Press, 1970.

Neyrey, Jerome H. *The Anchor Bible (Commentary), 2 Peter, Jude*. New York: Doubleday, 1993.

Orr, James. *The International Standard Bible Encyclopedia*, Vol. IV. Grand Rapids, Michigan: Wm. B. Eerdmans Publishing Co., 1956.

Purkiser, W. T. *Beacon Bible Expositions: Hebrews, James, and Peter.* Kansas City, Missouri: Beacon Hill Press, 1974.

Roberts, Oral. *Christ in Every Book of the Bible.* Tulsa, Oklahoma: Oral Roberts Univesity Press, 1965.

Spurgeon, Charles H. *John Ploughman's Talks*. Grand Rapids, Michigan: Baker Book House, 1976.

Stamps, Donald C., ed., and John Wesley Adams, assoc. ed. *The Full Life Study Bible*. Grand Rapids, Michigan: Zondervan Publishing House, 1975.

Stedman, Ray C. *The IVP New Testament Commentary Series: Hebrews.* Downers Grove, Illinois: InterVarsity Press, 1992.

Stott, John R. W. *The Message of Acts: The Spirit, the Church and the World.* Downers Grove, Illinois: InterVarsity Press, 1994.

Stronstad, Roger. *Spirit, Scripture, & Theology*. Baguio City, Philippines: Asia Pacific Theological Seminary Press, 1995.

Tan, Paul Lee. *Encyclopedia of 7700 Illustrations: Signs of the Times*. Rockville, Maryland: Assurance Publishers, 1984.

Tenney, Merrill C. *New Testament Survey*. Grand Rapids, Michigan: Wm. B. Eerdmans Publishing Co., 1961.

Walvoord, John F. *The Revelation*. Chicago, Illinois: Moody Press, 1980.

_____, and Roy B. Zuck. *The Bible Knowledge Commentary*. Wheaton, Illinois: Victor Books, 1997.

Wesley, John. *Explanatory Notes Upon the New Testament*, Vol. 2. Grand Rapids, Michigan: Baker Book House, 1983.

Westlake, George W., Jr. *Daniel and Revelation*. Irving, Texas: ICI University Press, 1995.

Wiersbe, Warren. *The Bible Exposition Commentary: Ephesians–Revelations*. Vol. 2. Wheaton, Illinois: Victor Books, 1989.

Wood, George O. *Study in Acts*, Introduction. (cassette tape) Costa Mesa, California: Newport-Mesa Christian Center, 1987.

_____. *Study in Acts*, Acts 18, (cassette tape) Costa Mesa, California: Newport-Mesa Christian Center, 1988.

_____. *Acts–A Study Guide*. Irving, Texas: ICI University Press, 1996.

_____. *Acts of the Holy Spirit*. 3rd ed. Springfield, Missouri: Resource and Development Ministries, 2005.

http://www.angelfire.com/ms/spiritual/page16.html accessed 11/05/01

http://www.gospelcom.net/chi/GLIMPSEF/Glimpses/glmps064.shtml-accessed 11/05/01

http://www.bib-arch.org/bswb_BAR/bswbbar2806f1.html.-accessed 11/12/02

Endnotes

Chapter 1

[1] F. F. Bruce, *New Testament History* (New York: Doubleday, 1971), pp. 69-72.

[2] J. D. Douglas, ed., *The New Bible Dictionary* (Grand Rapids, Michigan: Wm. B. Eerdmans Publishing Co., 1978), p. 981.

[3] Kenneth Barker, gen. ed., *The NIV Study Bible* (Grand Rapids, Michigan: Zondervan Publishing House, 1985), p. 1430.

[4] Walter M. Dunnet, *New Testament Survey, Matthew–Revelation, Broadening Your Biblical Horizons* (Wheaton, Illinois: Evangelical Training Association, 1963), p. 6.

[5] Norman Geisler, *A Popular Survey of the Old Testament* (Grand Rapids, Michigan: Baker Book House, 1982), pp. 21-24.

[6] Henrietta Mears, *What the Bible Is All About* (Ventura, California: Regal Books, 1983), pp. 337-649.

[7] Oral Roberts, *Christ in Every Book of the Bible* (Tulsa, Oklahoma: Oral Roberts University Press, 1965).

Chapter 2

[1] Mears, p. 340.

[2] Merrill C. Tenney, *New Testament Survey* (Grand Rapids, Michigan: Wm. B. Eerdmans Publishing Co., 1961), p. 146.

[3] Donald C. Stamps, gen. ed., and J. Wesley Adams, assoc. ed., *The Full Life Study Bible* (Grand Rapids, Michigan: Zondervan Publishing House, 1992), p. 1403.

[4] Norval Geldenhuys, *The New International Commentary on the New Testament: Commentary on the Gospel of Luke* (Grand Rapids, Michigan: Wm. B. Eerdmans Publishing Co., 1977), pp. 43-44.

[5] Geldenhuys, p. 45.

[6] Joe Harding, *Don't Blame Mary*, printed sermon (Richland, Washington: Central United Protestant Church, 1984).

Chapter 3

[1] Interview with Missionary Dan Lund from Malawi, September, 2001.

[2] Mears, p. 397.

[3] Leon Morris, *New International Commentary on the New Testament: The Gospel According to John* (Grand Rapids, Michigan: Wm. B. Eerdmans Publishing Co., 1971), p. 226.

[4] Morris, p. 248.

[5] Paul Lee Tan, *Encyclopedia of 7700 Illustrations: Signs of the Times* (Rockville, Maryland: Assurance Publishers, 1984), p. 403.

[6] Tenney, p. 190.

Chapter 4

[1] John Lindell, Pastor at James River Assembly in Springfield, Missouri, Sermon "The first Christian martyr" preached September 2, 2001.

[2] Carl Gibbs, *Acts of the Apostles*, The Barnabas Series–A Faculty Enrichment Packet, November, 1999, p. 33.

[3] Stanley M. Horton, *The Book of Acts* (Springfield, Missouri: Gospel Publishing House, 1994), p. 9.

[4] George O. Wood, *Study in Acts,* Introduction, cassette tape (Costa Mesa, California: Newport-Mesa Christian Center, 1987).

[5] Horton, p. 11.

[6] George O. Wood, *Acts—A Study Guide* (Irving, Texas: ICI University Press, 1996), p. 7.

[7] Horton, p. 10.

[8] John F. Walvoord and Roy B. Zuck, *The Bible Knowledge Commentary* (Wheaton, Illinois: Victor Books, 1997), p. 89.

[9] Horton, p. 184.

[10] William W. Menzies and Robert Menzies, *Spirit and Power* (Grand Rapids, Michigan: Zondervan Publishing House, 2000), p. 41.

[11] Bill Lasley, Missionary and editor at Global University, Interview on the relationship between history and doctrine, July, 2000.

[12] Roger Stronstad, *Spirit, Scripture, & Theology* (Baguio City, Philippines: Asia Pacific Theological Seminary Press, 1995), p. 42.

[13] *The NIV Study Bible*, p. 1642.

[14] Glen D. Cole, "Waiting for the Promise," *Cassette Series on Acts,* Sermon Number One (Sacramento, California: Capital Christian Center).

[15] Lindell, Sermon on Romans 12, September, 2000.

[16] David Barrett, *International Bulletin of Missionary Research,* Fall 2000, p. 25.

[17] Stronstad, pp. 189-192.

[18] Gary B. McGee, *Initial Evidence* (Peabody, Massachusetts: Hendrickson, 1991), p. 164.

[19] Dunnett, p. 29.

[20] Adapted from Robert H. Gundry, *A Survey of the New Testament* (Grand Rapids, Michigan: Zondervan Publishing House, 1994), pp. 313-314.

[21] David Barrett, p. 25.

Chapter 5

[1] Willard Teague, Missionary to Africa for 27 years, supplied this illustration.

[2] *The NIV Study Bible*, p. 1672.

[3] George O. Wood, *Acts of the Holy Spirit,* 3rd ed. (Springfield, Missouri: Global University Press, 2001), p. 156.

Chapter 5 (continued)

4 John R. W. Stott, *The Message of Acts: The Spirit, the Church and the World* (Downers Grove, Illinois: InterVarsity Press, 1994), p. 383.

5 Wood, *Acts* (ICI), p. 388.

6 Adams, *The Full Life Study Bible*, p. 1705.

7 G. K. Gillespie, *Englishman's Greek Concordance of the New Testament* (Grand Rapids, Michigan: Zondervan Publishing House, 1970), pp. 7-8.

8 Gundry, pp. 257-259.

9 Adams, *The Full Life Study Bible*, pp. 1806-1807.

10 Stamps, *The Full Life Study Bible*, "Personal Apostasy," pp. 1918-1919.

Chapter 6

1 Adams, *The Full Life Study Bible*, p. 1748.

2 Bruce, p. 367.

3 Stott, p. 296.

4 Wood, *Acts* (ICI), p. 289.

5 Stott, pp. 295-296.

6 Wood, *Acts* (ICI), p. 289.

7 George O. Wood, *Study in Acts*, Acts 18, cassette tape (Costa Mesa, California: Newport-Mesa Christian Center, 1988).

8 Stott, p. 293.

9 Charles Pfeiffer, Howard Vos, and John Rea, *Wycliffe Bible Encyclopedia*, vol. 1 (Chicago, Illinois: Moody Press, 1975), p. 380.

10 *The NIV Study Bible*, p. 1732.

11 David Barrett, p. 25.

12 Stott, p. 292.

13 Stamps, *The Full Life Study Bible*, Acts 28:30, p. 1704.

14 Tenney, p. 297.

15 Ralph W. Harris, ed., *The Complete Biblical Library: The New Testament Study Bible, Romans–Corinthians*, vol. 7 (Springfield, Missouri: World Library Press, Inc., 1989), p. 313.

16 D. A. Carson, Douglas J. Moo, and Leon Morris, *An Introduction to the New Testament* (Grand Rapids, Michigan: Zondervan Publishing House, 1992), pp. 264-283.

17 Walter A. Elwell and Robert W. Yarbrough, *Encountering The New Testament* (Grand Rapids, Michigan: Baker Book House, 1998), p. 293.

18 Gundry, 285.

19 Philip E. Hughes, *The Second Epistle to the Corinthians* (Grand Rapids, Michigan: Wm. B. Eerdmans Publishing Co., 1977), p. xvii.

20 C. K. Barrett, *The Second Epistle to the Corinthians* (London: Adam and Charles Black, 1976), pp. 17-19.

21 Hughes, p. xvi.

22 Hughes, p. xxii.

23 Gundry, p. 286.

24 Gundry, p. 285.

25 Hughes, p. xvii.

Chapter 7

1 http://www.angelfire.com/ms/spiritual/page16.html and http://www.gospelcom.net/chi/GLIMPSEF/Glimpses/glmps064.shtml—accessed 11/05/01

2 J. D. Douglas, ed., *The New Bible Dictionary* (Grand Rapids, Michigan: Wm. B. Eerdmans Publishing Co., 1978), p. 380.

3 Robert E. Cooley, "The Apocalypse: 7 Letters to the Church," *The Pentecostal Evangel*, April 11, 1999, p. 22.

4 Robert H. Mounce, *New International Commentary on the New Testament: The Book of Revelation* (Grand Rapids, Michigan: Wm. B. Eerdmans Publishing Co., 1977), p. 85.

5 Douglas, p. 380.

6 Stott, p. 293.

7 Douglas, p. 381.

8 *The NIV Study Bible*, p. 1789.

9 Douglas, p. 311.

10 George O. Wood, *Study in Acts*, Acts 18, cassette tape (Costa Mesa, California: Newport-Mesa Christian Center, 1988).

11 Bruce, p. 387.

12 Stamps, *The Full Life Study Bible*, "Election and Predestination," pp. 1824-25.

13 John Eadie, *A Commentary on the Greek Text of the Epistle of Paul to the Ephesians* (Grand Rapids, Michigan: Baker Book House, 1979), p. xlviii.

14 Douglas, p. 23.

Chapter 8

1 Dale Carnegie, *How to Win Friends and Influence People* (London, Great Britain: Cedar, 1981), p. 33.

2 *The NIV Study Bible*, p. 1819.

3 Gundry, p. 270.

4 Ralph W. Harris, ed., *The Complete Biblical Library: The New Testament Study Bible, Galatians–Philemon*, vol. 8 (Springfield, Missouri: World Library Press, Inc., 1995), p. 353.

5 Stamps, *The Full Life Study Bible*, "The Age of the Antichrist," p. 1872.

6 Gundry, p. 271.

Chapter 9

1 Adams, *The Full Life Study Bible*, p. 1877.

2 Gundry, p. 325.

3 Stamps, *The Full Life Study Bible*, "Moral Qualifications for Overseers," p. 1882.

4 Adams, *The Full Life Study Bible*, p. 1901-02.

5 Adams, *The Full Life Study Bible*, pp. 1889-1890.

6 Elwell and Yarbrough, p. 364.

7 Tenney, p. 341.

8 Gundry, pp. 327-328.

Chapter 10

[1] Tenney, p. 358.

[2] Stamps, *The Full Life Study Bible*, p. 1912.

[3] Tenney, pp. 355-357.

[4] *The NIV Study Bible*, pp. 1857-58.

[5] Ray C. Stedman, *The IVP New Testament Commentary Series: Hebrews* (Downers Grove, Illinois: InterVarsity Press, 1992), p. 135.

[6] Tenney, p. 362.

[7] Gundry, p. 342.

[8] Elwell and Yarbrough, p. 354.

[9] Adams, *The Full Life Study Bible*, p. 1940.

[10] James Orr, *The International Standard Bible Encyclopedia*, vol. IV (Grand Rapids, Michigan: Wm. B. Eerdmans Publishing Co., 1956), p. 1560.

[11] Adams, *The Full Life Study Bible*, p. 1940.

[12] *The NIV Study Bible*, p. 1879.

[13] Tenney, p. 262.

[14] Elwell and Yarbrough, p. 354.

[15] Elwell and Yarbrough, p. 355.

[16] Elwell and Yarbrough, p. 356.

[17] Bill Hybels, *Live Wisely: James* (Grand Rapids, Michigan: Zondervan Publishing House, 1999), p. 24.

[18] Elwell and Yarbrough, p. 353.

[19] William W. Klein, Craig L. Blomberg, and Robert L. Hubbard, Jr., *Introduction to Biblical Interpretation* (Dallas, Texas: Word, 1993), pp. 386-387.

[20] Orr, p. 1566.

[21] Gundry, p. 343.

[22] William Barclay, *The Letters to James and Peter* (Philadelphia, Pennsylvania: The Westminster Press, 1976), pp. 140-141.

[23] W. T. Purkiser, *Beacon Bible Expositions: Hebrews, James, and Peter* (Kansas City, Missouri: Beacon Hill Press, 1974), pp. 170-171.

[24] Elwell and Yarbrough, p. 362.

[25] *The NIV Study Bible* textual footnote on John 1:42, p. 1595.

[26] Stamps, *The Full Life Study Bible*, John 21:18, p. 1629.

[27] Tenney, pp. 351-352.

[28] Ralph W. Harris, ed., *The Complete Biblical Library: The New Testament Study Bible, Hebrews–Jude*, vol. 9 (Springfield, Missouri: World Library Press, Inc., 1986), p. 315.

[29] Tenney, p. 358.

[30] André Lemair, "Evidence of Jesus Written in Stone," *Biblical Archaeology Review (online),* Nov./Dec. 2002, http://www.bib-arch.org/bswb_BAR/bswbbar2806f1.html. Accessed 11/12/02. Also: http://www.bib-arch.org/bswbOOossuary_IAAreport.html (Nov. 12, 2004)

Chapter 11

[1] Ralph W. Harris, ed., *The Complete Biblical Library: The New Testament Study Bible, Matthew,* vol. 1 (Springfield, Missouri: World Library Press, 1989), p. 355.

[2] Elwell and Yarbrough, p. 366.

[3] Stamps, *The Full Life Study Bible*, article on the relationship of faith and grace, p. 1720.

[4] Stamps, *The Full Life Study Bible*, Ephesians 2:9 note, pp. 1826-1827.

[5] Gundry, p. 355.

[6] Gundry, p. 355.

[7] *The NIV Study Bible*, p. 1905.

[8] Adams, *The Full Life Study Bible*, p. 1971.

[9] Elwell and Yarbrough, p. 367.

[10] Robert H. Mounce, *The New International Commentary on the New Testament: The Book of Revelation*, rev. ed. (Grand Rapids, Michigan: Wm. B. Eerdmans Publishing Co., 1998), p. 15.

[11] John Drane, *Introducing the New Testament* (Minneapolis, Minnesota: Fortress Press, 2001), pp. 452-453.

[12] Orr, p. 2798.

[13] Douglas, pp. 1189-1190.

[14] Charles H. Spurgeon, "Thoughts about thought," *John Ploughman's Talks* (Grand Rapids, Michigan: Baker Book House, 1976), pp. 50-53.

[15] John Wesley, *Explanatory Notes Upon the New Testament*, vol. 2 (Grand Rapids, Michigan: Baker Book House, 1983), 1 John 3:5.

[16] Orr, p. 2801.

Chapter 12

[1] James H. Hewett, ed., *Illustrations Unlimited* (Wheaton, Illinois: Tyndale House Publishers, Inc., 1988), p. 481.

[2] Adams, *The Full Life Study Bible*, p. 1985.

[3] William Barclay, *The Letters to John and Jude* (Philadelphia, Pennsylvania: The Westminster Press, 1976), p. 138.

[4] Barclay, *The Letters to John and Jude*, p. 139.

[5] Barclay, *The Letters to John and Jude*, p. 153.

[6] Jerome H. Neyrey, *The Anchor Bible (Commentary), 2 Peter, Jude* (New York: Doubleday, 1993), p. 28.

[7] Adams, *The Full Life Study Bible*, p. 1993.

[8] *Merriam Webster's Collegiate Dictionary*, 10th ed. (Springfield, Massachusetts: Merriam-Webster, Inc., 1993).

[9] A. R. C. Leaney, *The Cambridge Bible Commentary on the New English Bible: The Letters of Peter and Jude* (London: Cambridge University Press, 1967), pp. 101-104.

[10] Carl Gibbs, Missionary and Dean of the School of Graduate Studies at Global University, interview on January 25, 2002.

[11] Laird Harris, *The Inspiration and Canonicity of Scripture* (Grand Rapids, Michigan: Zondervan Publishing House 1975), p. 183.

Chapter 12 (continued)

12 Gundry, pp. 44-46.

13 Elwell and Yarbrough, p. 28.

14 Klein, Blomberg, and Hubbard, p. 55.

15 Elwell and Yarbrough, p. 28.

16 Douglas, p. 197.

17 Gundry, p. 57.

18 Elwell and Yarbrough, p. 21.

19 Douglas, p. 186.

20 Laird Harris, p. 180.

21 Orr, p. 2728.

22 Laird Harris, p. 183.

23 Bruce Metzger, *The Oxford Annotated Apocrypha* (New York: Oxford University Press, 1977), p. xi.

24 "Introduction to the Apocrypha," *The New English Bible with the Apocrypha* (Great Britain, Oxford University Press, 1970), p. v.

Chapter 13

1 Stanley M. Horton, *The Ultimate Victory, An Exposition of the Book of Revelation* (Springfield, Missouri: Gospel Publishing House, 1991), p. 15.

2 Warren Wiersbe, *The Bible Exposition Commentary: Ephesians to Revelation,* vol. 2 (Wheaton, Illinois: Victor Books, 1989), p. 566.

3 *The NIV Study Bible*, p. 1923.

4 George W. Westlake, Jr., *Daniel and Revelation* (Irving, Texas: ICI University Press, 1995), p. 84.

5 *The NIV Study Bible*, p. 1923.

6 Gundry, p. 383.

7 Mounce, *New International Commentary on the New Testament: The Book of Revelation*, rev. ed., p. 15.

8 Adams, *The Full Life Study Bible*, p. 2002.

9 Horton, *Revelation*, p. 17.

10 Gundry, p. 385.

11 *The NIV Study Bible*, p. 1923.

12 David A. deSilva, *Exegesis of the Apocalypse: Graduate Study Guide* (Irving, Texas: ICI University Press, 1997), p. 28.

13 Horton, *Revelation*, p. 19.

14 Horton, *Revelation*, pp. 18-19.

15 Horton, *Revelation*, pp. 19-20.

16 Horton, *Revelation*, p. 20.

17 Mounce, *New International Commentary on the New Testament: The Book of Revelation*, rev. ed., p. 30.

18 Walvoord, pp. 47-48.

19 J. Nelson Kraybill, "Apocalypse Now," *Christianity Today* (Volume 43, No. 12, October 25, 1999), p. 35.

20 Glen D. Cole and Quentin R. McGhee, *Revelation & Daniel,* 3rd ed. (Springfield, Missouri: Resource and Development Ministries, 2005), pp. 165-168.

21 Wiersbe, p. 567.

22 John F. Walvoord, *The Revelation* (Chicago, Illinois: Moody Press, 1980), pp. 29-30. (The chart in this book is adapted from Walvoord's list.)

23 Cole and McGhee, pp. 148-150.

Definitions

1 Douglas, pp. 614-615.

2 Charles Pfeiffer, *Baker's Bible Atlas* (Grand Rapids, Michigan: Baker Book House, 1979), p. 25.

God's Plan of Salvation

1. Introduction: God is holy, good, and pure—completely righteous. *"God is light; in him there is no darkness at all"* (1 John 1:5).

2. The Problem: Our sins have separated us from God. Because we have sinned—done things we know are wrong—we cannot fellowship with God. Our sins make us too dirty to come into God's holy presence. As we cannot enter a clean room with muddy shoes, we cannot come into God's presence with our sins. *"All have sinned"* (Rom. 3:23). The wages for our sin is death—spiritual death—which is separation from God, now and forever. Those who reject Jesus will die in their sins. They will spend eternity tormented in the flames of hell, away from the presence of God.

3. God's Solution: God loves us so much that he sent Jesus to rescue us. Jesus said, *"I am the way and the truth and the life. No one comes to the Father except through me"* (John 14:6). His name is Jesus, which means Savior, because He saves us from our sins (Matt. 1:21). Jesus saves us from both the penalty and the power of sin–now and forever. Jesus, the Son of God, became a man and lived a perfect, sinless life (John 1:14; Heb. 4:15). He died on the cross as our substitute—He took the penalty for our sins (Rom. 6:23; 2 Cor. 5:21; 1 Pet. 2:24-25. Those who submit their lives to Jesus—God declares to be forgiven, clean and righteous (Rom. 5:1-2).

4. God's Invitation: Jesus says, *"Here I am! I stand at the door (of your heart) and knock. If anyone hears my voice and opens the door, I will come in"* (Rev. 3:20). God's favorite word is "Come". He wants to come to all people, and He wants them to come to him. *"The Spirit and the bride say, "Come!" And let him who hears say, "Come!" Whoever is thirsty, let him come; and whoever wishes, let him take the free gift of the water of life"* (Rev. 22:17). Accept God's invitation. Come to Jesus. Repent of your sins, that is, turn away from what you know is wrong. Put your trust in Jesus as your Savior and Lord. Believe that He died to save you from your sins. Ask Him to forgive your past sins and free you from being a slave to sin. *"If we confess our sins, He is faithful and just and will forgive us our sins, and cleanse us from all unrighteousness"* (1 John 1:9). Welcome Jesus into your life and He will enter. To all who receive Him, He gives the right to become God's children (1 John 1:12).

5. Your Commitment: Welcome to the family of God! God's plan of salvation has a beginning, a middle, and a completion–when we reach heaven. By walking through steps 1–4 above, you have begun to follow God's plan of salvation. Your name is now written in God's book of life (Phil. 4:3; Rev. 3:5; 20:12). The middle part of God's plan is following Jesus as we live on earth. As a child of God, seek to obey the teachings of Jesus in the Bible (Matt. 28:19-20). As you follow Him, He will lead and strengthen you in your relationship with God. As a baby grows into an adult, you will grow from a new child of God into to a mature family member. Be baptized in water (Matt. 28:19; Acts 8:36-38; Rom. 6:4; Mark 16:16). Become part of a local church that preaches and teaches the Bible (Acts 2:41; 9:31). Seek to be filled with the Holy Spirit (Acts 1:8; 2:4; 4:31; 8:17; 10:44-46; 19:1-7; Eph. 5:18-20). Learn to walk in the Spirit, so you can overcome sinful desires that come through the flesh (Rom. 8:5; Gal. 5:16). Grow in grace, and in the knowledge of our Lord and Savior Jesus Christ, and in maturity (2 Pet. 3:18; 2 Pet. 1:5-18). Fellowship with other believers who will encourage you. Share your testimony with others, and lead them to Jesus (John 1:40-42; 4:39). The completion of salvation occurs when Jesus Christ returns. At that time, He will give you a new body, and complete His glorious plan of salvation in your life (Rom. 8:18-25; 1 Cor. 15:20-58; 1 Thess. 4:13-17). We do not know the exact time Jesus will return. For now, enjoy the presence of God, and His Spirit in you, as you grow in grace. You have been saved from your past sins. You are being saved daily, as you abide and grow in Christ. And your salvation has a glorious completion ahead.